# Lecture Notes in Computer Science 3866

Commenced Publication in 1973
Founding and Former Series Editors:
Gerhard Goos, Juris Hartmanis, and Jan van Leeuwen

T0218641

Theo Dimitrakos   Fabio Martinelli
Peter Y.A. Ryan   Steve Schneider (Eds.)

# Formal Aspects in Security and Trust

Third International Workshop, FAST 2005
Newcastle upon Tyne, UK, July 18-19, 2005
Revised Selected Papers

 Springer

Volume Editors

Theo Dimitrakos
Security Research Centre
BT Group Chief Technology Office
2A Rigel House, Adastral Park, Martlesham, Ipswich IP5 3RE, UK
E-mail: Theo.Dimitrakos@bt.com

Fabio Martinelli
Istituto di Informatica e Telematica - IIT
National Research Council - C.N.R.
Pisa Research Area, Via G. Moruzzi, Pisa, Italy
E-mail: fabio.martinelli@iit.cnr.it

Peter Y.A. Ryan
University of Newcastle upon Tyne
School of Computing Science
Newcastle upon Tyne, NE1 7RU, UK
E-mail: Peter.Ryan@newcastle.ac.uk

Steve Schneider
University of Surrey
Department of Computing
Guildford, Surrey, GU2 7XH, UK
E-mail: S.Schneider@surrey.ac.uk

Library of Congress Control Number: 2006921788

CR Subject Classification (1998): C.2.0, D.4.6, E.3, K.4.4, K.6.5

LNCS Sublibrary: SL 4 – Security and Cryptology

ISSN        0302-9743
ISBN-10     3-540-32628-6 Springer Berlin Heidelberg New York
ISBN-13     978-3-540-32628-1 Springer Berlin Heidelberg New York

Springer is a part of Springer Science+Business Media

springer.com

© Springer-Verlag Berlin Heidelberg 2006
Printed in Germany

Typesetting: Camera-ready by author, data conversion by Scientific Publishing Services, Chennai, India
Printed on acid-free paper     SPIN: 11679219     06/3142     5 4 3 2 1 0

# Preface

This volume contains the post-proceedings of the Third International Workshop on Formal Aspects in Security and Trust (FAST 2005), held in Newcastle upon Tyne, July 18-19, 2005. FAST is an event affiliated with the Formal Methods 2005 Congress (FM05).

FAST 2005 aimed at continuing the successful effort of the previous two FAST workshop editions for fostering the cooperation among researchers in the areas of security and trust. The new challenges offered by the so-called ambient intelligence space, as a future paradigm in the information society, demand for a coherent and rigorous framework of concepts, tools and methodologies to increase users' trust&confidence in the underlying communication/interaction infrastructure. It is necessary to address issues relating to both guaranteeing security of the infrastructure and the perception of the infrastructure being secure. In addition, user confidence in what is happening must be enhanced by developing trust models which are not only effective but also easily comprehensible and manageable by users.

FAST sought original papers focusing on formal aspects in: security and trust policy models; security protocol design and analysis; formal models of trust and reputation; logics for security and trust; distributed trust management systems; trust-based reasoning; digital assets protection; data protection; privacy and ID issues; information flow analysis; language-based security; security and trust aspects in ubiquitous computing; validation/analysis tools; Web service security/trust/privacy; GRID security; security risk assessment; case studies etc.

This volume contains revised versions of 17 papers selected out of 37 submissions and the extended abstract of one invited contribution. Each paper was reviewed by at least three members of the international Program Committee (PC).

We wish to thank the PC members for their valuable efforts in properly evaluating the submissions, and the FM05 organizers for accepting FAST as an affiliated event and for providing a perfect environment for running the workshop.

Thanks are also due to BCS-FACS and IIT-CNR for the financial support for FAST 2005.

October 2005

Theo Dimitrakos
Fabio Martinelli
Peter Y.A. Ryan
Steve Schneider
FAST 2005 Co-chairs

# Preface

This volume contains the post-proceedings of the Third International Workshop on Formal Aspects in Security and Trust (FAST 2005), held in Newcastle upon Tyne, July 18-19, 2005. FAST is an event affiliated with the Formal Methods 2005 Congress (FM05).

FAST 2005 aimed at continuing the successful effort of the previous two FAST workshop editions for fostering the cooperation among researchers in the areas of security and trust. The new challenges offered by the so-called ambient intelligence space, as a future paradigm in the information society, demand for a coherent and rigorous framework of concepts, tools and methodologies to increase users' trust&confidence in the underlying communication/interaction infrastructure. It is necessary to address issues relating to both guaranteeing security of the infrastructure and the perception of the infrastructure being secure. In addition, user confidence in what is happening must be enhanced by developing trust models which are not only effective but also easily comprehensible and manageable by users.

FAST sought original papers focusing on formal aspects in: security and trust policy models; security protocol design and analysis; formal models of trust and reputation; logics for security and trust; distributed trust management systems; trust-based reasoning; digital assets protection; data protection; privacy and ID issues; information flow analysis; language-based security; security and trust aspects in ubiquitous computing; validation/analysis tools; Web service security/trust/privacy; GRID security; security risk assessment; case studies etc.

This volume contains revised versions of 17 papers selected out of 37 submissions and the extended abstract of one invited contribution. Each paper was reviewed by at least three members of the international Program Committee (PC).

We wish to thank the PC members for their valuable efforts in properly evaluating the submissions, and the FM05 organizers for accepting FAST as an affiliated event and for providing a perfect environment for running the workshop.

Thanks are also due to BCS-FACS and IIT-CNR for the financial support for FAST 2005.

October 2005

Theo Dimitrakos
Fabio Martinelli
Peter Y.A. Ryan
Steve Schneider
FAST 2005 Co-chairs

# Workshop Organization

## Workshop Organizers

Theo Dimitrakos, BT, UK
Fabio Martinelli, IIT-CNR, Italy
Peter Y.A. Ryan, University of Newcastle, UK
Steve Schneider, University of Surrey, UK

## Invited Speakers

Cédric Fournet, Microsoft Research (Cambridge), UK
Brian Randell, University of Newcastle, UK

## Program Committee

Elisa Bertino, Purdue University, USA
John A. Clark, University of York, UK
Frédéric Cuppens, ENST Bretagne, France
Rino Falcone, ISTC-CNR, Italy
Simon Foley, University College Cork, Ireland
Roberto Gorrieri, University of Bologna, Italy
Masami Hagiya, University of Tokyo, Japan
Chris Hankin, Imperial College (London), UK
Valerie Issarny, INRIA, France
Christian Jensen, DTU, Denmark
Audun Jøsang, DSTC, Australia
Jan Jürjens, TU München, Germany
Yuecel Karabulut, SAP, Germany
Igor Kotenko, SPIIRAS, Russia
Heiko Krumm, University of Dortmund, Germany
Fabio Massacci, University of Trento, Italy
Stefan Poslad, Queen Mary College, UK
Catherine Meadows, Naval Research Lab, USA
Ron van der Meyden, University of New South Wales, Australia
Andrew Myers, Cornell University, USA
Mogens Nielsen, University of Aarhus, Denmark
Indrajit Ray, Colorado State University, USA
Babak Sadighi Firozabadi, SICS, Sweden
Pierangela Samarati, University of Milan, Italy
Ketil Stølen, SINTEF, Norway
Kymie Tan, Carnegie Mellon University, USA
William H. Winsborough, George Mason University, USA

## Local Organization

Alessandro Falleni, IIT-CNR, Italy
Ilaria Matteucci, IIT-CNR, Italy

# Table of Contents

# Voting Technologies and Trust

## (Extended Abstract)

Brian Randell and Peter Y. A. Ryan

School of Computing Science, University of Newcastle upon Tyne
{brian.randell, peter.ryan}@ncl.ac.uk

In this extended abstract we describe initial steps towards a secure voting scheme that could gain as high a level of public trust as is achieved by the existing UK voting scheme. Such a scheme would, we suggest, need to be regarded by the general public as being as understandable as well as at least as trustworthy (*i.e.* dependable and secure) as the system they are already used to. Note that trustworthiness is a necessary, but by no means always sufficient condition for achieving trusted status. The challenge we are addressing is thus as much a socio-technical as a technical one.

The present-day voting process used in the UK national elections is a manual one which involves the use of pre-printed paper ballots. These have a column of candidates' names printed down the left-hand column, and a right-hand column which provides a corresponding set of boxes in which a vote or votes can be marked. The entire voting process takes place under the close supervision of a set of independent officials and, in the case of the vote-counting process, also representatives of the rival candidates, under the protection of a strict legal regime.

Voters must previously have ensured that their names are on the electoral register. They have to cast their votes at a particular voting station, and each such station has a list of the voters who are registered to vote there. This list is marked as each voter is given a ballot paper. Thus the same individual attempting to vote more than once, or different individuals trying to vote using the same identity, especially at the same voting station, is fairly readily detected, though using means which cause some to have concerns regarding vote secrecy.

The current level of trust in the manual system used in UK national elections appears to be due to its many years of largely unchallenged use, and the fact that the general public can readily understand the system. The fact that it involves a large number of independent, and probably rather hostile, observers, suggests that a large number of votes cannot be subverted (changed, replicated or lost) other than by the malicious activities of a large number of individuals, who would have to act for the most part in collusion. This has led us to propose a rather simplistic but useful and generally understandable measure of the merit of a voting system that we term its *insubvertibility*, a robustness-related characteristic that is assessed by dividing the number of votes that could be altered, faked or lost into the number of people who are needed to achieve such alteration, faking or loss.

We take ballot secrecy, insubvertibility and understandability as the key characteristics that need to be maximised. These are all too easily undermined by ill-thought-out schemes of electronic voting, in which a very small number of people in the right position might well be able to subvert the entire election! The approach we

T. Dimitrakos et al. (Eds.): FAST 2005, LNCS 3866, pp. 1–4, 2006.

take is to explore some possible improvements to the existing manual UK voting system, in particular with regard to vote secrecy, accuracy and overall system efficiency (via the introduction of automation), without compromising the system's existing merits. In this extended abstract we describe just the initial step in this exploration.

In order to improve the voter secrecy provided by the existing manual system we suggest use of a ballot paper based on that used in the Prêt à Voter scheme[1]. In this scheme:

- the ballot papers are perforated vertically so that the column with the list of candidates can readily be separated from that on which the voter has recorded her vote,
- the order in which the candidates are listed varies randomly from ballot paper to ballot paper, and
- the voter is allowed to choose a ballot paper for herself at random from a large well-shuffled bundle of such papers.

However, as shown in the Figure, and in contrast to the Prêt à Voter scheme, at the foot of *each* column is printed a unique vote identification number (VIN). The left-hand column of the ballot paper (LHC) constitutes a vote receipt that can be retained by the voter, while the right-hand portion (RHC) is carried forward into the vote counting process. Although the LHC does not, once separated from the RHC, provide any indication of how the voter cast her vote, it does provide an identifiable record of the fact that a vote has been cast.

The crucial aspect of our scheme, inspired by the cryptographic technique involved in the Prêt à Voter scheme, is that the RHC is, in effect, a so-called "scratch card", in that it contains a small rectangle of opaque coating which is initially obscuring a pre-printed code. This code (OCN) identifies the order in which the candidates' names were printed in the left-hand column. The copy of the VIN at the foot of this RHC is printed *on* this opaque coating. This coating can be scratched off, simultaneously destroying the VIN and revealing the OCN.

As well as permitting the voter to choose her own ballot paper at random, she would also be permitted – indeed encouraged – to take other ballot papers and (i) assure herself that they varied with regard to the ordering of the candidates, (ii) scratch off the VINs (thereby invalidating their use as ballots) and verify that the revealed OCNs match the order of the candidates. (Such testing and discarding of RHCs should be done under the supervision of the polling station officials to prevent multiple voting.).

Actual vote casting requires the voter to proceed to a booth with a single ballot paper with its VIN strip still intact. In the booth, she indicates her vote by placing a cross in the appropriate cell on the RHC against the candidate of her choice in the usual fashion. She then splits the ballot paper along the perforation down the middle

---

[1] David Chaum, Peter Y.A. Ryan and Steve A. Schneider. *A Practical, Voter-verifiable Election Scheme.* Proc. 10th European Symposium on Research in Computer Security - ESORICS. Springer Verlag (2005).

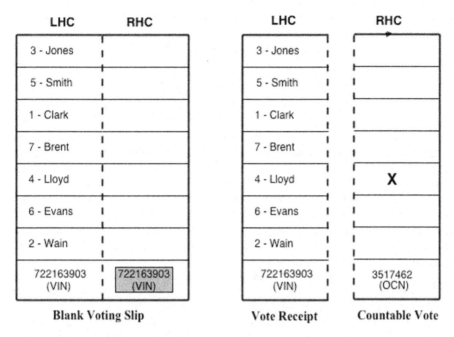

**Fig. 1.** A ballot paper – before voting and after it has been split and its OCN made visible

and, leaving the scratch strip intact so as to preserve the secrecy of her vote, posts the RHC into a locked ballot box. When the vote casting period has ended, the secure boxes of votes (RHCs) are taken from each voting station to a vote counting centre. In order to interpret the vote value encoded on each RHC, the VIN strip must be scratched off under supervision. (This is so as to minimise the possibility that ballots are lost, altered or injected whilst at the same time ensuring that no-one can link the VIN numbers to the resulting ballot papers reveal the OCN hidden underneath.) Before the RHCs have their VINs scratched off, however, the VINs would be recorded and published (e.g. via a secure web bulletin board) so that each voter can use her vote receipt to check that her vote was indeed entered into the counting process.

Once their OCNs have been revealed the RHCs can be used in a near-conventional process of (well-scrutinised) manual vote counting. Given the general public's experience of and trust in scratch cards (which are likely to be even more familiar to them than ballot papers) and in the act of shuffling playing cards, we believe that this vote counting process and indeed the whole voting scheme could gain a level of acceptance from the public regarding its overall trustworthiness comparable to that enjoyed by the manual scheme that is currently in use in the UK. The additional vote secrecy it provides should also be manifest to the general public.

However, major trust concerns arise when one moves away from the use of paper ballots either partly (in that paper voting receipts might still be retained) or completely, so that the vote casting as well as counting is all done essentially invisibly, *e.g.* electronically. Even if the public have good reason to believe that electronic versions of their votes are reaching the vote counting process safely, the problem is to provide the public with continued reason to trust a vote counting process that is not directly visible to ordinary officials and scrutineers.

For example, vote counting machines, or indeed voting machines, i.e. DRE (direct recording electronic) devices, that have a conventional general-purpose computer and operating system incorporated into them are problematic and likely to remain controversial. Their use normally requires a degree of trust that the more technically-aware voters in particular are, quite correctly, likely to be reluctant to provide. Indeed, with electronic votes various forms of "online" manual checking by multiple observers will normally have to be replaced or supplemented by (i) prior checking of the design of possibly very sophisticated algorithms and devices, and (ii) ensuring the continued relevance of the results of these checks up to and during the actual voting process.

The Voter Verifiable Paper Audit Trail (VVPAT) scheme has therefore been advocated as an adjunct to an electronic voting casting and counting system. Such an approach depends on somehow ensuring (i) that the audit trail mechanism, rather than the actual voting system *per se*, is adequately trustworthy, and (ii) that recourse will be had to this audit trail mechanism whenever necessary.

An alternative approach is to use cryptographic mechanisms to make the counting process highly transparent and auditable, within the constraints of ballot secrecy, and to make the auditing processes public and open to scrutiny– this is the approach taken in the Prêt à Voter scheme, for example. However, although with such voting schemes the computers and the software involved need not be trusted, the arguments for the trustworthiness of the overall voting system are subtle and require specialist knowledge in order to be properly appreciated.

In our full paper, to appear in the IEEE Journal of Security & Privacy, we go on to explore various developments of the basic scratch-card system, in a series of steps towards actual e-voting. However, we have deliberately tried - in pursuit of user acceptance and trust - to retain the familiarity and simplicity of current well-accepted devices and systems. As a result, in most of our proposals we have deliberately sought to retain at least some use of paper, and to avoid, or at least minimize the use of, electronics and computers.

# On the Formal Analyses of the Zhou-Gollmann Non-repudiation Protocol

Susan Pancho-Festin[1] and Dieter Gollmann[2]

[1] Dept. of Computer Science, University of the Philippines-Diliman
sbpancho@up.edu.ph
[2] TU Hamburg-Harburg, Germany
diego@tu-harburg.de

**Abstract.** Most of the previous comparisons of formal analyses of security protocols have concentrated on the tabulation of attacks found or missed. More recent investigations suggest that such cursory comparisons can be misleading. The original context of a protocol as well as the operating assumptions of the analyst have to be taken into account before conducting comparative evaluations of different analyses of a protocol. In this paper, we present four analyses of the Zhou-Gollmann non-repudiation protocol and trace the differences in the results of the four analyses to the differences in the assumed contexts. This shows that even contemporary analyses may unknowingly deviate from a protocol's original context.

## 1 Introduction

The observations derived from the comparative evaluation of formalisations and analyses of the Needham-Schroeder public key and shared key protocols [1] suggest that different protocol models affect the resulting analysis results, to the extent that it explains why some analyses fail to find attacks detected by other methods [2]. Although it is now generally accepted that this explains the previously undocumented attack discovered by Lowe [3] on the Needham-Schroeder public key protocol, the wider effects of protocol models have not been always considered in previous comparisons of protocol results. This results in the continued misinterpretation of a protocol's security particularly when it is implicitly assumed that different analyses are directly comparable without recourse to the details of their protocol models.

Contemporary protocols encompass a larger scope. Some attempt to offer security guarantees that do not fit traditional definitions of authentication, confidentiality or integrity. The scope of newer protocols is broader, their properties often more complex and the implementation details more convoluted. This provides a richer ground for misinterpretation of requirements and conflicts in both formalisation and implementation. Intuition suggests that if differences in formalisation are already observed in relatively simple protocols such as those in the Needham-Schroeder family, then the more recent and more complex protocols are even more susceptible to the production of different protocol models, and possibly, to different analysis results. In this paper we present the Zhou-Gollmann

T. Dimitrakos et al. (Eds.): FAST 2005, LNCS 3866, pp. 5–15, 2006.

Non-repudiation protocol as an example of a contemporary, non-conventional security protocol where differences in the results from several analyses are attributed to changes in the assumed protocol context.

## 2   The Zhou-Gollmann Non-repudiation Protocol

The Zhou-Gollmann non-repudiation protocol [4] was analysed by its authors using the SVO logic [5], by Schneider using CSP/FDR [6] and by Bella and Paulson using the Isabelle theorem prover [7]. These analyses did not report the more recent attacks reported by Gürgens and Rudolph [8] using asynchronous product automata (APA) and the simple homomorphism verification tool (SHVT). The primary cause for the conflicting results is in the differences in assumptions among the four analyses with respect to the storage of evidence and the behaviour of participants, particularly the trusted third party (TTP).

Non-repudiation is a fairly new security requirement compared to authentication and confidentiality. As such, there are fewer protocols that provide this property; there are even fewer formal analyses of these protocols. The Zhou-Gollmann (ZG) protocol [4] is unique in the sense that there are several existing analyses of it; this allows us to compare how different methods formalise the new concept of non-repudiation.

Non-repudiation is the property wherein both the message sender and recipient obtain evidence of having sent or received a message, respectively. This evidence must be independently verifiable by a third party. Evidence of receipt is given to the message sender to prove that the recipient has received a message. Evidence of origin is given to the message recipient to prove that the sender has indeed sent a message.

In the ZG protocol, there is an additional requirement of fairness. It should not be possible for either sender or recipient to be in a more advantageous position over the other. Fairness ensures that both evidence of receipt and origin can only be held after the protocol completes. If one party abandons a protocol session, no acceptable evidence must be generated for that session.

The ZG protocol is shown in Figure 1. Note that, even if the commitment $C$ is produced via the encryption of the message $M$ with key $K$, this is not undertaken to ensure message secrecy. Rather, the commitment is first sent to the recipient who signs it and returns it to the sender. Both the sender and recipient's signature on this commitment and its corresponding label $L$ comprises the first part of the evidence of receipt and evidence of origin respectively. To complete both evidence, the sender and recipient must individually obtain $con\_K$ from the trusted third party via an *ftp-get* operation.

If $A$ denies having sent the message $M$, $B$ presents to the judge $M$, $C$, $L$, $K$, $EOO$ and $con\_K$. The judge will check if [4]:

- $con\_K$ was signed by the TTP.
- $EOO$ was signed by $A$.
- $M = \{C\}_{K^{-1}}$

1. $A \rightarrow B : f_{EOO}, B, L, C, EOO$
2. $B \rightarrow A : f_{EOR}, A, L, EOR$
3. $A \rightarrow TTP : f_{SUB}, B, L, K, sub\_K$
4. $B \leftrightarrow TTP : f_{CON}, A, B, L, K, con\_K$
5. $A \leftrightarrow TTP : f_{CON}, A, B, L, K, con\_K$

where

- $A \leftrightarrow B : X : A$ fetches message $X$ from $B$ via an *ftp-get* operation or some analogous means. TTP is the trusted third party.
- $L$ is a unique label
- $K$ is the key
- $C$ is the commitment, where $C = \{M\}_K$
- $f_{EOO}, f_{EOR}, f_{SUB}, f_{CON}$ : flags to indicate the purpose of a (signed) message
- $EOO = (f_{EOO}, B, L, C)_{S_A}$ : evidence of origin of commitment $C$
- $EOR = (f_{EOR}, A, L, C)_{S_B}$ : evidence of receipt of commitment $C$
- $sub\_K = (f_{SUB}, B, L, K)_{S_A}$ : evidence of submission of key $K$
- $con\_K = (f_{CON}, A, B, L, K)_{S_{TTP}}$ : evidence of confirmation of key $K$ issued by the $TTP$

**Fig. 1.** Zhou-Gollmann Non-repudiation Protocol

If these checks are confirmed then the judge upholds $B$'s claim. A similar procedure is followed if the dispute concerns B's denial of receipt of $M$. However, the checks carried out by the judge rest on several assumptions which we will discuss within our framework.

## 3  Modelling Protocol Goals

The protocol is defined by two general goals:

1. Non-repudiation, both of origin and receipt, and
2. Fairness

The first general goal requires that both $A$ and $B$ have evidence of receipt and origin respectively. The second goal is an additional requirement, and has been defined by the protocol authors as:

"A non-repudiation protocol is fair if it provides the originator and the recipient with valid irrefutable evidence after completion of the protocol, without giving a party an advantage over the other at any stage of the protocol run." [4]

### 3.1  Zhou and Gollmann's Analysis

In [5], the authors used the SVO logic [9] to verify their protocol. The protocol goals were formalised from the point of view of the judge who will preside over a dispute. Thus, the two general non-repudiation goals were formalised as:

G1   The judge $J$ believes ($A$ said $M$).
G2   The judge $J$ believes ($B$ received $M$).

There are certain assumptions under which these goals are checked; in particular, the authors assumed that $J$ holds the public signature verification keys of $A$, $B$ and the $TTP$ as well as the evidence presented by $A$, $B$, or both. Other assumptions relate to the behaviour of the $TTP$. This analysis did not formalise fairness as an explicit protocol goal, which seems to be due to the limitations of the belief logic SVO [5].

## 3.2   Schneider's Analysis

In Schneider's CSP analysis [6], the protocol goals were analysed from two different perspectives: the judge's and the participants'. From the judge's point of view, the validity of origin and/or receipt claims is determined purely from the evidence presented. The judge is assumed not to have observed the protocol run. From each participant's point of view, fairness is expected during the protocol's execution. Schneider asserts that participants can only expect fairness if they follow the protocol [6].

Both non-repudiation and fairness were formalised in Schneider's analysis.

1. Non-repudiation of Origin:
   – $B$ possesses $EOO = (f_{EOO}, B, L, C)_{S_A}$
   – $B$ possesses $con\_K = (f_{CON}, A, B, L, K)_{S_{TTP}}$
   It is assumed that if $B$ has these signed messages as evidence as well as the components $L,C,M$, and $K$, then $A$ must have sent $(f_{EOO}, B, L, C)_{S_A}$ and $(f_{SUB}, B, L, K)_{S_A}$.
2. Non-repudiation of Receipt:
   – $A$ possesses $EOR = (f_{EOR}, A, L, C)_{S_B}$
   – $A$ possesses $con\_K = (f_{CON}, A, B, L, K)_{S_{TTP}}$
   It is assumed that if $A$ has these signed messages as evidence as well as $L, C$, $M$ and $K$, then $B$ must have sent $(f_{EOR}, A, L, C)_{S_B}$ and that $B$ can obtain $(f_{CON}, A, B, L, K)_{S_{TTP}}$ from the $TTP$.
3. Fairness for $A$: If $B$ has proof of origin for $M$, then the proof of receipt must be available to $A$. This relies on the assumption that only $A$ knows the key $K$, and that $A$ sends this key only once to the $TTP$. Thus, $B$ will only obtain the message $M$ only when the $TTP$ has made the key available to both $A$ and $B$.
4. Fairness for $B$: If $A$ has proof of receipt for $M$, then the proof of origin must be available to $B$.

## 3.3   Bella and Paulson's Analysis

In [7], Bella and Paulson used the Isabelle theorem prover to analyse the ZG protocol. Their formalisation of the protocol's goals follows the same line as that pursued by Schneider, i.e., both validity of evidence and fairness were modelled.

In their analysis, the validity of evidence and fairness was specified in terms of the guarantees that each party may expect from the protocol.

1. Guarantees for A: (To justify $A$'s claim that $B$ did receive the message $M$.)
   - Validity of Evidence.
     - $con\_K$ shows that $A$ bound the key $K$ to the label $L$. This means that, since $con\_K$ is available, the $TTP$ has received $sub\_K$ from $A$. In $sub\_K$, $A$ has bound $K$ to $L$.
     - The other evidence in $A$'s possession is $EOR$. This proves that $B$ has received $A$'s $EOO$, where $A$ binds $C$ to $L$.
   - Fairness. If $B$ holds $con\_K$, then either $A$ has it, or it is made available to $A$. This fairness guarantee for $A$ also states that $con\_K$ will not be available if $A$ has not submitted $sub\_K$; and $A$ will not submit $sub\_K$ until $A$ has received $EOR$ from $B$.
2. Guarantees for B: (To justify $B$'s claim that $A$ did send the message $M$.)
   - Validity of Evidence.
     - As with $A$, if $B$ holds $con\_K$, then $B$ could only have obtained this via the *ftp-get* operation from the $TTP$. The $TTP$ would have made this available only if $A$ has submitted $sub\_K$ to the $TTP$.
     - $B$ also presents as evidence $EOO$, which shows that $A$ has bound the commitment $C$ to the key $K$ via the label $L$.
   - Fairness. If $A$ holds $con\_K$ then it is also available to $B$.

### 3.4 Gürgens and Rudolph's Analysis

In their analysis [8], Gürgens and Rudolph defined the protocol goals in terms of predicates that must hold true for each participant.

1. For party $A$ (originator), the predicate that must hold true is $(NRR(B))$. This predicate states that if $B$ has a valid $EOO$ and $con\_K$ for a particular message $M$, then $A$ must have a valid $EOR$ and either possesses or has access to $con\_K$.
2. For party $B$ (recipient), the predicate that must hold true is $(NRO(A))$. This predicate states that if $A$ has a valid $EOR$ and $con\_K$ for a particular message $M$, then $B$ must have a valid $EOO$ and either possesses or has access to $con\_K$.

### 3.5 Remarks

Of the four analyses, three defined the protocol's goals in terms of the correctness of evidence as well as fairness. Only the SVO logic analysis [5] did not explicitly formalise fairness. Thus, the SVO analysis is limited to results with respect to the validity of evidence only. For the other analyses, goals were defined in terms of the evidence each participant holds as well as what may be assumed with respect to the availability of evidence to the other party.

## 4   Modelling Cryptographic Schemes

The ZG protocol makes non-standard use of encryption wherein it is utilised not to keep a message secret, but rather to split a message $M$ into a commitment $C$ and a key $K$. The commitment $C = \{M\}_K$ is first sent out by the sender to the recipient together with the sender's signature on the commitment. The recipient sends back its own signature on the commitment. The key $K$ that will allow $B$ to decrypt the message is sent by $A$ to the trusted third party $TTP$ who checks that the key and the label is signed by $A$. If this is the case, the $TTP$ signs the key, the label and the identity of the two parties. This signed message will now be made available to both $A$ and $B$ via an ftp-like server allowing them to have access to it.

All of the analyses we have considered have formalised the cryptographic functions in an abstract manner and assumed perfect encryption. Keys cannot be guessed and certain parties keep their private keys secret. Zhou and Gollmann did not require specific properties as to the uniqueness of the key $K$. Bella and Paulson [7] explicitly allowed for $A$ re-using an old key to encrypt a message $M$; their only restriction was that $A$ does not use private signature keys for this purpose. They also assumed that the $TTP$ checks if the key sent in message 3 is indeed a shared key and not a private signature key[1]. Gürgens and Rudolph [8] explicitly state that, in their interpretation of the ZG protocol, $A$ must choose a new label $L$ and a new key $K$ for each protocol run. Schneider [6] did not specify an explicit assumption for the uniqueness of $K$. The implication of $A$'s re-use of an old key is that other participants who have a copy of the key $K$ (perhaps from previous protocol runs conducted with $A$) can try out this key for decrypting $A$'s commitments.

## 5   Modelling Communications

The protocol makes three important assumptions on protocol communications:

1. The communications link is not permanently broken. Since the protocol relies on an *ftp-get* operation to allow parties $A$ and $B$ fair access to *con_K* in the last part of the protocol, it has to be assumed that, eventually, both parties will be able to obtain this evidence from the TTP.
2. The $TTP$ does not store evidence indefinitely. In [4], it was suggested that timestamps be used to set a lifetime for the availability of the evidence from the TTP. It is further assumed that the $TTP$ does not overwrite existing evidence stored in the public directory.
3. A message label is unique and creates a link between the commitment and the key [4]. Zhou and Gollmann gave several suggestions on how this label may be constructed:
   - $L$, where $L$ is independent of the message $M$. $M$ can be defined at a later stage in the protocol (step 3).

---

[1] The check they perform relies on the length of shared keys and signature keys.

- $L = H(M)$ where $H$ is a collision-free, one-way hash function. This links $L$ to $M$ at step 1.
- $L = H(M, K)$, if $M$ belongs to a small message space.

We shall now see how these assumptions were formalised by the four analyses.

## 5.1  Zhou and Gollmann's Analysis

In the protocol authors' own analysis using SVO logic [5], they maintained the same assumptions on communications, but did not formally model them.

## 5.2  Schneider's Analysis

Schneider modelled communications via a *medium* through which all messages are sent, received, or retrieved (in the case of the *ftp-get* operation). Schneider further allowed for this medium to be unreliable with the following restrictions:

1. Messages cannot be altered in transit. Errors can occur in the transmission but it is not possible for corrupted messages to be delivered; these messages will be detected and disposed of. Schneider allows for deliberately altered messages and assumes that the modification has been carried out by some agent.
2. Messages cannot be mis-delivered. Initially, Schneider considered a more unreliable medium which allows for messages to be mis-delivered. In that context, however, Schneider discovered that fairness for party $A$ cannot be guaranteed since it is possible for the key $K$ to be mis-delivered to $B$ and never reach the $TTP$.

Schneider did not model the expiry of the evidence stored at the $TTP$ but assumed a liveness property wherein, once a message has been made available via *ftp* to an agent $i$, then it will "...always be available to any agent $i'$..." [6].

Schneider did not specifically model the uniqueness of the labels used in the messages but did note that the label has to be unique for each protocol run.

## 5.3  Bella and Paulson's Analysis

In Bella and Paulson's analysis [7], a *trace* is a list of network events consisting of either of the following:

- Says A B X: $A$ sends $X$ to $B$
- Gets A X: $A$ receives $X$
- Notes A X: $A$ notes down $X$

Their model does not force events to happen, i.e., it is possible that the preconditions for a certain event have been met but the event does not occur. This allows for assumption of an unreliable communications medium, i.e., a message that has been sent may not be received and protocol runs may be abandoned. However, they did assume that messages cannot alter during transmission.

The uniqueness of labels was assumed and a label was modelled as a nonce. They assumed that, for the first message in the protocol, $A$ chooses a fresh label. Bella and Paulson did not seem to consider setting a lifetime on the evidence stored at the $TTP$.

### 5.4    Gürgens and Rudolph's Analysis

In Gürgens and Rudolph's analysis [8], they modelled the assumption that the communications medium is not permanently broken by putting a restriction on the behaviour of a dishonest agent. They assumed that a dishonest agent cannot permanently block the delivery of $sub\_K$ from $A$ to the $TTP$ nor the retrieval of $con\_K$ from the $TTP$. Thus, they assumed that a dishonest agent can only remove messages to which it is explicitly named as the intended recipient.

They further assumed that the evidence in the $TTP$ has a limited lifetime. However, they imposed their own policy on the storage and lifetime of evidence at the $TTP$. Evidence is available only until $A$ and $B$ have retrieved it. They further assumed that the $TTP$ has some way of determining whether $A$ and $B$ have retrieved the evidence. These are additional assumptions and were not part of the original protocol description. Although Zhou and Gollmann acknowledged that the evidence cannot be kept at the $TTP$ indefinitely, they did not specify that the evidence be deleted soon after it is retrieved by both $A$ and $B$. They had proposed to use a timestamp defined by $A$ relative to the $TTP$'s clock; this timestamp $T$ specifies a deadline for the storage of evidence at the $TTP$. $B$ can refuse to acknowledge a commitment sent by $A$ if $B$ does not agree with the deadline. This suggestion does not require additional actions on the part of the $TTP$. Furthermore, the protocol authors did not require that $A$ and $B$ inform the $TTP$ that they have retrieved the evidence; they assumed that the $TTP$ only notarises message keys and provides directory services.

**Gürgens and Rudolph's Attack No. 1**
$\alpha.1\ A \rightarrow B\quad : f_{EOO}, B, L, C, EOO$
$\alpha.2\ B \rightarrow A\quad : f_{EOR}, A, L, EOR$
$\alpha.3\ A \rightarrow TTP : f_{SUB}, B, L, K, sub\_K$
$\alpha.4\ A \leftrightarrow TTP : f_{CON}, A, B, L, K, con\_K$
$\alpha.5\ B \leftrightarrow TTP : f_{CON}, A, B, L, K, con\_K$
$\beta.1\ A \rightarrow B\quad : f_{EOO}, B, L, C_2, EOO_2$
$\beta.2\ B \rightarrow A\quad : f_{EOR}, A, L, EOR_2$

This attack requires $A$ to first complete a protocol run with $B$. After this run, $A$ possesses $EOR$ signed by $B$ and $con\_K$ signed by the $TTP$. $con\_K$ will be deleted by the $TTP$ after steps $\alpha.4$ and $\alpha.5$. In the second protocol run, $A$ uses the same key $K$ and label $L$ that it used in the first run but sends a new commitment $C_2$, where $C_2 = \{M_2\}_K$. After receiving $EOR_2$ from $B$, $A$ can present this together with the $con\_K$ it received from the first run as *"evidence"* of receipt for $M_2$ although $A$ will never complete the second protocol run.

In the second attack, Gürgens and Rudolph considered that $L = H(M, K)$.

**Gürgens and Rudolph's Attack No. 2**
$\alpha.1\ A \to B \qquad : f_{EOO}, B, L, C_1, EOO_1$
$\qquad\qquad\qquad\ : \text{where } L = H(M_2, K), C_1 = \{M_1\}_K$
$\alpha.2\ B \to A \qquad : f_{EOR}, A, L, EOR_1$
$\alpha.3\ A \to TTP : f_{SUB}, B, L, K, sub\_K$
$\alpha.4\ A \leftrightarrow TTP : f_{CON}, A, B, L, K, con\_K$
$\alpha.5\ B \leftrightarrow TTP : f_{CON}, A, B, L, K, con\_K$
$\beta.1\ A \to B \qquad : f_{EOO}, B, L, C_2, EOO_2$
$\qquad\qquad\qquad\ : \text{where } L \text{ is the same and } C_2 = \{M_2\}_K$
$\beta.2\ B \to A \qquad : f_{EOR}, A, L, EOR_2$

The label $L$ is constructed from the second message, $M_2$ of $A$ and the key $K$ that $A$ will use for both runs. After $\alpha.5$, $B$ has $K$ and $C_1$. Although Zhou and Gollmann did not explicitly state that $A$ and $B$ check the evidence they obtained, it is reasonable to expect that $A$ and $B$ check their respective evidence since it is assumed that the $TTP$ is a lightweight notary only. When $B$ detects that $L$ and $C_1$ do not match, he would be warned against proceeding in protocol run $\beta$ with $A$.

Gürgens and Rudolph's third attack is against a variation of the ZG protocol that utilises timestamps [10]; we do not discuss this attack since the other analyses refer to the original protocol.

## 6   Modelling Participants

In a non-repudiation protocol, it is expected that both parties at the outset do not trust each other. It is for this reason that both parties wish to obtain evidence of the other party's participation in the protocol. In the SVO logic analysis [5], it was assumed that the $TTP$ is trustworthy. It was further assumed that either party may abort a protocol run, without disputes, at certain stages. Since this analysis was conducted from the point of view of a judge that will preside over disputes, there were additional assumptions with respect to the public signature verification keys of $A$, $B$ and the $TTP$. It was assumed that these keys are valid.

Schneider [6] allowed for participants not following the protocol; however, he assumed that a participant does not divulge his secret signing key. Each participant is modelled in terms of the messages it can transmit and receive, retrieve from the $TTP$ and present as evidence in case of disputes. Schneider further assumed that a participant can only expect fairness if it follows the protocol. Bella and Paulson [7] assumed that $A$, $B$, and the $TTP$ do not belong to the set of compromised agents. Without this assumption, the intruder would have access to $S_A$, $S_B$, and $S_{TTP}$.

Gürgens and Rudolph analysed scenarios wherein $A$ deliberately tries to obtain unfair evidence for a message. However, their attacks work not because $A$ was "allowed" to misbehave. The ZG non-repudiation protocol is motivated by the possibility that $A$ or $B$ will not follow protocol rules. The Gürgens and Rudolph attacks work because they redefined the behaviour of the $TTP$.

## 7   Modelling the Intruder

In the SVO logic analysis [5], no intruder is modelled and the objective was to determine the beliefs that may be derived by parties $A$ and $B$. This was due to the limited scope of a belief logic method [5]. In Schneider's analysis [6], it was observed that the two parties essentially need protection from each other. Bella and Paulson [7] analysed the protocol both with and without a spy. The spy is assumed to be capable of faking messages and is in control of a set of bad agents. However, they did not include the $TTP$, $A$, or $B$ in the set of bad agents. Gürgens and Rudolph assumed that only $B$ and the $TTP$ are honest.

## 8   Conclusion

Schneider did not detect the Gürgens and Rudolph attacks since he did not assume that evidence in the $TTP$ server expires. Thus, in Schneider's model, if $A$ attempts to re-use an old label, there will be duplicate entries in the $TTP$'s server and it is assumed that the $TTP$ will detect this. Bella and Paulson did not detect the attack since they also assumed the same properties for evidence storage. Zhou and Gollmann's SVO logic analysis was not intended to find flaws in the protocol. Gürgens and Rudolph modified the original context by assuming that evidence stored in the TTP is immediately deleted after $A$ and $B$ have retrieved the evidence. They further assumed that the server would know when to delete such a message. Thus, the two attacks they found are only relevant to their version of the ZG protocol.

The Zhou-Gollmann non-repudiation protocol and its analyses presented reinforce the observation that incompatibilities in formalisations are not restricted to the well-known discrepancies in the analyses of the Needham-Schroeder public key and conventional key protocols. In order to objectively compare the results of different analyses, it is clearly vital that we must take due account of the protocol's original security context as well as the assumptions in the formal protocol models.

Different analyses may be compared by comparing their security contexts. This includes the definition of goals (both of the protocol and the analyses) and the drawing out of assumptions with respect to communications, participants, cryptographic functions, and the intruder. Discrepancies in at least one of these areas could render differences in analyses results. Such observation may seem trivial, but there is still a tendency in some comparative discussions to forget the security contexts and instead concentrate on the discovery of supposedly *new* attacks.

## 9   Future Work

The observations derived from the four analyses of the Zhou-Gollmann protocol were based on an informal comparison of five aspects of the protocol model. An interesting extension of our work would be to determine if these five aspects (and possibly others) could be formalised in a specific framework of analysis.

It was shown how a *"new"* attack was discovered by one analysis through the differences in its formalisation of the protocol. It would be natural to ask whether such differences have resulted in the omission of attacks on this and other protocols.

# References

1. Needham, R., Schroeder, M.: Using encryption for authentication in large networks of computers. Communications of the ACM **21** (1978) 993–999
2. Pancho, S.: Paradigm shifts in protocol analysis. In: Proceedings of the 1999 ACM New Security Paradigms Workshop, ACM Press (1999) 70–79
3. Lowe, G.: Breaking and fixing the Needham-Schroeder public-key protocol using FDR. In: Tools and Algorithms for the Construction and Analysis of Systems. Lecture Notes in Computer Science 1055, Springer-Verlag (1996) 147–166
4. Zhou, J., Gollmann, D.: A fair non-repudiation protocol. In: Proceedings of the 1996 IEEE Symposium on Security and Privacy. (1996) 55–61
5. Zhou, J., Gollmann, D.: Towards verification of non-repudiation protocols. In: Proceedings of 1998 International Refinement Workshop and Formal Methods Pacific, Canberra, Australia. (1998) 370–380
6. Schneider, S.: Formal analysis of a non-repudiation protocol. In: Proceedings of the 11th IEEE Computer Security Foundations Workshop. (1998)
7. Bella, G., Paulson, L.C.: Mechanical proofs about a non-repudiation protocol. In Boulton, R.J., Jackson, P.B., eds.: Proceedings of the 14th International Conference on Theorem Proving in Higher Order Logics. Number 2152 in Lecture Notes in Computer Science, Springer Verlag (2001) 91–104
8. Gürgens, S., Rudolph, C.: Security analysis of (un-)fair non-repudiation protocols. In: Proceedings of the Conference on Formal Aspects of Security. (2002)
9. Syverson, P.F., van Oorschot, P.C.: On unifying some cryptographic protocol logics. In: Proceedings of the IEEE Symposium on Research in Security and Privacy. (1994) 14–28
10. Zhou, J., Deng, R., Bao, F.: Evolution of fair non-repudiation with TTP. In: Proceedings of the 1999 Australasian Conference on Information Security and Privacy (ACISP). (1999)

# Formal Reasoning About a Specification-Based Intrusion Detection for Dynamic Auto-configuration Protocols in Ad Hoc Networks

Tao Song[1], Calvin Ko[2], Chinyang Henry Tseng[1], Poornima Balasubramanyam[1], Anant Chaudhary[1], and Karl N. Levitt[1]

[1] Computer Security Laboratory, University of California, Davis
{tsong, ctseng, pbala, achaudhary, knlevitt}@ucdavis.edu
[2] Sparta Inc., Saratoga, CA 95070
calvin.ko@sparta.com

**Abstract.** As mobile ad hoc networks (MANETs) are increasingly deployed in critical environments, security becomes a paramount issue. The dynamic and decentralized nature of MANETs makes their protocols very vulnerable to attacks, for example, by malicious insiders, who can cause packets to be misrouted or cause other nodes to have improper configuration. This paper addresses security issues of auto-configuration protocols in ad hoc networks. Auto-configuration protocols enable nodes to obtain configuration information (e.g., an IP address) so that they can communicate with other nodes in the network. We describe a formal approach to modeling and reasoning about auto-configuration protocols to support the detection of malicious insider nodes. With respect to this family of protocols, our approach defines a global security requirement for a network that characterizes the "good" behavior of individual nodes to assure the global property. This behavior becomes local detection rules that define a distributed specification-based intrusion detection system aimed at detecting malicious insider nodes. We formally prove that the local detection rules (identifying activity that is monitored) together with "assumptions" that identify system properties which are not monitored imply the global security requirement. This approach, novel to the field of intrusion detection, can, in principle, yield an intrusion detection system that detects any attack, even unknown attacks, that can imperil the global security requirement.

**Keywords:** Formal reasoning, Intrusion Detection, Ad hoc network, Network Security.

## 1 Introduction

Mobile ad hoc networks (MANETs), which offer infrastructure-less communication over wireless channels, are envisioned to be an integral part of future computing. MANETs are particularly attractive in application areas in which a fixed network infrastructure either does not exist or is temporarily disabled because the MANET is being employed in an environment subject to natural or malicious faults. Often, these MANETs are deployed in highly critical environments and should be protected.

T. Dimitrakos et al. (Eds.): FAST 2005, LNCS 3866, pp. 16–33, 2006.

MANETs present a highly challenging environment [21, 6], requiring new approaches to keeping them secure. The dynamic and distributed nature of a MANET makes it vulnerable to security attacks. Unlike wired networks in which an attacker must gain physical access to the wired link or sneak through security holes in routers or firewalls, wireless attacks may come from anywhere. An important consideration is the security of the protocols employed in MANETs. Protocols designed for MANETs are highly cooperative, relying on all the participating nodes to follow the protocol. A malicious node which deliberately performs bad operations in a MANET could highly impact the operation of the entire network.

We take a specification-based intrusion-detection approach [10] to address the problem of detecting insider attacks in MANETs. Specification-based intrusion detection has been applied to successfully detect attacks on traditional [9] and ad hoc network protocols [18]. Briefly, the approach requires that the valid behavior of a node be identified (by an "expert", by discovery, or a combination of these two approaches); network monitoring is employed to check the operations of nodes, where any activity inconsistent with the specification is judged to be a violation. This approach can be retrofitted on to existing protocols and complements other preventive approaches. A unique contribution of this paper is that we employ formal reasoning to analyze whether the detection rules, that constitute the specifications, are sufficiently strong to detect all attacks, even unknown attacks, that violate security requirements. The readers might be suspicious of our claim that *all* attacks are detectable. The keys, as demonstrated in [16] are the assumptions used in the proof that, in effect, rule out behavior not expected to occur and the fact that the proof of the detection rules guarantee that any activity that threatens the overall network policy is detectable.

A specification-based Intrusion detection approach in a MANET is discussed in [15]. In this paper, we focus the investigation on an auto-configuration protocol for MANETs, namely the Dynamic Registration and Configuration Protocol (DRCP) [11, 20]. DRCP is a subnet configuration protocol that enables a node to obtain configuration information (e.g., an IP address) in order to communicate in wireless networks. Besides ad hoc routing protocols, auto-configuration protocols, such as DRCP, are critical elements in a MANET. DRCP has been proposed to overcome shortcomings of Dynamic Host Configuration Protocol (DHCP) and facilitates dynamic, rapid and efficient configuration in the unpredictable ad hoc wireless network environment. Due to mobility, instability of wireless links, and other unpredictable environmental characteristics, auto-configuration protocols designed for MANETs usually allow multiple nodes to provide configuration information to improve performance. These extensions, coupled with mobility, make it difficult to assure the security posture of the network. Thus, the design of the intrusion detection system benefits from a formal approach to reasoning about security – the focus of this paper.

We define a global security requirement for the subnet operating with the DRCP protocol and analyze the local detection rules that are intended to restrict the behavior of individual nodes. We have developed a proof framework for reasoning about security, through which we formally prove that the local detection rules ensure the global security requirements.

There are two significant contributions to this paper. First, we analyze security aspects of DRCP, including security requirements and possible generic attack methods on DRCP, and propose a specification-based intrusion detection mechanism to ensure that these security requirements are met; our intrusion detection system is requirements-driven rather than attack-driven. Second, we developed a formal model for DRCP and verified the enforcement of the security requirements; the proof is carried out using the ACL2 theorem prover [8]. We chose the DRCP protocol for study since it possesses features that are characteristic of other auto configuration protocols that may be used in MANETs, making the general results of the study applicable and useful for other MANET auto-configuration protocols.

Specification-based intrusion detection is an IDS methodology that compares, at run time, the behavior of objects with their associated security specifications, the latter capturing the correct behavior of the objects. The specifications are usually manually crafted based on the security policy, the expected functional behavior of the objects, and the expected usage. Specification-based detection does not detect intrusions directly -- it detects the effect of the intrusions as run-time violations of the specifications. This approach has been successfully applied to monitor security-critical programs [9], applications [7], and protocols [9, 18, 19], and is beginning to be used in commercial host-based intrusion detection products. Since the approach provides a systematic framework for developing specifications/constraints such that security breaches may be described as violations of these constraints, it can detect known as well as unknown attacks. An added benefit is that such an approach, as it rests on specifications, can support reasoning which in our case demonstrates that the rules that define the intrusion detection system together with certain assumptions are sufficiently strong to guarantee that the intrusion detection system will detect all attacks that could case the overall security requirements of the MANET to be violated.

The remainder of the paper is organized as follows. A framework for reasoning is introduced in Section 2. Section 3 provides a brief overview of the DRCP protocol and attacks against the protocol. We present a specification-based IDS in Section 4. Formalization and verification are covered in Section 5. Section 6 discusses our work relative to others' in intrusion detection and in formal methods as applied to security reasoning. Section 7 concludes the paper along with a brief description of our ongoing and future work.

## 2   Formal Network Model and Hierarchical Framework

### 2.1   A Hierarchical Framework for Formal Reasoning

Figure 1 depicts a hierarchical framework to verify security aspects of protocols, DRCP being the one under study in this paper. In this framework, a formal network model is used to focus on abstract security-critical properties of ad hoc networks. We define security requirements of DRCP and reason about the enforcement of the security requirements by a specification-based intrusion detection system, characterized itself by a formal model. There are two important components for the specification-based intrusion detection - formal specifications and monitoring mechanisms. The formal specifications define valid behavior of DRCP nodes, and the monitoring mechanisms collect information from the ad hoc network and analyze

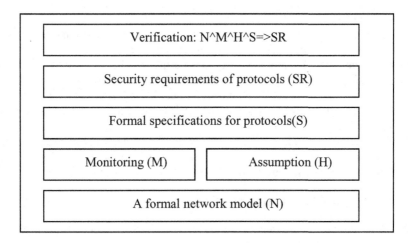

**Fig. 1.** Hierarchical Framework for Verification

the behavior of DRCP nodes according to the formal specifications. The main goal of our verification is to prove that the specification-based IDS can achieve the stated global security requirements of a DRCP network. Assumptions are introduced to cover some properties that may not be covered by the intrusion detection approach, for example functionality that (we assure and believe) cannot be impacted by an attacker. A similar framework was used to reason the detection rules of host-based IDS [14, 16].

### 2.2 A Formal Network Model

The network model defines security-critical elements of a MANET. A network is defined as a tuple *(N, S, OP, $s_0$, $\delta$)*, where *N* is a set of nodes, *S* is a set of possible states, *OP* is a set of network operations, $s_0$ is the initial state and $\delta$ is a function which maps  network operations from a previous state to a current state.

A network trace is a sequence of events, e.g. $e_1,...e_k$, that occurs in the network.

The sequence of events moves the network from $s_0$, to $s_1$, ...to $s_k$. Denote T as the set of possible traces (T = {E*}).

The state of a network comprises the states of individual nodes. Let NS be a function that return the state of a node *i*, when the network is in state S, NS(*S, i*) -> state of node *i*.

A Connection matrix C is an important component of the current state. C[i][j] denotes the whether there is a direct link between node i and node j. The connection matrix will be updated according to dynamic changes of the DRCP network.

Security requirements describe properties of systems inspired by the traditional concerns: confidentiality, integrity, and availability of resources. A security requirement is defined as a function *SR*, which accepts network traces as input and returns true if these network traces satisfy the requirement. A security requirement *SR* characterizes a set of authorized network traces *AT*, which includes all network traces that satisfy the security requirement.

In our approach, formal specifications are used as detection rules in specification-based intrusion detection. Each specification is denoted as a function *SP* and defines a set of valid network traces *VT*, which includes all finite traces of a network accepted by the specification. Any trace violating the specification will not be members of the valid set *VT*, and will be detected by the intrusion detection.

In our verification, we attempt to answer the question of whether a valid trace defined by formal specifications is an authorized trace defined by security requirements. We claim that security requirements are enforced by specifications if a set of valid traces *VT* defined by the specifications is a subset of the set of authorized traces *AT* defined by the security requirements. If the security requirements are enforced, any trace violating the security requirements (outside authorized set *AT*) will be detected by the specifications (outside valid set *VT*). The verification is carried out with ACL2 theorem prover, and the enforcement of security requirements is defined and proved as theorems in ACL2.

### 2.3  Automated Verification with ACL2

ACL2 is a re-implemented extended version of Nqthm [5], intended for large scale verification efforts. The ACL2 system consists of a programming language based on Common Lisp, a theory based first order logic and total recursive functions, and a theorem prover [8].

ACL2 has two significant advantages for our purposes: scalability and automatic proof. ACL2 has been successfully used to reason about the logic of industrial applications, including the AMD5K86 floating-point division proof [4] and the JAVA virtual machine proof [12]. Proofs of theorems in ACL2 are automatically established by the theorem prover using mathematical induction and other methods, but human intervention is usually required to introduce lemmas that guide a proof. In the mechanization of our framework, structures and functions in ACL2 are used to formalize declarative components of the framework, including an abstract network model, formal specifications of DRCP, assumptions, and security requirements. To perform the verifications, we define appropriate theorems in ACL2 and prove them using mathematical induction and the other proof mechanism of ACL2.

## 3  Overview of DRCP

DRCP provides rapid client configuration and reconfiguration in a MANET. In particular, DRCP allows rapid configuration and detects the need to reconfigure without relying on signals from other layers. The primary configuration data obtained using DRCP is an IP address. Once a node has an IP address, it can then communicate with other servers to obtain additional information. Other configuration information such as IP addresses of DNS servers and of DCDP (Distributed Configuration Distribution Protocol) [11] servers can be provided using DRCP.

A node with a DRCP process running is initially assumed only to know which of its interfaces are configured using DRCP. If there are multiple interfaces, then some interfaces may be configured by DRCP, others are configured manually. After boot-up, a node assumes all of its DRCP interfaces are configured to be DRCP clients and attempts to discover a DRCP node acting as a DRCP server. The client continues to send DRCP_DISCOVER messages broadcast on the local subnet to the DRCP_SERVER_PORT. On discovering a DRCP server, the node gets configuration information and starts communicating within the network.

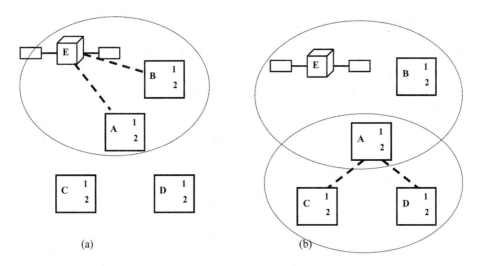

**Fig. 2.** Example Operation of DRCP

If a DRCP interface does not have a local address pool, it remains a DRCP client. A node becomes a DRCP server for an interface when it has configuration information, including an address pool. A DRCP node does not get this configuration information through DRCP, but from preset information (e.g., in a configuration file) or another protocol like DCDP.

A DRCP server takes the first address from its address-pool and other configuration information to configure its own interface for that subnet. The node is then ready to serve other nodes on that subnet. An interesting but security-challenging characteristic of DRCP is that a node can act as a DRCP Server on some of its interfaces and a DRCP Client on other interfaces. We illustrate how a node could be both a server and a client using an example network shown in Figure 2.

The example shows five network nodes, A, B, C, D each having two network interfaces, and a border gateway node E. The border gateway runs both DRCP and DCDP protocols. Initially, A, B, C, and D are not configured. The DRCP server program running on node E periodically broadcasts a DRCP_ADVERTISE message, which reaches nodes A and B. Nodes C and D do not get the message because they are not sufficiently close to E. Upon receiving a DRCP_ADVERTISE message, node A broadcasts a DRCP_DISCOVER message. Node E then sends back a DRCP_OFFER message to A with the configuration data (IP address). Node B performs similar actions to obtain configuration data. After these message exchanges, nodes E, A, B form a subnet.

In figure 2(a), after the subnet E, A, B, is formed, Node A obtains an IP address pool from E and becomes a DRCP server for interface 2. Nodes C and D then can obtain configuration information from Node A (figure 2(b)) and form a subnet (A, C, D). This example illustrates that multiple subnets can be formed, and a node can serve as a DRCP client on one interface and as a DRCP server on another interface. Nevertheless, a node is either a DRCP client or a DRCP server for a single interface.

## 3.1  DRCP Vulnerabilities and Attacks

In general, DRCP node vulnerabilities fall into three categories:

1.  intentional overuse of scarce resources by the rogue node itself,
2.  intentionally causing other nodes to overuse scarce resources by a rogue node improperly using its forwarding function,
3.  lying about the content of configuration information either by a rogue node corrupting messages that it is forwarding, or by supplying incorrect configuration information when acting as a DRCP server.

According to these vulnerabilities, a rogue node can:

1.  continuously send DRCP_DISCOVER messages requesting new IP addresses to cause the DRCP server run out of IP addresses
2.  continuously send DRCP_DISCOVER messages with other nodes' MAC addresses
3.  provide incorrect DNS server address or IP address in DRCP_OFFER message sent from a DRCP server
4.  pretend to be a legitimate DRCP server and send DRCP_OFFER with incorrect DNS information or IP address

A rogue node can use these generic attack methods to launch very sophisticated attacks. For example, the rogue node could identify itself as the DNS server, field DNS queries from a victim node, and supply answers that cause information to be sent to incorrect rogue nodes. Or a rogue node can erroneously report another as of yet un-compromised node as a standard server in hopes that the volume of requests misdirected to that other node will result in a successful DOS attack on that node.

Also, a rogue DRCP server can:

1.  intentionally ignore DRCP_DISCOVER messages from a victim node
2.  send DRCP_OFFER with incorrect DNS information or IP address. Without initial configuration information, the victim cannot obtain an IP address and is therefore not able to communicate with any other node. Note that because of the hierarchical manner in which nodes become DRCP servers, incorrect data supplied by a rogue DRCP server will be propagated to all lower nodes, thus amplifying the extent of corruption.

## 3.2  Example DRCP Attacks

Figure 3 depicts an example attack that makes use of a DRCP vulnerability, the effect being to deny a legitimate node from communicating with the network. In particular, the attacker (a rogue node) provides incorrect configuration information (e.g., IP address, DNS address) to a newly arrived node E. The effect could be that node E is denied from communication with the network In addition, node E could be fooled into using wrong information that causes further damage to the network. The scenario is described as follows.

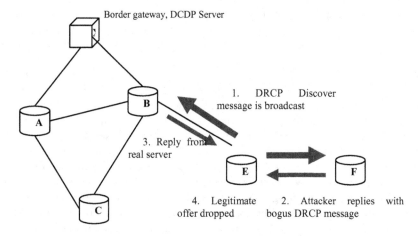

**Fig. 3.** Example DRCP Attack

1. A node E moves to the subnet and broadcasts a DRCP Discover message to obtain an IP address and other information for communication with the subnet.
2. An attacker node, after observing the DRCP Discover message from node E, replies to E with a bogus DRCP Offer message that has incorrect information. This message reaches node E first and is used by node E to configure its node.
3. Node B, which is a DRCP, receives the DRCP Discover message and replies with a correct DRCP Offer message.

Node E, having already obtained the bogus DRCP Offer message, drops the DRCP Offer message forwarded by node E.

We do not claim that the vulnerabilities presented are exhaustive, but they permit a wide variety of attacks – too many and too rich to be amenable to conventional signature-based intrusion detection. In the next section, we describe our specification-based intrusion detection approach that is capable of detecting any attack that exploits the vulnerabilities.

## 4  A Formal Specification-Based Intrusion-Detection

This section introduces the specification-based intrusion-detection approach we employ to protect a DRCP network. Other intrusion detection approaches include signature-based detection [13, 2] and anomaly detection approaches [1]. While signature-based detection offers low detection latency and a low number of false positives, it requires well-established signatures to be in place. In the case of the anomaly detection approach, "normal" profiles, usually statistical, need to be built from network and individual system events, including possible user and system activities. It will be a significant challenge to establish and dynamically tune normal profile in this domain so that the false positive rate is not unacceptably high. While statistical anomaly detection, in principle, can detect unknown attacks, the success of this methodology depends greatly on establishing effective normative profiles - a considerable challenge in a noisy wireless dynamic environment. As opposed to these approaches, the primary goal of the specification-based approach is to detect when a system / network fails to meet certain global security requirements. In addition, the approach identifies the root cause of the failure so that corrective action can be taken to deal with an intrusion.

Our approach involves decomposition of the global security requirements into formal specifications of individual network nodes. Cooperative network monitors are used to observe the behavior of individual nodes and report alerts when a node violates the local behavioral specifications. The approach has the advantage that the security officers are able to understand at a high level the security property that the intrusion detection system guarantees. In addition, the approach can, in principle detect all attacks (known or unknown) that cause the system to fail to meet the global security requirements but with few false positives. False positives may be caused by specifications that are too strong for the global security requirements or by their being a similarity between attacks and normal behavior of the system. For example, a very mobile node can cause a DOS attack. In contrast, signature-based intrusion detection can only detect known or variants of known attacks but with few false positives, and anomaly-based intrusion detection can detect unknown attacks but at the expense of many false positives which are caused by non-proficiency of the statistical rules.

### 4.1  Global Security Requirement

Our formal network model consists of a collection of mobile computing nodes, each running a DRCP agent. In our approach, the ultimate goal of the intrusion detection system is to ensure that the network of DRCP nodes can meet certain global security requirements that are critical to the mission of the MANET. The security requirements can encompass many aspects of security (e.g., integrity, availability) in addition to cryptographic requirements on the messages being exchanged. Our focus for the IDS is to achieve security requirements that are related to the integrity and the availability of a DRCP network. Informally, a general critical security requirement for DRCP is:

**An unconfigured network node in a subnet must be configured with a correct IP address (as well as DNS, default router, networking mask) within X seconds.**

**Table 1.** System Requirement for DRCP

|   | Security requirements | Aspects | Corresponding attacks |
|---|---|---|---|
| 1. | A network node in a subnet will be configured with an unused IP address of the subnet. | Safety | Rogue server, IP spoof |
| 2. | No two nodes have the same IP address. | Safety | IP spoof |
| 3. | A network node in a subnet will be given correct configuration information, including default router, DNS server, and network mask. | Safety | Man-in-the-middle attack |
| 4. | A node without an IP address will be given one within X seconds | Liveness | DOS attack |

Such a requirement is obviously important since a network node needs correct configuration information in order to communicate with other nodes in the network. To support reasoning with respect to the requirement, we break it down into the four properties listed in Table 1; we view a requirement as being safety-related if it bears on integrity, and liveness-related if it bears on availability.

The identification of global security requirements of a DRCP network determines what activity the IDS must detect. Give a global security requirement, one can reason about, informally, about whether a given attack will be detected. For example, given the stated security requirements of DRCP, it is easy to see that the IDS can detect the attack described in Section 3. Obviously, a more formal analysis is needed to further assure that the IDS can really detect the attack. This can be performed using the formal framework described in section 5.

One simple way to detect breaches of the global security requirement is to observe the activity of the whole network and check whether it breaks the global security requirements. As the global security requirements are usually concerned with global properties of the network, checking for these global security requirements requires collection of all activity in the network and keeping track of the global state. As an example, in order to check whether property 1 has been breached, one could keep track of all assigned IP addresses and the network messages that are associated with the assignment of IP addresses. Nevertheless, such a *centralized* monitoring approach is inappropriate for a MANET because of the mobility of nodes and bandwidth limitations – an IDS that requires as much bandwidth as the normal functions of the MANET is unacceptable.

In contrast, our intrusion detection approach focuses on the behavior at individual network nodes. We enforce the global security requirements by deploying local behavioral specifications for individual network nodes such that the local behavioral specifications imply the global security requirements as depicted in figure 4. The local behavioral specifications are constraints on the operation of the nodes that can be checked by external monitoring (i.e., monitoring the messages it sends and receives). We assume that an aggregating mechanism is

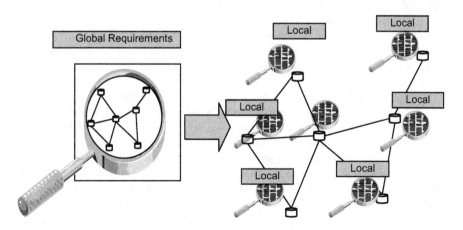

**Fig. 4.** Global Requirements and Local Specification for DRCP protocol

used to collect states of the network. Network activities of individual nodes are monitored to detect breaches of the local behavioral specifications with respect to local data and some (not all!) system data collected from other nodes, e.g. IP address of other nodes. For the most part, if no violation of local behavioral specifications is detected in any node, one can be assured that the global security requirements are satisfied.

## 4.2  Motivation for Local Behavioral Specifications

Towards producing a local behavioral specification of the protocol, we formalize parts of the protocol specification that are security-relevant (i.e., related to the global security requirements). The local behavioral specification captures, formally, the behavioral of a node in sending and responding to protocol messages. Then, we employ formal verification techniques to guarantee that the set of local behavioral specifications imply the global security requirements.

Suppose it is true that the specification is strong enough so that the global security requirement can be guaranteed if all the DRCP agents adhere to the specification. Then, one should be able to formally verify that the specification implies the system requirements. Otherwise, there are weaknesses in the specification, and the verification system may output a counterexample showing a sequence of events that leads to the undesirable situation. This sequence if synthesized by the theorem prover, constitutes a "signature" of an attack that is not noted by the IDS. One could, in principle, monitor the entire system to see whether this sequence occurs – but focusing the IDS on local rules is more efficient.

Again, why do we monitor for violation of the individual constraints of DRCP agents instead of directly monitoring activity with respect to the global system requirements? While it is nice to know that some global DRCP system requirement has been violated, it is more informative to know what is the root cause. A major benefit of our specification-based approach is that it provides knowledge of the latter. If we monitor for violation of global requirements, additional reasoning is required to determine the root cause. An example of such a requirement is "if a client sends a request it must obtain a valid IP address within a fixed amount of time". Detecting that this requirement is violated does not tell anything about potential root causes such as: (a) the server sends out incorrect IP addresses and invalid messages in general (b) the server ignores requests, or (c) there is an agent that requests IP addresses at abnormally high rates and has therefore depleted the server's address pool.

In addition, in many cases it not practical to monitor for the system requirement directly. This is because the detector usually possesses only local information, and evaluation of the global system requirement usually requires global knowledge about the current state of the system. Therefore, if we are able to enforce global system requirements with local behavioral specifications (i.e., those that must be satisfied by DRCP processes) and detect an alert, we simultaneously obtain a root cause. No further reasoning is required. In fact, the reasoning has already been performed by formal verification that shows how local behavioral specifications imply global requirements.

### 4.3   Generation of Local Behavioral Specification

We choose ESTELLE[3] to formally capture the  behavior of the DRCP protocol; later we translate this description into ACL2 to support verification. ESTELLE is an ISO standard and has been used in formal description and analysis of several military link-layer and network-layer protocols. ESTELLE, which is based on Extended Finite State Machine (EFSM) theory, is well-suited to model network protocols.

Figure 5 depicts the server part of the DRCP Local behavioral specification. The specification is derived from an informal protocol specification as well as from other DRCP documents. The DRCP agent will move to the "Server Init" state if it has obtained a configuration pool (e.g., locally configured or obtained through DCDP). The server can send a DRCP_ADVERTISE message periodically send a Gratuitous DRCP_OFFER for existing IP address. Upon receiving a DISCOVER message, it will send a DRCP_OFFER to offer an unused IP address to the requesting client. The local behavioral specification of DRCP in ESTELLE is listed below. The specification basically describes the possible states of a DRCP node and how the node transitions from one state to another state when an event occurs.

*body Node_BODY for NODE;*
*state INIT, DISCOVERING, BINDING, SERVER,WAITING;*
*initialize to INIT; //initial state*
*trans when GetIPPool() from Init to Server_Init; //change the state to Server if an IP pool is*

                                                        *available*
*trans when SetIPPool()  from Server_Init to Listen;//ready to accept DRCP requests after*

                                                     *being  configured*
*trans when send(unicast.Gratuitous_Offer) from Listen to Listen;//send out Gratuitous offers*
*trans when broadcast.DISCOVER // broadcast DRCP Discover*
    *from Listen to Reply;*
    *from Reply to Reply;*
*trans when unicast.DISCOVER //unicast DRCP Discover*
    *from Listen to Reply;*
*trans when send(unicast.OFFER(ipinfo)) //send out DRCP offers*
    *from Reply to Listen;......*

If the original DRCP design is sufficient to guarantee all required properties, then one can just use the formal protocol specification as the detection rule to detect the presence of network activity such that the properties will not hold. Otherwise, we need to define additional constraints on the behavior of the DRCP agent in order to guarantee the required properties. Formal reasoning techniques can tell whether the specification is sufficiently strong to guarantee certain security properties. In this paper we first consider properties that can be assured with the current DRCP design. In particular, we focus on two top-level requirements:

- DRCP nodes will be configured with an IP address in the subnet, and
- No two nodes have the same IP address

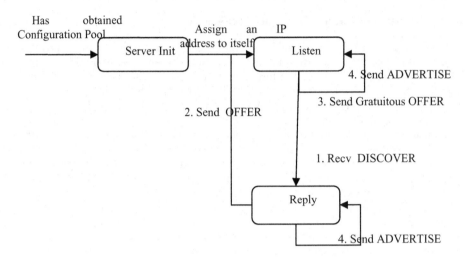

**Fig. 5.** An EFSM Model of DRCP – Server Part

## 5  Formalization and Verification

This section discusses our experience in applying formal methods to assure that the specification-based intrusion detection system can achieve what it claims: it can guarantee the detection of any activity that impacts the global security requirements. In general, formal methods are mathematically based techniques that rely on descriptions of system elements and properties, and enable one to show that the system elements achieve more abstract properties of the system. Formal methods provide a framework in which one can specify, develop, and verify systems in a systematic manner.

### 5.1  Formalization of Security Requirements

We have developed a framework for formal reasoning about the cooperative monitoring of the DRCP protocol. This framework consists of a network model, a monitoring model, behavioral specifications, assumptions, and security requirements. Security requirements are abstract properties that represent what it means for the DRCP protocol to be secure; we believe our requirements capture such behavior, but recognize that other requirements are possible – and can be dealt with in our methodology. Formal methods, including formal specification and analysis techniques, are used to describe the behavioral specification as well as in mathematically proving that the behavioral specification is strong enough to guarantee certain critical system requirements. The security requirements are formalized as functions in ACL2. These functions accept audit traces of DRCP nodes as parameters and verify security-related properties according to current packets and history information. For instance, the second security property, "No two nodes have the same IP address," is formalized as a function that rejects any audit trace containing two DRCP_OFFER packets with the same IP address. The ACL2 function is defined as below:

*(defun uniqueoffer (packet historyinfo)*
  *(if (endp historyinfo)*
    *t*
    *(and (uniqueofferrec packet (car (getofferlist historyinfo)))*
                         *//a unique IP address for the current offer*
       *(uniqueoffer packet (cdr (getofferlist historyinfo)))*
                        *// unique IP addresses for all offers  )))*

The security property, "A node without an IP address will be given one within X seconds", is defined as a function that only accepts audit traces that have corresponding DRCP_OFFERs for each request from a DRCP client within X seconds. Any request without a corresponding DRCP OFFER will be considered as a starved request.

*(defun no_starve_req (packet historyinfo network)*
  *(if (endp historyinfo)*
    *t*
    *(and (no_starve_req_rec packet (car (getreqlist historyinfo)))*
                      *//no starved request for current record*
      *(no_starve_req (cdr (getreqrlist historyinfo))) //no starved request for all*
*records*
  *) ))*

### 5.2 Formalization of Specifications of DRCP

We formally specify the activities of a DRCP server and a client. Our model, codified in ACL2, is in essence a server and client's actions expressed as an extended finite state machines (EFSM) and formalize them using ACL2.

The local behavioral specifications of DRCP protocol are defined as a function which uses incoming packets and current states as inputs to determine the next state and outgoing packets. A network buffer stores the packets through the wireless network. The state transitions are defined as below:

*(defun statetransition(currstate inpacket outpacket iplist)*
  *(cond*
   *((and (equal currstate 'Server_init) (getippool))// get IP Pool from DRCP server*
    *'Listen)*
   *((and (equal currstate 'Listen) (equalpackettype inpacket 'Discover)(validip iplist)*
    *'Reply) //send out an offer if a valid IP is available*
   *((and (equal currstate 'Listen) (equalpackettype inpacket 'Discover)(not(validip*
*iplist)))*
      *'Server_init) // request new IP pool if no valid IP available*
  *...*

We now describe how we prove that these formal DRCP local behavioral specifications imply the global security requirements.

### 5.3 Verification About Enforcement of Security Requirements

In verification, we try to demonstrate whether the local behavioral specifications are strong enough to guarantee the security requirements. We have formalized and verified a few availability requirements like whether a unique IP will be provided to a DRCP client in a timely manner, which we say is X seconds. In the verification, we prove that under certain assumptions, if any audit trail does not violate the local behavioral specifications of DRCP, these audit trail do not violate the security requirements either. The theorem is defined as:

> *(defthm specification-requirement*
>   *(implies*
>     *(and*
>       *(assumptions packetlist) // assumptions A1 to A4*
>       *(spec packetlist network) //local specification for DRCP nodes*
>     *)*
>     *(requirement packetlist nil network)// global requirements for DRCP networks*
>   *))*

Assumptions are made in our verification to cover properties that may not be monitored by the behavioral IDS specifications. These assumptions include:

A1: a DRCP server always gets a valid IP pool;
A2: a DRCP server only uses each IP address in the IP pool once;
A3: only one DRCP server is in a subnet;
A4: a DRCP server sends out an offer in T1 seconds after receiving a request; network delay is less than T2; and T1+2*T2 less than X.

These assumptions are important in analyzing the enforcement of security requirements. They are sufficient but not certainly the weakest possible assumptions; in our methodology, assumptions can be reviewed and relaxed, if possible to still carry out the verification.  We can use formal reasoning to determine which assumptions are necessary. For now we ask the reader to accept the reasonableness of these assumptions.

Some of the assumptions are not always true and may be violated by some unusual behavior of DRCP nodes. For example, assumption A1 may not hold during the process in which a DRCP server, which uses up all IP addresses, sends out a request asking for a new IP pool from a DCDP server. Some of the assumptions can be removed or weakened by using an improved DRCP specification that can describe the behavior of DRCP more precisely. These assumptions may also be sources for attacks when they do not hold. Additional detection rules can be developed to monitor whether the assumptions are violated. For example, DRCP servers get IP pools from DCDP servers by sending out DCDP requests. Deploying a monitoring scheme with proper DCDP specifications will detect the violation of assumption A1.

## 6  Discussions

Monitoring mechanisms are important for achieving security when a network might be subject to attacks – that exploit vulnerabilities in the protocol design, or the protocol implementation, or that arise when a node is under the control of an attacker. Since we wish to detect unknown attacks, we reject a signature-based approach in favor of specification-based intrusion detection. In the IDS approach presented in this paper, we could have assumed that a centralized monitoring scheme is employed to collect a complete set of information about the MANET. This centralized approach, although feasible, scales poorly since every node needs to collect information and send it to a server for analysis. An alternate mechanism is to employ a cooperative monitoring approach - IDS monitors at each node make decisions based upon local information and necessary but limited correlated information from other monitors. Bandwidth costs as well as processing costs associated with message gathering will improve as compared with centralized monitoring. Further improvement could be obtained if a subset of nodes is used for monitoring instead of all the nodes. In [17], it is observed that all malicious packets can be detected by executing the IDS in only a small fraction of the nodes (typically less than 15%). For example, a set of nodes, that represents a minimum vertex cover of an ad hoc network, can be used to monitor all the traffic in the network. We are pursuing these ideas in our current research.

Our verification methodology makes progress towards the achievement of an important claim of specification-based intrusion detection: a zero false negative rate in detecting all attacks that violate the security requirements. Since we have proved that the specifications can ensure that the security requirements will not be violated, it is trivial to prove the any violation of the security requirements implies violations of the specification. This means all attacks that violate the security requirements will be detected by the specification-based intrusion detection. Another important aspect of the specification-based approach is a low false positive rate. This aspect is not addressed in our verification presently, but we believe that determining a near-minimal rule set that is necessary to carry out the proof is a possible approach. Right now, the amount of search to determine such a rule set is expensive but we are considering heuristic search methods to reduce the search.

## 7 Conclusions and Future Work

We have applied specification-based intrusion detection to detect insider attacks on DRCP. DRCP is used to automatically configure nodes in a MANET with IP addresses, and other data, a newly arriving node requires to interface to the network. It is especially important to secure this protocol since if it is compromised, no IP layer connectivity can be established or there will be unintended sharing of addresses.

We defined global security requirements and created rules that characterize a specification-based intrusion detection system that enforces these global requirements, i.e., detect activity that could cause the security requirements to be violated. Local behavioral specifications are developed to define normal behavior of DRCP. In our results, we have proved that the local behavioral specifications of DRCP can ensure that the global security requirements will hold. Any violation of global security requirements will result in a violation of local specifications and raise an alert. We claim that the intrusion detection system is efficient (because it monitors behavior of individual nodes), has no false negatives (with respect to the global requirements we defined).

Future work includes improving the formal specifications of DRCP as the basis for arguing that the IDS issues few (hopefully no) false positives, reasoning about other wireless protocols like OLSR and simulating the specification-based intrusion detection on a test bed as a way to validate our proof and our claim about IDS overhead.

# References

[1]  J. P. Anderson, "Computer security threat monitoring and surveilance," Technical report, James P. Anderson Co., Fort Washington, PA, April 1980.

[2]  Matthew A. Bishop, Computer Security: Art and Science, Addison Wesley Longman, 2002.

[3]  S. Budkowski and P. Dembinski, "An Introduction to Estelle: A specification language for distributed systems," Computer Networks and ISDN Systems, vol. 14, no. 1, pp. 3--24, 1991.

[4]  Bishop Brock, Matt Kaufmann and J Moore,"ACL2 Theorems about Commercial Microprocessors," in proceedings of Formal Methods in Computer-Aided Design (FMCAD'96), Springer-Verlag, pp. 275-293, 1996

[5]  R. S. Boyer and J S. Moore, A computational logic, Academic Press, New York, 1979.

[6]  Yian Huang and Wenke Lee, "Attack Analysis and Detection for Ad Hoc Routing Protocols," in proceedings of The 7th International Symposium on Recent Advances in Intrusion Detection (RAID 2004), Sophia Antipolis, France, September 2004

[7]  K. Ilgun, R. Kemmerer, and P. Porras , "State Transition Analysis: A Rule-based Intrusion Detection Approach", In IEEE Transactions of Software Engineering, 2(13):181-199, March 1995.

[8]  Matt Kaufmann, Panagiotis Manolios, and J Strother Moore, "Computer-Aided Reasoning: An Approach", Kluwer Academic Publishers, June, 2000

[9]  C. Ko, J. Rowe, P. Brutch, K. Levitt, "System Health and Intrusion Monitoring Using a hierarchy of Constraints", In Proceedings of the 4th International Symposium on Recent Advances in Intrusion Detection (RAID), 2001.

[10] C. Ko, M. Ruschitzka and K. Levitt, "Execution Monitoring of Security-Critical Programs in Distributed Systems: A Specification-based Approach," In Proceedings of the 1997 IEEE Symposium on Security and Privacy, May 1997.

[11] A. J. McAuley, K. Manousakis, "Self-Configuring Networks", IEEE Milcom 2000, Los Angeles, October 2000.

[12] J Moore,"Proving Theorems about Java-like Byte Code," in Correct System Design - Issues, Methods and Perspectives, 1999.

[13] M. Roesch, "Snort: Lightweight Intrusion Detection for Networks", Proc. Of USENIX LISA '99, Seattle, Washington, November 1999, pp. 229-238.

[14] Tao Song, Jim Alves-Foss, Calvin Ko, Cui Zhang, Karl Levitt, "Using ACL2 to Verify Security Properties of Specification-based Intrusion Detection Systems," In Proceedings of the Fourth International Workshop on the ACL2 Theorem Prover and Its Applications, 2003.

[15] D. Sterne, P. Balasubramanyam, D. Carman, B. Wilson, R. Talpade, C. Ko, R. Balupari, C-Y. Tseng, T. Bowen, K. Levitt and J. Rowe, "A General Cooperative Intrusion Detection Architecture for MANETs," In Proceedings of the 3rd IEEE International Workshop on Information Assurance, March 2005

[16] Tao Song, Calvin Ko, Jim Alves-Foss, Cui Zhang and Karl Levitt, "Formal Reasoning about Intrusion Detection Systems," In Proceedings of the 7th International Symposium on Recent Advances in Intrusion Detection (RAID), 2004.

[17] Dhanant Subhadrabandhu, Saswati Sarkar, and Farooq Anjum, "Efficacy of Misuse Detection in Adhoc Networks, " In proceeding of IEEE Communications Society Conference on Sensor and Ad Hoc Communications and Networks, 2004.

[18] C.Y. Tseng, P. Balasubramanyam, C. Ko, R. Limprasittiporn, J. Rowe, K. Levitt, "A Specification-Based Instrusion Detection system for AODV," 2003 ACM Workshop on security of Ad Hoc and Sensor Networks (SASN '03), October 21, 2003.

[19] Chinyang Henry Tseng, Tao Song, Poornima Balasubramanyam, Calvin Ko, Karl Levitt, "A Specification-based Intrusion Detection Model for OLSR," submited to International Symposium on Recent Advances in Intrusion Detection (RAID), 2005

[20] Ravi Vaidyanathan, Latha Kant, Anthony McAuley, Michael Bereschinsky, "Performance Modeling and Simulation of Dynamic and Rapid Auto-configuration Protocols for Ad-hoc Wireless Networks," in proceeding of Annual Simulation Symposium 2003.

[21] Lidong Zhou and Zygmunt J. Haas. Securing ad hoc networks. IEEE Network Magazine, 13(6), November/ December 1999.

# A Formal Approach for Reasoning About a Class of Diffie-Hellman Protocols

Rob Delicata and Steve Schneider

Department of Computing, University of Surrey, Guildford, GU2 7XH, UK
{R.Delicata, S.Schneider}@surrey.ac.uk

**Abstract.** We present a framework for reasoning about secrecy in a class of Diffie-Hellman protocols. The technique, which shares a conceptual origin with the idea of a rank function, uses the notion of a message-template to determine whether a given value is generable by an intruder in a protocol model. Traditionally, the rich algebraic structure of Diffie-Hellman messages has made it difficult to reason about such protocols using formal, rather than complexity-theoretic, techniques. We describe the approach in the context of the MTI A(0) protocol, and derive the conditions under which this protocol can be considered secure.

## 1 Introduction

Formal protocol analysis techniques have a simplicity which is due, in part, to the high level of abstraction at which they operate. Such abstractions are justified since any attack discovered at the abstract level will tend to be preserved in a more concrete model. In general, however, failure to discover an attack does not imply correctness, and in seeking to establish correctness we must be mindful of the assumptions on which our abstractions are based.

Protocols based on the Diffie-Hellman scheme [DH76] present an interesting verification challenge since, in this context, we cannot assume such an abstract view of cryptography. Certain algebraic properties (such as the homomorphism of exponentiation in $(g^x)^y = (g^y)^x$) must be represented for the protocol to reach its functional goal, and other properties (such as the cancellation of multiplicative inverses) must also be considered if we wish to prove a meaningful security result. As a consequence, such protocols have tended to be evaluated in complexity-theoretic models (see [BCP01], for example) which aim to reduce the correctness of the protocol to some well-defined hard problem, such as the computation of discrete logarithms in a finite field. The resulting proofs tend to be difficult to conduct and evaluate, and a small change in the protocol will often require an entirely new proof to be constructed.

With some exceptions [Mea00, PQ01, AC04] formal techniques have been slow in rising to the challenge of Diffie-Hellman. This paper presents a theorem-proving approach to the verification of a class of Diffie-Hellman protocols. Although our approach is quite general we present it in the context of the MTI A(0) protocol of Matsumoto, Takashima and Imai [MTI86]. This protocol is chosen for

T. Dimitrakos et al. (Eds.): FAST 2005, LNCS 3866, pp. 34–46, 2006.
© Springer-Verlag Berlin Heidelberg 2006

the simplicity of its messages and non-standard use of Diffie-Hellman (in particular, the computation of a shared key as $g^x \cdot g^y = g^{x+y}$). Some of the MTI protocols satisfy an interesting property—which we call I/O-independence—that enables us to model the protocols at a very abstract level. The protocols and the concept of I/O-independence are described in Section 2. Our model revolves around the idea of a message-template which, suitably instantiated, can represent any value that an intruder can deduce (under a defined set of capabilities). A particular value remains secret if it cannot be realised via any instantiation of the message-template. This model, and its associated definition of secrecy, is described in Section 3 and applied to the MTI A(0) protocol in Section 4. Although we do not describe it in such language, our approach shares a conceptual origin with the notion of a rank function [Sch97], and is informed by the approach of Pereira and Quisquater [PQ01]; we explore these relationships, and conclude, in Section 5.

## 2    The MTI Protocols

Three infinite classes of authenticated key agreement protocols fall under the banner of MTI [MTI86]. All of the MTI protocols appear amenable to analysis in our framework but, in this paper, we focus on one particular protocol, A(0). The protocol combines long-term and ephemeral key contributions to provide authentication in the Diffie-Hellman scheme. A summary of notation, following [BM03], is given in Figure 1. In protocol A(0) (Figure 2) principal $A$ (who wishes to establish a shared-secret with $B$) generates a long-term secret, $x_A$, and publishes the corresponding public-key $y_A = g^{x_A}$. $B$ does the same with $x_B$ and $y_B$. $A$ randomly chooses $r_A$, computes $z_A = g^{r_A}$ and sends it to $B$. In response, $B$ randomly chooses $r_B$, computes $z_B = g^{r_B}$ and sends it to $A$. $B$ then computes $Z_{AB} = z_A^{x_B} y_A^{r_B} = (g^{r_A})^{x_B} \cdot (g^{x_A})^{r_B} = g^{r_A x_B + x_A r_B}$ and $A$ computes $Z_{AB} = g^{r_B x_A + x_B r_A}$.

| | |
|---|---|
| $r_A, r_B, r_C$ | Random integers, chosen by $A$, $B$ and $C$ respectively |
| $t_A, t_B$ | Ephemeral public-keys, $t_A = g^{r_A}$, $t_B = g^{r_B}$ |
| $x_A, x_B, x_C$ | Private long-term keys of $A$, $B$ and $C$ respectively |
| $y_A, y_B$ | Public keys of $A$ and $B$: $y_A = g^{x_A}$, $y_B = g^{x_B}$ |
| $Z_{AB}$ | The shared secret between $A$ and $B$ |
| $x \in_R X$ | An element $x$ chosen at random from the set $X$ |

**Fig. 1.** Protocol notation

$$A \qquad\qquad\qquad B$$

$$r_A \in_R \mathbb{Z}_q$$
$$z_A = g^{r_A} \quad \xrightarrow{\quad z_A \quad} \quad r_B \in_R \mathbb{Z}_q$$
$$z_B = g^{r_B}$$
$$Z_{AB} = z_B^{x_A} y_B^{r_A} \quad \xleftarrow{\quad z_B \quad} \quad Z_{AB} = z_A^{x_B} y_A^{r_B}$$

**Fig. 2.** MTI A(0) protocol

The protocol aims to convince each principal that no one, aside from the other protocol participant, can learn the shared-secret $Z_{AB}$. This property is often termed *implicit key authentication*; here we simply refer to it as *secrecy*.

All of the MTI protocols involve the exchange of two messages, $z_A$ and $z_B$, each of which is computed within the principal and not as a function of a previously received message. (Contrast this with protocols like Cliques, where a principal $B$ may receive an input $m$ from $A$, apply some function to $m$ and send the result on to $C$.) We capture this notion in the property of Input/Output-independence:

**Definition 1.** *In a Diffie-Hellman protocol a principal $P$ is I/O-independent if $P$ does not transmit any message which is dependent on the value of a previously received message.*

We say that a protocol is I/O-independent if every honest principal is I/O-independent.

**Proposition 1.** *Protocol $A(0)$ is I/O-independent.*

We will see in the next section that the property of I/O-independence enables us to model protocols at a very abstract level.

# 3    A Model for I/O-Independent Diffie-Hellman Protocols

In this section we present a model for I/O-independent protocols based around the idea of a *message-template* which defines the general form of any message generable by an intruder in a given protocol.

We begin by noting that transmitted messages are elements of some group $G$ in which the Decisional Diffie-Hellman problem is believed to be hard. A generator $g$ of $G$ is agreed by all principals and there exists an identity element 1 such that $1 \cdot x = 1$, for all $x \in G$. We assume that elements of $G$ can be expressed as $g$ raised to the power of a sum of products of random numbers. This assumption permits, for example, $g^{xy+z}$, where $x$, $y$ and $z$ are random numbers, but excludes values such as $g^{(g^x)}$ since the exponent is itself a group element. The users of the system therefore manipulate two types of element, (i) random exponents, and (ii) powers of $g$, and we assume that only the latter will be sent on the network.

## 3.1    The Intruder

We divide the users of the system into a set of honest principals, $\{A, B\}$, who will always adhere to the protocol, and a malevolent intruder, $C$, whose goal is to subvert the protocol.

Some elements of (i) (from above) will be known initially to the intruder (such as random numbers he has chosen himself), and some elements of (ii) will become known to the intruder during the course of the protocol. The I/O-independent nature of the protocols means that an active intruder cannot influence any of the values sent by honest participants, since the functions which produce these values are not dependent on any external input. This is important, since it is then sufficient to assume that the intruder knows these values from the start.

Following [PQ01], we divide the intruder's initial knowledge into a set $E$ of exponents and a set $P$ of known powers of $g$, where $x \in P$ indicates knowledge of $g^x$ but not of $x$ (unless $x \in E$). We then define the computations that the intruder can perform.

**Definition 2 (intruder capabilities).** *Given a set $P$ of initially known powers of $g$ and a set $E$ of initially known exponents, the intruder can* grow *$P$ based on the following operations:*
1. *given $m_1 \in P$ and $m_2 \in P$ add $m_1 + m_2$ to $P$*
2. *given $m \in P$ and $n \in E$ add $mn$, $m(n^{-1})$ to $P$*
3. *given $m \in P$ add $-m$ to $P$*

In other words, we allow the intruder to (1) compute $g^{m_1} \cdot g^{m_1} = g^{m_1+m_2}$ given knowledge of $g^{m_1}$ and $g^{m_2}$, (2) compute the exponentiations $(g^m)^n$, $(g^m)^{n^{-1}}$ given knowledge of $g^m$ and $n$, and (3) compute the inverse $\frac{1}{g^m} = g^{-m}$ given $g^m$. Moreover, these capabilities can be combined:

*Example 1.* Suppose that $P = \{1, r_A\}$ and $E = \{r_C\}$. The intruder can deduce (i) $-r_A \in P$ by rule 3 from $r_A$, (ii) $1r_C \in P$ by rule 2 and $-r_A + 1r_C \in P$ by rule 1 from (i) and (ii), representing the computation of $g^{r_C - r_A}$.

Crucially, the intruder is not able to use $m_1 \in P$ and $m_2 \in P$ to deduce $m_1 m_2$.                                                                                ∎

In this model, the intruder's entire knowledge can be defined as the closure of $P$ under the deductions of Definition 2 and set $E$. In any useful protocol, $E$ and $P$ will initially be non-empty, and the resulting knowledge sets will be infinite. For this reason, it will be infeasible to enumerate these sets by *growing* $P$ via successive application of rules 1–3.

## 3.2   System Definition

An examination of the sorts of values that can be deduced by an intruder leads to the following observation: a generable value can be written as some number of elements of $P$ multiplied by some product of (possibly inverted) elements from $E$. For instance, the value derived in Example 1 can be written as $-1(r_A)(r_C^0) + 1(1)(r_C^1)$ (noting the difference between the group identity 1 and the integer 1). In fact, we can go further by defining a polynomial over the variables of $E$ and $P$ which represents any value generable by the intruder using rules 1–3, above.

**Definition 3.** *Let $F$ be a finite family of functions that map elements of $E$ to integer powers: $F \subseteq_{fin} E \to \mathbb{Z}$.*

Given $E = \{x_C\}$, for example, we may define $F = \{\{x_C \mapsto -1\}\}$.

**Definition 4.** *Let $h$ be a higher-order function which, for a member of $F$, maps elements of $P$ to integers: $h : F \to (P \to \mathbb{Z})$.*

As an example, given $P = \{r_A\}$ and $F = \{\{x_C \mapsto -1\}\}$, we might choose to define $h(\{x_C \mapsto -1\}) = \{r_A \mapsto 1\}$.

**Definition 5 (message-template).** *Fix some $E$ and $P$. Then:*

$$v(F, h) = \sum_{f \in F} \left( \sum_{p \in P} h_{f,p} \cdot p \right) \left( \prod_{e \in E} e^{f_e} \right)$$

We call $v$ the *message-template* for a system defined by $E$ and $P$. Intuition is little help here, so consider a simple example:

*Example 2.* Given the system defined by $P = \{r_A\}$ and $E = \{x_C\}$, consider how the value $g^{-r_A x_C^{-1} + 5 r_A x_C}$ can be expressed. $P$ and $E$ result in the following polynomial:

$$v(F, h) = \sum_{f \in F} \left( h_{f,r_A} \cdot x_C^{f_{x_C}} \right)$$

To express a particular generable value we must define $F$ and $h$. Recall that $F$ is a family of functions. Suppose that $F = \{\{x_C \mapsto -1\}, \{x_C \mapsto 0\}, \{x_C \mapsto 1\}\}$, then we have:

$$v(F, h) = (h_{\{x_C \mapsto -1\}, r_A} \cdot x_C^{-1}) + (h_{\{x_C \mapsto 0\}, r_A} \cdot x_C^0) + (h_{\{x_C \mapsto 1\}, r_A} \cdot x_C^1)$$

Finally, suppose that $h$ is defined such that $h(\{x_C \mapsto -1\}) = \{r_A \mapsto 1\}$, $h(\{x_C \mapsto 0\}) = \{r_A \mapsto 0\}$ and $h(\{x_C \mapsto 1\}) = \{r_A \mapsto 5\}$. This results in:

$$v(F, h) = (-1 \cdot r_A) \cdot (x_C^{-1}) + (0 \cdot r_A) \cdot (x_C^0) + (5 \cdot r_A)(x_C^1)$$

which is the value $-r_A x_C^{-1} + 5 r_A x_C$. ∎

As a more complex example, consider the following:

*Example 3.* Let $P = \{1, r_A, r_B\}$, $E = \{x_C, r_C\}$. Then:

$$v(F, h) = \sum_{f \in F} (h_{f,1} \cdot 1 + h_{f,r_A} \cdot r_A + h_{f,r_B} \cdot r_B) \left( x_C^{f_{x_C}} \cdot r_C^{f_{r_C}} \right)$$

In this polynomial, the value $g^{r_C - r_A}$ from Example 1 can be represented by defining:

$$F = \{\{x_C \mapsto 0, r_C \mapsto 0\}, \{x_C \mapsto 0, r_C \mapsto 1\}\}$$

and $h$ such that:

$$h(\{x_C \mapsto 0, r_C \mapsto 0\}) = \{1 \mapsto 0, r_A \mapsto -1, r_B \mapsto 0\}$$
$$h(\{x_C \mapsto 0, r_C \mapsto 1\}) = \{1 \mapsto 1, r_A \mapsto 0, r_B \mapsto 0\}$$

We then obtain: $v(F, h) = (0 \cdot 1 + -1 \cdot r_A + 0 \cdot r_B)(x_C^0 \cdot r_C^0) + (1 \cdot 1 + 0 \cdot r_A + 0 \cdot r_B)(x_C^0 \cdot r_C^1) = -r_A + r_C$. ∎

As stated, our intention is that, for a given system (defined by $E$ and $P$), the polynomial $v(F, h)$ expresses the general form of all values deducible by an intruder, from $P$ and $E$, by appeal to the deduction rules of Definition 2. We embed the ability of a polynomial to take a certain value in the concept of realisability:

**Definition 6.** *A value $m$ is realisable (written realisable($m$)) if there exists functions $F$ and $h$ such that $v(F, h) = m$.*

That is, a value $m$ is realisable if there exists a solution to the equation $v(F, h) - m = 0$. If $m$ is not realisable we write $\neg realisable(m)$. Define $Pub$ to be a closure containing all possible polynomials for a given system. $Pub$ is the set containing all realisable values of that system: the set of *public* messages.

**Theorem 1 (Faithfulness).** *Fix some $P$ and $E$ and $Pub$ as defined above. $Pub$ is closed under the deductions of Definition 2.*

*Proof.* By induction. For the base case we show that, whenever $p \in P$, $p$ is realisable.

**Base case:** Given some $p \in P$, $p$ is realisable with $v(F, h)$ by defining

$$F = \{\{e \mapsto 0 \mid e \in E\}\}$$

and:

$$h(\{e \mapsto 0 \mid e \in E\}) = \{p \mapsto 1\} \cup \{q \mapsto 0 \mid q \in P \setminus \{p\}\}$$

**Inductive step:** There are three cases, corresponding to the three intruder deduction rules: (i) $realisable(m_1) \wedge realisable(m_2) \implies realisable(m_1 + m_2)$, (ii) $realisable(m_1) \wedge n \in E \implies realisable(m_1 n) \wedge realisable(m_1 n^{-1})$, and (iii) $realisable(m_1) \implies realisable(-m_1)$.

(i) Assume $m_1 = v(F_1, h_1)$ and $m_2 = v(F_2, h_2)$. Then $m_1 + m_2$ is realisable with $v(F_3, h_3)$ by defining $F_3 = F_1 \cup F_2$ and $h$ such that:

$$h_3(f) = \begin{cases} h_1(f) & \text{if } f \in dom(h_1) \setminus dom(h_2) \\ h_2(f) & \text{if } f \in dom(h_2) \setminus dom(h_1) \\ \lambda p.h_1(f)(p) + h_2(f)(p) & \text{if } f \in dom(h_1) \cap dom(h_2) \end{cases}$$

(ii) For the first conjunct assume $m_1 = v(F_1, h_1)$ and $n \in E$. Then, $m_1 n$ is realisable with $v(F_2, h_2)$ by defining:

$$F_2 = \{f \oplus \{n \mapsto (F_1(n) + 1)\} \mid f \in F_1\}$$

and $h_2$ such that:

$$h_2(f) = h_1(f \oplus \{n \mapsto (f(n) - 1)\})$$

The second conjunct follows the above, with addition in place of the subtraction in the definition of $h_2$.

(iii) Assume $m_1 = v(F_1, h_1)$. Then $-m_1$ is realisable with $v(F_1, h_2)$ where $h_2$ is defined such that $h_2(f)(p) = -(h_1(f)(p))$. ∎

Our intention is for the model to respect the fact that some values are impossible for an intruder to guess. We achieve this by assuming that the variables ($r_A$, $x_C$ etc.) are *symbolic*, that each is distinct from all others, and that the set of variables is disjoint from the set of integers.

**Assumption 1.** $(P \cup E) \cap \mathbb{Z} = \emptyset$

The following example makes clear why this restriction is necessary:

*Example 4.* Consider the system defined by $P = \{1\}$ and $E = \{x_C\}$. If variables are numbers, then any group value $g^X$ can be realised by defining $X = v(F, h)$, where $F = \{\{x_C \mapsto 0\}\}$ and $h(\{x_C \mapsto 0\}) = \{1 \mapsto X\}$, yielding $v(F, h) = (1 \cdot X)x_C^0 = X$. ∎

Assumption 1 means that, for the group identity 1, we have that $1 \notin \mathbb{Z}$ and, in particular, $1 \neq 1$. However, we grant special privileges to the group identity such that $1 \cdot m = m$, for all $m$. Note that an element $n \in E \setminus P$ will typically only be realisable if $1 \in P$. That is, $n$ is realisable by $v(F, h)$, where $F = \{\{n \mapsto 1\}\}$ and $h(\{n \mapsto 1\}) = \{1 \mapsto 1\}$, giving $1 \cdot (1 \cdot n^1) = n$.

**Condition 1.** $1 \in P \implies P \cap E = \emptyset$

We require that the above condition be true of any protocol model. To see why this is necessary consider the system given by $E = \{x_C\}$, $P = \{1, x_C\}$. The value $x_C$ can be realised in two ways, $x_C = v(F, h_1) = v(F, h_2)$, where $F = \{\{x_C \mapsto 0\}, \{x_C \mapsto 1\}\}$, and $h_1$, $h_2$ are defined such that:

- $h_1(\{x_C \mapsto 0\}) = \{1 \mapsto 0, x_C \mapsto 1\}$, $h_1(\{x_C \mapsto 1\}) = \{1 \mapsto 0, x_C \mapsto 0\}$
- $h_2(\{x_C \mapsto 0\}) = \{1 \mapsto 0, x_C \mapsto 0\}$, $h_2(\{x_C \mapsto 1\}) = \{1 \mapsto 1, x_C \mapsto 0\}$

The first case yields $v(F, h_1) = (x_C)x_C^0 + (0)x_C^1 = x_C$ and the second results in $v(F, h_2) = (0)x_C^0 + (1)x_C^1 = x_C$. Since $h_1 \neq h_2$, but $v(F, h_1) = v(F, h_2)$, the example allows the same value to be derived in two separate ways.

## 3.3   Secrecy

In a Diffie-Hellman protocol, a principal $u$ performs some key computation function on an input $z$ to derive a secret $Z_{uv}$ believed to be shared with $v$. We denote this function $k_{uv}$ with $Z_{uv} = k_{uv}(z)$.

*Example 5.* In the standard Diffie-Hellman protocol [DH76], a principal $A$, apparently running with $B$ and using the ephemeral secret $x_A$ performs the key computation $k_{AB}(z) = zx_A$ representing the shared secret $Z_{AB} = g^{zx_A}$. ∎

**Definition 7 (Secrecy).** *Given a system defined by $E$ and $P$, a key computation function $k$ maintains secrecy iff:*

$$\forall m.realisable(m) \implies \neg realisable(k(m))$$

Intuitively, secrecy is defined as an anti-closure property of the set of generable values: the result of applying $k$ to a realisable value should never result in a realisable value. If this property does not hold then an intruder will possess two values, $x$ and $y$, such that, if $x$ is sent to some principal she will compute $y$, wrongly believing it to be secret.

## 4  Reasoning About the MTI A(0) Protocol

A complete model of an I/O-independent protocol is a combination of the message-template with an appropriate key computation function. In this section we present a model of the MTI A(0) protocol and use it to deduce the conditions under which the protocol guarantees the secrecy of a shared key.

Define $E^{A(0)} = \{r_C, x_C\}$, $P^{A(0)} = \{1, r_A, r_B, x_A, x_B\}$, representing a run of the MTI A(0) protocol. We wish to show that the key computation function $k_{ab}^{A(0)}(z) = zx_a + x_b r_a$ maintains secrecy. There are eight cases to consider:

$$
\begin{array}{ll}
1.\ a = A \wedge b = C & 5.\ a = A \wedge b = A \\
2.\ a = B \wedge b = C & 6.\ a = B \wedge b = B \\
3.\ a = C \wedge b = A & 7.\ a = A \wedge b = B \\
4.\ a = C \wedge b = B & 8.\ a = B \wedge b = A
\end{array}
$$

We treat each in turn.

### Cases 1–4

Let $a = A$ and $b = C$. We are trying to show that, for any $z$ where $realisable(z)$, $\neg realisable(k_{AC}^{A(0)}(z))$. There exists some $F_1$ and $h_1$ such that $v(F_1, h_1) = z$. If we can find some $F_2$ and $h_2$ such that $v(F_2, h_2) = k_{AC}^{A(0)}(z)$ we will have shown that $k_{AC}^{A(0)}(z)$ is realisable and is therefore, not secret.

Note that $k_{AC}^{A(0)}(z) = zx_A + x_C r_A$ is a linear combination, and that the linear combination will be realisable if each of its components is realisable. In general $zx_A$ will be realisable if $z$ does not mention $x_A$ (since $x_A \in P$ but $x_A \notin E$). Consider, then, $z = r_C$, given by $v(F_1, h_1)$ where:

$$
\begin{aligned}
F_1 &= \{\{r_C \mapsto 1\}\} \\
h_1(\{r_C \mapsto 1\}) &= \{1 \mapsto 1\} \cup \{p \mapsto 0 \mid p \in P \setminus \{1\}\}
\end{aligned}
$$

then $zx_A = r_C x_A$ is realisable by $v(F_1, h_3)$ where $h_3(\{r_C \mapsto 1\}) = \{x_A \mapsto 1\}$. Similarly, $x_C r_A$ is realisable by $v(F_3, h_4)$, where:

$$
\begin{aligned}
F_3 &= \{\{x_C \mapsto 1\}\} \\
h_4(\{x_C \mapsto 1\}) &= \{r_A \mapsto 1\} \cup \{p \mapsto 0 \mid p \in P \setminus \{r_A\}\}
\end{aligned}
$$

Theorem 1 then tells us that, since $realisable(r_C x_A)$ and $realisable(x_C r_A)$, the sum $r_C x_A + x_C r_A$ is also realisable, and is given by $v(F_2, h_2)$, where:

$$
\begin{aligned}
F_2 &= F_1 \cup F_3 = \{\{r_C \mapsto 1\}, \{x_C \mapsto 1\}\} \\
h_2(\{r_C \mapsto 1\}) &= \{x_A \mapsto 1\} \cup \{p \mapsto 0 \mid p \in P \setminus \{x_A\}\} \\
h_2(\{x_C \mapsto 1\}) &= \{r_A \mapsto 1\} \cup \{p \mapsto 0 \mid p \in P \setminus \{r_A\}\}
\end{aligned}
$$

From this we conclude that the intruder can deduce a pair of values, $r_C$ and $r_C x_A + x_C r_A$, related by the key computation function $k_{AC}^{A(0)}$, and so secrecy fails. This failure should come as no surprise since $b = C$ represents the intruder's legitimate participation in the protocol. Any honest principal who willingly engages in a protocol run with the intruder cannot hope to maintain secrecy of the resulting session-key. We note that similar conclusions can be reached in cases 2–4.

### Cases 5 and 6 ($b = a$)

Let $a = A$, $b = A$. The corresponding key computation is given by $k_{AA}^{A(0)}(z) = z x_A + x_A r_A$. Note that $x_A r_A$ is the multiplication of two elements from $P$. The intruder model only allows the addition of elements from $P$ and, since $x_A \notin E$ and $r_A \notin E$, the component $x_A r_A$ is unrealisable. Consequently, for $z x_A + x_A r_A$ to be realisable, $z x_A$ must be a linear combination that includes $-x_A r_A$ (since $-x_A r_A + x_A r_A = 0$ is realisable). Consider the simplest case, where $z = -r_A$, which is realisable, since $r_A \in P$. The result of $k_{AA}^{A(0)}(-r_A) = -r_A x_A + x_A r_A = 0$ is realisable by $v(F_5, h_5)$, where, for instance:

$$F_5 = \{\{r_C \mapsto 0\}, \{x_C \mapsto 0\}\}$$
$$h_5(\{r_C \mapsto 0\}) = \{p \mapsto 0 \mid p \in P\}$$
$$h_5(\{r_C \mapsto 0\}) = \{p \mapsto 0 \mid p \in P\}$$

As a result, the intruder can deduce a pair of values $-r_A$ and $0$ such that $0 = k_{AA}^{A(0)}(-r_A)$ and, again, secrecy fails. A similar result holds for case 6, where $a = b = B$. This attack is a simpler version of one discovered by Just and Vaudenay [JV96] and described by Boyd and Mathuria [BM03]. In the original attack, $z$ was set to be $r_C - r_A$ and the resulting session-key computed as $g^{x_A r_C}$ (where $x_A r_C$ is realisable). The attack depends on the willingness of $A$ to engage in the protocol with someone claiming her identity, and can be seen as stipulating a condition on an implementation: namely, that a principal should only engage in the protocol if the other party has a distinct identity.

### Cases 7 and 8 ($b \neq a$)

For the final cases, assume $a = A$ and $b = B$ (a similar result holds for $a = B$ and $b = A$). The key computation is given by $k_{AB}^{A(0)}(z) = z x_A + x_B r_A$. For secrecy to fail there must exist some $z = v(F_1, h_1)$ and $k_{AB}^{A(0)}(z) = v(F_2, h_2)$ such that:

$$v(F_1, h_1) \cdot x_A + x_B r_A = v(F_2, h_2)$$

Consider the coefficient of $x_C^0 r_C^0$. We have:

$$h_2(\{x_C \mapsto 0, r_C \mapsto 0\}) = \{1 \mapsto n_1, r_A \mapsto n_2, r_B \mapsto n_3, x_A \mapsto n_4, x_B \mapsto n_5\}$$
$$h_1(\{x_C \mapsto 0, r_C \mapsto 0\}) = \{1 \mapsto m_1, r_A \mapsto m_2, r_B \mapsto m_3, x_A \mapsto m_4, x_B \mapsto m_5\}$$

for some $m_1 \ldots m_5 \in \mathbb{Z}$, $n_1 \ldots n_5 \in \mathbb{Z}$ where the coefficients on both sides are the same:

$$m_1 x_A + m_2 r_A x_A + m_3 r_B x_A + m_4 x_A^2 + m_5 x_B x_A + x_B r_A$$
$$=$$
$$n_1 + n_2 r_A + n_3 r_B + n_4 x_A + n_5 x_B$$

By assumption we have that variables are symbolic and that a given symbol $x$ is distinct from all others. Specifically, we note that $x_B r_A$ is distinct from all other terms on either side of the equation and, therefore, there are no values of the coefficients which enable the equality to be met. We conclude that, for any realisable $z$, $k_{AB}^{A(0)}(z)$ is unrealisable.

### Results

The analysis enables us to state the following result:

**Theorem 2.** *Given* $E^{A(0)} = \{r_C, x_C\}$, $P^{A(0)} = \{1, r_A, r_B, x_A, x_B\}$,

$$a \neq C \wedge b \neq C \wedge a \neq b \implies k_{ab}^{A(0)} \text{ maintains secrecy} \qquad \blacksquare$$

This tells us that protocol A(0) maintains the secrecy of the session-key precisely when the initiator and responder are distinct entities and neither of them is the intruder $C$.

## 5  Discussion

### 5.1  The Link with Rank Functions

Although we have not described our approach in such terms, it shares a conceptual origin with the notion of a *rank function*. In the context of protocol verification, a rank function describes an invariant property of a system [Sch97]. This property will define the sorts of messages that may pass through the system, crucially distinguishing certain values that should remain secret. The rank function effectively partitions the message-space of a protocol by assigning a rank of pub to public and sec to secret messages. Traditionally a rank function is defined over the message-space of a protocol model expressed in the process algebra CSP [Sch00], and a central rank theorem gives a series of proof obligations on the rank function whose achievement allows us to conclude that only messages of rank pub ever appear on the network. Previous work has applied the rank function approach in the context of Diffie-Hellman protocols [DS05]. However, a fundamental difficulty with this approach is the necessity to statically assign a rank to messages. It is interesting to note that the present work side-steps this issue by defining (via the message-template) the set $Pub$ of public messages. This set corresponds to the set of messages assigned a rank of pub by the rank approach.[1]

---

[1] In fact, $Pub$ is similar to Heather's concept of a minimal rank function [Hea01].

## 5.2    Pereira and Quisquater's Approach

Recently, Pereira and Quisquater [PQ01] developed a formal model of the Cliques conference key agreement protocols [AST00], based on linear logic, and discovered attacks on each of the claimed security properties. In the model, secrecy is defined as the inability of an intruder to discover a pair of values $(g^x, g^y)$ such that, if a principal is sent $g^x$, he will compute the key $g^y$. Values are assumed to take the form of $g$ raised to a product of exponents, and secrecy becomes the inability of an intruder to learn a pair of messages separated by the ratio $\frac{y}{x}$. The model allows the intruder to *grow* a set of known ratios, in the hope that some secret ratio(s) remain unobtainable. This ratio-centric view of secrecy seems particularly natural for Diffie-Hellman exchanges, and our initial attempts at modelling the MTI protocols sought to embrace this approach. However, it turns out that this view of secrecy does not generalise in the obvious way. Consider, for example, a value $z$ in the A(0) protocol, and the key computation function $k_{ab}^{A(0)}(z) = zx_a + x_b r_a$. The ratio between $k_{ab}^{A(0)}(z)$ and $z\,(x_a + \frac{x_b r_a}{z})$ is still in terms of $z$, due to the presence of addition in the exponents. This fact makes it difficult to derive the set of secret ratios, since a ratio cannot be stated without recourse to the argument to the key computation function. The present work can be viewed as an attempt to provide a more general view of Diffie-Hellman key computation.

In a different respect, Pereira's and Quisquater's model is more general than ours, since it applies to protocols which fail to satisfy the property of I/O-independence. This property, recall, tells us that no user of the protocol ever sends out any message which is dependent on a previously received message. In the Cliques protocols, protocol participants tend to receive a message, perform some computation on that message and send out the result. Pereira and Quisquater call such user operations *services*.[2] These services are encoded in terms of the values added to the exponent of an incoming message. For instance, a principal may receive a message $g^x$ and generate and send the message $g^{xyz}$ (where $y$ and $z$ are known to that principal). The intruder can then (with some restrictions) use the principal as an oracle, enabling him to send a spurious message $g^c$ and receive $g^{cyz}$ in return. The fact that the property of I/O-independence does not allow such services to be expressed in our model is not a fundamental limitation but a restriction which enables us to describe our work in a clean manner. One could envisage weakening this assumption by internalising such services in the intruder (in the style of Broadfoot and Roscoe[BR02]) where, for example, the multiplication of a value with $yz$ is encoded as an additional intruder deduction. The message-template would need to be redesigned to account for these additional capabilities. In contrast to the present work, such a message-template would tend to be protocol specific.

## 5.3    Conclusion and Further Work

We have presented a framework for reasoning about secrecy in a class of Diffie-Hellman protocols, and demonstrated the approach by a consideration of

---

[2] In these terms, a principal is I/O-independent if it provides no services.

secrecy in the MTI A(0) protocol. The work hinges around the idea of a message-template, an object which defines, in a highly abstract way, the values that can be deduced by an intruder under a given set of capabilities. A protocol model is given as a combination of a message-template and a function representing the key computation applied by a principal to derive a shared secret.

This work is nascent, but we are currently applying it to other protocols, both within and without the MTI suite. This requires us to relax the condition of I/O-independence and widen our model to address situations in which protocol participants provide *services*. In many cases, this extension appears straightforward. The *ad hoc* nature of the secrecy proof in Section 4 is unfortunate, and it would be useful to derive a general framework for such proof (as is achieved in [PQ01], for instance). There also appears to be interesting links between the idea of a message-template and the concept of *ideal* used within the strand space approach [THG99]. Future work will investigate whether this correspondence enables us to deduce general principles with which a protocol can be proven correct.

## Acknowledgements

Thanks to David Pitt, Joshua Guttman and James Heather for interesting discussions on this work and to the anonymous referees for their careful reviewing.

## References

[AC04]    Martín Abadi and Véronique Cortier. Deciding knowledge in security protocols under equational theories. In *31st International Colloquium on Automata, Languages and Programming: ICALP'04*, volume 3142 of *Lecture Notes in Computer Science*. Springer-Verlag, 2004.

[AST00]   Giuseppe Ateniese, Michael Steiner, and Gene Tsudik. Authenticated group key agreement and friends. In *Proceedings of the 5th ACM Conference on Computer and Communication Security*. ACM Press, 2000.

[BCP01]   Emmanuel Bresson, Olivier Chevassut, and David Pointcheval. Provably authenticated group Diffie-Hellman key exchange — the dynamic case. In *Advances in Cryptology: Proceedings of ASIACRYPT '01*, volume 2248 of *Lecture Notes in Computer Science*. Springer-Verlag, 2001.

[BM03]    Colin Boyd and Anish Mathuria. *Protocols for Authentication and Key Establishment*. Springer-Verlag, 2003.

[BR02]    Philippa Broadfoot and A. W. Roscoe. Internalising agents in CSP protocol models. In *Workshop on Issues in the Theory of Security: WITS '02*, 2002.

[DH76]    Whitfield Diffie and Martin E. Hellman. New directions in cryptography. *IEEE Transactions on Information Theory*, IT-22(6), 1976.

[DS05]    Rob Delicata and Steve Schneider. Temporal rank functions for forward secrecy. In *Proceedings of the 18th Computer Security Foundations Workshop: CSFW-18*. IEEE Computer Society Press, 2005.

[Hea01]   James Heather. 'Oh! ... Is it *really* you?' *using rank functions to verify authentication protocols*. Ph.D Thesis, Royal Holloway, University of London, 2001.

[JV96]     Mike Just and Serge Vaudenay. Authenticated multi-party key agreement. In *Advances in Cryptology: Proceedings of ASIACRYPT '96*, volume 1163 of *Lecture Notes in Computer Science*. Springer-Verlag, 1996.

[Mea00]    Catherine Meadows. Extending formal cryptographic protocol analysis techniques for group protocols and low-level cryptographic primitives. In *Workshop on Issues in the Theory of Security: WITS '00*, 2000.

[MTI86]    Tsutomu Matsumoto, Youichi Takashima, and Hideki Imai. On seeking smart public-key-distribution systems. *Transactions of the IECE of Japan*, E69(2), 1986.

[PQ01]     Olivier Pereira and Jean-Jacques Quisquater. Security analysis of the Cliques protocols suites. In *Proceedings of the 14th IEEE Computer Security Foundations Workshop: CSFW-14*. IEEE Computer Society Press, 2001.

[Sch97]    Steve Schneider. Verifying authentication protocols with CSP. In *Proceedings of The 10th Computer Security Foundations Workshop: CSFW-10*. IEEE Computer Society Press, 1997.

[Sch00]    Steve Schneider. *Concurrent and Real-time Systems: The CSP Approach*. John Wiley and Sons, Ltd, 2000.

[THG99]    F. Javier Thayer Fábrega, Jonathan Herzog, and Joshua Guttman. Strand spaces: Proving security protocols correct. *Journal of Computer Security*, 7(2/3), 1999.

# Eliminating Implicit Information Leaks by Transformational Typing and Unification

Boris Köpf[1] and Heiko Mantel[2,*]

[1] Information Security, ETH Zürich, Switzerland
boris.koepf@inf.ethz.ch
[2] Department of Computer Science, RWTH Aachen University, Germany
mantel@cs.rwth-aachen.de

**Abstract.** Before starting the security analysis of an existing system, the most likely outcome is often already clear, namely that the system is not entirely secure. Modifying a program such that it passes the analysis is a difficult problem and usually left entirely to the programmer. In this article, we show that and how unification can be used to compute such program transformations. This opens a new perspective on the problem of correcting insecure programs. We demonstrate that integrating our approach into an existing transforming type system can also improve the precision of the analysis and the quality of the resulting programs.

## 1 Introduction

Security requirements like confidentiality or integrity can often be adequately expressed by restrictions on the permitted flow of information. This approach goes beyond access control models in that it controls not only the access to data, but also how data is propagated within a program after a legitimate access.

Security type systems provide a basis for automating the information flow analysis of concrete programs [SM03]. If type checking succeeds then a program has secure information flow. If type checking fails then the program might be insecure and should not be run. After a failed type check, the task of correcting the program is often left to the programmer. Given the significance of the problem, it would be very desirable to have automated tools that better support the programmer in this task. For the future, we envision a framework for the information flow analysis that, firstly, gives more constructive advice on how a given program could be improved and, secondly, in some cases automatically corrects the program, or parts thereof, without any need for interaction by the programmer. The current article focuses on the second of these two aspects.

Obviously, one cannot allow an automatic transformation to modify programs in completely arbitrary ways as the transformed program should resemble the original program in some well-defined way. Such constraints can be captured by defining an equivalence relation on programs and demanding that the transformed program is equivalent to the original program under this relation.

---

* The author gratefully acknowledges support by the DFG and the ETH Zürich.

T. Dimitrakos et al. (Eds.): FAST 2005, LNCS 3866, pp. 47–62, 2006.
© Springer-Verlag Berlin Heidelberg 2006

A second equivalence relation can be used to capture the objective of a transformation. The problem of removing implicit information leaks from a program can be viewed as the problem of making alternative execution paths observationally equivalent. For instance, if the guard of a conditional depends on a secret then the two branches must be observationally equivalent because, otherwise, an untrusted observer might be able to deduce the value of the guard and, thereby, the secret. The PER model [SS99] even reduces the problem of making an entire program secure to the problem of making the program equivalent to itself.

In our approach, meta-variables are inserted into a program and are instantiated with programs during the transformation. The problem of making two program fragments equivalent is cast as a unification problem, which allows us to automatically compute suitable substitutions using existing unification algorithms. The approach is parametric in two equivalence relations. The first relation captures the semantic equivalence to be preserved by the transformation while the second relation captures the observational equivalence to be achieved.

We define two concrete equivalence relations to instantiate our approach and integrate this instance into an existing transforming type system [SS00]. This results in a security type system that is capable of recognizing some secure programs and of correcting some insecure programs that are rejected by the original type system. Moreover, the resulting programs are faster and often substantially smaller in size. Another advantage over the cross-copying technique [Aga00], which constitutes the current state of the art in this area, is that security policies with more than two levels can be considered. Besides these technical advantages, the use of unification yields a very natural perspective on the problem of making two programs observationally equivalent. However, we do not claim that using unification will solve all problems with repairing insecure programs or that unification would be the only way to achieve the above technical advantages.

The contributions of this article are a novel approach to making the information flow in a given program secure and the demonstration that transforming security type systems can benefit from the integration of this approach.

## 2    The Approach

The observational capabilities of an attacker can be captured by an equivalence relation on configurations, i.e. pairs consisting of a program and a state. Namely, $(C_1, s_1)$ is observationally equivalent to $(C_2, s_2)$ for an attacker $a$ if and only if the observations that $a$ makes when $C_1$ is run in state $s_1$ equal $a$'s observations when $C_2$ is run in $s_2$. The programs $C_1$ and $C_2$ are observationally equivalent for $a$ if, for all states $s_1$ and $s_2$ that are indistinguishable for $a$, the configurations $(C_1, s_1)$ and $(C_2, s_2)$ are observationally equivalent for $a$. The resulting relation on programs is only a partial equivalence relation (PER), i.e. a transitive and symmetric relation that need not be reflexive. If a program $C$ is not observationally equivalent to itself for $a$ then running $C$ in two indistinguishable states may lead to different observations and, thereby, reveal the differences between the states or, in other words, let $a$ learn secret information. This observation is the key to capturing secure information flow in the PER model [SS99] in which a program is secure if and only if it is observationally equivalent to itself.

In this article, we focus on the removal of implicit information leaks from a program. There is a danger of implicit information leakage if the flow of control depends on a secret and the alternative execution paths are not observationally equivalent for an attacker. The program if $h$ then $l{:=}1$ else $l{:=}0$, for instance, causes information to flow from the boolean guard $h$ into the variable $l$, and this constitutes an illegitimate information leak if $h$ stores a secret and the value of $l$ is observable for the attacker. Information can also be leaked in a similar way, e.g., when the guard of a loop depends on a secret, when it depends on a secret whether an exception is raised, or when the target location of a jump depends on a secret. For brevity of the presentation, we focus on the case of conditionals.

We view the problem of making the branches of a conditional equivalent as a unification problem under a theory that captures observational equivalence. To this end, we insert meta-variables into the program under consideration that can be substituted during the transformation. For a given non-transforming security type system, the rule for conditionals is modified such that, instead of checking whether the branches are equivalent, the rule calculates a unifier of the branches and applies it to the conditional. Typing rules for other language constructs are lifted such that they propagate the transformations that have occurred in the analysis of the subprograms. In summary, our approach proceeds as follows:

1. Lift the given program by inserting meta-variables at suitable locations.
2. Repair the lifted program by applying lifted typing rules.
3. Eliminate all remaining meta-variables.

The approach is not only parametric in the given security type system and in the theory under which branches are unified, but also in where meta-variables are placed and how they may be substituted. The latter two parameters determine how similar a transformed program is to the original program. They also limit the extent to which insecure programs can be corrected. For instance, one might decide to insert meta-variables between every two sub-commands and to permit the substitution of meta-variables with arbitrary programs. For these choices, lifting $P_1 = $ if $h$ then $l{:=}1$ else $l{:=}0$ results in if $h$ then $(\alpha_1; l{:=}1; \alpha_2)$ else $(\alpha_3; l{:=}0; \alpha_4)$ and the substitution $\{\alpha_1\backslash l{:=}0,\ \alpha_2\backslash\epsilon, \alpha_3\backslash\epsilon,\ \alpha_4\backslash l{:=}1\}$ (where $\epsilon$ is denotes the empty program) is a unifier of the branches under any equational theory as the substituted program is if $h$ then $(l{:=}0; l{:=}1)$ else $(l{:=}0; l{:=}1)$. Alternatively, one might decide to restrict the range of substitutions to sequences of skip statements. This ensures that the transformed program more closely resembles the original program, essentially any transformed program is a slowed-down version of the original program, but makes it impossible to correct programs like $P_1$. However, the program $P_2 = $ if $h$ then $(\mathsf{skip}; l{:=}1)$ else $l{:=}1$, which is insecure in a multi-threaded setting (as we will explain later in this section), can be corrected under these choices to if $h$ then $(\mathsf{skip}; l{:=}1)$ else $(\mathsf{skip}; l{:=}1)$. Alternatively, one could even decide to insert higher-order meta-variables such that lifting $P_1$ leads to if $h$ then $\alpha_1(l{:=}1)$ else $\alpha_2(l{:=}0)$ and applying, e.g., the unifier $\{\alpha_1\backslash(\lambda x.\text{skip}), \ \alpha_2\backslash(\lambda x.\text{skip})\}$ results in if $h$ then skip else skip while applying the unifier $\{\alpha_1\backslash(\lambda x.x), \ \alpha_2\backslash(\lambda x.l{:=}1)\}$ results in if $h$ then $l{:=}1$ else $l{:=}1$. These examples just illustrate the wide spectrum of possible choices for defining in which sense a transformed program must be equivalent to the original program. Ultimately it depends on the application, how flexible one is in dealing with the trade-off between being able to correct more insecure programs and having transformed programs that more closely resemble the original programs.

There also is a wide spectrum of possible choices for defining the (partial) observational equivalence relation. For simplicity, assume that variables are classified as either low or high depending on whether their values are observable by the attacker (low variables) or secret (high variables). As a convention, we denote low variables by $l$ and high variables by $h$, possibly with indexes and primes. Given that the values of low variables are only observable at the end of a program run, the programs $P_3 = (\text{skip}; l := 0)$ and $P_4 = (l := h; l := 0)$ are observationally equivalent and each is equivalent to itself (which means secure information flow in the PER model). However, if the attacker can observe also the intermediate values of low variables then they are not equivalent and, moreover, only $P_3$ is secure while $P_4$ is insecure. If the attacker can observe the timing of assignments or the duration of a program run then $P_2 = $ if $h$ then $(\text{skip}; l{:=}1)$ else $l{:=}1$ is insecure and, hence, not observationally equivalent to itself. In a multi-threaded setting, $P_2$ should be considered insecure even if the attacker cannot observe the timing of assignments or the duration of a program run. If $P_3 = (\text{skip}; l := 0)$ is run in parallel with $P_2$ under a shared memory and a round-robin scheduler that re-schedules after every sub-command then the final value of $l$ is 0 and 1 if the initial value of $h$ is 0 and 1, respectively. That is, a program that is observationally equivalent to itself in a sequential setting might not be observationally equivalent to itself in a multi-threaded setting – for the same attacker.

## 3   Instantiating the Approach

We are now ready to illustrate how our approach can be instantiated. We introduce a simple programming language, a security policy, an observational equivalence, and a program equivalence to be preserved under the transformation.

*Programming Language.* We adopt the multi-threaded while language (short: MWL) from [SS00], which includes assignments, conditionals, loops, and a command for dynamic thread creation. The set $Com$ of commands is defined by

$$C ::= \text{skip} \mid Id{:=}Exp \mid C_1; C_2 \mid \text{if } B \text{ then } C_1 \text{ else } C_2 \mid \text{while } B \text{ do } C \mid \text{fork}(CV)$$

where $V$ is a command vector in $\boldsymbol{Com} = \bigcup_{n\in\mathbb{N}} Com^n$. *Expressions* are variables, constants, or terms resulting from applying binary operators to expressions. A *state* is a mapping from variables in a given set $Var$ to values in a given set $Val$. We use the judgment $\langle Exp, s\rangle \downarrow n$ for specifying that expression $Exp$ evaluates to value $n$ in state $s$. Expression evaluation is assumed to be total and to occur atomically. We say that expressions $Exp$ and $Exp'$ are *equivalent* to each other (denoted by $Exp \equiv Exp'$) if and only if they evaluate to identical values in each state, i.e. $\forall s \in S : \forall v \in Val : \langle Exp, s \rangle \downarrow v \Leftrightarrow \langle Exp', s \rangle \downarrow v$.

The operational semantics for MWL is formalized in Figures 5 and 6 in the appendix. *Deterministic judgments* have the form $\langle C, s \rangle \rightarrow \langle W, t \rangle$ expressing that command $C$ performs a computation step in state $s$, yielding a state $t$ and a vector of commands $W$, which has length zero if $C$ terminated, length one if it has neither terminated nor spawned any threads, and length $> 1$ if threads were spawned. That is, a command vector of length $n$ can be viewed as a *pool of $n$ threads* that run concurrently. *Nondeterministic judgments* have the form $\langle V, s \rangle \rightarrow \langle V', t \rangle$ expressing that some thread $C_i$ in the thread pool $V$ performs a step in state $s$ resulting in the state $t$ and some thread pool $W$. The global thread pool $V'$ results then by replacing $C_i$ with $W$. For simplicity, we do not distinguish between commands and command vectors of length one in the notation and use the term *program* for referring to commands as well as to command vectors. A *configuration* is then a pair $\langle V, s \rangle$ where $V$ specifies the threads that are currently active and $s$ defines the current state of the memory.

In the following, we adopt the naming conventions used above. That is, $s, t$ denote states, $Exp$ denotes an expression, $B$ denotes a boolean expression, $C$ denotes a command, and $V, W$ denote command vectors.

*Security Policy and Labellings.* We assume a two-domain security policy, where the requirement is that there is no flow of information from the *high domain* to the *low domain*. This is the simplest policy under which the problem of secure information flow can be studied. Each program variable is associated with a security domain by means of a *labeling lab* : $Var \rightarrow \{low, high\}$. The intuition is that values of *low* variables can be observed by the attacker and, hence, should only be used to store public data. *High variables* are used for storing secret data and, hence, their values must not be observable for the attacker. As mentioned before, we use $l$ and $h$ to denote high and low variables, respectively. An expression $Exp$ has the security domain *low* (denoted by $Exp : low$) if all variables in $Exp$ have domain *low* and, otherwise, has security domain *high* (denoted by $Exp : high$). The intuition is that values of expressions with domain *high* possibly depend on secrets while values of *low* expressions can only depend on public data.

*Observational Equivalence.* The rules in Figure 1 inductively define a relation $\cong_L \subseteq \mathbf{Com} \times \mathbf{Com}$ that will serve us as an observational equivalence relation.

The relation $\cong_L$ captures observational equivalence for an attacker who can see the values of low variables at any point during a program run and cannot distinguish states $s_1$ and $s_2$ if they are low equal (denoted by $s_1 =_L s_2$), i.e. if $\forall var \in Var : lab(var) = low \implies s_1(var) = s_2(var)$. He cannot distinguish two program runs that have equal length and in which every two corresponding states are low equal. For capturing this intuition, Sabelfeld and Sands introduce the notion of a strong low bisimulation. The relation $\cong_L$ also captures this intuition and, moreover, programs that are related by $\cong_L$ are also strongly bisimilar. That is, $\cong_L$ is a decidable approximation of the strong bisimulation relation.

$$\frac{}{\text{skip} \mathrel{\widehat{\simeq}_L} \text{skip}} \; [Skip] \qquad \frac{Id : high}{\text{skip} \mathrel{\widehat{\simeq}_L} Id{:=}Exp} \; [SHA_1] \qquad \frac{Id : high}{Id{:=}Exp \mathrel{\widehat{\simeq}_L} \text{skip}} \; [SHA_2]$$

$$\frac{Id : high \quad Id' : high}{Id{:=}Exp \mathrel{\widehat{\simeq}_L} Id'{:=}Exp'} \; [HA] \qquad \frac{Id : low \quad Exp : low \quad Exp' : low \quad Exp \equiv Exp'}{Id{:=}Exp \mathrel{\widehat{\simeq}_L} Id{:=}Exp'} \; [LA]$$

$$\frac{C_1 \mathrel{\widehat{\simeq}_L} C_1', \ldots, C_n \mathrel{\widehat{\simeq}_L} C_n'}{\langle C_1, \ldots, C_n \rangle \mathrel{\widehat{\simeq}_L} \langle C_1', \ldots, C_n' \rangle} \; [PComp] \qquad \frac{C \mathrel{\widehat{\simeq}_L} C' \quad V \mathrel{\widehat{\simeq}_L} V'}{\text{fork}(CV) \mathrel{\widehat{\simeq}_L} \text{fork}(C'V')} \; [Fork]$$

$$\frac{B, B' : low \quad B \equiv B' \quad C_1 \mathrel{\widehat{\simeq}_L} C_1' \quad C_2 \mathrel{\widehat{\simeq}_L} C_2'}{\text{if } B \text{ then } C_1 \text{ else } C_2 \mathrel{\widehat{\simeq}_L} \text{if } B' \text{ then } C_1' \text{ else } C_2'} \; [LIte] \qquad \frac{B, B' : low \quad B \equiv B' \quad C \mathrel{\widehat{\simeq}_L} C'}{\text{while } B \text{ do } C \mathrel{\widehat{\simeq}_L} \text{while } B' \text{ do } C'} \; [WL]$$

$$\frac{B, B' : high \quad C_1 \mathrel{\widehat{\simeq}_L} C_1' \quad C_1 \mathrel{\widehat{\simeq}_L} C_2' \quad C_1 \mathrel{\widehat{\simeq}_L} C_2}{\text{if } B \text{ then } C_1 \text{ else } C_2 \mathrel{\widehat{\simeq}_L} \text{if } B' \text{ then } C_1' \text{ else } C_2'} \; [HIte] \qquad \frac{C_1 \mathrel{\widehat{\simeq}_L} C_1' \quad C_2 \mathrel{\widehat{\simeq}_L} C_2'}{C_1; C_2 \mathrel{\widehat{\simeq}_L} C_1'; C_2'} \; [SComp]$$

$$\frac{B' : high \quad C_1 \mathrel{\widehat{\simeq}_L} C_1' \quad C_1 \mathrel{\widehat{\simeq}_L} C_2'}{\text{skip}; C_1 \mathrel{\widehat{\simeq}_L} \text{if } B' \text{ then } C_1' \text{ else } C_2'} \; [SHIte_1] \qquad \frac{Id, B' : high \quad C_1 \mathrel{\widehat{\simeq}_L} C_1' \quad C_1 \mathrel{\widehat{\simeq}_L} C_2'}{Id{:=}Exp; C_1 \mathrel{\widehat{\simeq}_L} \text{if } B' \text{ then } C_1' \text{ else } C_2'} \; [HAHIte_1]$$

$$\frac{B : high \quad C_1 \mathrel{\widehat{\simeq}_L} C_1' \quad C_2 \mathrel{\widehat{\simeq}_L} C_1'}{\text{if } B \text{ then } C_1 \text{ else } C_2 \mathrel{\widehat{\simeq}_L} \text{skip}; C_1'} \; [SHIte_2] \qquad \frac{Id', B : high \quad C_1 \mathrel{\widehat{\simeq}_L} C_1' \quad C_2 \mathrel{\widehat{\simeq}_L} C_1'}{\text{if } B \text{ then } C_1 \text{ else } C_2 \mathrel{\widehat{\simeq}_L} Id'{:=}Exp'; C_1'} \; [HAHIte_2]$$

**Fig. 1.** A notion of observational equivalence

**Definition 1 ([SS00]).** *The* strong low-bisimulation $\approx_L$ *is the union of all symmetric relations $R$ on command vectors $V, V' \in \boldsymbol{Com}$ of equal size, i.e. $V = \langle C_1, \ldots, C_n \rangle$ and $V' = \langle C_1', \ldots, C_n' \rangle$, such that*

$$\forall s, s', t \in S : \forall i \in \{1 \ldots n\} : \forall W \in \boldsymbol{Com}:$$
$$[(V \, R \, V' \wedge s =_L s' \wedge \langle C_i, s \rangle \rightarrow \langle W, t \rangle)$$
$$\Rightarrow \exists W' \in \boldsymbol{Com}: \exists t' \in S: (\langle C_i', s' \rangle \rightarrow \langle W', t' \rangle \wedge W \, R \, W' \wedge t =_L t')]$$

**Theorem 1 (Adequacy of $\mathrel{\widehat{\simeq}_L}$).** *If $V \mathrel{\widehat{\simeq}_L} V'$ is derivable then $V \approx_L V'$ holds.*

The proofs of this and all subsequent results are provided in an accompanying Technical Report [KM05].

*Remark 1.* Note that $\mathrel{\widehat{\simeq}_L}$ and $\approx_L$ are only partial equivalence relations, i.e. they are transitive and symmetric, but not reflexive. For instance, the program $l{:=}h$ is not $\mathrel{\widehat{\simeq}_L}$-related to itself because the precondition of $[LA]$, the only rule in Figure 1 applicable to assignments to low variables, rules out that high variables occur on the right hand side of the assignment. Moreover, the program $l{:=}h$ is not strongly low bisimilar to itself because the states $s$ and $t$ (defined by $s(l) = 0$, $s(h) = 0$, $t(l) = 0$, $t(h) = 1$) are low equal, but the states $s'$ and $t'$ resulting after $l{:=}h$ is run in $s$ and $t$, respectively, are not low equal ($s'(l) = 0 \neq 1 = t'(l)$).

However, $\mathrel{\widehat{\simeq}_L}$ is an equivalence relation if one restricts programs to the language *Slice* that we define as the largest sub-language of *Com* without assignments of high expressions to low variables, assignments to high variables, and loops or conditionals having high guards. On *Slice*, $\mathrel{\widehat{\simeq}_L}$ even constitutes a congruence relation. This sub-language is the context in which we will apply unification and, hence, using the term *unification under an equational theory* is justified. ◇

*Program Equivalence.* We introduce an equivalence relation $\simeq$ to constrain the modifications caused by the transformation. Intuitively, this relation requires a transformed program to be a slowed down version of the original program. This is stronger than the constraint in [SS00].

**Definition 2.** *The* weak possibilistic bisimulation $\simeq$ *is the union of all symmetric relations $R$ on command vectors such that whenever $V\ R\ V'$ then for all states $s, t$ and all vectors $W$ there is a vector $W'$ such that*

$$\langle V, s \rangle \twoheadrightarrow \langle W, t \rangle \implies (\langle V', s \rangle \twoheadrightarrow^* \langle W', t \rangle \wedge W R W')$$
$$and\ V = \langle \rangle \implies \langle V', s \rangle \twoheadrightarrow^* \langle \langle \rangle, s \rangle .$$

# 4   Lifting a Security Type System

In this section we introduce a formal framework for transforming programs by inserting and instantiating meta-variables. Rather than developing an entirely new formalism from scratch, we adapt an existing security type system from [SS00]. We show that any transformation within our framework is sound in the sense that the output is secure and the behavior of the original program is preserved in the sense of Definition 2.

*Substitutions and Liftings.* We insert meta-variables from a set $\mathcal{V} = \{\alpha_1, \alpha_2, \dots\}$ into a program by sequential composition with its sub-terms. The extension of MWL with meta-variables is denoted by $\mathrm{MWL}_{\mathcal{V}}$. The set $Com_{\mathcal{V}}$ of commands in $\mathrm{MWL}_{\mathcal{V}}$ is defined by[1]

$$C ::= \mathsf{skip} \mid Id{:=}Exp \mid C_1; C_2 \mid C; X \mid X; C$$
$$\mathsf{if}\ B\ \mathsf{then}\ C_1\ \mathsf{else}\ C_2 \mid \mathsf{while}\ B\ \mathsf{do}\ C \mid \mathsf{fork}(CV) ,$$

where placeholders $X, Y$ range over $\mathcal{V}$. Analogously to MWL, the set of all command vectors in $\mathrm{MWL}_{\mathcal{V}}$ is defined by $\boldsymbol{Com_{\mathcal{V}}} = \bigcup_{n \in \mathbb{N}} (Com_{\mathcal{V}})^n$. Note that the *ground programs* in $\mathrm{MWL}_{\mathcal{V}}$ are exactly the programs in MWL. The operational semantics for such programs remain unchanged, whereas programs with meta-variables are not meant to be executed.

Meta-variables may be substituted with programs, meta-variables or the special symbol $\epsilon$ that acts as the neutral element of the sequential composition operator ("$;$"), i.e. $\epsilon; C = C$ and $C; \epsilon = C^2$. When talking about programs in $Com_{\mathcal{V}}$ under a given substitution, we implicitly assume that these equations have been applied (from left to right) to eliminate the symbol $\epsilon$ from the program. Moreover, we view sequential composition as an associative operator and implicitly identify programs that differ only in the use of parentheses for sequential composition. That is, $C_1; (C_2; C_3)$ and $(C_1; C_2); C_3$ denote the same program.

A mapping $\sigma : \mathcal{V} \rightarrow (\{\epsilon\} \cup \mathcal{V} \cup Com_{\mathcal{V}})$ is a *substitution* if the set $\{\alpha \in \mathcal{V} \mid \sigma(\alpha) \neq \alpha\}$ is finite. A substitution mapping each meta-variable in a program

---

[1] Here and in the following, we overload notation by using $C$ and $V$ to denote commands and command vectors in $Com_{\mathcal{V}}$, respectively.

[2] Note that skip is not a neutral element of ("$;$") as skip requires a computation step.

$V$ to $\{\epsilon\} \cup Com$ is a *ground substitution of $V$*. A substitution $\pi$ mapping all meta-variables in $V$ to $\epsilon$ is a *projection of $V$*. Given a program $V$ in **Com**, we call every program $V'$ in $\textbf{Com}_{\mathcal{V}}$ with $\pi V' = V$ a *lifting of $V$*.

For example, the program if $h$ then $(\alpha_1; \text{skip}; \alpha_2; l{:=}1)$ else $(\alpha_3; l{:=}1)$ is in fact a lifting of if $h$ then $(\text{skip}; l{:=}1)$ else $l{:=}1$. In the remainder of this article, we will focus on substitutions with a restricted range.

**Definition 3.** *A substitution with range $\{\epsilon\} \cup Stut_{\mathcal{V}}$ is called* preserving, *where $Stut_{\mathcal{V}}$ is defined by $C ::= X \mid \text{skip} \mid C_1; C_2$ (the $C_i$ range over $Stut_{\mathcal{V}}$).*

The term *preserving* substitution is justified by the fact that such substitutions preserve a given program's semantics as specified in Definition 2.

**Theorem 2 (Preservation of Behavior).**

1. *Let $V \in \textbf{Com}_{\mathcal{V}}$. For all preserving substitutions $\sigma, \rho$ that are ground for $V$, we have $\sigma(V) \simeq \rho(V)$.*
2. *Let $V \in \textbf{Com}$. For each lifting $V'$ of $V$ and each preserving substitution $\sigma$ with $\sigma(V')$ ground, we have $\sigma(V') \simeq V$.*

*Unification of Programs.* The problem of finding a substitution that makes the branches of conditionals with high guards observationally equivalent can be viewed as the problem of finding a unifier for the branches under the equational theory $\backsimeq_L$.[3] To this end, we lift the relation $\backsimeq_L \subseteq \textbf{Com} \times \textbf{Com}$ to a binary relation on $\textbf{Com}_{\mathcal{V}}$ that we also denote by $\backsimeq_L$.

**Definition 4.** *$V_1, V_2 \in \textbf{Com}_{\mathcal{V}}$ are* observationally equivalent *($V_1 \backsimeq_L V_2$) iff $\sigma V_1 \backsimeq_L \sigma V_2$ for each preserving substitution $\sigma$ that is ground for $V_1$ and $V_2$.*

**Definition 5.** *A $\backsimeq_L$-unification problem $\Delta$ is a finite set of statements of the form $V_i \backsimeq^?_L V'_i$, i.e. $\Delta = \{V_0 \backsimeq^?_L V'_0, \ldots, V_n \backsimeq^?_L V'_n\}$ with $V_i, V'_i \in \textbf{Com}_{\mathcal{V}}$ for all $i \in \{0, \ldots, n\}$. A substitution $\sigma$ is a* preserving unifier *for $\Delta$ if and only if $\sigma$ is preserving and $\sigma V_i \backsimeq_L \sigma V'_i$ holds for each $i \in \{0, \ldots, n\}$. A $\backsimeq_L$-unification problem is* solvable *if the set of preserving unifiers $\mathcal{U}(\Delta)$ for $\Delta$ is not empty.*

*A Transforming Type System.* The transforming type system in Figure 2 has been derived from the one in [SS00]. We use the judgment $V \hookrightarrow V' : S$ for denoting that the MWL$_{\mathcal{V}}$-program $V$ can be transformed into an MWL$_{\mathcal{V}}$-program $V'$. The intention is that $V'$ has secure information flow and reflects the semantics of $V$ as specified by Definition 2. The *slice $S$* is a program that is in the sub-language *Slice$_{\mathcal{V}}$* and describes the timing behavior of $V'$. The novelty over [SS00] is that our type system operates on $\textbf{Com}_{\mathcal{V}}$ (rather than on **Com**) and that the rule for high conditionals has been altered. In the original type system, a high conditional is transformed by sequentially composing each branch with the slice of the respective other branch. Instead of cross-copying slices, our rule instantiates the meta-variables occurring in the branches using preserving unifiers. The advantages of this modification are discussed in Section 6. Note that the

---

[3] The term *equational theory* is justified as we apply unification only to programs in the sub-language *Slice$_{\mathcal{V}}$* for which $\backsimeq_L$ constitutes a congruence relation (see Remark 1).

$$\frac{}{\mathsf{skip} \hookrightarrow \mathsf{skip} : \mathsf{skip}} \; [Skp] \qquad \frac{Id : high}{Id := Exp \hookrightarrow Id := Exp : \mathsf{skip}} \; [Ass_h] \qquad \frac{C_1 \hookrightarrow C_1' : S_1 \quad C_2 \hookrightarrow C_2' : S_2}{C_1 ; C_2 \hookrightarrow C_1' ; C_2' : S_1 ; S_2} \; [Seq]$$

$$\frac{Id : low \quad Exp : low}{Id := Exp \hookrightarrow Id := Exp : Id := Exp} \; [Ass_l] \qquad \frac{B : low \quad C \hookrightarrow C' : S}{\mathsf{while} \; B \; \mathsf{do} \; C \hookrightarrow \mathsf{while} \; B \; \mathsf{do} \; C' : \mathsf{while} \; B \; \mathsf{do} \; S} \; [Whl]$$

$$\frac{C_1 \hookrightarrow C_1' : S_1 \quad \ldots \quad C_n \hookrightarrow C_n' : S_n}{\langle C_1, \ldots, C_n \rangle \hookrightarrow \langle C_1', \ldots, C_n' \rangle : \langle S_1, \ldots, S_n \rangle} \; [Par] \qquad \frac{C_1 \hookrightarrow C_1' : S_1 \quad V_2 \hookrightarrow V_2' : S_2}{\mathsf{fork}(C_1 V_2) \hookrightarrow \mathsf{fork}(C_1' V_2') : \mathsf{fork}(S_1 S_2)} \; [Frk]$$

$$\frac{B : low \quad C_1 \hookrightarrow C_1' : S_1 \quad C_2 \hookrightarrow C_2' : S_2}{\mathsf{if} \; B \; \mathsf{then} \; C_1 \; \mathsf{else} \; C_2 \hookrightarrow \mathsf{if} \; B \; \mathsf{then} \; C_1' \; \mathsf{else} \; C_2' : \mathsf{if} \; B \; \mathsf{then} \; S_1 \; \mathsf{else} \; S_2} \; [Cond_l]$$

$$\frac{B : high \quad C_1 \hookrightarrow C_1' : S_1 \quad C_2 \hookrightarrow C_2' : S_2 \quad \sigma \in \mathcal{U}(\{S_1 \overset{?}{\eqsim}_L S_2\})}{\mathsf{if} \; B \; \mathsf{then} \; C_1 \; \mathsf{else} \; C_2 \hookrightarrow \mathsf{if} \; B \; \mathsf{then} \; \sigma C_1' \; \mathsf{else} \; \sigma C_2' : \mathsf{skip} ; \sigma S_1} \; [Cond_h] \qquad \frac{}{X \hookrightarrow X : X} \; [Var]$$

**Fig. 2.** A transforming security type system for programs with meta-variables

rule $[Cond_h]$ does not mandate the choice of a specific preserving unifier of the branches. Nevertheless, we can prove that the type system meets our previously described intuition about the judgment $V \hookrightarrow V' : S$. To this end, we employ Sabelfeld and Sands's strong security condition for defining what it means for a program to have secure information flow. Many other definitions are possible (see e.g. [SM03]).

**Definition 6.** *A program $V \in \boldsymbol{Com}$ is strongly secure if and only if $V \eqsim_L V$ holds. A program $V \in \boldsymbol{Com_V}$ is strongly secure if and only if $\sigma V$ is strongly secure for each substitution $\sigma$ that is preserving and ground for $V$.*

**Theorem 3 (Soundness Type System).** *If $V \hookrightarrow V' : S$ can be derived then (1) $V'$ has secure information flow, (2) $V \simeq V'$ holds,[4] and (3) $V' \eqsim_L S$ holds.*

The following corollary is an immediate consequence of Theorems 2 and 3. It shows that lifting a program and then applying the transforming type system preserves a program's behavior in the desired way.

**Corollary 1.** *If $V^* \hookrightarrow V' : S$ is derivable for some lifting $V^* \in \boldsymbol{Com_V}$ of a program $V \in \boldsymbol{Com}$ then $V'$ has secure information flow and $V \simeq V'$.*

## 5 Automating the Transformation

In Section 4, we have shown our type system to be sound for any choice of liftings and preserving unifiers in the applications of rule $[Cond_h]$. For automating the transformation, we have to define more concretely where meta-variables are inserted and how unifiers are determined.

*Automatic Insertion of Meta-Variables.* When lifting a program, one is faced with a trade off: inserting meta-variables means to create possibilities for correcting the program, but it also increases the complexity of the unification

---

[4] Here and in the following, we define $\simeq$ on $Com_V$ by $C \simeq C'$ iff $\sigma C \simeq \sigma C'$ for any substitution $\sigma$ that is preserving and ground for $C$ and for $C'$.

problem. Within this spectrum our objective is to minimize the number of inserted meta-variables without losing the possibility of correcting the program.

To this end, observe that two programs $C_1$ and $C_2$ within the sub-language $Pad_V$, the extension of $Stut_V$ with high assignments, are related via $\simeq_L$ whenever they contain the same number of constants, i.e., skips and assignments to high variables (denoted as $const(C_1) = const(C_2)$), and the same number of occurrences of each meta-variable $\alpha$ (denoted by $|C_1|_\alpha = |C_2|_\alpha$). Note that the positioning of meta-variables is irrelevant.

**Lemma 1.** *For two commands $C_1$ and $C_2$ in $Pad_V$ we have $C_1 \simeq_L C_2$ if and only if $const(C_1) = const(C_2)$ and $\forall \alpha \in \mathcal{V}: |C_1|_\alpha = |C_2|_\alpha$.*

Moreover, observe that inserting one meta-variable next to another does not create new possibilities for correcting a program. This, together with Lemma 1, implies that inserting one meta-variable into every subprogram within $Pad_V$ is sufficient for allowing every possible correction. We use this insight to define a mapping $\rightharpoonup: \textbf{Com} \rightarrow \textbf{Com}_V$ that calculates a lifting of a program by inserting one fresh meta-variable at the end of every sub-program in $Pad_V$, and between every two sub-programs outside $Pad_V$. The mapping is defined inductively: A fresh meta-variable is sequentially composed to the right hand side of each subprogram. Another fresh meta-variable is sequentially composed to the left hand side of each assignment to a low variable, fork, while loop, or conditional. A lifting of a sequentially composed program is computed by sequentially composing the liftings of the subprograms while removing the terminal variable of the left program. The three interesting cases are illustrated in Figure 3. The liftings computed by $\rightharpoonup$ are *most general* in the sense that if two programs can be made observationally equivalent for some lifting then they can be made equivalent for the lifting computed by $\rightharpoonup$. In other words, $\rightharpoonup$ is *complete*.

**Theorem 4.** *Let $V_1'$, $V_2'$, $\overline{V_1}$, and $\overline{V_2}$ be in $\textbf{Com}_V$ and let $V_1, V_2 \in \textbf{Com}$.*

1. *If $V_i \rightharpoonup \overline{V_i}$ can be derived then $\overline{V_i}$ is a lifting of $V_i$ $(i = 1, 2)$.*
2. *Suppose $\overline{V_1}$ $(\overline{V_2})$ shares no meta-variables with $V_1'$, $V_2'$, and $\overline{V_2}$ $(V_1'$, $V_2'$, and $\overline{V_1})$. If $V_1 \rightharpoonup \overline{V_1}$ and $V_2 \rightharpoonup \overline{V_2}$ can be derived and $V_1'$ and $V_2'$ are liftings of $V_1, V_2$, respectively, then $\mathcal{U}(\{V_1' \simeq_L^? V_2'\}) \neq \emptyset$ implies $\mathcal{U}(\{\overline{V_1} \simeq_L^? \overline{V_2}\}) \neq \emptyset$. Furthermore, $\mathcal{U}(\{V_1' \simeq_L^? V_1'\}) \neq \emptyset$ implies $\mathcal{U}(\{\overline{V_1} \simeq_L^? \overline{V_1}\}) \neq \emptyset$.*

*Integrating Standard Unification Algorithms.* Standard algorithms for unification modulo an associative and commutative operator with neutral element and constants (see, e.g., [BS01] for background information on $AC_1$ unification) build on a characterization of equality that is equivalent to the one in Lemma 1. This

$$\frac{Id : high \quad X \text{ fresh}}{Id{:=}Exp \rightharpoonup Id{:=}Exp; X} \qquad \frac{C_1 \rightharpoonup C_1' \quad V_2 \rightharpoonup V_2' \quad X, Y \text{ fresh}}{\mathsf{fork}(C_1 V_2) \rightharpoonup X; (\mathsf{fork}(C_1' V_2')); Y} \qquad \frac{C_1 \rightharpoonup C_1'; X \quad C_2 \rightharpoonup C_2'}{C_1; C_2 \rightharpoonup C_1'; C_2'}$$

**Fig. 3.** A calculus for computing most general liftings

correspondence allows one to employ existing algorithms for $AC_1$-unification problems with constants and free function symbols (like, e.g., the one in [HS87]) to the unification problems that arise when applying the rule for conditionals and then to filter the output such that only preserving substitutions remain.[5]

*Automating Unification.* In the following, we go beyond simply applying an existing unification algorithm by exploiting the specific shape of our unification problems and the limited range of substitutions in the computation of unifiers. Recall that we operate on programs in $Slice_V$, i.e., on programs without assignments to high variables, without assignments of high expressions to low variables, and without loops or conditionals having high guards.

The operative intuition behind our problem-tailored unification algorithm is to scan two program terms from left to right and distinguish two cases: if both leftmost subcommands are free constructors, (low assignments, loops, conditionals and forks) they are compared and, if they agree, unification is recursively applied to pairs of corresponding subprograms and the residual programs. If one leftmost subcommand is skip, both programs are decomposed into their maximal initial subprograms in $Stut_V$ and the remaining program. Unification is recursively applied to the corresponding subprograms. Formally, we define the language $NSeq_V$ of commands in $Slice_V \setminus \{\text{skip}\}$ without sequential composition as a top-level operator, and the language $NStut_V$ of commands in which the leftmost subcommand is not an element of $Stut_V$. $NStut_V$ is given by $C ::= C_1; C_2$, where $C_1 \in NSeq_V$ and $C_2 \in Slice_V$.

$$\frac{C_1 \hat{\simeq}_L^? C_2 :: \eta \quad C_1, C_2 \in Stut_V}{X; C_1 \hat{\simeq}_L^? C_2 :: \eta[X \backslash \epsilon]} \, [Seq_1] \qquad \frac{C_1 \hat{\simeq}_L^? C_2 :: \eta \quad C_1, C_2 \in Stut_V}{\text{skip}; C_1 \hat{\simeq}_L^? \text{skip}; C_2 :: \eta} \, [Seq_2]$$

$$\frac{C_1 \hat{\simeq}_L^? C_1' :: \eta_1 \quad C_2 \hat{\simeq}_L^? C_2' :: \eta_2 \quad C_1, C_1' \in NSeq_V}{C_1; C_2 \hat{\simeq}_L^? C_1'; C_2' :: \eta_1 \cup \eta_2} \, [Seq_3] \qquad \frac{C \in Stut_V \cup \{\epsilon\}}{X \hat{\simeq}_L^? C :: \{X \backslash C\}} \, [Var_1]$$

$$\frac{C_1 \hat{\simeq}_L^? C_1' :: \eta_1 \quad C_2 \hat{\simeq}_L^? C_2' :: \eta_2 \quad C_1, C_1' \in Stut_V \cup \{\epsilon\}, C_2, C_2' \in NStut_V}{C_1; C_2 \hat{\simeq}_L^? C_1'; C_2' :: \eta_1 \cup \eta_2} \, [Seq_4]$$

$$\frac{Id : low \quad Exp_1 \equiv Exp_2}{Id := Exp_1 \hat{\simeq}_L^? Id := Exp_2 :: \emptyset} \, [Asg] \qquad \frac{C \hat{\simeq}_L^? C' :: \eta \quad V \hat{\simeq}_L^? V' :: \eta_2}{\text{fork}(CV) \hat{\simeq}_L^? \text{fork}(C'V') :: \eta_1 \cup \eta_2} \, [Frk]$$

**Fig. 4.** Unification calculus

The unification algorithm in Figure 4 is given in form of a calculus for deriving judgments of the form $C_1 \hat{\simeq}_L^? C_2 :: \eta$, meaning that $\eta$ is a preserving unifier of the commands $C_1$ and $C_2$. The symmetric counterparts of rules $[Seq_1], [Var_1]$ are omitted, as are the rules for loops, conditionals and command vectors,

---

[5] For the reader familiar with $AC_1$ unification: In the language $Stut_V$ one views $\epsilon$ as the neutral element, skip as the constant, and ; as the operator. For $Slice_V$, the remaining language constructs, i.e., assignments, conditionals, loops, forks, and ; (outside the language $Stut_V$) must be treated as free constructors.

because they are analogous to [Frk]. Note that the unifiers obtained from recursive application of the algorithm to sub-programs are combined by set union. This is admissible if the meta-variables in all subprograms are disjoint, as the following lemma shows:

**Lemma 2.** *Let* $V_1, V_2 \in \textbf{\textit{Slice}}_{\mathcal{V}}$ *and let every variable occur at most once in* $(V_1, V_2)$. *Then* $V_1 \mathbin{\hat{=}}_L^? V_2 :: \eta$ *implies* $\eta \in \mathcal{U}(\{V_1 \mathbin{\hat{=}}_L^? V_2\})$.

Observe that the stand-alone unification algorithm is not complete, as it relies on the positions of meta-variables inserted by $\rightharpoonup$. However, we can prove a completeness result for the combination of both calculi.

*Completeness.* If conditionals with high guards are nested then the process of transformational typing possibly involves repeated applications of substitutions to a given subprogram. Hence, care must be taken in choosing a substitution in each application of rule [$Cond_h$] because, otherwise, unification problems in later applications of [$Cond_h$] might become unsolvable.[6] Fortunately, the instantiation of our framework presented in this section does not suffer from such problems.

**Theorem 5 (Completeness).** *Let* $V \in \textbf{\textit{Com}}$, $\overline{V}, W \in \textbf{\textit{Com}}_{\mathcal{V}}$, $W$ *be a lifting of* $V$, *and* $V \rightharpoonup \overline{V}$.

1. *If there is a preserving substitution* $\sigma$ *with* $\sigma W \mathbin{\hat{=}}_L \sigma W$, *then* $\overline{V} \hookrightarrow' V' : S$ *for some* $V', S \in \textbf{\textit{Com}}_{\mathcal{V}}$.
2. *If* $W \hookrightarrow W' : S$ *for some* $W', S \in \textbf{\textit{Com}}_{\mathcal{V}}$ *then* $\overline{V} \hookrightarrow' V' : S'$ *for some* $V', S' \in \textbf{\textit{Com}}_{\mathcal{V}}$.

Here, the judgment $V \hookrightarrow' V' : S$ denotes a successful transformation of $V$ to $V'$ by the transformational type system, where the precondition $\sigma \in \mathcal{U}(\{S_1 \mathbin{\hat{=}}_L^? S_2\})$ is replaced by $S_1 \mathbin{\hat{=}}_L^? S_2 :: \sigma$ in rule [$Cond_h$].

# 6   Related Work and Discussion

Type-based approaches to analyzing the security of the information flow in concrete programs have received much attention in recent years [SM03]. This resulted in security type systems for a broad range of languages (see, e.g., [VS97, SV98, HR98, Mye99, Sab01, SM02, BN02, HY02, BC02, ZM03, MS04]).

Regarding the analysis of conditionals with high guards, Volpano and Smith [VS98] proposed the atomic execution of entire conditionals for enforcing observational equivalence of alternative execution paths. This somewhat restrictive constraint is relaxed in the work of Agat [Aga00] and Sabelfeld and Sands [SS00] who achieve observational equivalence by cross-copying the slices of branches. The current article introduces unification modulo an equivalence relation as another alternative for making the branches of a conditional observationally equivalent to each other. Let us compare the latter two approaches more concretely for the relation $\mathbin{\hat{=}}_L$ that we have introduced to instantiate our approach.

---

[6] A standard solution would be to apply *most general unifiers*. Unfortunately, they do not exist in our setting.

The type system introduced in Section 4 is capable of analyzing programs where assignments to low variables appear in the branches of conditionals with high guards, which is not possible with the type system in [SS00].

*Example 1.* If one lifts $C =$ if $h_1$ then $(h_2:=Exp_1; l:=Exp_2)$ else $(l:=Exp_2)$ where $Exp_2 : low$ using our lifting calculus, applies our transforming type system, and finally removes all remaining meta-variables by applying a projection then this results in if $h_1$ then $(h_2:=Exp_1; l:=Exp_2)$ else (skip; $l:=Exp_2$), a program that is strongly secure and also weakly bisimilar to $C$. Note that the program $C$ cannot be repaired by applying the type system from [SS00].    ◊

Another advantage of our unification-based approach over the cross-copying technique is that the resulting programs are faster and smaller in size.

*Example 2.* The program if $h$ then $(h_1:=Exp_1)$ else $(h_2:=Exp_2)$ is returned unmodified by our type system, while the type system from [SS00] transforms it into the bigger program if $h$ then $(h_1:=Exp_1; skip)$ else (skip; $h_2:=Exp_2$). If one applies this type system a second time, one obtains an even bigger program, namely if $h$ then $(h_1:=Exp_1; skip; skip; skip)$ else (skip; skip; skip; $h_2:=Exp_2$). In contrast, our type system realizes a transformation that is idempotent, i.e. the program resulting from the transformation remains unmodified under a second application of the transformation.    ◊

Non-transforming security type systems for the two-level security policy can be used to also analyze programs under a policy with more domains. To this end, one performs multiple type checks where each type check ensures that no illegitimate information flow can occur into a designated domain. For instance, consider a three-domain policy with domains $\mathcal{D} = \{top, left, right\}$ where information may only flow from *left* and from *right* to *top*. To analyze a program under this policy, one considers all variables with label *top* and *left* as if labeled *high* in a first type check (ensuring that there is no illegitimate information flow to *right*) and, in a second type check, considers all variables with label *top* and *right* as if labeled *high*. There is no need for a third type check as all information may flow to *top*. When adopting this approach for transforming type systems, one must take into account that the guarantees established by the type check for one domain might not be preserved under the modifications caused by the transformation for another domain. Therefore, one needs to iterate the process until a fixpoint is reached for all security domains.

*Example 3.* For the three-level policy from above, the program $C =$ if $t$ then $(t:=t'; r:=r'; l:=l')$ else $(r:=r'; l:=l')$ (assuming $t, t' : top$, $r, r' : right$ and $l, l' : left$) is lifted to $\overline{C} =$ if $t$ then $(t:=t'; r:=r'; \alpha_1; l:=l'; \alpha_2)$ else $(r:=r'; \alpha_3; l:=l'; \alpha_4)$ and transformed into if $t$ then $(t:=t'; r:=r'; l:=l')$ else $(r:=r'; skip; l:=l')$ when analyzing security w.r.t. an observer with domain *left*. Lifting for *right* then results in if $t$ then $(t:=t'; \alpha_1; r:=r'; l:=l'; \alpha_2)$ else $(\alpha_3; r:=r'; skip; l:=l'; \alpha_4)$. Unification and projection gives if $t$ then $(t:=t'; r:=r'; l:=l'; skip)$ else (skip; $r:=r'; skip; l:=l'$). Observe that this program is not secure any more from the viewpoint of a *left*–observer. Applying the transformation again for domain *left* results in the secure program if $t$ then $(t:=t'; r:=r'; \text{skip}; l:=l'; \text{skip})$ else $(\text{skip}; r:=r'; \text{skip}; l:=l'; \text{skip})$, which is a fixpoint of both transformations.                                                                        ◇

Note that the idempotence of the transformation is a crucial prerequisite (but not a sufficient one) for the existence of a fixpoint and, hence, for the termination of such an iterative approach. As is illustrated in Example 2, the transformation realized by our type system is idempotent, whereas the transformation from [SS00] is not.

Another possibility to tackle multi-level security policies in our setting is to unify the branches of a conditional with guard of security level $D'$ under the theory $\bigcap_{D \not\geq D'} \,\hat{=}_D$. An investigation of this possibility remains to be done.

The chosen instantiation of our approach preserves the program behavior in the sense of a weak bisimulation. Naturally, one can correct more programs if one is willing to relax this relationship between input and output of the transformation. For this reason, there are also some programs that cannot be corrected with our type system although they can be corrected with the type system in [SS00] (which assumes a weaker relationship between input and output).

*Example 4.* if $h$ then (while $l$ do $(h_1:=Exp)$) else $(h_2:=1)$ is rejected by our type system. The type system in [SS00] transforms it into the strongly secure program if $h$ then (while $l$ do $(h_1:=Exp)$; skip) else (while $l$ do (skip); $h_2:=1$). Note that this program is not weakly bisimilar to the original program as the cross-copying of the while loop introduces possible non-termination.                                     ◇

If one wishes to permit such transformations, one could, for instance, choose a simulation instead of the weak bisimulation when instantiating our approach. This would result in an extended range of substitutions beyond $Stut_\mathcal{V}$. For instance, to correct the program in Example 4, one needs to instantiate a meta-variable with a while loop. We are confident that, in such a setting, using our approach would even further broaden the scope of corrections while retaining the advantage of transformed programs that are comparably small and fast.

## 7   Conclusions

We proposed a novel approach to analyzing the security of information flow in concrete programs with the help of transforming security type systems where the key idea has been to integrate unification with typing rules. This yielded a very natural perspective on the problem of eliminating implicit information flow.

We instantiated our approach by defining a program equivalence capturing the behavioral equivalence to be preserved during the transformation and an observational equivalence capturing the perspective of a low-level attacker. This led to a novel transforming security type system and calculi for automatically inserting meta-variables into programs and for computing substitutions. We proved that the resulting analysis technique is sound and also provided a relative completeness result. The main advantages of our approach include that the precision of type checking is improved, that additional insecure programs can be corrected, and that the resulting programs are faster and smaller in size.

It will be interesting to see how our approach performs for other choices of the parameters like, e.g., observational equivalences that admit intentional declassification [MS04]). Another interesting possibility is to perform the entire information flow analysis and program transformation using unification without any typing rules, which would mean to further explore the possibilities of the PER model. Finally, it would be desirable to integrate our fully automatic transformation into an interactive framework for supporting the programmer in correcting insecure programs.

# References

[Aga00]   J. Agat. Transforming out Timing Leaks. In *Proceedings of the 27th ACM Symposium on Principles of Programming Languages*, pages 40–53, 2000.

[BC02]   G. Boudol and I. Castellani. Noninterference for Concurrent Programs and Thread Systems. *Theoretical Computer Science*, 281:109–130, 2002.

[BN02]   A. Banerjee and D. A. Naumann. Secure Information Flow and Pointer Confinement in a Java-like Language. In *Proceedings of the 15th IEEE Computer Security Foundations Workshop*, pages 253–270, Cape Breton, Nova Scotia, Canada, 2002.

[BS01]   F. Baader and W. Snyder. Unification theory. In A. Robinson and A. Voronkov, editors, *Handbook of Automated Reasoning*, volume I, chapter 8, pages 445–532. Elsevier Science, 2001.

[HR98]   N. Heintze and J. G. Riecke. The SLam Calculus: Programming with Secrecy and Integrity. In *Proceedings of the 25th ACM Symposium on Principles of Programming Languages*, pages 365–377, 1998.

[HS87]   A. Herold and J. Siekmann. Unification in Abelian Semigroups. *Journal of Automated Reasoning*, 3:247–283, 1987.

[HY02]   K. Honda and N. Yoshida. A uniform type structure for secure information flow. In *Proceedings of the 29th ACM Symposium on Principles of Programming Languages*, pages 81–92. ACM Press, 2002.

[KM05]   Boris Köpf and Heiko Mantel. Eliminating Implicit Information Leaks by Transformational Typing and Unification. Technical Report 498, ETH Zürich, 2005.

[MS04]   Heiko Mantel and David Sands. Controlled Declassification based on Intransitive Noninterference. In *Proceedings of the 2nd ASIAN Symposium on Programming Languages and Systems, APLAS 2004*, LNCS 3303, pages 129–145, Taipei, Taiwan, November 4–6 2004. Springer-Verlag.

[Mye99]   A. Myers. JFlow: Practical mostly-static information flow control. In *Symposium on Principles of Programming Languages*, pages 228–241, 1999.

[Sab01]   A. Sabelfeld. The Impact of Synchronisation on Secure Information Flow in Concurrent Programs. In *Proceedings of Andrei Ershov 4th International Conference on Perspectives of System Informatics*, volume 2244 of *LNCS*, pages 225–239, 2001.

[SM02]   A. Sabelfeld and H. Mantel. Static Confidentiality Enforcement for Distributed Programs. In *Proceedings of the 9th International Static Analysis Symposium, SAS'02*, volume 2477 of *LNCS*, pages 376–394, Madrid, Spain, 2002.

[SM03]   A. Sabelfeld and A. C. Myers. Language-based Information-Flow Security. *IEEE Journal on Selected Areas in Communication*, 21(1):5–19, 2003.

[SS99]   A. Sabelfeld and D. Sands. A Per Model of Secure Information Flow in Sequential Programs. In *Proceedings of the 8th European Symposium on Programming*, LNCS, pages 50–59, 1999.

[SS00]   A. Sabelfeld and D. Sands. Probabilistic Noninterference for Multi-threaded Programs. In *Proceedings of the 13th IEEE Computer Security Foundations Workshop*, pages 200–215, Cambridge, UK, 2000.

[SV98]   G. Smith and D. Volpano. Secure Information Flow in a Multi-Threaded Imperative Language. In *25th ACM Symposium on Principles of Programming Languages, San Diego, California*, pages 355–364, 1998.

[VS97]   D. Volpano and G. Smith. A Type-Based Approach to Program Security. In *TAPSOFT 97*, volume 1214 of *LNCS*, pages 607–621, 1997.

[VS98]   D. Volpano and G. Smith. Probabilistic Noninterference in a Concurrent Language. In *Proceedings of the 11th IEEE Computer Security Foundations Workshop*, pages 34–43, Rockport, Massachusetts, 1998.

[ZM03]   S. Zdancewic and A. Myers. Observational determinism for concurrent program security. In *Proceedings of the 16th IEEE Computer Security Foundations Workshop, 2003*, pages 29–47. IEEE Computer Society, 2003.

# A   Semantics of MWL

The operational semantics for MWL are given in Figures 5 and 6.

$$\frac{\langle C_i, s\rangle \rightarrow \langle W', t\rangle}{\langle\langle C_0 \ldots C_{n-1}\rangle, s\rangle \rightarrow \langle\langle C_0 \ldots C_{i-1}\rangle W'\langle C_{i+1} \ldots C_{n-1}\rangle, t\rangle}$$

**Fig. 5.** Small-step nondeterministic semantics

$$\langle \text{skip}, s\rangle \rightarrow \langle\langle\rangle, s\rangle \qquad \frac{\langle Exp, s\rangle \downarrow n}{\langle Id{:=}Exp, s\rangle \rightarrow \langle\langle\rangle, [Id = n]s\rangle}$$

$$\frac{\langle C_1, s\rangle \rightarrow \langle\langle\rangle, t\rangle}{\langle C_1; C_2, s\rangle \rightarrow \langle C_2, t\rangle} \qquad \frac{\langle C_1, s\rangle \rightarrow \langle\langle C_1'\rangle V, t\rangle}{\langle C_1; C_2, s\rangle \rightarrow \langle\langle C_1'; C_2\rangle V, t\rangle} \qquad \langle \text{fork}(CV), s\rangle \rightarrow \langle\langle C\rangle V, s\rangle$$

$$\frac{\langle B, s\rangle \downarrow \text{True}}{\langle \text{if } B \text{ then } C_1 \text{ else } C_2, s\rangle \rightarrow \langle C_1, s\rangle} \qquad \frac{\langle B, s\rangle \downarrow \text{False}}{\langle \text{if } B \text{ then } C_1 \text{ else } C_2, s\rangle \rightarrow \langle C_2, s\rangle}$$

$$\frac{\langle B, s\rangle \downarrow \text{True}}{\langle \text{while } B \text{ do } C, s\rangle \rightarrow \langle C; \text{while } B \text{ do } C, s\rangle} \qquad \frac{\langle B, s\rangle \downarrow \text{False}}{\langle \text{while } B \text{ do } C, s\rangle \rightarrow \langle\langle\rangle, s\rangle}$$

**Fig. 6.** Small-step deterministic semantics

# Abstract Interpretation to Check Secure Information Flow in Programs with Input-Output Security Annotations

N. De Francesco and L. Martini

Dipartimento di Ingegneria dell'Informazione, Università di Pisa,
Via Diotisalvi, 2, 52126 Pisa, Italy
{nico, luca.martini}@iet.unipi.it

**Abstract.** We present a method based on abstract interpretation to check secure information flow in programs with dynamic structures where input and output channels are associated with security levels. In the concrete operational semantics each value is annotated with a security level dynamically taking into account both the explicit and the implicit information flows. We define a collecting semantics associating to each program point the set of concrete states of the machine when the point is reached. The abstract domains are obtained from the concrete ones by keeping the security levels and forgetting the actual values. An element of the abstract domain of states is a table whose rows correspond to the instructions of the program. An abstract operational semantics is defined on the abstract domain, and an efficient implementation is shown, operating a fixpoint iteration similar to that of the Java bytecode verification. The approach allows certifying a larger set of programs with respect to the typing approaches to check secure information flow.

## 1 Introduction

The secure information flow within programs in multilevel secure systems requires that information at a given security level does not flow to lower levels ([14]). Analyzing secure information flow allows a finer inspection of confidentiality than that obtained by using access control mechanisms. In fact access control mechanisms control only the release of information, but are not able to check the propagation of the information within the accessed entity. Instead, checking information flows makes it possible to control, once given an access right, whether the accessed information is properly used, according to some confidentiality policy.

We consider sequential programs communicating with the external environment by means of input and output channels. The program defines also a security policy by assigning a security level to each channel. A program has secure information flow if the observation of a channel having some security level does not reveal any information about the values input from channels associated with higher security levels. The language includes dynamic structures and pointers.

We analyze secure information flow by means of abstract interpretation (AI). Abstract interpretation [11, 12, 13] is a method for analyzing programs in order

T. Dimitrakos et al. (Eds.): FAST 2005, LNCS 3866, pp. 63–80, 2006.

to collect approximate information about their run-time behavior. It is based on a non-standard semantics, that is a semantic definition in which a simpler (abstract) domain replaces the standard (concrete) one, and the operations are interpreted on the new domain. Using this approach different analyses can be systematically defined. Moreover, the proof of the correctness of the analysis can be done in a standard way. In the paper first we define a concrete operational semantics which handles, in addition to execution aspects, the level of the flow of information of the program. The basis of the approach is that each value is annotated by a security level. Also each channel is associated with a security level, representing the lub of the levels of the data present in the channel. The level of the input data is assumed to be that specified for the channel by the security policy. The level of data flowing through the variables and structures of the program is calculated dynamically taking into account the information flows. We then define a collecting semantics associating to each program point (instruction) the set of concrete states in which the machine can be when the point is reached. We prove that the program is secure if in all states of the collecting semantics the level of each channel is less than or equal to that specified by the policy defined by the program. The proofs of all theorems can be found in the internal report [16].

The abstract domains are obtained from the concrete ones by keeping the security levels and forgetting the actual values. A main point is the domain of references. A state of the abstract semantics is a table having a row for each instruction. Each row is the abstraction of all concrete states in which the machine can be when executing the corresponding instruction. The table may be built by a fixpoint iteration algorithm similar to that used by bytecode verification in the Java Virtual Machine [24]. As a consequence, it is particularly efficient.

## 2   The Model

We consider the simple language illustrated in Figure 1. We indicate with $k$ a literal value and with $s, f, x, a$, respectively, generic structure, field, variable and channel name. $E$ represents the expressions and $C$ the commands. Each instruction is labeled by a label $t \in \mathcal{B} = \{0, 1, \ldots, n-1\}$ , where $n$ is the number of instructions in the program. Besides basic data, the language handles dynamic structures. We denote by New the subset of the new instructions in $\mathcal{B}$.

$$P ::= \{D; C\}$$
$$D ::= T\ x\ |\text{in}\ \sigma\ a\ |\ \text{out}\ \sigma\ a|\ D\ ;\ D$$
$$T ::= \text{int}\ |\ S$$
$$S ::= \text{struct}\ s\ \{D\}$$
$$C ::= t : x = E\ |\ t : x.f = E\ |\ t : x = \text{new}\ s\ |\ t : a?x\ |\ t : a!E\ |\text{skip}$$
$$\qquad t : \text{if}(E)\ C\ \text{else}\ C;\ |\ t : \text{while}(E)\ C;\ |\ C; C$$
$$E ::= k\ |\ E\ Op\ E\ |\ x\ |\ x.f$$

**Fig. 1.** Language grammar

Every program $P$ can retrieve data from a set of input channels and can send data to a set of output channels. If $a$ is an input channel, the command $a?x$ takes an item from $a$ and assign it to variable $x$. The command $a!e$ sends the value of expression $e$ over the output channel $a$, provided that $e$ is an expression returning a basic type (int). In the following, we denote as $\mathtt{Names}_I$ (respectively, $\mathtt{Names}_O$) the set of input (output) channels used by a program; moreover $\mathtt{Names} = \mathtt{Names}_I \cup \mathtt{Names}_O$ and $\mathtt{Names}_I \cap \mathtt{Names}_O = \emptyset$. We assume that programs are type correct.

The input and output channels represent the external environment in which the program is executed, that is all the interactions of the program occur by means of the channels and an external server is not able to inspect the internal state of the program. A *security policy* assigns to each input and output channel a security level, representing a fixed degree of secrecy. The security policy is expressed by the declaration of the channels. A channel $a$ is declared by using the keyword in (out) to indicate that is an input (output) channel and by indicating also its security level. Security levels are defined as a finite lattice $(\mathcal{L}, \sqsubseteq_{\mathcal{L}})$, ranged over by $\sigma, \tau, \ldots$ and partially ordered by $\sqsubseteq_{\mathcal{L}}$. In the following we indicate by $\mathcal{S} : \mathtt{Names} \rightarrow \mathcal{L}$ the security policy specified by the channels declarations.

**Definition 1 (secure information flow).** *Let $P$ be a program and $\mathcal{S}$ a security policy for $P$. Given $\sigma \in \mathcal{L}$, let us denote by $\mathtt{Names}_I^{\sqsubseteq \sigma}$ ($\mathtt{Names}_O^{\sqsubseteq \sigma}$) the set of channels $a$ belonging to $\mathtt{Names}_I$ ($\mathtt{Names}_O$) such that $\mathcal{S}(a) \sqsubseteq \sigma$. $P$ has $\sigma$-secure information flow (is $\sigma$-secure) under $\mathcal{S}$ if all concrete executions starting from the same configuration of input channels $\mathtt{Names}_I^{\sqsubseteq \sigma}$, input the same sequence of values from channels in $\mathtt{Names}_I^{\sqsubseteq \sigma}$ and output the same sequence of values on channels in $\mathtt{Names}_O^{\sqsubseteq \sigma}$. $P$ has secure information flow (is secure) if it is $\sigma$-secure for each $\sigma \in \mathcal{L}$.*

An external attacker having secrecy level $\sigma$ cannot infer information that is more secret than $\sigma$ from a $\sigma$-secure program if he can inspect only input and output channels with level less than or equal to $\sigma$.

Let us show some examples of programs. Consider the programs in Figure 2 and suppose that $a$ and $d$ are input channels and $b$ is an output channel. Moreover $\mathcal{S}(a) = h$, $\mathcal{S}(b) = \mathcal{S}(d) = l$, with $l \sqsubseteq h$. Since in this example there are only two security levels, we can say that channels $b$ and $d$ are public, while channel $a$ is private.

Program P1 shows an explicit insecure information flow, since the value output on channel $b$ depends on the value input from $a$: private information is made available to a public observer. Program P2 is insecure because it is possible to know if the private input is zero by observing the value present on the public output channel. In program P3 the private value affects the contents of input channel $d$, from which an item is taken only if the input is zero. Note that we consider observable both the input and the output channels. In program P4 the number of the values output on channel $b$ depends on the input value. In program P5 the first iteration of the while is driven by a low value, while the following iterations depend on high level information. Also program P6 may have an illicit

```
P1. 1: a?x; 2: b!x;
P2. 1: y=1; 2:a?x; 3: if (x==0) 4: y=0; else 5: skip; 6: b!y
P3. 1: a?x; 2: if (x==0) 3: d?y; else skip;
P4. 1: a?x; 2: while (x>0) (3: b!1; 4: x=x-1;)
P5. 1: d?x; 2: while (x>0) (3: b!1; 4: a?x;)
P6. 1: a?x; 2: while (x>0) 3: x=x-1; 4: b!1;
P7. 1: a?y; 2: y:=0; 3: b!y;
P8. 1: s1=new S; 2: s2=new S; 3: a?x; 4: if(x) 5: s3=s1; else 6: s3=s2; 7: s3.f=1;
```

**Fig. 2.** Some examples

information flow, even if the value output on channel $b$ is always the same: it is possible that, due to an infinite loop, no value is output on channel $b$. Program P7 is secure, since the output value, which is constant, does not depend on the input: even if y it is written with a high value, afterward it is assigned a constant value, and this one is given as an output. Consider program P8 and suppose that S is an user-defined structure with two int fields f and g, and that s1, s2, s3 are references of type S. Please notice that, depending on the value taken from the high level input channel a, instruction 7 updates field f of two different objects (created at the first two instructions). Now consider the two cases in which instruction 7 is followed by: (i) 8:b!s1.g; (ii) 8:b!s1.f;. In case (i) the program is secure because field g of object created at instruction 1 is the same in any computation. On the contrary, in case (ii), the value of the field s1.f depends on the input: by aliasing, the assignment in instruction 7 could have modified it.

## 3   Concrete Semantics

In this section we define the concrete semantics of the language. To take into account the security level of data, we annotate each value $v$ flowing through the variables and the structure fields with a security level, representing the least upper bound of the security levels of the explicit and implicit information flows on which $v$ depends. A value is a pair $(v^e, \sigma)$, where $v^e$ is an execution value and $\sigma$ a security level. The domains of the concrete semantics are shown in Figure 3. An execution value may be an integer $k \in \mathbb{Z}$ or a reference to an user-defined structure. A reference is in turn a pair $(\ell, t)$, where $\ell \in \mathcal{A}^e$ is a heap address and $t \in \text{New}$ is the label of the instruction which created the corresponding structure. This tag will be useful in the abstraction to coalesce into a same abstract structure all structures created at the same instruction. The memory

$$
\begin{array}{ll}
v \in \mathcal{V} = (\mathbb{Z} \cup \mathcal{A}) \times \mathcal{L} & \mathcal{A} = \mathcal{A}^e \times \text{New} \\
\mu \in \mathcal{M} = Var \to \mathcal{V} & \xi \in \Xi = \mathcal{A} \to \mathcal{M}_{\text{struct}} \\
c \in \mathcal{C} = \text{Names} \to (\mathbb{Z}^\star \times \mathcal{L}) & q \in \mathcal{Q} = \mathcal{B} \times Env \times \mathcal{M} \times \Xi \times \mathcal{C}
\end{array}
$$

**Fig. 3.** Domains of the concrete semantics

$$\text{Const} \frac{}{\langle k, \mu, \xi \rangle \xrightarrow{E} (k, \perp_{\mathcal{L}})} \qquad \text{Op} \frac{\langle E_1, \mu, \xi \rangle \xrightarrow{E} (v_1^e, \sigma_1), \ \langle E_2, \mu, \xi \rangle \xrightarrow{E} (v_2^e, \sigma_2)}{\langle E_1 \ op \ E_2, \mu, \xi \rangle \xrightarrow{E} (v_1^e \ \underline{op} \ v_2^e, \sigma_1 \sqcup_{\mathcal{L}} \sigma_2)}$$

$$\text{Value} \frac{}{x \quad \langle x, \mu, \xi \rangle \xrightarrow{E} \mu(x)} \qquad \text{Value} \frac{\mu(x) = ((\ell, t), \sigma_1), \ \xi(\ell, t)(f) = (v^e, \sigma_2)}{x.f \quad \langle x.f, \mu, \xi \rangle \xrightarrow{E} (v^e, \sigma_1 \sqcup_{\mathcal{L}} \sigma_2)}$$

**Fig. 4.** Concrete semantics of expressions

is represented by means of two functions: one denoted by $\mu$, that associates every variable with its value, and the other, denoted by $\xi$, that associates the addresses (references) with the respective structure instances. Every structure in the heap can be represented by a memory whose variables are the fields. Valid fields names are in the domain $\mathcal{F}$. We denote by $\mathcal{M}_S$ the domain of memories having the fields of structure $S$ as variables, and by $\mathcal{M}_{\text{struct}}$ the set: $\mathcal{M}_{\text{struct}} = \bigcup \{\mathcal{M}_S | S \text{ used in } P\}$. The state of input and output channels $c \in \mathcal{C}$ is a mapping from the names of the channels to pairs $(s, \sigma)$, where $s \in \mathbb{Z}^\star$ is a finite sequence of values and $\sigma$ a security level. Initially, the security level of each input channel $a$ is set to $\mathcal{S}(a)$, that is the security level defined for $a$ by the security specification. As a consequence, each value taken from an input channel $a$ is annotated with $\mathcal{S}(a)$. The security level of the output channels is initially set to the minimum level $\perp_{\mathcal{L}}$. The security level of the channels can be modified by the computation, when the channel is accessed.

The concrete semantics is defined by means of a set of rules: the rules for expressions are shown in Figure 4 and the rules for instructions in Figure 5. Let us consider the rules for expressions, defining a relation $\xrightarrow{E} \subseteq (expr \times \mathcal{M} \times \Xi) \times \mathcal{V}$. Rule **Const** assigns the bottom security level to any constant value. Rule **Op** calculates the security level of the result of an operation as the lub of the security levels of the operands. Rule **Value**$_x$ returns the value of the variable in the memory. Rule **Value**$_{x.f}$ annotates the resulting value with the lub of the security levels of the reference and of the value stored in the field.

The rules for instructions (Figure 5) define a relation $\longrightarrow \subseteq \mathcal{Q} \times \mathcal{Q}$ between the states of the computation. The set of concrete states is $\mathcal{Q} = \mathcal{B} \times Env \times \mathcal{M} \times \Xi \times \mathcal{C}$, where $Env = \mathcal{B} \to \mathcal{L}$. Each state $q \in \mathcal{Q}$ is a tuple $\langle t, \rho, \mu, \xi, c \rangle$ describing the configuration of the machine when executing the command $t$: $\mu$ and $\xi$ define the values of variables and structures fields, while $c$ represent the status of the channels. We also keep in each state a *security environment* $\rho \in Env$, assigning to every program point a security level representing the level of the implicit flow under which the corresponding command is executed. In the following, given an instruction label $t$ and a set $Q$ of states, we use the notation $Q(t)$ to denote the set of states in $Q$ corresponding to instruction $t$. A value $(v^e, \tau)$ evaluated, assigned or tested while the execution is under a security environment $\sigma$, changes its security level into $\sigma \sqcup \tau$. The environment, initially set to $\perp_{\mathcal{L}}$ for all commands, can be updated by the conditional and repetitive commands. With $succ(t)$ we indicate the successive instruction to be executed. All commands

$$\mathbf{Assign}_{t:\mathtt{x=E}}\ \frac{\langle E,\mu,\xi\rangle \xrightarrow{E}(v^e,\sigma)}{\langle t,\rho,\mu,\xi,c\rangle \longrightarrow \langle succ(t),\rho,\mu\,[x \leftarrow (v^e,\rho(t)\sqcup_{\mathcal{L}}\sigma)]\,,\xi,c\rangle}$$

$$\mathbf{Assign}_{t:\mathtt{x.f=E}}\ \frac{\langle E,\mu,\xi\rangle \xrightarrow{E}(v^e,\sigma_1),\ \mu(x)=((\ell,t_1),\sigma_2),\ \sigma_3=\sigma_1\sqcup_{\mathcal{L}}\sigma_2\sqcup_{\mathcal{L}}\rho(t)}{\langle t,\rho,\mu,\xi,c\rangle \longrightarrow \langle succ(t),\rho,\mu,\xi\,[(\ell,t_1),f \leftarrow (v^e,\sigma_3)]\,,c\rangle}$$

$$\mathbf{New}_{t:\mathtt{x=new\ S}}\ \frac{\mathrm{fresh}(\xi)=\ell}{\langle t,\rho,\mu,\xi,c\rangle \longrightarrow \langle succ(t),\rho,\mu\,[x \leftarrow ((\ell,t),\rho(t))]\,,\xi\,[(\ell,t)\leftarrow \mu_{S\perp}]\,,c\rangle}$$

$$\mathbf{Input}_{t:\mathtt{a?x}}\ \frac{c(a)=(k\cdot s,\sigma),a\in \mathrm{Names}_I}{\langle t,\rho,\mu,\xi,c\rangle \longrightarrow \langle succ(t),\rho,\mu\,[x \leftarrow (k,\rho(t)\sqcup_{\mathcal{L}}\sigma)]\,,\xi,c\,[a \leftarrow (s,\rho(t)\sqcup_{\mathcal{L}}\sigma)]\rangle}$$

$$\mathbf{Output}_{t:\mathtt{b!E}}\ \frac{\langle E,\mu,\xi\rangle \xrightarrow{E}(k,\sigma_1),\ c(b)=(s,\sigma_2),\ b\in \mathrm{Names}_O}{\langle (t,\rho,\mu,\xi,c\rangle \longrightarrow \langle succ(t),\rho,\mu,\xi,c\,[b \leftarrow (k\cdot s,\rho(t)\sqcup_{\mathcal{L}}\sigma_1\sqcup_{\mathcal{L}}\sigma_2)]\rangle}$$

$$\mathbf{If}_{\substack{t:\mathtt{if\ (E)\ C}\\ \mathtt{else\ C,\ (true)}}}\ \frac{\langle E,\mu,\xi\rangle \xrightarrow{E}(\mathit{true},\sigma)}{\langle t,\rho,\mu,\xi,c\rangle \longrightarrow \Big\langle succ_{true}(t),\rho\,[t' \leftarrow \rho(t')\sqcup_{\mathcal{L}}\sigma]_{\forall t'\in scope(t)}\,,\mu,\xi,c\Big\rangle}$$

$$\mathbf{While}_{\substack{t:\mathtt{while\ (E)\ C}\\ \mathtt{(true)}}}\ \frac{\langle E,\mu,\xi\rangle \xrightarrow{E}(\mathit{true},\sigma)}{\langle t,\rho,\mu,\xi,c\rangle \longrightarrow \Big\langle succ_{true}(t),\rho\,[t' \leftarrow \rho(t')\sqcup_{\mathcal{L}}\sigma]_{\forall t'\in scope(t)}\,,\mu,\xi,c\Big\rangle}$$

**Fig. 5.** Concrete semantics of commands

have only one successor, except the conditional and repetitive commands that have two successors, depending on the value of the guard; they are denoted by $succ_{true}(t)$ and $succ_{false}(t)$. We assume that the first instruction of the program has label $t_0$ and that for the last instruction is $succ(t)=\mathsf{end}$.

Rule **Assign**$_{t:x=e}$ annotates the security level of the value to be assigned with the lub of the security level resulted by the evaluation of the expression and the environment of the instruction $t$. The notation $\mu\,[x \leftarrow (v^e,\sigma)]$ stands for the memory obtained by $\mu$ by updating the contents for the variable $x$ with the value $(v^e,\sigma)$. Rule **Assign**$_{t:x.f=e}$ annotates the value to be assigned with the lub of 1) the security level resulted by the evaluation of the expression, 2) the security level of the reference, and 3) the environment of $t$. In the rule, the notation $\xi\,[(\ell,t),f \leftarrow v]$ indicates the heap $\xi'$ obtained from $\xi$ by updating the field $f$ of the structure located at address $\ell$ (and created at instruction $t$) with the value $v$.

Rule **New** contains the notation $\xi\,[(\ell,t)\leftarrow \mu_{S\perp}]$, meaning that, during the execution of instruction $t$, in the heap $\xi$ a new structure of type $S$ is created at address $\ell$, its fields containing the default value. We assume the default value is the pair $(0,\perp_{\mathcal{L}})$. In the premise of the rule the function fresh $:\ \Xi \to \mathcal{A}$ is used to find a free location in the heap to store the new structure.

Rule **Input** takes a value from the specified input channel and assigns it to the destination variable, annotated with the lub of the level $\sigma$ of the channel and the environment of $t$. Also the level of the channel is updated in the same way. As a consequence, if $\rho(t)$ is higher than $\sigma$, the level of the channel is upgraded, to record the fact that the manipulation of the channel depends on an information flow with level $\sigma \sqsubseteq_{\mathcal{L}} \rho(t)$. Analogously, in the **Output** rule, the level of the specified output channel is possibly upgraded taking into account the level of the value and that of the environment of the instruction.

The **If** and **While** rules, whatever branch is chosen, affect the environment of all the instructions belonging to the scope of the command, taking into account the level of the condition. The set $scope(t)$ contains all the instructions that can be executed or not depending on the condition. In the **If** case, $scope(t)$ includes all the instructions belonging to only one branch starting from the **If**. For the **While** command, $scope(t)$ includes all instructions following the **While**, that is the instructions belonging to the loop (the *true* part of the **While**) and also all instructions after the loop until the end of the program (the *false* part). The inclusion of these instructions takes into account the possibility of an infinite loop: in this case, the commands following the loop will never be executed. Updating the environment is necessary to trace implicit flow: the value of the condition (with its security level) drives the execution of the instructions in $scope(t)$. The table shows only the rule to be applied when the condition is true. The rule to be applied when the condition is false (not shown) is equal except that has $succ_{false}$ instead of $succ_{true}$.

**Definition 2 (initial state).** *Given an initial configuration $i_0$ : $\mathrm{Names}_I \rightarrow \mathbb{Z}^\star$ of the input channels, the initial state is defined as $q(i_0) = \langle t_0, \rho_\perp, \mu_0, \xi_\lambda, c_0 \rangle$, where $\rho_\perp$ associates $\perp_{\mathcal{L}}$ to all instruction labels, $\mu_0$ associates to every variable declared in the program the default value, $\xi_\lambda$ is the heap with empty domain (that is, the everywhere undefined function). The state $c_0$ is such that for all $a \in \mathrm{Names}_I, c_0(a) = (i_0(a), \mathcal{S}(a))$ and for all $a \in \mathrm{Names}_O, c_0(a) = (\lambda, \perp_{\mathcal{L}})$.*

We now define a collecting semantics, associating with each instruction the set of states in which the instruction can be executed in any computation.

First we define an alignment operation $\mathsf{align}(Q)$ which, given a set of states $Q$, aligns all the states corresponding to the same instruction. $\mathsf{align}(Q)$ increments $Q$ with some extra states: for each instruction $t$ and each state $q \in Q(t)$, a state $q'$ is added to $Q$ having the same execution values occurring in $q$, but where the security levels of the environment, memory variables, fields of structures and channels are upgraded to the lub in $\mathcal{L}$ of the levels occurring in the states in $Q(t)$ for the same items. In Fig. 6 are shown some auxiliary functions used in the alignment process.

Let $Q$ be a set of states: then $\mathsf{max}_{\mathcal{M}}(Q, x)$ is the lub of the security levels of $x$ in the memories occurring in the states of $Q$. For each $t \in \mathcal{B}$, $\mathsf{max}_E(Q, t)$ is the lub of the values of $\rho(t)$ in the environment occurring in the states of $Q$. For each field $f$ of each structure created at instruction $(\ell, t) \in \mathcal{A}$, $\mathsf{max}_{\Xi}(Q, \ell, t, f)$ is the lub of the values held by the field $f$ in the heap occurring in the states of $Q$. For each channel $a \in \mathrm{Names}$, $\mathsf{max}_C(Q, a)$ is the lub of the security levels held by the channel $a$ in the states of $Q$. Finally, given a value $v = (v^e, \tau)$, with

| | | |
|---|---|---|
| $\mathsf{max}_E : \mathcal{Q} \times \mathcal{B} \to \mathcal{L}$ | $\mathsf{max}_E(Q,t)$ | $= \bigsqcup_{\mathcal{L}} \{\rho(t) \mid \langle t', \rho, \mu, \xi, c \rangle \in Q\}$ |
| $\mathsf{max}_{\mathcal{M}} : \mathcal{Q} \times Var \to \mathcal{L}$ | $\mathsf{max}_{\mathcal{M}}(Q,x)$ | $= \bigsqcup_{\mathcal{L}} \{\sigma \mid \langle t, \rho, \mu, \xi, c \rangle \in Q, \mu(x) = (v^e, \sigma)\}$ |
| $\mathsf{max}_{\Xi} : \mathcal{Q} \times \mathcal{A} \times \mathcal{F} \to \mathcal{L}$ | $\mathsf{max}_{\Xi}(Q,\ell,t,f)$ | $= \bigsqcup_{\mathcal{L}} \{\sigma \mid \langle t, \rho, \mu, \xi, c \rangle \in Q, \xi(\ell,t)(f) = (v^e, \sigma)\}$ |
| $\mathsf{max}_{\mathcal{C}} : \mathcal{Q} \times \mathtt{Names} \to \mathcal{L}$ | $\mathsf{max}_{\mathcal{C}}(Q,a)$ | $= \bigsqcup_{\mathcal{L}} \{\sigma \mid \langle t, \rho, \mu, \xi, c \rangle \in Q, c(a) = (s, \sigma)\}$ |

**Fig. 6.** Auxiliary functions for merging

$v^e \in (\mathbb{Z} \cup \mathcal{A})$, $\mathsf{up}(v, \sigma) = (v^e, \tau \sqcup_{\mathcal{L}} \sigma)$ is the value obtained by keeping unaltered the execution part of the value and upgrading the annotation of $v$.

Now we can define the align function. Consider a set $Q \subseteq \mathcal{Q}$ of states. Given a state $q = \langle t, \rho, \mu, \xi, c \rangle \in Q$ let $\mathsf{align}_t(q, Q) = \langle t, \rho', \mu', \xi', c' \rangle\}$ with:

$$\forall t' \in \mathcal{B} : \rho'(t') = \mathsf{max}_E(Q(t), t') \quad \forall x \in Var : \mu'(x) = \mathsf{up}(\mu(x), \mathsf{max}_{\mathcal{M}}(Q(t), x))$$
$$\forall (\ell, t') \in dom(\xi), f \in dom(\xi(\ell, t')) : \xi'(\ell, t')(f) = \mathsf{up}(\xi(\ell, t')(f), \mathsf{max}_{\Xi}(Q(t), \ell, t', f))$$
$$\forall a \in \mathtt{Names} : c'(a) = \mathsf{up}(c(a), \mathsf{max}_{\mathcal{C}}(Q, a))$$
$$\mathsf{align}(Q) = (\bigcup_{q \in Q} \mathsf{align}_t(q, Q)) \cup Q$$

**Definition 3 (concrete next operator next).** *Given a set of concrete states $Q \subseteq \mathcal{Q}$, the application of the* next *operator yields the aligned set of states that are either in $Q$, or reached in one step of computation starting from a state in $Q$.*

$$\mathsf{next}(Q) = \mathsf{align}(Q \cup \{q \mid \exists q' \in Q : q' \longrightarrow q\})$$

**Proposition 1 (monotonicity of next).** next *is monotone in $(\wp(\mathcal{Q}), \subseteq)$.*

The concrete collecting semantics $sem \in \wp(\mathcal{Q})$ is the set of all aligned concrete states belonging to all executions.

**Definition 4 (collecting semantics).** *The concrete collecting semantics sem $\in \wp(\mathcal{Q})$ is the lub of the following increasing chain, defined for all $n \in \mathbb{N}$:*

$$sem_0 = \{q(i_0) \mid \forall i_0 \in (\mathtt{Names}_I \to \mathbb{Z}^\star)\}$$
$$sem_{n+1} = \mathsf{next}(sem_n)$$

Performing align at each step of $sem_n$ aligns the security annotations of the states corresponding to the join point of different branches of a conditional instruction, in order to properly manage implicit flows. Consider, for example, program P2 of figure 2. If we consider an execution in which the input value is 0, the branch *true* of the if command is executed, and at instruction 5 the state is $q = \langle 5, \perp_\rho, \mu, \perp_\xi, c \rangle$, with $\mu(y) = (0, \sigma)$ where the annotation $\sigma$ of 0 records the implicit flow of level $\sigma$ under which the assignment to $y$ has been performed. If, instead, the input value is different from 0, variable $x$ is not affected in the conditional command and the state $q' = \langle 5, \perp_\rho, \mu', \perp_\xi, c' \rangle$ is reached, where $\mu'(y) = (1, \perp_{\mathcal{L}})$. This state does not represent the implicit flow, since the level of the value held by $y$ is low. Instead, the contents of $y$ has been affected also in this case by the implicit flow of level $\sigma$. The violation becomes evident only if there exists another execution in which $y$ is updated in another branch of the conditional command. Since the alignment operation is applied to the chain $sem_n$, there exists at least one $j$ such that $sem_j$ contains a state $\langle 5, \perp_\rho, \mu'', \perp_\xi, c' \rangle$ where $\mu''(y) = (1, \sigma)$. This state derives from the alignment of $q$ and $q'$ and represents the effect of the implicit flow on $y$ in the case in which the *false* branch has been chosen. The following theorem states that the collecting semantics correctly represents the secure information flow property.

**Theorem 1 (secure information flow).** *A program $P$ has secure information flow under a security policy $\mathcal{S}$ if for each concrete state $\langle t, \rho, \mu, \xi, c \rangle \in sem$, for each channel $a$, if $c(a) = (\delta, \sigma), \delta \in \mathbb{Z}^\star$, then $\sigma \sqsubseteq \mathcal{S}(a)$.*

*Proof Sketch.* The proof is made by proving $\sigma$-security for a generic $\sigma$. We define a notion of $\sigma$-equivalence between states, such that two states are equivalent iff 1) each annotation on memory, heap, environment and channels is either $\sqsubseteq \sigma$ or $\not\sqsubseteq \sigma$ on both states and 2) they agree (have the same execution values) on data annotated by security levels $\sqsubseteq \sigma$. It holds that, under the hypothesis of the theorem, two $\sigma$-equivalent states have the same execution values on input/output channels with level $\sqsubseteq \sigma$. Consider two executions starting from same values on channels in $\mathtt{Names}_I^{\sqsubseteq \sigma}$. Until a conditional or repetitive instruction is reached with a high ($\not\sqsubseteq \sigma$) guard, the two executions perform the same instructions reaching at each step $\sigma$-equivalent states. When a conditional command is reached with a high guard it is possible that the two executions make different sequences of instructions, possibly leading to not $\sigma$-equivalent states. However all instructions executed until the end of the command is reached have a high environment in both executions. Thus, if a variable is updated, the value is annotated with a level $\not\sqsubseteq \sigma$. Analogously for the fields of the structures and for the input and output channels. Note that, while we are in the scope of the conditional command, no input and/or output channel $a$ can be affected with $\mathcal{S}(a) \sqsubseteq \sigma$, otherwise *sem* does not respect the condition of the theorem. Let both computations reach the end of the conditional commands, say instruction $t$, at states $q_1$ and $q_2$, respectively. Let $i$ and $j$ be the corresponding indexes of the chain $sem_n$, that is $q_1 \in sem_i$ and $q_2 \in sem_j$. We have that, due to the alignment applied by next, there are in $sem_{max(i,j)}(t)$ two states, say $q_1'$ and $q_2'$, corresponding resp. to the alignment of $q_1$ and $q_2$, that is with the same execution values of $q_1$ and $q_2$, but with the security levels upgraded to the maximum values between the two execution paths. It holds that $q_1'$ and $q_2'$ are $\sigma$-equivalent, since only the elements not updated in any of the two branches can have a low annotation. The above reasoning can be iterated starting from $q_1'$ and $q_2'$. If at least one of the two executions does not reach the end of the command, this means that a $\mathtt{while}$ with a high condition has been reached, but in this case all instructions of the program reachable from the $\mathtt{while}$ are given a high environment and no input/output operation on a channel may be executed without raising the security level of the channel to a high value. By hypothesis, channels with security level $\sqsubseteq \sigma$ cannot be affected from this point on. The same occurs when a $\mathtt{while}$ with a high guard is reached not belonging to a conditional command. □

## 4   Abstract Domains

The method consists in definining a concrete and an abstract domain and two functions between them: an abstraction function $\alpha$ and a concretization function $\gamma$. The kind of abstraction and concretization function are choosen according to the property that one need to prove. Neverthless, to ensure the correctness of the method, the two functions have to be related by a Galois Connection or a Galois Insertion, satisfying the properties Galois and Connection or Galois and Insertion in the definition below.

**Definition 5 (Galois Connection/Insertion).** *Let* $(C, \subseteq)$ *and* $(A, \sqsubseteq)$ *be two complete lattices. Two functions* $\alpha \colon C \mapsto A$ *and* $\gamma \colon A \mapsto C$ *form a Galois inser-tion between* $(C, \subseteq)$ *and* $(A, \sqsubseteq)$, *iff all the following conditions hold:*

- $\alpha$-**Monotonicity**: $\forall y, y' \in C.\ y \subseteq y' \Rightarrow \alpha(y) \sqsubseteq \alpha(y')$
- $\gamma$-**Monotonicity**: $\forall a, a' \in A.\ a \sqsubseteq a' \Rightarrow \gamma(a) \subseteq \gamma(a')$
- **Galois**: $\forall y \in C.\ y \subseteq \gamma(\alpha(y))$
- **Connection**: $\forall a \in A.\ \alpha(\gamma(a)) \sqsubseteq_A a$
- **Insertion**: $\forall a \in A.\ \alpha(\gamma(a)) = a$

For both connection and insertion, it must hold that, if $y \in C$ and $\alpha(y) = a \in A$, then, if we concretize $a$, we obtain a set that contains the original one $(y)$ (Galois) ; if moreover we concretize $a$ and then we abstract the result of the concretization, we obtain an abstract element which is less than or equal to $a$ (connection) or equal to the starting element (insertion). Thus the insertion represents a more precise and non redundant abstraction with respect to the connection. Once defined the domains, given a concrete semantics acting on objects belonging to the concrete domain, the abstract interpretation theory provides systematic methods to design an abstract semantics such that it cor-rectly approximates the concrete one. Moreover, showing that the concrete and the abstract domains are connected by a Galois Insertion will be useful to prove that the abstract flow equations converge to a fixpoint [20].

The abstract domains are obtained by eliminating from the concrete values both the execution values and execution addresses. Every value maintains instead its security annotation. Simple values (int) are no longer held and are repre-sented with a · symbol. In order to make the heap finite we abstract onto the same element different structures created at the same label. Moreover, an abstract ad-dress $\ell^{\natural}$ is composed of a set of labels in New. In this way $\ell^{\natural}$ records all the possible creation points of the structures pointed to by it during the computation. The operations defined on the lattice of abstract values $(\mathcal{V}^{\natural}, \sqsubseteq_{\mathcal{V}}^{\natural}, \sqcup_{\mathcal{V}}^{\natural}, \sqcap_{\mathcal{V}}^{\natural}, \perp_{\mathcal{V}}^{\natural}, \top_{\mathcal{V}}^{\natural})$ are reported in Figure 7. The abstraction of a set of simple values is the least upper bound of their security levels. We assume that $\alpha_{\mathcal{V}}$ returns the bottom element of $\mathcal{V}^{\natural}$ if applied to the empty set. Dually for the concretization function. The same for the other abstraction functions. The abstraction of a set of concrete references is an abstract reference that contains both the least upper bound of their secu-rity levels and a set $T \subseteq$ New of instruction points. $T$ contains all the instructions at which the structure referenced is created. For example, if $v_1 = ((\ell_1, t_1), \sigma_1)$ and $v_2 = ((\ell_2, t_2), \sigma_2)$, then $v^{\natural} = \alpha_{\mathcal{V}}(\{v_1, v_2\}) = (\{t_1, t_2\}, \sigma_1 \sqcup_{\mathcal{L}} \sigma_2)$.

$$\mathcal{A}^\natural = \wp(\mathtt{New}), \quad \mathcal{V}^\natural = (\{\cdot\} \cup \{\bot, \top\} \cup \mathcal{A}^\natural) \times \mathcal{L} \text{ ranged over by } v_1^\natural, v_2^\natural, \ldots$$

$$\sqsubseteq_\mathcal{V}: \quad v_1^\natural \sqsubseteq_\mathcal{V} v_2^\natural \text{ iff } v_1^\natural = (T_1, \sigma_1) \wedge v_2^\natural = (T_2, \sigma_2) \wedge T_1 \subseteq T_2 \wedge \sigma_1 \sqsubseteq_\mathcal{L} \sigma_2 \vee$$
$$\vee \, v_1^\natural = (\cdot, \sigma_1) \wedge v_2^\natural = (\cdot, \sigma_2) \wedge \sigma_1 \sqsubseteq_\mathcal{L} \sigma_2$$

$$\sqcup_\mathcal{V}: \quad v_1^\natural \sqcup_\mathcal{V} v_2^\natural = \begin{cases} (T_1 \cup T_2, \sigma_1 \sqcup_\mathcal{L} \sigma_2) & \text{if } v_1^\natural = (T_1, \sigma_1) \wedge v_2^\natural = (T_2, \sigma_2) \\ (\cdot, \sigma_1 \sqcup_\mathcal{L} \sigma_2) & \text{if } v_1^\natural = (\cdot, \sigma_1) \wedge v_1^\natural = (\cdot, \sigma_2) \\ \top_\mathcal{V} & \text{otherwise} \end{cases}$$

$$\sqcap_\mathcal{V}: \quad v_1^\natural \sqcap_\mathcal{V} v_2^\natural = \begin{cases} (T_1 \cap T_2, \sigma_1 \sqcap_\mathcal{L} \sigma_2) & \text{if } v_1^\natural = (T_1, \sigma_1) \wedge v_2^\natural = (T_2, \sigma_2) \\ (\cdot, \sigma_1 \sqcap_\mathcal{L} \sigma_2) & \text{if } v_1^\natural = (\cdot, \sigma_1) \wedge v_1^\natural = (\cdot, \sigma_2) \\ \bot_\mathcal{V} & \text{otherwise} \end{cases}$$

$$\bot_\mathcal{V} = (\bot, \bot_\mathcal{L}) \quad \top_\mathcal{V} = (\top, \top_\mathcal{L})$$

$$\alpha_\mathcal{V}^1(v) = \begin{cases} (\cdot, \sigma) & v = (k, \sigma), k \in \mathbb{Z} \\ (\{t\}, \sigma) & v = ((\ell, t), \sigma), (\ell, t) \in \mathcal{A} \end{cases} \quad y \in \wp(\mathcal{V}), \alpha_\mathcal{V}(y) = \bigsqcup_{v_i \in y} {}_\mathcal{V} \, \alpha_\mathcal{V}^1(v_i)$$

$$\gamma_\mathcal{V}(v^\natural) = \begin{cases} \{(k, \sigma') | k \in \mathbb{Z}, \sigma' \sqsubseteq_\mathcal{L} \sigma\} & v^\natural = (\cdot, \sigma) \\ \{((\ell, t), \sigma') | t \in T, (\ell, t) \in \mathcal{A}, \sigma' \sqsubseteq_\mathcal{L} \sigma\} & v^\natural = (T, \sigma) \\ \mathcal{V} & v^\natural = \top_\mathcal{V} \\ \emptyset & v^\natural = \bot_\mathcal{V} \end{cases}$$

**Fig. 7.** Lattice of abstract values

$$\alpha_\mathcal{M}(y)(x) = \alpha_\mathcal{V}(\{\mu(x) | \mu \in y\})$$
$$\gamma_\mathcal{M}(\mu^\natural) = \{\mu \in \mathcal{M} | \forall x \in X. \mu(x) \in \gamma_\mathcal{V}(\mu^\natural(x))\}$$
$$\alpha_\Xi(y)(t) = \alpha_\mathcal{M}(\{\xi(\ell, t) | \xi \in y, (\ell, t) \in dom(\xi)\})$$
$$\gamma_\Xi(\xi^\natural) = \{\xi \in \Xi | \forall t \in \mathtt{New}.\xi(t) \in \gamma_\mathcal{M}(\xi^\natural(t))\}$$
$$\alpha_\mathcal{C}(y)(a) = \bigsqcup_\mathcal{L} \{\sigma | c(a) = (\delta, \sigma), c \in y\}$$
$$\gamma_\mathcal{C}(c^\natural) = \{c \in \mathcal{C} | \forall a \in \mathtt{Names}.c(a) = (s, \sigma), s \in \mathbb{Z}^\star, \sigma \sqsubseteq_\mathcal{L} c^\natural(a)\}$$

**Fig. 8.** Abstraction and concretization functions for the abstract domains

An abstract memory $\mu^\natural \in \mathcal{M}_X^\natural = X \to \mathcal{V}^\natural$ maps every variable in the set $X$ to an abstract value. Two abstract memories can be compared only if their domains are the same. When $X = Var$ we omit the subscript and indicate the domain with $\mathcal{M}^\natural$. An abstract heap $\xi^\natural \in \Xi^\natural = \mathtt{New} \to \mathcal{M}_{\mathtt{struct}}^\natural$ is a map from structure creation points to abstract memories representing fields contents. Two heaps $\xi_1^\natural, \xi_2^\natural$ can be compared only if each abstract address points to structures of the same type, i.e. $\forall t \in \mathtt{New}, \xi_1^\natural(t)$ and $\xi_2^\natural(t)$ are comparable memories. Input and output channels are represented in the abstract domain $\mathcal{C}^\natural = \mathtt{Names} \to \mathcal{L}$ with tuples of security levels, one for each channel. Here, for brevity, we omit the description of lattice operations (that are defined in a standard way) on the domains $\mathcal{M}^\natural$, $\Xi^\natural$ and $\mathcal{C}^\natural$, showing in Figure 8 their corresponding abstraction/concretization functions.

The abstract domain of states is $\mathcal{Q}^\natural = \mathcal{B} \to (\mathcal{L} \times \mathcal{M}^\natural \times \Xi^\natural \times \mathcal{C}^\natural)$. It contains all functions associating the instruction labels $\mathcal{B}$ with elements in $(\mathcal{L} \times \mathcal{M}^\natural \times \Xi^\natural \times \mathcal{C}^\natural)$. Given an abstract state $q^\natural \in \mathcal{Q}^\natural$, and an instruction label $t \in \mathcal{B}$, $q^\natural(t) = \langle \sigma, \mu^\natural, \xi^\natural, c^\natural \rangle$ is a tuple composed of a security level representing the security environment of $t$, an abstract memory, heap and channels. We use $q^\natural(t).env$ to denote $\sigma$. We denote by $dom(q^\natural) = \{t \mid q^\natural(t) = \langle \sigma, \mu^\natural, \xi^\natural, c^\natural \rangle \wedge \mu^\natural \neq \perp_\mathcal{M}^\natural \wedge \xi^\natural \neq \perp_\Xi^\natural \wedge c^\natural \neq \perp_\mathcal{C}^\natural\}$ the instruction addresses to which $q^\natural$ assigns a defined value for memory, heap and channels. We have that $(\mathcal{Q}^\natural, \sqsubseteq_\mathcal{Q})$ is a lattice, where, the operation $\sqsubseteq_\mathcal{Q}$ is defined as the pointwise application of the corresponding operation on the fields of the abstract states. Let us now consider the abstraction and concretization functions between the concrete and abstract domains of the states.

$\alpha_\mathcal{Q} : \wp(\mathcal{Q}) \to \mathcal{Q}^\natural$ is defined as follows. Let $Q$ be a set of concrete states in $\mathcal{Q} = \mathcal{B} \times Env \times \mathcal{M} \times \Xi \times \mathcal{C}$. For each $t \in \mathcal{B}$, it is $\alpha_\mathcal{Q}(Q)(t) = \langle \sigma, \mu^\natural, \xi^\natural, c^\natural \rangle$ where

$$\sigma = \bigsqcup_\mathcal{L}\{\rho(t) \mid \langle t', \rho, \mu, \xi, c \rangle \in Q\} \quad \mu^\natural = \alpha_\mathcal{M}(\{\mu \mid \langle t, \rho, \mu, \xi, c \rangle \in Q\})$$
$$\xi^\natural = \alpha_\Xi(\{\xi \mid \langle t, \rho, \mu, \xi, c \rangle \in Q\}) \quad c^\natural = \alpha_\mathcal{C}(\{c \mid \langle t, \rho, \mu, \xi, c \rangle \in Q\})$$

If an instruction $t$ does not occur in $Q$, then the abstraction functions $\alpha_\mathcal{M}$, $\alpha_\Xi$ and $\alpha_\mathcal{C}$ will produce bottom values, excluding $t$ from $dom(\alpha_\mathcal{Q}(Q))$. Note that the security environment of an instruction $t$ (whether $t$ is in $dom(\alpha_\mathcal{Q}(Q))$ or not) in the abstract state is the lub of the security environments assigned to $t$ by all states in $Q$. On the contrary, the abstract memory, heap and channels associated to $t$ are the lub of the abstractions of the concrete memories, heaps and channels, respectively, occurring the states of $Q$ corresponding to the execution of the instruction with label $t$. For the concretization function $\gamma_\mathcal{Q} : \mathcal{Q}^\natural \to \wp(\mathcal{Q})$ we have:

$$\gamma_\mathcal{Q}(q^\natural) = \{ \langle t, \rho, \mu, \xi, c \rangle \mid t \in dom(q^\natural), \forall t' \in \mathcal{B}, \rho(t') \sqsubseteq q^\natural(t').env, q^\natural(t) = \langle \sigma, \mu^\natural, \xi^\natural, c^\natural \rangle,$$
$$\mu = \gamma_\mathcal{M}(\mu^\natural), \xi = \gamma_\Xi(\xi^\natural), c = \gamma_\mathcal{C}(c^\natural)\}$$

**Proposition 2.** *The pairs of functions* $(\alpha_\mathcal{V}, \gamma_\mathcal{V})$, $(\alpha_\mathcal{M}, \gamma_\mathcal{M})$, $(\alpha_\Xi, \gamma_\Xi)$, $(\alpha_\mathcal{C}, \gamma_\mathcal{C})$ *and* $(\alpha_\mathcal{Q}, \gamma_\mathcal{Q})$ *are Galois Insertions.*

## 5   Abstract Semantics and Correctness

In this section we give an abstract semantics of the language allowing to finitely execute the program in the abstract domain.

Figure 9 describes the abstract semantics of expressions. The rules of the abstract semantics for instructions are shown in Figure 10. They define a relation $\xrightarrow{C^\natural}$ between the abstract states: if the premise of the rule is true, the rule

$$\text{Const} \frac{}{k, \mu^\natural, \xi^\natural \xrightarrow{E^\natural} (\cdot, \perp_\mathcal{L})} \qquad \text{Op} \frac{E_1, \mu^\natural, \xi^\natural \xrightarrow{E^\natural} (\cdot, \tau_1), \ E_2, \mu^\natural, \xi^\natural \xrightarrow{E^\natural} (\cdot, \tau_2)}{E_1 \ op \ E_2, \mu^\natural, \xi^\natural \xrightarrow{E^\natural} (\cdot, \tau_1 \sqcup_\mathcal{L} \tau_2)}$$

$$\text{Value}_x \frac{}{x, \mu^\natural, \xi^\natural \xrightarrow{E^\natural} \mu^\natural(x)} \qquad \text{Value}_{x.f} \frac{\mu^\natural(x) = (T, \sigma), \ \bigsqcup_{\forall v \in T} \xi^\natural(t)(f) = (w, \tau), \ w \in \mathcal{A}^\natural \cup \{\cdot\}}{x.f, \mu^\natural, \xi^\natural \xrightarrow{E^\natural} (w, \tau \sqcup_\mathcal{L} \sigma)}$$

**Fig. 9.** Abstract expressions semantics

$$\textbf{Assign}_{\text{t:x=e}} \quad \frac{q^\natural(t) = \sigma, \mu^\natural, \xi^\natural, c^\natural \;,\; q^\natural(succ(t)) = \sigma', \mu'^\natural, \xi'^\natural, c'^\natural \;,\; E, \mu^\natural, \xi^\natural \xrightarrow{E^\natural} (w, \tau)}{\bar{q}^\natural(succ(t)) = \sigma', \mu'^\natural \sqcup_{\mathcal{M}} \mu^\natural \, [x \leftarrow (w, \sigma \sqcup_{\mathcal{L}} \tau)], \xi'^\natural \sqcup_{\Xi} \xi^\natural, c'^\natural \sqcup_{\mathcal{C}} c^\natural}$$

$$\textbf{Assign}_{\text{t:x.f=e}} \quad \frac{\begin{array}{c} q^\natural(t) = \sigma, \mu^\natural, \xi^\natural, c^\natural \;,\; q^\natural(succ(t)) = \sigma', \mu'^\natural, \xi'^\natural, c'^\natural \;,\; E, \mu^\natural, \xi^\natural \xrightarrow{E^\natural} (w, \tau_1), \\ \mu^\natural(x) = (T, \tau_2), \;\; \tau_3 = \sigma \sqcup_{\mathcal{L}} \tau_1 \sqcup_{\mathcal{L}} \tau_2 \end{array}}{\bar{q}^\natural(succ(t)) = \left\langle \sigma', \mu'^\natural \sqcup_{\mathcal{M}} \mu^\natural, \xi'^\natural \sqcup_{\Xi} \xi^\natural[t_j, f \leftarrow (w, \tau_3)]_{\forall t_j \in T}, c'^\natural \sqcup_{\mathcal{C}} c^\natural \right\rangle}$$

$$\textbf{New}_{\text{t:x=new S}} \quad \frac{q^\natural(t) = \sigma, \mu^\natural, \xi^\natural, c^\natural \;,\; q^\natural(succ(t)) = \sigma', \mu'^\natural, \xi'^\natural, c'^\natural}{\bar{q}^\natural(succ(t)) = \sigma', \mu'^\natural \sqcup_{\mathcal{M}} \mu^\natural \, [x \leftarrow (t, \sigma)], \xi'^\natural \sqcup_{\Xi} \xi^\natural, c'^\natural \sqcup_{\mathcal{C}} c^\natural}$$

$$\textbf{Input}_{\text{t:a?x}} \quad \frac{q^\natural(t) = \sigma, \mu^\natural, \xi^\natural, c^\natural \;,\; q^\natural(succ(t)) = \sigma', \mu'^\natural, \xi'^\natural, c'^\natural \;,\; \tau = c^\natural(a) \sqcup_{\mathcal{L}} \sigma}{\bar{q}^\natural(succ(t)) = \sigma', \mu'^\natural \sqcup_{\mathcal{M}} \mu^\natural \, [x \leftarrow \tau], \xi'^\natural \sqcup_{\Xi} \xi^\natural, c'^\natural \sqcup_{\mathcal{C}} c^\natural \, [a \leftarrow \tau]}$$

$$\textbf{Output}_{\text{t:b!E}} \quad \frac{q^\natural(t) = \sigma, \mu^\natural, \xi^\natural, c^\natural \;,\; q^\natural(succ(t)) = \sigma', \mu'^\natural, \xi'^\natural, c'^\natural \;,\; E, \mu^\natural, \xi^\natural \xrightarrow{E^\natural} (\cdot, \tau)}{\bar{q}^\natural(succ(t)) = \sigma', \mu'^\natural \sqcup_{\mathcal{M}} \mu^\natural, \xi'^\natural \sqcup_{\Xi} \xi^\natural, c'^\natural \sqcup_{\mathcal{C}} c^\natural \, [b \leftarrow \sigma \sqcup_{\mathcal{L}} \tau]}$$

$$\substack{\textbf{If, while} \\ \text{t:if (E) C} \\ \text{else C} \\ \text{while E C}} \quad \frac{\begin{array}{c} q^\natural(t) = \sigma, \mu^\natural, \xi^\natural, c^\natural \;,\; E, \mu^\natural, \xi^\natural \xrightarrow{E^\natural} (\cdot, \tau), \\ q^\natural(succ_{true}(t)) = \sigma', \mu'^\natural, \xi'^\natural, c'^\natural \;,\; q^\natural(succ_{false}(t)) = \sigma'', \mu''^\natural, \xi''^\natural, c''^\natural \;, \end{array}}{\begin{array}{c} \bar{q}^\natural(succ_{true}(t)) = \sigma' \sqcup_{\mathcal{L}} \tau, \mu'^\natural \sqcup_{\mathcal{M}} \mu^\natural, \xi'^\natural \sqcup_{\Xi} \xi^\natural, c'^\natural \sqcup_{\mathcal{C}} c^\natural \\ \bar{q}^\natural(succ_{false}(t)) = \sigma'' \sqcup_{\mathcal{L}} \tau, \mu''^\natural \sqcup_{\mathcal{M}} \mu^\natural, \xi''^\natural \sqcup_{\Xi} \xi^\natural, c''^\natural \sqcup_{\mathcal{C}} c^\natural \;, \\ \forall t' \in scope(t) : \bar{q}^\natural(t').env = \tau \sqcup_{\mathcal{L}} q^\natural(t').env \end{array}}$$

**Fig. 10.** Abstract semantics of commands

transforms the state $q^\natural$ in the state $\bar{q}^\natural$ as described by the rule. There is only one rule for if and while: in both cases, besides propagating the state unchanged to the successors, the field *env* of all the instructions in *scope(t)* are updated. Rules **Value**$_{x.f}$ and **Assign**$_{x.f=e}$ need some explanations. In the abstract semantics, the structure addresses are lost and the references, besides the security level, contain the set $T$ of possible creation points. Then, in order to obtain the abstract value x.f needed by Rule **Value**$_{x.f}$, it is necessary to compute the lub of $\xi^\natural(t_i)(f)$ for all the $t_i$ in the set $T$. Similarly, to execute Rule **Assign**$_{x.f=e}$, an assignment must be performed for each abstract structure that $x$ might refer to.

**Definition 6 (next$^\natural$ operator).** *Given an abstract state $q^\natural$, the application of the* next$^\natural$ *operator yields the state reached in one step of computation from each instruction:*

$$\text{next}^\natural(q^\natural) = \bigsqcup \{ \bar{q}^\natural | q^\natural \xrightarrow{C^\natural} \bar{q}^\natural \}$$

**Proposition 3 (monotonicity of next$^\natural$).** next$^\natural$ *is monotone in $(\mathcal{Q}^\natural, \sqsubseteq^\natural)$.*

**Definition 7 (initial abstract state $q_0^\natural$).** *For the initial state $q_0^\natural$ we have $dom(q_0^\natural) = \{t_0\}$ and $q_0^\natural(t_0) = \left\langle \bot_{\mathcal{L}}, \bot_{\mathcal{M}}, \bot_{\Xi}, c_0^\natural \right\rangle$, where for all $a \in \text{Names}_I, c_0^\natural(a) = \mathcal{S}(a)$ and for all $a \in \text{Names}_O, c_0^\natural(a) = \bot_{\mathcal{L}}$.*

**Definition 8 (abstract semantics).** *The abstract semantics $sem^\natural \in \mathcal{Q}^\natural$ is the least upper bound in $(\mathcal{Q}^\natural, \sqsubseteq^\natural)$ of the following increasing chain, defined for all $n \in \mathbb{N}$:*

$$sem_0^\natural = q_0^\natural$$
$$sem_{n+1}^\natural = \mathsf{next}^\natural(A_n)$$

**Proposition 4 (Local correctness).** $\mathsf{next}^\natural$ *is a safe approximation of* $\mathsf{next}$*:*

$$\forall Q \in \wp(\mathcal{Q}) : \mathsf{next}(Q) \sqsubseteq_\mathcal{Q} \gamma \mathcal{Q}(\mathsf{next}^\natural(\alpha \mathcal{Q}(Q)))$$

**Theorem 2 (Global correctness).** $\alpha(sem) \sqsubseteq^\natural sem^\natural$.

A consequence of the above theorem is the following corollary. Its meaning is that we can use the abstract as a means to check secure information flow.

**Corollary 1.** *If, given $t \in \mathcal{B}$ with $sem^\natural(t) = \langle t, \mu^\natural, \xi^\natural, c^\natural \rangle$, then $\forall a \in \mathtt{Names}, c(a) \sqsubseteq_\mathcal{L} \mathcal{S}(a)$, then the considered program has secure information flow.*

## 6   A Prototype Tool

A prototype tool (Iflow[1]) that, given a program, constructs its abstract semantics $sem^\natural$, has been developed. Iflow accepts programs written in the language described in Section 2. The lattice $\mathcal{L}$ has been defined as the simplest two-level chain $\{L, H\}$, with $L \sqsubset_\mathcal{L} H$, but the tool can be easily extended to manage with generic lattices. Iflow has been written in C++, using Flex [27] and Bison [15] as scanner and parser generators. After having parsed the input file, Iflow builds the initial abstract state $q_0^\natural$. Then, starting from $q_0^\natural$, it performs a least fixed computation using the Kildall working list algorithm [22]. Finally, it dumps $sem^\natural$. Giving Iflow a "verbose" switch, it is possible to dump also each step of the fixpoint calculation.

As an example, consider the application of the algorithm to programs P5 and P8 in Figure 2. In Figure 11, we summarize the abstract execution, showing the result of the algorithm ($sem^\natural$) in the two cases. Let us briefly explain how the state in Figure 11(a) is computed for P5. Initially, the entry point of the program is inserted in the working list and abstractly executed. Every instruction brings its successor into the working list, and, until instruction 4 is executed, the states are unchanged from their default value. Execution of instruction 4 lifts the value of $x$ to $h$. Then, when the while instruction is newly executed, the environment of all the instructions in its scope (3,4) is upgraded. The new execution of the loop lifts the security level of channel $b$ to $h$ (because of the environment, see Rule **Output**), thus making the program insecure. In Figure 11(b) we show the abstract semantics for program P8. We can notice that, before executing instruction 7, s3 may refer either to the object created at 1 or to the object created at 2. After the abstract execution of instruction 7, the field f of both the two abstract objects is upgraded.

---

[1] Iflow is freely available at the URL: http://www.ing.unipi.it/~o1103499

| Instruction | env | x | s1 | s2 | s3 | 1.f | 1.g | 2.f | 2.g |
|---|---|---|---|---|---|---|---|---|---|
| 1:s1=new S | $l$ | $l$ | $\emptyset,l$ | $\emptyset,l$ | $\emptyset,l$ | $l$ | $l$ | $l$ | $l$ |
| 2:s2=new S | $l$ | $l$ | $1,l$ | $\emptyset,l$ | $\emptyset,l$ | $l$ | $l$ | $l$ | $l$ |
| 3:a?x | $l$ | $l$ | $1,l$ | $2,l$ | $\emptyset,l$ | $l$ | $l$ | $l$ | $l$ |
| 4:if(x) 5: else 6: | $l$ | $h$ | $1,l$ | $2,l$ | $\emptyset,l$ | $l$ | $l$ | $l$ | $l$ |
| 5:s3=s1 | $h$ | $h$ | $1,l$ | $2,l$ | $\emptyset,l$ | $l$ | $l$ | $l$ | $l$ |
| 6:s3=s2 | $h$ | $h$ | $1,l$ | $2,l$ | $\emptyset,l$ | $l$ | $l$ | $l$ | $l$ |
| 7:s3.f=1 | $h$ | $h$ | $1,l$ | $2,l$ | $\{1,2\},l$ | $l$ | $l$ | $l$ | $l$ |
| 8:??? | $h$ | $h$ | $1,l$ | $2,l$ | $\{1,2\},l$ | $h$ | $l$ | $h$ | $l$ |

| Instruction | env | x | a | b | d |
|---|---|---|---|---|---|
| 1:d?x | $l$ | $l$ | $h$ | $l$ | $l$ |
| 2:While (x > 0) | $l$ | $h$ | $h$ | $h$ | $l$ |
| 3:b!1 | $h$ | $h$ | $h$ | $h$ | $l$ |
| 4:a?x | $h$ | $h$ | $h$ | $h$ | $l$ |
| end: | $h$ | $h$ | $h$ | $h$ | $l$ |

(a)                                 (b)

**Fig. 11.** Abstract semantics of the programs a) P5 and b) P8, calculated using Iflow

Let us now give a short account of the complexity of such analysis: for space complexity, it is $O(N \cdot \log(M) \cdot n)$ where $N = \sharp(Var) + \sharp(\texttt{New})$ if the maximum number of fields of each structure is constant, $M$ is the number of elements in $\mathcal{L}$ and $n$ is the number of program points. The time complexity is theoretically $O(N^2 \cdot M \cdot n)$: every application of an abstract rule has a linear complexity in $N$ due to the least upper bound operation on the abstract memory and heap, and, in the worst case, the abstract state of every instruction can assume up to $O(N \cdot M)$ different values during the verification process. However, in practice, the number of abstract executions is much smaller. As suggested in [23] the dataflow analysis can be conducted at the level of the basic blocks instead of single instructions, saving only the state for the beginning of each basic block and calculating the others on the fly: this can reduce the space complexity to $O(N \cdot \log(M) \cdot B)$, and the time complexity to $O(N^2 \cdot M \cdot B)$, where $B$ is the number of basic blocks.

## 7   Related Work and Conclusions

A recent survey of works on secure information flow is [30]. The problem has been coped with mainly by means of typing. In type-based approaches, each variable is assigned a security level, which is part of the type of the variable and secure information flow is checked by means of a type system; see, for example, [31, 1, 25, 7, 33]. The work [3] handles secure information flow in object-oriented languages, with particular attention to pointers and objects. In [28, 29] references, exceptions and let-polymorphism are treated for a call-by-value $\lambda$-calculus.

With respect to typing, AI can give a finer inspection of information flows. In fact, in order to check input/output non-interference, it is not necessary to associate security levels to variables: a variable, during its life, can hold data with different security levels without affecting non-interference, provided that the output channels contain data with level less that or equal to the channel's level. Consider for example program P7 in section 2. Here variable $y$ first holds a high level datum (input from a high level channel), and after it is overwritten with a low level one (a constant): since it is this constant to be output on the low level channel, the program is correct. This program is certified by our approach, while it is not accepted by typing approaches. We think that also declassification (see, for example [26]) can be suitably handled by abstract interpretation. Other papers based on AI [32, 18] takes as abstract domain the lattice of levels and perform an AI with almost the same power of typing (in terms of class of certified programs). Thus they do not exploit all the power of abstract interpretation. For example, they do not certify program P7 above. On the other hand, the focus of [18] is the definition of a framework based on AI able to represent a parameterized notion of non-interference. Approaches that are able to cope with "temporary breaking of security", similar to that presented by program P7, are based on theorem proving [19, 21]. AI is also exploited in [2] to annotate programs with pre and postconditions defining variable dependences.

Some previous papers of the team to which the authors belong cope with the definition of abstractions suitable to check secure information flow, based on the annotation of data with security levels. The works [8, 6, 4, 9] handle secure information flow in stack based machine languages, while the papers [5, 17] consider high level languages, including parallel ones. In these papers abstract transition systems are used, possibly having a high number of states: the same instruction may belong to different states, characterized by different security environments and memories. The number of states being high, the abstraction is not suitable to be directly used for a definition of an analysis tool for checking secure information flow. In fact there is a need for other techniques to be combined with this abstraction method: in the above papers we used model checking to complete the verification process (a similar combination of abstraction and model checking is used in [10]). In the present paper, instead, the abstract semantics is a table composed of a row for each program point and is built by an efficient fixpoint algorithm using the abstract rules. Finally, the previous papers of the authors do not cope with pointers and dynamic structures, here handled by a suitable abstract domain.

# References

1. M. Abadi, A. Banerjee, N. Heintze, and J. Riecke. A core calculus of dependency. In *26th Annual ACM SIGPLAN-SIGACT Symposium on Principles of Programming Languages Proceedings*, pages 147–160. Texas, Usa, 1999.

2. T. Amtoft and A. Banerjee. Information flow analysis in logical form. In R. Giacobazzi, editor, *SAS 2004 (11th Static Analysis Symposium), Verona, Italy, August 2004*, volume 3148 of *LNCS*, pages 100–115. Springer-Verlag, 2004.

3. A. Banerjee and D. A. Naumann. Representation independence, confinement and access control. In *29th ACM Symposium on Principles of Programming Languages Proceedings*, pages 166–177, 2002.

4. R. Barbuti, C. Bernardeschi, and N. De Francesco. Analyzing information flow properties in assembly code by abstract interpretation. *Computer Journal*, 47(1):25–45, 2004.

5. R. Barbuti, C. Bernardeschi, and N. D. Francesco. Abstract interpretation of operational semantics for secure information flow. *Information Processing Letters*, 83(2):101–108, 2002.
6. R. Barbuti, C. Bernardeschi, and N. D. Francesco. Checking security of java byte-code by abstract interpretation. In *The 17th ACM Symposium on Applied Computing: Special Track on Computer Security Proceedings*, pages 229–236. Madrid, March 2002.
7. G. Barthe and T. Rezk. Non-interference for a JVM-like language. In *The ACM SIGPLAN Workshop on Types in Language Design and Implementation (TLDI)*, January 2005.
8. C. Bernardeschi and N. D. Francesco. Combining abstract interpretation and model checking for analysing security properties of Java bytecode. In *Third International Workshop on Verification, Model Checking and Abstract Interpretation Proceedings*, pages 1–15. LNCS 2294, Venice, January 2002.
9. C. Bernardeschi, N. D. Francesco, and G. Lettieri. An abstract semantics tool for secure information flow of stack-based assembly programs. *Microprocessors and Microsystems*, 26(8):391–398, 2002.
10. P. Bieber, J. Cazin, P. Girard, J.-L. Lanet, V.Wiels, and G. Zanon. Checking secure interactions of smart card applets. In *ESORICS 2000 Proceedings*, 2000.
11. P. Cousot and R. Cousot. Abstract interpretation: a unified lattice model for static analysis of programs by construction or approximation of fixpoints. In *4th Annual ACM SIGPLAN-SIGACT Symposium on Principles of Programming Languages Proceedings*, pages 238–252. Los Angeles, California, 1977.
12. P. Cousot and R. Cousot. Abstract interpretation frameworks. *Journal of Logic and Comp.*, 2:511–547, 1992.
13. P. Cousot and R. Cousot. Inductive definitions, semantics and abstract interpretations. In *ACM POPL'92 Proceedings*, pages 83–94, 1992.
14. D. E. Denning. A lattice model of secure information flow. *Comm. ACM*, 19(5):236–243, 1976.
15. C. Donnely and R. Stallman. *Bison, the YACC-compatible parser generator*. Free Software Foundation, November 1995.
16. N. D. Francesco and L. Martini. Technical Report IET-05-01, IET - Dipartimento di Ingegneria dell'Informazione, Università di Pisa, 2005.
17. N. D. Francesco, A. Santone, and L. Tesei. Abstract interpretation and model checking for checking secure information flow in concurrent systems. *Fundam. Inf.*, 54(2-3):195–211, 2003.
18. R. Giacobazzi and I. Mastroeni. Abstract non-interference: Parameterizing non-interference by abstract interpretation. In *Proc. ACM Symp. on Principles of Programming Languages*, pages 186–197, January 2004.
19. B. Jacobs, W. Pieters, and M. Warnier. Statically checking confidentiality via dynamic labels. In *Workshop on Issues in the Theory of Security proceedings*. ACM, 2005.
20. N. D. Jones and F. Nielson. Abstract interpretation: a semantic based tool for program analysis. *S. Abramsky, D.M. Gabbay, T.S.E. Maibaum(Eds.), Handbook of Logic in Computer Science*, Vol. 4:527–636, Oxford University Press, Oxford 1995.
21. R. Joshi and K. Leino. A semantic approach to secure information flow. *Science of Computer Programming*, 37(1-3):113–138, May 2000.
22. G. Kildall. A unified approach to global program optimization. In *Proceedings of the $1^{st}$ Annual ACM Symposium on Principles of Programming Languages*, pages 194–206, 1973.

23. X. Leroy. Java bytecode verification: Algorithms and formalizations. *Journal of Automated Reasoning*, 30(3-4):235–269, 2003.
24. T. Lindholm and F. Yellin. *The Java virtual machine specification.* Addison-Wesley Publishing Company, Reading, Massachusetts, 1996.
25. A. C. Myers. Jflow: Practical mostly-static information flow control. In *ACM POPL'99 Proceedings*, pages 228–241, 1999.
26. A. C. Myers, A. Sabelfeld, and S. Zdancewic. Enforcing robust declassification. In *CSFW*, pages 172–186. IEEE Computer Society, 2004.
27. V. Paxson. *Flex, a fast scanner generator, version 2.5*, March 1995.
28. F. Pottier and S. Conchon. Information flow inference for free. In *ACM ICFP'00 Proceedings*, pages 46–57, 2000.
29. F. Pottier and V. Simonet. Information flow inference for ML. In *29th Annual ACM Symposium on Principles of Programming Languages (POPL'02) Proceedings*, pages 319–330. Portland, Usa, 2002.
30. A. Sabelfeld and A. Myers. Language-based information-flow security. *IEEE Journal on Selected Areas in Communications*, 21(1):5–19, 2003.
31. D. Volpano, G. Smith, and C. Irvine. A sound type system for secure flow analysis. *Journal of Computer Security*, 4(3):167–187, 1996.
32. M. Zanotti. Security typings by abstract interpretation. In *Proc. of The 9th Static Analysis Symp.*, pages 360–375. LNCS 2477, 2002.
33. S. Zdancewic and A. Myers. Secure information flow via linear continuations. *Higher Order and Symbolic Computation*, 15(2/3), Kluwer Academic Publishers, The Netherlands 2002.

# Opacity Generalised to Transition Systems

Jeremy W. Bryans[1], Maciej Koutny[1], Laurent Mazaré[2], and Peter Y.A. Ryan[1]

[1] School of Computing Science, University of Newcastle,
Newcastle upon Tyne, NE1 7RU, United Kingdom
{jeremy.bryans, maciej.koutny, peter.ryan}@ncl.ac.uk
[2] Laboratoire VERIMAG; 2, av. de Vignates, Gières, France
laurent.mazare@imag.fr

**Abstract.** Recently, opacity has proved a promising technique for describing security properties. Much of the work has been couched in terms of Petri nets. Here, we extend the notion of opacity to the model of labelled transition systems and generalise opacity in order to better represent concepts from the literature on information flow. In particular, we establish links between opacity and the information flow concepts of anonymity and non-inference. We also investigate ways of verifying opacity when working with Petri nets. Our work is illustrated by an example modelling requirements upon a simple voting system.

**Keywords:** opacity, non-deducibility, anonymity, non-inference, Petri nets, observable behaviour, labelled transition systems.

## 1 Introduction

The notion of secrecy has been formulated in various ways in the computer security literature. However, two views of security have been developed over the years by two separate communities. The first one starts from the notion of information flow, describing the knowledge an intruder could gain in terms of properties such as non-deducibility or non-interference. The second view was initiated by Dolev and Yao's work and focussed initially on security protocols [7]. The idea here is to describe properly the capability of the intruder. Some variants of secrecy appeared, such as strong secrecy, giving more expressivity than the classical secrecy property but still lacking the expressivity of information flow concepts.

Recently, opacity has been shown to be a promising technique for describing security properties. Early work was couched in terms of Petri nets. In this paper, we extend the notion of opacity to the more general framework of labelled transition systems. When using opacity we have fine-grained control over the observation capabilities of the players, and we show one way that these capabilities may be encoded. The essential idea is that a predicate is opaque if an observer of the system will never be able to determine the truth of that predicate.

In the first section, after recalling some basic definitions, we present a generalisation of opacity, and show how this specialises into the three previously defined variants. In Section 3, we show how opacity is related to previous work

T. Dimitrakos et al. (Eds.): FAST 2005, LNCS 3866, pp. 81–95, 2006.

in security. In Section 4, we consider the question of opacity checking. After restricting ourselves to Petri nets, we give some decidability and undecidability properties. As opacity is undecidable as soon as we consider systems with infinite number of states, we present an approximation technique which may provide a way of model checking even in such cases. Finally, in Section 5, we consider a voting scheme, and show how the approximation technique might be used. All the proofs are available in [6].

## 2   Basic Definitions

The set of finite sequences over a set $A$ will be denoted by $A^*$, and the empty sequence by $\epsilon$. The length of a finite sequence $\lambda$ will be denoted by $len(\lambda)$, and its projection onto a set $B \subseteq A$ by $\lambda|_B$.

**Definition 1.** *A labelled transition system (LTS) is a tuple $\Pi = (S, L, \Delta, S_0)$, where $S$ is the (potentially infinite) set of states, $L$ is the (potentially infinite) set of labels, $\Delta \subseteq S \times L \times S$ is the transition relation, and $S_0$ is the nonempty (finite) set of initial states. We consider only deterministic LTSs, and so for any transitions $(s, l, s'), (s, l, s'') \in \Delta$, it is the case that $s' = s''^1$.*

*A run of $\Pi$ is a pair $(s_0, \lambda)$, where $s_0 \in S_0$ and $\lambda = l_1 \ldots l_n$ is a finite sequence of labels such that there are states $s_1, \ldots, s_n$ satisfying $(s_{i-1}, l_i, s_i)$, for $i = 1, \ldots, n$. We will denote the state $s_n$ by $s_0 \oplus \lambda$, and call it reachable from $s$.*

*The set of all runs is denoted by $run(\Pi)$, and the language generated by $\Pi$ is defined as $\mathcal{L}(\Pi) = \{\lambda \mid \exists s_0 \in S_0 : (s_0, \lambda) \in run(\Pi)\}$.*

Let $\Pi = (S, L, \Delta, S_0)$ be an LTS fixed for the rest of this section, and $\Theta$ be a set of elements called *observables*. We will now aim at modelling the different capabilities for observing the system modelled by $\Pi$. First, we introduce a general observation function and then, specialise it to reflect limited information about runs available to an observer.

**Definition 2.** *Any function $obs : run(\Pi) \to \Theta^*$ is an observation function. It is called label-based and: static / dynamic / orwellian / m-orwellian $(m \geq 1)$ if respectively the following hold (below $\lambda = l_1 \ldots l_n$):*

- *static: there is a mapping $obs' : L \to \Theta \cup \{\epsilon\}$ such that for every run $(s, \lambda)$ of $\Pi$, $obs(s, \lambda) = obs'(l_1) \ldots obs'(l_n)$.*
- *dynamic: there is a mapping $obs' : L \times L^* \to \Theta \cup \{\epsilon\}$ such that for every run $(s, \lambda)$ of $\Pi$, $obs(s, \lambda) = obs'(l_1, \epsilon) obs'(l_2, l_1) \ldots obs'(l_n, l_1 \ldots l_{n-1})$.*
- *orwellian: there is a mapping $obs' : L \times L^* \to \Theta \cup \{\epsilon\}$ such that for every run $(s, \lambda)$ of $\Pi$, $obs(s, \lambda) = obs'(l_1, \lambda) \ldots obs'(l_n, \lambda)$.*
- *m-orwellian: there is a mapping $obs' : L \times L^* \to \Theta \cup \{\epsilon\}$ such that for every run $(s, \lambda)$ of $\Pi$, $obs(s, \lambda) = obs'(l_1, \kappa_1) \ldots obs'(l_n, \kappa_n)$, where for $i = 1, \ldots, n$, $\kappa_i = l_{max\{1, i-m+1\}} l_{max\{1, i-m+1\}+1} \cdots l_{min\{n, i+m-1\}}$.*

---

[1] A nondeterministic LTS can be transformed into a deterministic one through a relabeling that assigns a unique label to each transition.

*In each of the above four cases, we will often use $obs(\lambda)$ to denote $obs(s, \lambda)$ which is possible as $obs(s, \lambda)$ does not depend on $s$.*

It is worth observing that both static and dynamic observation functions satisfy monotonicity w.r.t. prefixes, i.e., if $s \prec t$ then $obs(s) \prec obs(t)$. The orwellian observation functions do not in general satisfy this property.

Note that allowing $obs'$ to return $\epsilon$ allows one to model invisible actions. The different kinds of observable functions reflect different computational power of the observers. Static functions correspond to an observer which always interprets the same executed label in the same way. Dynamic functions correspond to an observer which has potentially infinite memory to store labels, but can only use knowledge of previous labels to interpret a label. Orwellian functions correspond to an observer which has potentially infinite memory to store labels, and can use knowledge of later labels to (re-)interpret a label. $m$-orwellian functions are a restricted version of the last class where the observer can store only a bounded number of labels. Static functions are nothing but 1-orwellian ones; static functions are also a special case of dynamic functions; and both dynamic and $m$-orwellian are a special case of orwellian functions.

Let us consider an observation function $obs$. We are interested in whether an observer can establish a property $\phi$ (a predicate over system states and traces) for some run having only access to the result of the observation function. We will identify $\phi$ with its characteristic set: the set of runs for which it holds.

Now, given an observed execution of the system, we would want to find out whether the fact that the underlying run belongs to $\phi$ can be deduced by the observer (note that we are not interested in establishing whether the underlying run does not belong to $\phi$; to do this, we would rather consider the property $\overline{\phi} = run(\Pi) \setminus \phi$).

What it means to deduce a property can mean different things depending on what is relevant or important from the point of view of a real application. Below, we give a general formalisation of opacity and then specialise it in three different ways.

**Definition 3.** *A predicate $\phi$ over $run(\Pi)$ is opaque w.r.t. the observation function $obs$ if, for every run $(s, \lambda) \in \phi$, there is a run $(s', \lambda') \notin \phi$ such that $obs(s, \lambda) = obs(s', \lambda')$. Moreover, $\phi$ is called: initial-opaque / final-opaque / total-opaque if respectively the following hold:*

- *there is a predicate $\phi'$ over $S_0$ such that for every run $(s, \lambda)$ of $\Pi$, we have $\phi(s, \lambda) = \phi'(s)$.*
- *there is a predicate $\phi'$ over $S$ such that for every run $(s, \lambda)$ of $\Pi$, we have $\phi(s, \lambda) = \phi'(s \oplus \lambda)$.*
- *there is a predicate $\phi'$ over $S^*$ such that for every run $(s, l_1 \ldots l_n)$ of $\Pi$, we have $\phi(s, l_1 \ldots l_n) = \phi'(s, s \oplus l_1, \ldots, s \oplus l_1 \ldots l_n)$.*

*In the first of above three cases, we will often write $s \in \phi$ whenever $(s, \lambda) \in \phi$.*

All these definitions of opacity are purely *possibilistic*: we make no reference to the probability of $\phi$ being true. For a probabilistic treatment of opacity, the reader is referred to [13].

Initial-opacity has been illustrated by the dining cryptographers example (in [4] with two cryptographers and [5] with three). It would appear that it is suited to modelling situations in which initialisation information such as crypto keys, etc., needs to be kept secret. More generally, situations in which confidential information can be modelled in terms of initially resolved non-determinism (i.e. non-determinism resolved before the first transition) can be captured in this way. Final-opacity models situations where the final result of a computation needs to be secret. Total-opacity is a generalisation of the two other properties asking not only the result of the computation and its parameters to be secret but also the states visited during computation.

**Proposition 1.** *Let $\phi$ and $\phi'$ be two predicates over $run(\Pi)$. If $\phi$ is opaque w.r.t. an observation function obs and $\phi' \Rightarrow \phi$, then $\phi'$ is opaque w.r.t. obs.*

## 3   Opacity in Security

The goal of this section is to show how our notion of opacity relates to other concepts commonly used in the formal security community. We will compare opacity to forms of anonymity and non-interference, as well as discuss its application to security protocols.

### 3.1   Anonymity

Anonymity is concerned with the preservation of secrecy of identity of a user through the obscuring of the actions of that user. It is a function of the behaviour of the underlying (anonymising) system, as well as being dependent on capability of the observer.

For concreteness, assume a system with $n$ users (indexed by $i$) each of whom can perform multiple instances of a single action $\alpha_i$. Intuitively, if the observer cannot distinguish these actions, and, as far as the observer is concerned, any $\alpha$ may have been performed by any of the users, then the system is anonymous with respect to the $\alpha$ actions.

The static, dynamic and orwellian forms of observation function presented in Definition 2 model three different strengths of observer. We now introduce two observation functions needed to render anonymity in terms of suitable opacity properties.

Let $\Pi = (S, L, \Delta, S_0)$ be an LTS fixed for the rest of this section, and $A = \{a_1, \ldots, a_n\} \subseteq L$ be a set of labels over which anonymity is being considered. Moreover, let $\alpha, \alpha_1, \ldots, \alpha_n \notin L$ be fresh labels.

The first observation function, $obs_A^s$, is static and defined so that $obs_A^s(\lambda)$ is obtained from $\lambda$ by replacing each occurrence of $a_i$ by $\alpha$. The second observation function, $obs_A^d$, is dynamic and defined thus: let $a_{i_1}, \ldots, a_{i_q}$ ($q \geq 0$) be all the distinct labels of $A$ appearing within $\lambda$ listed in the (unique) order in which they appeared for the first time in $\lambda$; then $obs(\lambda)$ is obtained from $\lambda$ by replacing each occurrence of $a_{i_j}$ by $\alpha_j$. For example,

$$obs_{\{a,b\}}^s(acdba) = \alpha cd\alpha\alpha \quad \text{and} \quad obs_{\{a,b\}}^d(acdba) = \alpha_1 cd\alpha_2\alpha_1.$$

**Strong anonymity.** In [23], a definition of strong anonymity is presented for the process algebra CSP. In our (LTS) context, this definition translates as follows.

**Definition 4.** $\Pi$ *is strongly anonymous w.r.t.* $A$ *if* $\mathcal{L}(\Pi) = \mathcal{L}(\Pi')$, *where* $\Pi'$ *is obtained from* $\Pi$ *by replacing each transition* $(s, a_i, s')$ *with* $n$ *transitions:* $(s, a_1, s'), \ldots, (s, a_n, s')$.

In our framework, we have that

**Definition 5.** $\Pi$ *is O-anonymous w.r.t.* $A$ *if, for every sequence* $\mu \in A^*$, *the predicate* $\phi_\mu$ *over the runs of* $\Pi$ *defined by*

$$\phi_\mu(s, \lambda) = \big(len(\lambda|_A) = len(\mu) \wedge \lambda|_A \neq \mu\big)$$

*is opaque w.r.t.* $obs_A^s$.

We want to ensure that every possible sequence $\mu$ (with appropriate length restrictions) of anonymised actions is a possible sequence within the LTS. In Definition 5 above, the opacity of the predicate $\phi_\mu$ ensures that the sequence $\mu$ is a possible history of anonymised actions, because it is the only sequence for which the predicate $\phi_\mu$ is false, and so $\phi_\mu$ can only be opaque if $\mu$ is a possible sequence.

**Theorem 1.** $\Pi$ *is O-anonymous w.r.t.* $A$ *iff it is strongly anonymous w.r.t.* $A$.

**Weak anonymity.** A natural extension of strong anonymity is *weak anonymity*[2]. This models easily the notion of *pseudo-anonymity*: actions performed by the same party can be correlated, but the identity of the party cannot be determined.

**Definition 6.** $\Pi$ *is weakly anonymous w.r.t.* $A$ *if* $\pi(\mathcal{L}(\Pi)) \subseteq \mathcal{L}(\Pi)$, *for every permutation* $\pi$ *over the set* $A$.

In our framework, we have that

**Definition 7.** $\Pi$ *is weak-O-anonymous if, for every sequence* $\mu \in A^*$, *the predicate* $\phi_\mu$ *over the runs of* $\Pi$ *introduced in Definition 5 is opaque w.r.t.* $obs_A^d$.

**Theorem 2.** $\Pi$ *is weak-O-anonymous w.r.t.* $A$ *iff it is weak-anonymous w.r.t.* $A$.

**Other observation functions.** Dynamic observation functions can model for example the *downgrading* of a channel. Before the downgrade nothing can be seen, after the downgrade the observer is allowed to see all transmissions on that channel. A suitable formulation would be as follows.

Suppose that $A$ represents the set of all possible messages on a confidential channel, and $\delta \in L \setminus A$ represents an action of downgrading that channel. Then $obs(\lambda)$ is obtained from $\lambda$ by deleting each occurrence of $a_i$ which is preceded (directly or indirectly) by an occurrence of $\delta$. In other words, if the downgrade action appears earlier in the run, then the messages on the channel are observed in the clear, otherwise nothing is observed.

---

[2] We believe that this formulation of weak anonymity was originally due to Ryan and Schneider.

Orwellian observation functions can model conditional or escrowed anonymity, where someone can be anonymous when they initially interact with the system, but some time in the future their identity can be revealed, as outlined below.

Suppose that there are $n$ identities $Id_i$, each identity being capable of performing actions represented by $a_i \in A$. Moreover, $\alpha \notin L$ represents the encrypted observation of any of these actions, and $\rho_i \in L \setminus A$ represents the action of identity $Id_i$ being revealed. Then $obs(\lambda)$ is obtained from $\lambda$ by replacing each occurrence of $a_i$ by $\alpha$, provided that $\rho_i$ never occurs within $\lambda$.

## 3.2   Non-interference

Opacity can be linked to a particular formulation of non-interference. A discussion of non-interference can be found in [10] and [22]. The basic idea is that labels are split into two sets, *High* and *Low*. *Low* labels are visible by anyone, whereas *High* labels are private. Then, a system is non-interfering if it is not possible for an outside observer to gain any knowledge about the presence of *High* labels in the original run (the observer only sees *Low* labels). This notion is in fact a restriction of standard non-interference. It was originally called non-inference in [19], and is called strong non-deterministic non-interference in [11].

**Definition 8.**  *$\Pi$ satisfies non-inference if $\mathcal{L}(\Pi)\,|_{Low} \subseteq \mathcal{L}(\Pi)$.*

In other words, for any run $(s, \lambda)$ of $\Pi$, there exists a run $(s', \lambda')$ such that $\lambda'$ is $\lambda$ with all the labels in *High* removed.

The notion of non-interference (and in particular non-inference) is close to opacity as stated by the two following properties. First, it is possible to transform certain initial opacity properties into non-inference properties.

**Proposition 2.** *Any initial opacity property involving static observation functions can be reduced to a non-inference property.*

A kind of converse result also holds, in the sense that one can transform any non-inference property to a general opacity property.

**Proposition 3.** *Any non-inference property can be reduced to an opacity property.*

Non-interference in general makes a distinction between public (*Low*) and private (*High*) messages, and any revelation of a high message breaks the non-interference property. We believe that the ability to fine-tune the *obs* function may make opacity better suited to tackling the problem of *partial information flow*, where a message could provide some partial knowledge and it may take a collection of such leakages to move the system into a compromised state.

## 3.3   Security Protocols

Opacity was introduced in the context of security protocols in [16]. With one restriction, the current version of opacity is still applicable to protocols. Namely, since we require the number of initial states to be finite, the initial choices made by the various honest agents must come from bounded sets.

To formalise opacity for protocols in the present framework, labels will be *messages* defined by the simple grammar

$$m ::= a \mid \langle m, m \rangle \mid \{m\}_m$$

where $a$ ranges over a set $A$ of *atomic* messages; $\langle m_1, m_2 \rangle$ represents the pairing (concatenation) of messages $m_1$ and $m_2$; and $\{m_1\}_{m_2}$ is the encoding of message $m_1$ using message $m_2$. A subset $K$ of $A$ is the set of *keys*, each key $k$ in $K$ having an inverse denoted by $k^{-1}$. The notation $E \vdash m$, where $m$ is a message and $E$ is a finite set of messages (environment), comes from Dolev-Yao theory [7] and denotes the fact that $m$ is deducible from $E$.

Two messages, $m_1$ and $m_2$, are *similar* for environment $E$ *iff* $E \vdash m_1 \sim m_2$ where $\sim$ is the smallest (w.r.t. set inclusion) binary relation satisfying the following:

$$\frac{a \in Atoms}{a \sim a} \qquad \frac{u_1 \sim u_2 \quad v_1 \sim v_2}{\langle u_1, v_1 \rangle \sim \langle u_2, v_2 \rangle} \qquad \frac{E \vdash k^{-1} \quad u \sim v}{\{u\}_k \sim \{v\}_k} \qquad \frac{\neg E \vdash k^{-1} \quad \neg E \vdash k'^{-1}}{\{u\}_k \sim \{v\}_{k'}}$$

In other words, messages are similar if it is not feasible for an intruder to distinguish them using the knowledge $E$. Such a notion was introduced in [2], where it was shown to be sound in the computational model, and its generalisation including the case of equational theories appears in [1].

To state which part of a message is visible from the outside, we will use the notion of a *pattern* [2], which adds a new message $\square$ to the above grammar, representing undecryptable messages. Then, $pattern(m, E)$ is the accessible skeleton of $m$ using messages in $E$ as knowledge and $E \vdash m_1 \sim m_2 \Leftrightarrow pattern(m_1, E) = pattern(m_2, E)$. It is defined thus:

$$pattern(a, E) = a$$
$$pattern(\langle m_1, m_2 \rangle, E) = \langle pattern(m_1, E), pattern(m_2, E) \rangle$$
$$pattern(\{m_1\}_{m_2}, E) = \begin{cases} \{pattern(m_1)\}_{m_2} & \text{if } E \vdash m_2 \\ \square & \text{otherwise} . \end{cases}$$

To simplify the presentation, we assume that a security protocol is represented by an LTS $\Pi = (S, L, \Delta, S_0)$ (for protocols semantics, see [15]). As protocols are commonly interested in initial opacity (opacity on the value of one of the parameter, e.g., a vote's value), the predicate $\phi$ will be a suitable subset of $S_0$. The observation function *obs* will be orwellian with $obs(l_i, \lambda) = pattern(l_i, E)$, where $E$ is the set of messages appearing in $\lambda$. (note that, in the case of a bounded protocol, an $m$-orwellian function will be sufficient). Then, opacity of $\phi$ w.r.t. *obs* is equivalent to the concept introduced in [16].

# 4   Opacity Checking

Opacity is a very general concept and many instantiations of it are undecidable. This is even true when LTSs are finite. We will formulate such a property as Proposition 5 (part 4), but first we state a general non-decidability result.

**Proposition 4.** *Opacity is undecidable.*

*Proof.* We will show that the reachability problem for Turing machines is reducible to (final) opacity. Let $TM$ be a Turing machine and $s$ be its (non-initial) state. We construct an instance of the final opacity as follows: $\Pi$ is given by the operational semantics of $TM$, the observation function $obs$ is constant, and $\phi$ returns true *iff* the final state of a run is different from $s$. Since $s$ is reachable in $TM$ *iff* $\phi$ is final opaque w.r.t. $obs$, opacity is undecidable.     ∎

It follows from the above proposition that the undecidability of the reachability problem for a class of machines generating LTSs renders opacity undecidable. We will therefore restrict ourselves to Petri nets, a rich model of computation in which the reachability problem is still decidable [21]. Furthermore, Petri nets are well-studied structures and there is a wide range of tools and algorithms for their verification.

## 4.1   Petri Nets

We will use Petri nets with weighted arcs [21], and give their operational semantics in terms of *transition sequences.*[3] Note that this varies slightly from the one used in [4] where the *step sequence* semantics allowed multiple transitions to occur simultaneously. Here, transitions are clearly separated.

A (weighted) *net* is a triple $N = (P, T, W)$ such that $P$ and $T$ are disjoint finite sets, and $W : (T \times P) \cup (P \times T) \to \mathbb{N}$. The elements of $P$ and $T$ are respectively the *places* and *transitions*, and $W$ is the *weight function* of $N$. In diagrams, places are drawn as circles, and transitions as rectangles. If $W(x, y) \geq 1$ for some $(x, y) \in (T \times P) \cup (P \times T)$, then $(x, y)$ is an *arc* leading from $x$ to $y$. As usual, arcs are annotated with their weight if this is 2 or more. The *pre-* and *post-multiset* of a transition $t \in T$ are multisets of places, $\text{PRE}_N(t)$ and $\text{POST}_N(t)$, respectively given by

$$\text{PRE}_N(t)(p) = W(p, t) \text{ and } \text{POST}_N(t)(p) = W(t, p),$$

for all $p \in P$. A *marking* of a net $N$ is a multiset of places. Following the standard terminology, given a marking $M$ of $N$ and a place $p \in P$, we say that $p$ is marked if $M(p) \geq 1$ and that $M(p)$ is the number of tokens in $p$. In diagrams, $M$ will be represented by drawing in each place $p$ exactly $M(p)$ tokens (black dots). Transitions represent actions which may occur at a given marking and then lead to a new marking. A transition $t$ is *enabled* at a marking $M$ if $M \geq \text{PRE}_N(t)$.

---

[3] It should be stressed that the transitions in the Petri net context correspond to the labels rather than arcs in the LTS framework.

Thus, in order for $t$ to be enabled at $M$, for each place $p$, the number of tokens in $p$ under $M$ should at least be equal to the total number of tokens that are needed as an input to $t$, respecting the weights of the input arcs. If $t$ is enabled at $M$, then it can be *executed* leading to the marking $M' = M - \text{PRE}_N(t) + \text{POST}_N(t)$. This means that the execution of $t$ 'consumes' from each place $p$ exactly $W(p, t)$ tokens and 'produces' in each place $p$ exactly $W(t, p)$ tokens. If the execution of $t$ leads from $M$ to $M'$ we write $M[t\rangle M'$ and call $M'$ *reachable* from $M$. A *marked Petri net* $\Sigma = (N, S_0)$ comprises a net $N = (P, T, W)$ and a finite set of initial markings $S_0$. It generates the LTS $\Pi_\Sigma = (S, T, \Delta, S_0)$ where $S$ is the set of all the markings reachable from the markings in $S_0$, $T$ is the set of labels, and $\Delta$ is defined by $(M, t, M') \in \Delta$ if $M[t\rangle M'$. The language of $\Sigma$ is that of $\Pi_\Sigma$.

In the case of Petri nets, there are still some undecidable opacity problems.

**Proposition 5.** *The following problems are undecidable for Petri nets:*

1. *Initial opacity when considering a static observation function.*
2. *Initial opacity when considering a state-based static observation function.*
3. *Initial opacity when considering an orwellian observation function even in the case of finite LTSs generated by marked nets.*
4. *Opacity when considering a constant observable function even in the case of finite LTSs generated by a marked nets.*

An analysis of the proof of the last result identifies two sources for the complexity of the opacity problem. The first one is the complexity of the studied property, captured through the definition of $\phi$. In particular, the latter may be used to encode undecidable problems and so in practice one should presumably restrict the interest to relatively straightforward versions of opacity, such as the initial opacity. The second source is the complexity of the observation function, and it is presumably reasonable to restrict the interest to some simple classes of observation functions, such as the static observation functions. This should not, however, be considered as a real drawback since the initial opacity combined with an $n$-orwellian observation function yields an opacity notion which is powerful enough to deal, for example, with bounded security protocols (section 3.3).

What now follows is a crucial result stating that initial opacity with an $n$-orwellian observation function is decidable provided that the LTS generated by a marked Petri net is finite[4]. In fact, this result could be generalised to any finite LTS; i.e., in the case of a finite LTS, initial opacity w.r.t. an $n$-orwellian observation function is decidable.

## 4.2   Approximation of Opacity

As initial opacity is, in general, undecidable when LTSs are allowed to be infinite, we propose in this section a technique which might allow us to verify it, at least in some cases, using what we call under/over-opacity.

---

[4] Note that the finiteness of LTS is decidable, and can be checked using the standard coverability tree construction [21].

**Definition 9.** *For $i = 1, 2, 3$, let $\Pi_i$ be an LTS. Moreover, let $obs_i$ be an observation function and $\phi_i$ a predicate for the runs of $\Pi_i$ such that the following hold:*

$$(\forall \xi \in run(\Pi_1) \cap \phi_1) \, (\exists \xi' \in run(\Pi_2) \cap \phi_2) \, obs_1(\xi) = obs_2(\xi')$$
$$(\forall \xi \in run(\Pi_3) \setminus \phi_3) \, (\exists \xi' \in run(\Pi_1) \setminus \phi_1) \, obs_3(\xi) = obs_1(\xi') \, .$$

*Then $\phi_1$ is under/over-opaque (or simply uo-opaque) w.r.t. $obs_1$ if for every $\xi \in run(\Pi_2) \cap \phi_2$ there is $\xi' \in run(\Pi_3) \setminus \phi_3$ such that $obs_3(\xi) = obs_1(\xi')$.*

Intuitively, $\Pi_2$ provides an over-approximation of the runs satisfying $\phi_1$, while $\Pi_3$ provides an under-approximation of those runs that do not satisfy $\phi_1$. One can then show that uo-opacity w.r.t. $obs_1$ *implies* opacity w.r.t. $obs_1$. Given $\Pi_1$, $obs_1$ and $\phi_1$, the idea then is to be able to construct an over-approximation and under-approximation to satisfy the last definition. A possible way of doing this in the case of marked Petri nets is described next.

**Uo-opacity for Petri nets.** Suppose that $\Sigma = (N, S_0)$ is a marked Petri net, $\Pi_1 = \Pi_\Sigma$, $obs_1$ is a static observation function for $\Pi_1$ and $\phi_1 \subseteq S_0$ is an initial opacity predicate for $\Pi_1$.

*Deriving over-approximation.* The over-approximation is obtained by generating the coverability graph $\Pi_2$ of $\Sigma$ (see [9] for details), starting from the initial nodes in $S_0 \cap \phi_1$. The only modification of the original algorithm needed is that in our setup there may be several starting nodes $S_0 \cap \phi_1$ rather than just one. However, this is a small technical detail. The observation function $obs_2$ is static and defined in the same way as $obs_1$. The predicate $\phi_2$ is true for all the initial nodes $S_0 \cap \phi_1$. Crucially, $\Pi_2$ is always a finite LTS.

**Proposition 6.** $(\forall \xi \in run(\Pi_1) \cap \phi_1) \, (\exists \xi' \in run(\Pi_2) \cap \phi_2) \, obs_1(\xi) = obs_2(\xi')$.

*Deriving under-approximation.* A straightforward way of finding under-approximation is to impose a maximal finite capacity *max* for the places of $\Sigma$ (for example, by using the complement place construction), and then deriving the LTS $\Pi_3$ assuming that the initial markings are those in $S_0 \setminus \phi_1$. The observation function $obs_3$ is static and defined in the same way as $obs_1$. The predicate $\phi_3$ is false for all the initial nodes $S_0 \setminus \phi_1$.

Clearly, $\Pi_3$ is always a finite LTS. However, for some Petri nets with an infinite reachability graph (as shown later on by our example), this under-approximation may be too restrictive, even if one takes arbitrarily large bound *max*. Then, in addition to using instance specific techniques, one may attempt to derive more generous under-approximation, in the following way.

We assume that there are some (invisible) transitions in $\Sigma$ mapped by $obs_1$ to $\epsilon$ transitions, and propagate the information that a place could become unbounded due to infinite sequence of invisible transitions. The construction resembles the coverability graph generation.

As in the case of the reachability graph, the states in $\Pi_3$ are $\omega$-markings (see the proof of Proposition 6). Then $\Pi_3$ is built by starting from the initial states

$S_0 \setminus \phi_1$, and performing a depth-first exploration. At each visited $\omega$-marking $M$, we find (for example, using a nested call to a coverability graph generation restricted to the invisible transitions starting from $M$) whether there exists $M' > M$ reachable from $M$ through invisible transitions only[5]; then we set $M(p) = \omega$, for every place $p$ such that $M'(p) > M(p)$. Note that the above algorithm may be combined with the capacity based approach and then it always produces a finite $\Pi_3$. In general, however, $\Pi_3$ is not guaranteed to be finite.

It should be pointed out that $\Pi_3$ generated in this way will not, in general, be a deterministic LTS, but this does not matter as the only thing we will be interested in is the language it generates.

**Proposition 7.** $(\forall \xi \in run(\Pi_3) \setminus \phi_3)\,(\exists \xi' \in run(\Pi_1) \setminus \phi_1)\; obs_3(\xi) = obs_1(\xi')$.

*Deciding uo-opacity.* Assuming that we have generated over- and under- approximations $\Pi_2$ and $\Pi_3$, uo-opacity holds *iff* $obs_2(\mathcal{L}(\Pi_2)) \subseteq obs_3(\mathcal{L}(\Pi_3))$. And the latter problem is decidable whenever $\Pi_2$ and $\Pi_3$ are *finite* LTSs as it then reduces to that of inclusion of two regular languages.

## 5   A Simple Voting Scheme

To illustrate our work, we give an example of a simple voting system. Another one, inspired by an anonymity requirement required in the chemical industry, is described in [6].

In this example, we consider a vote session allowing only two votes: 1 and 2. We then describe a simple voting scheme in the form of a Petri net (see figure 1). The voting scheme contains two phases. The first one called *voting phase* (when there is a token in Voting) allows any new voter to enter the polling station (transition $NV$) and vote (transitions $V1$ and $V2$). Votes are stored in two places *Results*1 and *Results*2. A particular voter $A$ is identified, and we formulate our properties with respect to $A$. After an indeterminate time, the election enters the *counting phase* (when there is a token in Counting, after executing transition $C$, and no token in Voting). Then the different votes are counted. Votes for 1 are seen via transition $C1$ and vote for 2 via $C2$. This net has one obvious limitation. At the end, there still can be some tokens left in places Results1 and Results2 so this scheme does not ensure that every vote is counted.

We want to verify that the vote cast by $A$ is secret: the two possible initial markings are $\{Voting, 1\}$ and $\{Voting, 2\}$. We prove that it is impossible to detect that "1" was marked (a symmetric argument would show that it is impossible to detect whether "2" was marked). The observation function is static and only transitions $C1$ and $C2$ are visible, i.e., $obs(C1) = C1$, $obs(C2) = C2$ and $obs(t) = \epsilon$ for any other transition $t$.

To verify opacity, we will use the under/over approximation method. The coverability graph (over-approximation) can be computed (see figure 1) using, for

---

[5] This search does not have to be complete for the method to work, however, the more markings $M'$ we find, the better the overall result is expected to be.

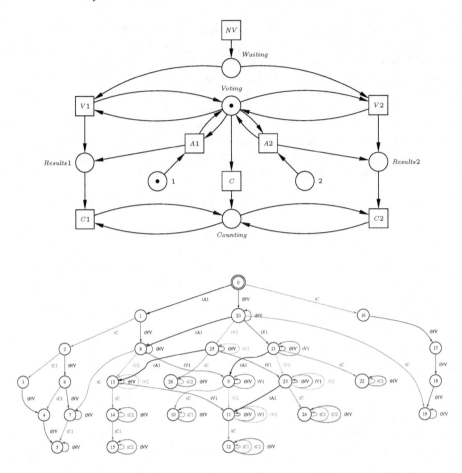

**Fig. 1.** Net for the voting system, and below its coverability graph

example, Tina [25]. After application of the observation function and simplification, we obtain that $obs_2(\mathcal{L}(\Pi_2)) = \{C_1, C_2\}^*$ (see section 4.2 for the definition of $\Pi_2$.)

However, the simple under approximation using bounded capacity places will not work in this case, as for any chosen maximal capacity $max$, the language $\mathcal{L}(\Pi_3)$ will be finite whereas $obs_2(\mathcal{L}(\Pi_2))$ is infinite. Thus, we use the second under approximation technique. The following array represents the reachable states of the system starting from marking $\{Voting, 2\}$ using this technique.

|   | Waiting | Voting | Results1 | Results2 | 1 | 2 | Counting |
|---|---------|--------|----------|----------|---|---|----------|
| A | $\omega$ | 1 | $\omega$ | $\omega$ | 0 | 1 | 0 |
| B | $\omega$ | 1 | $\omega$ | $\omega$ | 0 | 0 | 0 |
| C | $\omega$ | 0 | $\omega$ | $\omega$ | 0 | 1 | 1 |
| D | $\omega$ | 0 | $\omega$ | $\omega$ | 0 | 0 | 1 |

The behaviour of this reachability graph, i.e. $obs_3(\mathcal{L}(\Pi_3))$, is simple:

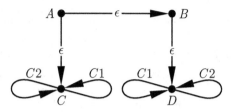

Thus, the under-approximation is in this case: $obs_3(\mathcal{L}(\Pi_3)) = \{C1, C2\}^*$, and so $obs_2(\mathcal{L}(\Pi_2)) \subseteq obs_3(\mathcal{L}(\Pi_3))$ holds. We can now conclude that opacity of $\phi$ w.r.t. $obs$ is verified and so the vote cast by $A$ is kept secret.

## 6  Related Work

Concepts similar to opacity have been studied using *epistemic logics*, or logics of knowledge [8]. These logics include a "knowledge" operator, representing the case where an agent knows a fact, and are particularly suitable for reasoning about security within a multi-agent context [17, 12, 3]. The semantics can be given within a "possible worlds" model: an agent knows a fact in a given world if it is true in every world that the agent considers possible. Opacity appears to be closely related to this knowledge operator, in that a property is opaque when the observer cannot be sure that it is true (see also below). That is, there is a world (a high level trace) that the observer considers possible, in which the fact does not hold. In [26] the notion of *ignorance* is developed, where an agent is ignorant of a fact $\phi$ when it cannot say for certain either that $\phi$ holds or that $\neg\, \phi$ holds. In our terms, an agent would be ignorant of $\phi$ if both $\phi$ and $\neg\, \phi$ were opaque.

There is a clear and strong relationship between our work and that contained in [14], and through it also with that in [8]. For example, final-opacity could be understood, using the terminology of [14], in the following way. To start with, we assume that an agent $i$ is modelled by our $obs$ function and, for every point $(r, m)$, we have $r_i(m) = obs(r, m)$. In other words, the $i$-th agent (in the sense of [14]) is observing the system. To model predicates within our approach, we then use information functions of [14], saying that $f$ is such a function and, for every point $(r, m)$, $f(r, m)$ returns a *true* or *false* value which only depends on the $m$-th state of the run $r$. Then, applying Definition 3.3 of [14], results in the following rendering of our notion of final-opacity: "for every point $(r, m)$ there is another point $(r', m')$ such that $obs(r, m) = obs(r', m')$ and $f(r, m) = \neg\, f(r', m')$". Indeed, this looks very similar to the definition used by us, but is in fact *strictly stronger*, since our definition should correspond to the following: "for every point $(r, m)$ with $f(r, m) = true$, there is another point $(r', m')$ such that $obs(r, m) = obs(r', m')$ and $f(r', m') = false$". And the notion based on Definition 3.3 of [14] is basically equivalent to opacity of both $f$ and $f' = \neg\, f$. We therefore feel that there is no straightforward way of embedding our approach within that proposed in [14] (and so also [8]). We also feel that the basic reason behind this is that our notion of information hiding is 'asymmetric' in a sense that different values are obscured in possibly different ways. To make this more concrete, we could propose a slight modification of the definition from [14] along the following lines:

> Assume additionally that for every $v$ in the range of $f$ there exists possibly empty set $Mask(v)$ of values in the domain of $f$. Then, if $f$ is a $j$-information function, then agent $j$ maintains $f$-secrecy w.r.t. $i$ in system $\mathcal{R}$ if, for all points $(r, m)$ and values $v \in Mask(f(r, m))$ there is a point $(r', m')$ such that $r_i(m) = r'_i(m')$ and $f(r', m') = v$.

Intuitively, $Mask(v)$ provides sufficient obscurity from the point of view of agent $j$ about the actual value of $v$. In our case we could then set $Mask(true) = false$ and $Mask(false) = \varnothing$ (the latter to indicate that we do not care about the states where our predicate is false). And final-opacity would then be expressible using the modified definition. Our hypothesis is that such a modification constitutes an interesting true weakening of the security notion discussed in [14], and consequently it deserves an investigation in its own right.

## 7   Conclusions

We have presented a general definition of opacity that extends previous work. This notion is no longer bound to the Petri net formalism and applies to any labelled transition system. However, restricting ourselves to initial opacity in the case of Petri nets allows us to find some decidability results. Furthermore, in this general model we can show how opacity relates to other information flow properties such as anonymity or non-inference.

Non-decidability results show that the opacity problem is a complex one. Its complexity is related to the complexity of the checked property, the complexity of the adversary's observational capabilities and the complexity of the system. The first point can be addressed by considering initial opacity which is still very expressive. The second one can be simplified by considering only $n$-orwellian observation functions. To solve the third problem, we can restrict ourselves to finite automata but this causes us to lose significant expressive power.

In the case of infinite Petri nets, over- and under- approximating gives a way of checking opacity. This technique works well in the case of our voting example. We intend in future work to find a better abstraction for Petri nets and some well suited abstractions for other formalisms.

Some of the work done within epistemic logic has been with a view to model checking (see [18, 20, 24] for recent examples). Automatic verification is also an important goal of our work, and so exploring the connections between epistemic logic and opacity should prove a strong basis for further research.

## Acknowledgments

This research was supported by DSTL, the EPSRC DIRC, GOLD and SCREEN projects, the RNTL project PROUVE-03V360, and the ACI project ROSSIGNOL.

# References

1. M.Abadi and V.Cortier: Deciding Knowledge in Security Protocols under Equational Theories. In: ICALP (2004)
2. M.Abadi and P.Rogaway: Reconciling two Views of Cryptography (The computational soundness of formal encryption). In: IFIP TCS2000 (2000)
3. P.Bieber: A Logic of Communication in a Hostile Environment. In: CSFW (1990)
4. J.W.Bryans, M.Koutny and P.Y.A.Ryan: Modelling Opacity using Petri Nets. ENTCS 121 (2005)
5. J.W.Bryans, M.Koutny and P.Y.A.Ryan: Modelling Dynamic Opacity using Petri Nets with Silent Actions. In: FAST (2004)
6. J.W.Bryans, M.Koutny, L.Mazaré and P.Y.A.Ryan: Opacity Generalised to Transition Systems. CS-TR 868, University of Newcastle (2004)
   http://www.cs.ncl.ac.uk/research/pubs/trs/abstract.php?number=868
7. D.Dolev and A.C.Yao: On the Security of Public Key Protocols. IEEE Transactions on Information Theory 29 (1983)
8. R.Fagin, J.Y.Halpern, Y.Moses and M.Y.Vardi: Reasoning about Knowledge. MIT press (1995)
9. A.Finkel: The Minimal Coverability Graph for Petri Nets. LNCS 674 (1993)
10. R.Focardi and R.Gorrieri: A Taxonomy of Trace-Based Security Properties for CCS. In: CSFW (1994)
11. R.Focardi and R.Gorrieri: Classification of Security Properties: Information flow. LNCS 2171 (2000)
12. J.Glasgow, G.Macewen and P.Panangaden: A Logic for Reasoning about Security. ACM Transactions on Computer Systems 10 (1992)
13. Y. Lakhnech and L. Mazaré: Probabilistic Opacity for a Passive Adversary and its Application to Chaum's Voting Scheme. Verimag Technical Report 2005-04, (2005).
14. J.Y.Halpern and K.O'Neill: Anonymity and Information Hiding in Multiagent Systems. In: CSFW (2003)
15. F.Jacquemard, M.Rusinowitch and L.Vigneron: Compiling and Verifying Security Protocols. In: LPAR (2000)
16. L.Mazaré: Using Unification For Opacity Properties. In: WITS (2004)
17. L.Moser: A Logic of Knowledge and Belief for Reasoning about Security. In: CSFW (1989)
18. W.Nabialek, A.Niewiadomski, W.Penczek, A.Polórla and M.Szreter: Verics 2004: A Model Checker of Real-Time and Multi-agent Systems. In: CS&P (2004)
19. C.O'Halloran: A Calculus of Information Flow. In: ESORICS (1990)
20. F.Raimondi and A.Lomuscio: Verification of Multiagent Systems via Ordered Binary Decision Diagrams: an Algorithm and its Implementation. TR-04-01, King's College (2004)
21. W.Reisig and G.Rozenberg (Eds.): Lectures on Petri Nets. LNCS 1491 & 1492 (1998)
22. P.Y.A.Ryan: Mathematical Models of Computer Security. LNCS 2171 (2000)
23. S.Schneider and A.Sidiropoulos: CSP and Anonymity. In: ESORICS (1996)
24. S.van Otterloo, W.van der Hoek and M.Woolridge: Model Checking a Knowledge Exchange Scenario. In: IJCAI (2003)
25. Time Petri Net Analyzer. http://www.laas.fr/tina/ (2004)
26. W.van der Hoek and A.Lomuscio: A Logic for Ignorance. ENTCS 85 (2004)

# Unifying Decidability Results on Protection Systems Using Simulations*

Constantin Enea

Faculty of Computer Science, "Al.I.Cuza" University of Iasi, Romania
`cenea@infoiasi.ro`

**Abstract.** We investigate two possible definitions of simulation between protection systems. The resulting simulation relations are used to unify the proofs of decidability of the safety problem for several classes of protection systems from the literature, notably the take-grant systems ([4]) and the MTAM systems with acyclic creation graphs([9]).

## 1 Introduction and Preliminaries

Access control is one of the facets of the implementation of security policies. In access control models, the security policy is implemented by an assignment of access rights to the objects composing the system and by the rules allowing the creation and/or destruction of new objects and the modification of their access rights.

A powerful model of access control systems is the *access matrix* model [2]. In this model, the *protection state* of the system is characterized by the set of access rights that different entities (*subjects* or *objects*) have over other entities and by the set of *commands* which may change this state, by creating/destroying subjects or objects or by adding/removing rights. The expressive power of this model is sufficiently large to include other models like take-grant systems ([4]), SPM systems ([8]), ESPM systems ([1]), TAM systems ([9]), etc.

The basic decision problem in an access matrix model is the *safety problem*: given two entities $A$ and $B$ and a right $R$, decide whether the system can evolve into a state in which $A$ has right $R$ over $B$. Very early, it was shown that this problem is undecidable ([2]) and remains like that, even for systems without subject/object destruction ([3]). Consequently, a number of restrictions have been proposed [2, 4, 9] for which the safety problem is decidable.

In this paper we propose two notions of simulation between protection systems that allow us to define a class of access control models for which the safety problem is decidable. We prove that several classes of protection systems from the litterature fall into this class, notably the *take-grant systems* and the *monotonic typed access matrix systems with an acyclic creation graph*.

---

* The research reported in this paper was partially supported by the program ECO-NET 08112WJ/2004-2005 and by the National University Research Council of Romania, grants CNCSIS 632/28/2004 and CNCSIS 632/50/2005.

T. Dimitrakos et al. (Eds.): FAST 2005, LNCS 3866, pp. 96–111, 2006.

Our contributions consist in defining such simulation relations on access matrix models of protection systems and using them to unify and clarify the proof of decidability of the safety problem for the classes of protection systems above. As to our knowledge, this is the first attempt to define simulation relations on such models. We also obtain a slight generalization of the decidability result in [9] as we will see in Subsect. 5.1.

The paper is organized as follows: in the second section we remind the notion of a protection system, in the access matrix presentation of [2]. We then define in Sect. 3 and 4, two notions of simulation between protection systems and show how we can use them to solve the safety problem. Also, these two simulation relations allow us to define, in the fifth section, a class of protection systems for which the safety problem is decidable. We then prove that the *mono-operational*, the *take-grant*, and the *monotonic typed access matrix systems with acyclic creation graphs* fall into this class. The last section contains some conclusions.

## 2 Protection Systems

We use protection systems modeled as in [2]. Here, the protection state of a system is modeled by an access matrix with a row for each subject and a column for each object. The cells hold the rights that subjects have on objects.

A protection system is defined over a finite set of generic rights and contains commands that specify how the protection state can be changed. The commands are formed of a conditional part which tests for the presence of rights in some cells of the access matrix and an operational part which specifies the changes made on the protection state. The changes are specified using primitive operations for subject/object creation and destruction and for entering/removing rights.

**Definition 2.1.** A *protection scheme* is a tuple $\mathcal{S} = (R, C)$, where $R$ is a finite set of *rights* and $C$ is a finite set of *commands* of the following form:

$$\text{command } c(x_1, x_2, \cdots, x_n)$$
$$\text{if} \quad r_1 \quad \text{in } [x_{s_1}, x_{o_1}]$$
$$\cdots$$
$$r_k \quad \text{in } [x_{s_k}, x_{o_k}]$$
$$\text{then}$$
$$op_1$$
$$\cdots$$
$$op_m$$

Above, $c$ is a name, $x_1, x_2, \cdots, x_n$ are formal parameters and each $op_i$ is one of the following *primitive operations*: enter $r$ into $[x_s, x_o]$, delete $r$ from $[x_s, x_o]$, create subject $x_s$, create object $x_o$, destroy subject $x_s$ and destroy object $x_o$. Also, $r, r_1, \cdots r_k$ are rights from $R$ and $s, s_1, \cdots, s_k, o, o_1, \cdots, o_k$ are integers between 1 and $n$.

We will call a command *mono-operational* if it contains only one primitive operation and *monotonic* if it does not contain "destroy subject", "destroy object" and "delete" operations.

**Definition 2.2.** A *configuration* over $R$ is a tuple $Q = (S, O, P)$, where $S$ is the set of *subjects*, $O$ the set of *objects*, $S \subseteq O$ and $P : S \times O \to \mathcal{P}(R)$ is the *access matrix*. We will denote by $Cf(R)$ the set of configurations over $R$.

As we can see, all subjects are also objects. This is a very natural assumption since, for example, processes in a computer system may be accessed by, or may access other processes. The objects from $O - S$ will be called *pure objects*.

**Definition 2.3.** A *protection system* is a tuple $\psi = (R, C, Q_0)$, where $(R, C)$ is a protection scheme and $Q_0$ a configuration over $R$, called the *initial configuration*. A protection system is *mono-operational* (*monotonic*) if all commands in $C$ are mono-operational (monotonic).

We will call the subjects (objects) from $S_0$ ($O_0$) *initial subjects (objects)*.

The six primitive operations mean exactly what their name imply (for details the reader is reffered [2]). We will denote by $\Rightarrow_{op}$ the application of a primitive operation $op$ in some configuration.

**Definition 2.4.** Let $\psi = (R, C, Q_0)$ be a protection system, $Q$ and $Q'$ two configurations over $R$ and $c(x_1, \cdots x_n) \in C$ a command like in Definition 2.1. We say that $Q'$ *is obtained from $Q$ in $\psi$, applying $c$ with the actual arguments* $o_1, \cdots, o_n$, denoted by $Q \to_{\psi}^{c(o_1, \cdots, o_n)} Q'$, if:

- $r_i \in P(o_{s_i}, o_{o_i})$, for all $1 \le i \le k$;
- there exist configurations $Q_1, \cdots, Q_m$ such that $Q \Rightarrow_{op'_1} Q_1 \Rightarrow_{op'_2} \cdots \Rightarrow_{op'_m} Q_m$ and $Q_m = Q'$ ($op'_i$ is the primitive operation obtained after substituting $x_1, \cdots, x_n$ with $o_1, \cdots, o_n$).

When the command $c$ and the actual arguments $o_1, \cdots, o_n$ are understood from the context, we will write only $Q \to_{\psi} Q'$. We consider also $\to_{\psi}^*$, the reflexive and transitive closure of $\to_{\psi}$. We say that a configuration $Q$ over $R$ is *reachable in $\psi$* if $Q_0 \to_{\psi}^* Q$.

For protection systems like above, we consider the following safety problem: given $s$ an initial subject, $o$ an initial object and a right $r$, decide if a state in which $s$ has right $r$ over $o$ is reachable. This is a less general safety problem than the one in [2], but it is more natural and used more frequently in the literature ([1, 4, 8, 9]).

**Definition 2.5.** Let $\psi = (R, C, Q_0 = (S_0, O_0, P_0))$ be a protection system, $s \in S_0$, $o \in O_0$ and $r \in R$. A configuration $Q = (S, O, P)$ over $R$ is called *leaky for $(s, o, r)$* if $s \in S$, $o \in O$ and $r \in P(s, o)$.

We say that $\psi$ is *leaky for $(s, o, r)$* if there exists a reachable configuration leaky for $(s, o, r)$. Otherwise, $\psi$ is called *safe for $(s, o, r)$*, denoted by $\psi \lhd (s, o, r)$.

Now we can define the safety problem as follows:

    **Safety problem** (SP)

        **Instance:** protection system $\psi$, $s \in S_0$, $o \in O_0$, $r \in R$;

        **Question:** is $\psi$ safe for $(s, o, r)$?

## 3    Simulations

The problem to decide if a protection system is safe was shown to be undecidable in [2], by designing a protection system that simulates a Turing machine. The most important source of undecidability is the creation of objects, which makes the system infinite-state. Hence, techniques to reduce the state space of the system are well suited. In this paper we will refer to an abstraction technique, namely the *simulation relation* ([6]).

**Definition 3.1.** Let $\psi_1 = (R_1, C_1, Q_0^1 = (S_0^1, O_0^1, P_0^1))$ and $\psi_2 = (R_2, C_2, Q_0^2 = (S_0^2, O_0^2, P_0^2))$ be two protection systems. Also, let $\rho_o \subseteq O_0^1 \times O_0^2$ and $\rho_r \subseteq R_1 \times R_2$ be two relations. For any $Q_1 = (S_1, O_1, P_1) \in Cf(R_1)$ and $Q_2 = (S_2, O_2, P_2) \in Cf(R_2)$, we say that $Q_2$ *simulates* $Q_1$ w.r.t. $\rho_o$ and $\rho_r$, denoted by $Q_1 \prec_{\rho_o, \rho_r} Q_2$, if:

1. $\rho_o(S_1 \cap S_0^1) \subseteq S_2 \cap S_0^2$;
2. $\rho_o(O_1 \cap O_0^1) \subseteq O_2 \cap O_0^2$;
3. for any $s \in S_1 \cap S_0^1$, $o \in O_1 \cap O_0^1$ and $r \in R_1$, if $r \in P_1(s, o)$ then there exist $s' \in \rho_o(s)$, $o' \in \rho_o(o)$ and $r' \in \rho_r(r)$ such that $r' \in P_2(s', o')$.

Above, $\rho(s) = \{s' | \rho(s, s')\}$, for any relation $\rho$.

The relations $\rho_o$ and $\rho_r$ are used to relate the "access powers" of subjects from two different protection systems. For example, having right $r$ over an object $o$ in the first system is considered to be the same as having a right $r' \in \rho_r(r)$ over an object $o' \in \rho_o(o)$ in the second system. In this context, a configuration $Q_2$ from $\psi_2$ simulates a configuration $Q_1$ from $\psi_1$, if every initial subject from $Q_2$ has at least the same "access power" as the initial subject from $Q_1$ to which is related by $\rho_o$.

The simulation relation we define next, is more general than the one in [6], because one transition step in the first system can be simulated by zero, one or more transition steps in the second system.

**Definition 3.2.** Let $\psi_1 = (R_1, C_1, Q_0^1)$ and $\psi_2 = (R_2, C_2, Q_0^2)$ be two protection systems, and $\rho_o, \rho_r$ relations like above. We say that $H \subseteq Cf(R_1) \times Cf(R_2)$ is a *simulation relation from $\psi_1$ to $\psi_2$* w.r.t. $\rho_o$ and $\rho_r$ if for any $Q_1 \in Cf(R_1)$ and $Q_2 \in Cf(R_2)$, $H(Q_1, Q_2)$ implies that:

1. $Q_1 \prec_{\rho_o, \rho_r} Q_2$;
2. for any $Q_1' \in Cf(R_1)$ such that $Q_1 \rightarrow_{\psi_1} Q_1'$ there exists $Q_2' \in Cf(R_2)$ such that $Q_2 \rightarrow_{\psi_2}^* Q_2'$ and $H(Q_1', Q_2')$.

**Definition 3.3.** Let $\psi_1 = (R_1, C_1, Q_0^1)$ and $\psi_2 = (R_2, C_2, Q_0^2)$ be two protection systems, and $\rho_o, \rho_r$ relations like above. We say that $\psi_2$ *simulates* $\psi_1$ w.r.t. $\rho_o$ and $\rho_r$, denoted by $\psi_1 \prec_{\rho_o, \rho_r} \psi_2$, if there exists a simulation relation $H$ from $\psi_1$ to $\psi_2$ w.r.t. $\rho_o$ and $\rho_r$ such that $H(Q_0^1, Q_0^2)$. We write $\psi_1 \prec \psi_2$ if there exist $\rho_o$ and $\rho_r$ like above such that $\psi_1 \prec_{\rho_o, \rho_r} \psi_2$.

The usefulness of the simulation relation is proved by the next theorem. We will show that solving some instances of SP in a protection system that simulates another may lead to solving an instance of SP in the initial system.

**Theorem 3.1.** Let $\psi_1 = (R_1, C_1, Q_0 = (S_0, O_0, P_0))$ and $\psi_2 = (R_2, C_2, Q_0' = (S_0', O_0', P_0'))$ be two protection systems, and $\rho_o$, $\rho_r$ two relations like above. If $\psi_1 \prec_{\rho_o, \rho_r} \psi_2$, then:

$$[(\forall s' \in \rho_o(s))(\forall o' \in \rho_o(o))(\forall r' \in \rho_r(r))(\psi_2 \lhd (s', o', r'))] \Rightarrow [\psi_1 \lhd (s, o, r)],$$

for any $s \in S_0$, $o \in O_0$ and $r \in R_1$.

**Proof.** Suppose by contradiction that $\psi_1$ is not safe for $(s, o, r)$. Then, there exists the follwing computation in $\psi_1$:

$$Q_0 \to_{\psi_1} Q_1 \to_{\psi_1} \cdots \to_{\psi_1} Q_l,$$

such that $Q_l$ is leaky for $(s, o, r)$.

$\psi_1 \prec_{\rho_o, \rho_r} \psi_2$ implies that there exists a simulation relation $H$ from $\psi_1$ to $\psi_2$ such that $H(Q_0, Q_0')$. Hence, we have in $\psi_2$ the following computation:

$$Q_0' \to_{\psi_2}^* Q_1' \to_{\psi_2}^* \cdots \to_{\psi_2}^* Q_l',$$

such that $H(Q_i, Q_i')$ for all $0 \le i \le l$.

Consequently, $Q_l \prec_{\rho_o, \rho_r} Q_l'$ and, since $r \in P_l(s, o)$, we obtain that there exists $s'$ in $\rho_o(s)$, $o'$ in $\rho_o(o)$ and $r'$ in $\rho_r(r)$ such that $r' \in P_l'(s', o')$, where $P_l$ is the access matrix of $Q_l$ and $P_l'$ the access matrix of $Q_l'$. So, $Q_l'$ is leaky for $(s', o', r')$ and $\psi_2$ is not safe for $(s', o', r')$, contradicting the supposition made above.    $\square$

The result above implies that $\psi_2$ is a *weak-preserving abstraction* of $\psi_1$ in the sense that only positive answers to instances of SP in $\psi_2$ may lead to solving instances of SP in $\psi_1$.

We will now prove that in some conditions, the existence of simulation relations in both senses may transform $\psi_2$ into a *strong-preserving abstraction* of $\psi_1$. This means that, also negative answers to instances of SP in $\psi_2$ are important for solving instances of SP in $\psi_1$.

We say that a relation $\rho \subseteq D_1 \times D_2$ is *injective* if $\rho(x_1) \cap \rho(x_2) = \emptyset$, for any $x_1$, $x_2 \in D_1$.

**Corollary 3.1.** Let $\psi_1 = (R_1, C_1, Q_0 = (S_0, O_0, P_0))$ and $\psi_2 = (R_2, C_2, Q_0' = (S_0', O_0', P_0'))$ be two protection systems, and $\rho_o$, $\rho_r$ two relations like above.
If $\psi_1 \prec_{\rho_o, \rho_r} \psi_2$, $\psi_2 \prec_{\rho_o^{-1}, \rho_r^{-1}} \psi_1$ and $\rho_o$, $\rho_r$ are injective then:

$$[(\forall s' \in \rho_o(s))(\forall o' \in \rho_o(o))(\forall r' \in \rho_r(r))(\psi_2 \lhd (s', o', r'))] \Leftrightarrow [\psi_1 \lhd (s, o, r)],$$

for any $s \in S_0$, $o \in O_0$ and $r \in R_1$.

**Proof.** The result is immediate, applying Theorem 3.1 for $\psi_1 \prec_{\rho_o, \rho_r} \psi_2$ and $\psi_2 \prec_{\rho_o^{-1}, \rho_r^{-1}} \psi_1$.    $\square$

Next, we exemplify the use of simulation relations in the analysis of protection systems. We will show that an weak-preserving abstraction of a protection system can be obtained by adding commands or by removing the non-monotonic primitive operations from all the commands. Then, for monotonic protection systems, we prove that an abstraction can be obtained by splitting each command into mono-operational commands.

**Example 3.1.** Let $\psi = (R, C, Q_0 = (S_0, O_0, P_0))$ and $\psi' = (R, C', Q_0)$ be two protection systems such that $C \subseteq C'$.

We say that two configurations $Q = (S, O, P)$ and $Q' = (S', O', P')$ from $Cf(R)$ are *equal up to names*, denoted by $Q \approx Q'$, if:

- $O \cap O_0 = O' \cap O_0$;
- there exists a bijection $\phi : O \to O'$ such that:
  - $\phi(o) = o$, for every $o \in O \cap O_0$ ($\phi$ preserves initial objects);
  - $\phi(S) = S'$ ($\phi$ preserves subjects);
  - $r \in P(s, o) \Leftrightarrow r \in P'(\phi(s), \phi(o))$, for any $s \in S$, $o \in O$ and $r \in R$.

It can be easily proved that $\psi \prec_{id_{O_0}, id_R} \psi'$, considering the simulation relation $H \subseteq Cf(R) \times Cf(R)$, given by $H(Q, Q')$ iff $Q \approx Q'$.

**Example 3.2.** Let $\psi = (R, C, Q_0 = (S_0, O_0, P_0))$ be a protection system. We suppose w.l.o.g. that the commands in $C$ do not delete a right that they have just entered or destroy an object that they have just created. We will prove that $\psi$ is simulated by its *monotonic restriction*, i.e., by the system which acts like $\psi$ but does not destroy any object and does not delete any right.

Let $\psi_m = (R, C_m, Q_0)$, where $C_m$ is the set of commands obtained from the ones in $C$, by removing all non-monotonic primitive operations.

We can prove that $\psi \prec_{id_{O_0}, id_R} \psi_m$, considering the following relation $H$: given $Q = (S, O, P)$ and $Q' = (S', O', P')$ from $Cf(R)$, we have $H(Q, Q')$ if:

- $O \cap O_0 \subseteq O' \cap O_0$;
- there exists an injection $\phi : O \to O'$, such that:
  - $\phi(o) = o$, for every $o \in O \cap O_0$;
  - $\phi(S) \subseteq S'$;
  - $r \in P(s, o) \Rightarrow r \in P'(\phi(s), \phi(o))$, for any $s \in S$, $o \in O$ and $r \in R$.

**Example 3.3.** Let $\psi = (R, C, Q_0)$ be a monotonic protection system. We can prove that $\psi$ is simulated by the mono-operational system that results by splitting all the commands from $C$ into mono-operational commands.

To this end, we will reuse the relation $H$ defined by $H(Q, Q')$ if $Q \approx Q'$ and prove that it is a simulation from $\psi$ to $\psi_{mo}$ w.r.t. $id_{O_0}$ and $id_R$.

## 4 Quasi-bisimulations

We present another type of simulation relation between protection systems, that resembles to a bisimulation relation ([7]) but does not induce an equivalence relation over protection systems. That is why we will call this relation a quasi-bisimulation. It differs from the simulation relation presented earlier by the fact that initial subjects must have the same "access power" and we must be able to simulate one step from a protection system with a sequence of zero or more steps in the other system.

**Definition 4.1.** Let $\psi_1 = (R_1, C_1, Q_0^1 = (S_0^1, O_0^1, P_0^1))$ and $\psi_2 = (R_2, C_2, Q_0^2 = (S_0^2, O_0^2, P_0^2))$ be two protection systems. Also, let $\rho_o \subseteq O_0^1 \times O_0^2$ and $\rho_r \subseteq R_1 \times R_2$ be two relations. For any $Q_1 = (S_1, O_1, P_1) \in Cf(R_1)$ and $Q_2 = (S_2, O_2, P_2) \in Cf(R_2)$, we say that $Q_2$ *is quasi-bisimilar to* $Q_1$ *w.r.t.* $\rho_o$ *and* $\rho_r$, denoted by $Q_1 \preceq_{\rho_o,\rho_r} Q_2$, if:

1. $\rho_o(S_1 \cap S_0^1) \subseteq S_2 \cap S_0^2$;
2. $\rho_o(O_1 \cap O_0^1) \subseteq O_2 \cap O_0^2$;
3. For any $s \in S_1 \cap S_0^1$, $o \in O_1 \cap O_0^1$ and $r \in R_1$, $r \in P_1(s,o)$ iff there exist $s' \in \rho_o(s)$, $o' \in \rho_o(o)$ and $r' \in \rho_r(r)$ such that $r' \in P_2(s',o')$.

**Definition 4.2.** Let $\psi_1 = (R_1, C_1, Q_0^1)$ and $\psi_2 = (R_2, C_2, Q_0^2)$ be two protection systems, and $\rho_o$, $\rho_r$ relations like above. We say that $B \subseteq Cf(R_1) \times Cf(R_2)$ is a *quasi-bisimulation relation from* $\psi_1$ *to* $\psi_2$ *w.r.t.* $\rho_o$ *and* $\rho_r$ if for any $Q_1 \in Cf(R_1)$ and $Q_2 \in Cf(R_2)$, $B(Q_1, Q_2)$ implies that:

1. $Q_1 \preceq_{\rho_o,\rho_r} Q_2$
2. for any $Q_1' \in Cf(R_1)$ such that $Q_1 \rightarrow_{\psi_1} Q_1'$ there exists $Q_2' \in Cf(R_2)$ such that $Q_2 \rightarrow_{\psi_2}^* Q_2'$ and $B(Q_1', Q_2')$.
3. for any $Q_2' \in Cf(R_2)$ such that $Q_2 \rightarrow_{\psi_2} Q_2'$ there exists $Q_1' \in Cf(R_1)$ such that $Q_1 \rightarrow_{\psi_1}^* Q_1'$ and $B(Q_1', Q_2')$.

**Definition 4.3.** Let $\psi_1 = (R_1, C_1, Q_0^1)$ and $\psi_2 = (R_2, C_2, Q_0^2)$ be two protection systems, and $\rho_o$, $\rho_r$ relations like above. We say that $\psi_2$ *is quasi-bisimilar to* $\psi_1$ *w.r.t.* $\rho_o$ *and* $\rho_r$, denoted by $\psi_1 \preceq_{\rho_o,\rho_r} \psi_2$, if there exists a quasi-bisimulation relation $B$ from $\psi_1$ to $\psi_2$ w.r.t. $\rho_o$ and $\rho_r$, such that $B(Q_0^1, Q_0^2)$. We write $\psi_1 \preceq \psi_2$ if there exist $\rho_o$ and $\rho_r$ like above such that $\psi_1 \preceq_{\rho_o,\rho_r} \psi_2$.

Next, we will prove the usefulness of the quasi-bisimulations, showing that if we have two protection systems such that $\psi_1 \preceq \psi_2$, solving an instance of SP in $\psi_1$ is equivalent with solving one or more instances of SP in $\psi_2$. This could still be more efficient if the state space of $\psi_2$ is much smaller than the one of $\psi_1$.

**Theorem 4.1.** Let $\psi_1 = (R_1, C_1, Q_0 = (S_0, O_0, P_0))$ and $\psi_2 = (R_2, C_2, Q_0' = (S_0', O_0', P_0'))$ be two protection systems, and $\rho_o$, $\rho_r$ two relations like above. If $\psi_1 \preceq_{\rho_o,\rho_r} \psi_2$, then:

$$[(\forall s' \in \rho_o(s))(\forall o' \in \rho_o(o))(\forall r' \in \rho_r(r))(\psi_2 \lhd (s', o', r'))] \Leftrightarrow [\psi_1 \lhd (s, o, r)],$$

for any $s \in S_0$, $o \in O_0$ and $r \in R_1$.

**Proof.** Similar to the proof of Theorem 3.1. $\qquad\square$

## 5   A Class of Decidable Protection Systems

**Definition 5.1.** A protection system $\psi = (R, C, Q_0)$ is called *a finite protection system* if the commands from $C$ do not contain "create" primitive operations.

It is well known ([5]) that the safety problem for finite protection systems is decidable.

**Definition 5.2.** We define $Dec$ to be the class of protection systems that has the following properties:

- if $\psi$ is a finite protection system then $\psi \in Dec$;
- if $\psi' \in Dec$ and $\psi \prec_{\rho_o, \rho_r} \psi'$, $\psi' \prec_{\rho_o^{-1}, \rho_r^{-1}} \psi$, for some $\rho_o$ and $\rho_r$ injective relations, then $\psi \in Dec$;
- if $\psi' \in Dec$ and $\psi \preceq \psi'$ then $\psi \in Dec$.

By Corollary 3.1 and Theorem 4.1, we obtain that the safety problem for the protection systems from $Dec$ is decidable.

We will show that it contains three other well-known classes of protection systems for which the safety problem is decidable: MTAM systems with acyclic creation graphs([9]), mono-operational protection systems([2]) and take-grant systems([4]).

By showing that these three classes of protection systems are included in $Dec$, we unify their proof of decidability for the safety problem. We show that the safety problem is decidable because these protection systems are simulated by systems that have all the needed objects created even from the initial configuration and no commands that can create objects afterwards.

## 5.1    MTAM Systems with Acyclic Creation Graphs

In [9], the authors propose an extension of the access matrix model, the typed access matrix model (TAM, for short), that assigns a type to each object of a configuration.

Formally, a TAM system is a tuple $\tau = (R, T, C, Q_0 = (S_0, O_0, t_0, P_0))$, where $R$ is a finite set of rights, $T$ a finite set of types, $C$ a finite set of typed commands and $Q_0$ the initial configuration.

Configurations are tuples $Q = (S, O, t, P)$, where $S$, $O$ and $P$ are as before, and $t : O \to T$ is a function that assigns a type to every object.

The typed commands differ from the commands of a protection system defined as in Sect. 2, by the fact that they test the type of each argument and the primitive operations used to create objects are: "create subject $s$ of type $t$" and "create object $o$ of type $t$".

$\tau$ is called a monotonic TAM system (MTAM, for short) if the commands from $C$ do not contain operations that delete rights or destroy objects.

We say that an MTAM system is in canonical form if the "create" commands (commands that contain at least one "create" primitive operation) are unconditional (the conditional part is empty). In [9] was proved that MTAM systems can always be considered to be in canonical form.

If $c$ is a typed command like in Fig. 1, $t_i$ is called a child type of $c$ if "create subject $x_i$ of type $t_i$" or "create object $x_i$ of type $t_i$" appears in $c$. Otherwise, $t_i$ is called a parent type of $c$.

command $c(x_1 : t_1, x_2 : t_2, \cdots, x_n : t_n)$  command $\gamma(c)(x_1, x_2, \cdots, x_n)$

    if    $r_1$  in $[x_{s_1}, x_{o_1}]$            if    $t_{i_1}$  in $[x_{i_1}, x_{i_1}]$

               $\cdots$                                  $\cdots$

        $r_k$  in $[x_{s_k}, x_{o_k}]$              $t_{i_l}$  in $[x_{i_l}, x_{i_l}]$

    then                               $r_1$  in $[x_{s_1}, x_{o_1}]$

        $op_1$                                  $\cdots$

        $\cdots$                                $r_k$  in $[x_{s_k}, x_{o_k}]$

        $op_m$                         then

                                      $op'_1$

                                      $\cdots$

                                      $op'_{m'}$

**Fig. 1.** The transformation $\gamma$

The creation graph of a TAM system $\tau = (R, T, C, Q_0)$ is a directed graph with the set of vertices $T$ and an edge from $t_1$ to $t_2$ if there exists a command $c \in C$ such that $t_1$ is a parent type of $c$ and $t_2$ a child type of $c$.

The safety problem SP can be defined analogously for TAM systems.

The main decidability result of [9] is:

**Theorem**
*SP for MTAM systems with acyclic creation graphs is decidable.*

A TAM system $\tau = (R, T, C, Q_0 = (S_0, O_0, t_0, P_0))$ can be described using a protection system $\psi_\tau = (R \cup T, C', Q'_0 = (O_0, O_0, P'_0))$, where:

$$P'_0(s, o) = \begin{cases} P_0(s, o), & \text{if } s \neq o \text{ and } s \in S_0 \\ P_0(s, o) \cup \{t_0(s)\}, & \text{if } s = o \text{ and } s \in S_0 \\ \{t_0(s)\}, & \text{if } s = o \text{ and } s \in O_0 - S_0 \\ \emptyset, & \text{otherwise.} \end{cases}$$

and $C' = \{\gamma(c) | c \in C\}$, with $\gamma$ the transformation from Fig. 1 ($i_1, \cdots, i_l$ are integers between 1 and n such that $x_{i_l}$ does not appear in a "create" operation).

The primitive operations of $\gamma(c)$ are obtained by copying the ones from $c$, excepting the case of a "create subject $s$ of type $t$" or "create object $s$ of type $t$" primitive operation, when we add in $\gamma(c)$ two operations: "create subject $s$" or "create object $s$" and "enter $t$ in [s,s]".

From now on, when we say TAM systems, we mean protection systems like $\psi_\tau$. Hence, an MTAM system is in canonical form if in the conditional part of every "create" command we test only rights from $T$.

In the following, we will obtain using quasi-bisimulations, the decidability of the safety problem for a class of protection systems more general than the MTAM systems with acyclic creation graphs.

If $\psi = (R, C, Q_0)$ is a protection system, denote by $\mathcal{T}_\psi(\mathcal{X})$ the set of terms defined over the set of variables $\mathcal{X}$ and the signature $\Sigma_\psi$, where

$$\Sigma_\psi = \{c_i \text{ of arity } n \mid c(x_1, \cdots, x_n) \in C \text{ and } 1 \leq i \leq n\} \cup \{o \text{ of arity } 0 \mid o \in O_0\}$$
$$\cup \{\emptyset \text{ of arity } 0\}$$

By $\mathcal{T}_\psi$ we will denote the set of ground terms.

For a command $c(x_1, \cdots, x_n) \in C$, we say that $x_i$, for some $1 \le i \le n$, is a *child argument* of $c$ if "create subject $x_i$" or "create object $x_i$" appears in $c$. Otherwise, $x_i$ is a *parent argument* of $c$. We define the relation $\equiv_Q$ over the objects of a configuration $Q = (S, O, P) \in Cf(R)$ as follows:

$o \equiv_Q o$ if $o \in O_0$;

$o \equiv_Q o'$ if $o$ and $o'$ were created as the $i$-th argument of a command $c$
  applied with $o_{p_1}, \cdots, o_{p_m}$ as parent arguments for $o$
  and with $o'_{p_1}, \cdots, o'_{p_m}$ as parent arguments for $o'$,
  and $o_{p_j} \equiv_Q o'_{p_j}$, for all $1 \le j \le m$.
  ($p_1, \cdots, p_m$ are the indexes of the parent arguments of $c$)

The fact that $o$ was created as the $i$-th argument of a command $c$ applied with $o_{p_1}, \cdots, o_{p_m}$ as parent arguments, can be memorized in a configuration $Q$ in many ways. For example, we can modify the system $\psi$ by adding a right *parent* and a right $c_i$, for all $c(x_1, \cdots, x_n) \in C$ and $1 \le i \le n$, and by transforming every command $c(x_1, \cdots, x_n) \in C$, such that after creating $x_i$, for some $1 \le i \le n$, we enter $c_i$ in $[x_i, x_i]$ and *parent* in $[x_{p_j}, x_i]$ for all $x_{p_j}$ parent arguments of $c$. In the following, for the simplicity of the exposition, we will not formalize this.

Clearly, the relation above is an equivalence and to every equivalence class we can uniquely associate a ground term from $\mathcal{T}_\psi$. Consequently, we will denote an equivalence class by $[t]_Q$, where $t$ is the corresponding term from $\mathcal{T}_\psi$.

In the following, when we say equivalence relation we mean the relation $\equiv_Q$ and when we say equivalence class, we mean an equivalence class of $\equiv_Q$.

**Definition 5.3.** Let $\psi = (R, C, Q_0)$ be a protection system. We say that a term from $\mathcal{T}_\psi$ is *accessible* if there exists $Q \in Cf(R)$ such that $Q_0 \to_\psi^* Q$ and $[t]_Q \ne \emptyset$. By $Acc(\psi)$ we will denote the set of accessible terms.

**Definition 5.4.** A monotonic protection system $\psi = (R, C, Q_0)$ is called *creation-independent* if $R$ can be partitioned into two disjunctive sets $R_c$ and $R_e$ such that:

- the "create" commands test for and enter only rights from $R_c$;
- the other commands (the commands that contain only "enter" operations) enter only rights from $R_e$.

We can easily see that MTAM systems are particular cases of creation-independent protection systems in which $R_c = T$, $R_e = R$ and the tests for the rights in $R_c$ are as in command $\gamma(c)$ from Fig. 1. ·

If $\psi = (R, C, Q_0)$ is a protection system, we will denote by $Reach_\psi(Q, C')$, where $Q \in Cf(R)$ and $C' \subseteq C$, the set of reachable configurations from $Q$ using only commands from $C'$.

Now, we prove that for any creation-independent system $\psi$, any $t \in Acc(\psi)$ and any reachable configuration $Q$, we can apply in $Q$ a sequence of "create" commands to create an object from an equivalence class represented by $t$.

**Lemma 5.1.** Let $\psi = (R, C, Q_0)$ be a creation-independent protection system and $C' \subseteq C$ the set of "create" commands. Then,

$$(\forall t \in Acc(\psi))(\forall Q \in Reach_\psi(Q_0, C))(\exists Q' \in Reach_\psi(Q, C'))(|[t]_{Q'}| = |[t]_Q| + 1)$$

**Proof.** From Definition 5.4, we can see that the application of a "create" command is not influenced in any way by the application of a command from $C - C'$.

Because, $\psi$ is also monotonic, we can easily obtain the result above.     $\square$

**Theorem 5.1.** Let $\psi = (R, C, Q_0)$ be a creation-independent protection system. If $Acc(\psi)$ is finite then, $\psi$ belongs to $Dec$.

**Proof.** If $\psi$ is a creation-independent protection system, then $R$ can be partitioned into $R_c$ and $R_e$ as in Definition 5.4.

Let $\psi_f = (R, C_f, Q'_0 = (S'_0, O'_0, P'_0))$ be a protection system, where $C_f \subseteq C$ is the set of commands that do not create objects and:

- $O'_0 = \{t | t \in Acc(\psi)\}$. Clearly, $O_0 \subseteq O'_0$;
- $S'_0$ is the set of subjects from $O'_0$;
- $P'_0$ is defined such as it's restriction to objects from $O_0$ is $P_0$ and in the cells of the other objects we have the rights from $R_c$ entered by the corresponding "create" commands.

In other words, $Q'_0$ is obtained from $Q_0$ applying "create" commands such that we obtain objects from equivalence classes represented by all terms in $Acc(\psi)$.

We will prove that $\psi$ is quasi-bisimilar to $\psi_f$ w.r.t $id_{O_0}$ and $id_R$.

In the following, for a configuration $Q = (S, O, P)$, $f_Q : O \rightarrow Acc(\psi)$ is a function such that $f(o) = t$ iff $o \in [t]_Q$.

We consider the following relation $B$: given $Q = (S, O, P)$ reachable in $\psi$ and $Q' = (S', O', P')$ configuration from $Cf(R)$, we have $B(Q, Q')$ if:

- $O_0 \subseteq O$ and $O' = Acc(\psi)$;
- $r \in P'(t_1, t_2)$ iff there exists $s \in [t_1]_Q$ and $o \in [t_2]_Q$ such that $r \in P(s, o)$.

To prove that $B$ is a quasi-bisimulation, let $Q$ and $Q'$ be two configurations like above such that $B(Q, Q')$.

Clearly, $Q \preceq_{id_{O_0}, id_R} Q'$.

Now, let $Q_1$ be a configuration such that $Q \rightarrow_\psi Q_1$. If we apply a "create" command then, we can find $Q'_1 = Q'$, such that $Q' \rightarrow^*_{\psi_f} Q'_1$ and $B(Q_1, Q'_1)$. Otherwise, suppose we apply a command $c(x_1, \cdots, x_n) \in C'$, with actual arguments $o_1, \cdots, o_n$. Since $B(Q, Q')$, we can apply $c(x_1, \cdots, x_n)$ with actual arguments $f_Q(o_1), \cdots, f_Q(o_n)$ in $Q'$ and obtain a configuration $Q'_1$ such that $B(Q_1, Q'_1)$.

For the reverse, suppose we have $Q' \rightarrow_{\psi_f} Q'_1$, for some configuration $Q'_1$. Clearly, in this step we apply a command $c(x_1, \cdots, x_n)$ that contain only "enter" primitive operations. Suppose it is applied using $t_1, \cdots, t_n \in Acc(\psi)$ as actual arguments.

Since $\psi$ is monotonic and create-independent, we can reach in $\psi$ from $Q$ a configuration $\overline{Q}$ such that $B(\overline{Q}, Q')$ and the access matrix of $\overline{Q}$ includes that of $Q$ and has in plus one object $o_i$ for each $t_i$ above, such that $o_i \in [t_i]_{\overline{Q}}$ and $o_i$

has in his cells the same rights as $t_i$ in $Q'$ (the creation of objects is possible by Lemma 5.1 and the rights can be entered in the cells of $o_i$ because, once we have applied in $\psi$ a command that contains only "enter" primitive operations, we can apply it later eventually with equivalent actual arguments).

Now, in $\overline{Q}$ we can apply $c$ with $o_1, \cdots, o_n$ as actual arguments and obtain a configuration $Q_1$ such that $B(Q_1, Q_1')$.

The fact that $B(Q_0, Q_0')$ ends our proof. $\qquad\qquad\square$

Using Theorem 5.1, we will prove that MTAM systems with acyclic creation graphs and mono-operational protection systems belong to $Dec$.

**Corollary 5.1.** MTAM systems with acyclic creation graphs belong to $Dec$.

**Proof.** As stated above we suppose that MTAM systems are in canonical form and consequently, they are creation-independent.

Since the creation graph is acyclic, we have also that the set of accessible terms is finite and we can apply Theorem 5.1, to obtain the statement of this corollary. $\qquad\qquad\square$

## 5.2 Mono-operational Protection Systems

Mono-operational protection systems ([2]) are protection systems with mono-operational commands. We will show that they are included in $Dec$ in two steps, by proving first that the subclass of monotonic mono-operational protection systems is included in $Dec$.

**Theorem 5.2.** Monotonic mono-operational protection systems belong to $Dec$.

**Proof.** In the following we will consider protection systems such that every object is also a subject. This can be assumed without loss of generality by introducing an otherwise empty row for each pure object.

Hence, let $\psi = (R, C, Q_0 = (O_0, O_0, P_0))$ be a monotonic mono-operational protection system, such that the commands in $C$ do not contain "create object" primitive operations.

We will prove that $\psi$ is quasi-bisimilar to some monotonic mono-operational system $\psi'$ that is creation-independent and has $Acc(\psi')$ finite. Consequently, by Theorem 5.1, $\psi' \in Dec$ and from the definition of $Dec$, $\psi \in Dec$.

Let $\psi' = (R \cup \{alive\}, C', Q_0' = (O_0, O_0, P_0'))$, where $P_0'$ is defined by:

$$P_0'(s, o) = \begin{cases} P_0(s, o) \cup \{alive\}, & \text{if } s = o; \\ P_0(s, o), & \text{otherwise.} \end{cases}$$

and $C'$ is obtained from $C$ in the following way:

- modify each conditional part of an "enter" command (command that contains an "enter" primitive operation) $c(x_1, \cdots, x_n) \in C$ by adding tests of the form: $alive$ in $[x_i, x_i]$, for all $1 \le i \le n$;
- add a command $c_s(x)$ that has the conditional part empty and only a primitive operation "create subject $x$".

– remove each "create" command $c(x_1, \cdots, x_n)$ that creates a subject $x_i$, for some $1 \leq i \leq n$, and add an "enter" command with the conditional part of $c$, modified as in the first case, and a primitive operation "enter $alive$ in $[x_i, x_i]$".

Now, we prove that $\psi \preceq_{id_{O_0}, id_R} \psi'$, using the following relation $B$: if $Q = (O, O, P) \in Cf(R)$ and $Q' = (O', O', P') \in Cf(R \cup \{alive\})$, we have $B(Q, Q')$ if:

– $O_0 \subseteq O$ and $O_0 \subseteq O'$;
– if $O'_{alive} = \{o | o \in O'$ and $alive \in P'(o, o)\}$ then, there exists a bijection $\phi : O \rightarrow O'_{alive}$, such that:
  • $\phi(o) = o$, for every $o \in O \cap O_0$;
  • $r \in P(o_1, o_2) \Leftrightarrow r \in P'(\phi(o_1), \phi(o_2))$, for all $o_1, o_2 \in S$ and $r \in R$.

We can easily prove that $B$ is a quasi-bisimulation relation, if we take in consideration the following:

– applying a "create" command in $\psi$ is equivalent with applying in $\psi'$ the "create" command $c_s$ and an "enter" command that gives to this new subject the $alive$ right to himself;
– in $\psi'$ we can create more subjects than in $\psi$, but if they do not have the $alive$ right to themselves, they are useless. In fact, only to commands that enter the $alive$ right in $\psi'$, we associate a "create" command in $\psi$.

Clearly, $\psi'$ is create-independent since the only "create" command does not test or enter any right. $Acc(\psi')$ is finite, because all the created objects in $\psi'$ are from an equivalence class represented by the same term $c_s(\emptyset)$.    □

**Theorem 5.3.** Mono-operational protection systems belong to $Dec$.

**Proof.** Let $\psi = (R, C, Q_0)$ be a mono-operational system.

From Example 3.2 we have that $\psi \prec_{id_{O_0}, id_R} \psi_m$, where $\psi_m = (R, C_m, Q_0)$ is the monotonic restriction of $\psi$.

As $C_m \subseteq C$, from Example 3.1 we have also that $\psi_m \prec_{id_{O_0}, id_R} \psi$.

The fact that $id_{O_0}$ and $id_R$ are injective and $\psi_m$ is a monotonic mono-operational protection system, which by Theorem 5.2 belongs to $Dec$, concludes our proof.    □

### 5.3    Take-Grant Systems

Take-grant systems ([4]) are protection systems $\psi = (R, C, Q_0 = (O_0, O_0, P_0))$, where $R = \{t, g, c\}$ and $C$ is the set of commands shown in Fig. 2, for all $\alpha, \beta, \gamma \in R$. It is clear that the system is monotonic and all objects are also subjects.

In the original paper, take-grant systems were presented as graph transformation systems. A configuration $Q = (O, O, P)$ is represented as a labeled directed graph, using subjects as nodes and cells in the matrix as labeled arcs (if $P(o_1, o_2) \neq \emptyset$, we have an arc from $o_1$ to $o_2$ labeled with $P(o_1, o_2)$ ). The

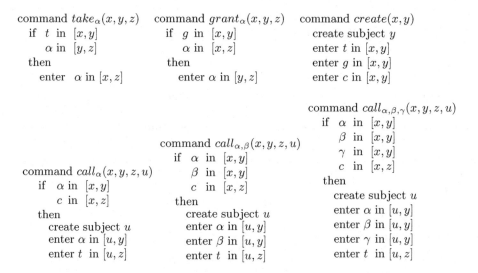

**Fig. 2.** Take-grant commands

commands in Fig. 2 are represented as graph transformations that introduce nodes and/or arcs.

We say that two nodes are *connected* if there exists a path between them, independent of the directionality or labels of the arcs. The decidability of the safety problem is obtained from the following theorem:

**Theorem**

*Let $\psi$ be a take-grant system. $\psi$ is leaky for $(o_1, o_2, r)$ iff in $\mathcal{G}_0$ (the graph that represents $Q_0$) $o_1$ and $o_2$ are connected and there exists an incoming arc in $o_2$ labeled with $t$ or $c$ if $r = t$ or with $r$ if $r \in \{g, c\}$.*

We will prove that take-grant protection systems are in *Dec*, by showing that they are quasi-bisimilar to a finite protection system with the same initial configuration.

**Theorem 5.4.** Take-grant systems belong to *Dec*.

**Proof.** If $\psi = (R, C, Q_0 = (O_0, O_0, P_0))$ is a take-grant protection system like above, let $\psi_f = (R, C', Q_0)$, where $C'$ contains all the commands of the following form:

$$\text{command } c_{i,\alpha}(x, y, z, x_1, \cdots, x_i)$$
$$\text{if } \text{connected}(x, y, x_1, \cdots, x_i)$$
$$\alpha \text{ in } [z, y]$$
$$\text{then}$$
$$\text{enter } \alpha \text{ in } [x, y]$$

where $0 \le i \le |O_0| - 2$ and $\alpha \in R$. connected$(x, y, x_1, \cdots, x_i)$ is a set of conditions obtained from the conditions below, choosing one from each line:

$$\beta_1 \text{ in } [x, x_1] \quad \text{or} \quad \beta_1 \text{ in } [x_1, x]$$
$$\beta_2 \text{ in } [x_1, x_2] \quad \text{or} \quad \beta_2 \text{ in } [x_2, x_1]$$
$$\cdots$$
$$\beta_{i+1} \text{ in } [x_i, y] \text{ or } \beta_{i+1} \text{ in } [y, x_i].$$

Above, $\beta_k$, for $1 \leq k \leq i+1$, can be any right from $R$.

Intuitively, $connected(x, y, x_1, \cdots, x_i)$ checks if in the graph that represents the configuration in which we apply $c_{i,\alpha}$, the nodes $x$ and $y$ are connected by a path of length $i + 2$ that passes through $x_1, \cdots, x_i$.

We will prove that $\psi \preceq_{id_{O_0}, id_R} \psi_f$, considering the following relation $B$: given $Q_1 = (S_1, O_1, P_1)$ reachable from $Q_0$ and $Q_2 = (S_2, O_2, P_2) \in Cf(R)$, we have $B(Q_1, Q_2)$ if:

- $O_2 = O_0$;
- $r \in P_1(s, o) \Leftrightarrow r \in P_2(s, o)$, for any $s \in S_0$, $o \in O_0$ and $r \in R$.

Now, we will prove that $B$ is a quasi-bisimulation relation between $\psi$ and $\psi_f$ w.r.t. $id_{O_0}$ and $id_R$.

$Q_1 \preceq_{id_{O_0}, id_R} Q_2$ is straightforward from the definition of $B$.

Now suppose that $Q_1 \rightarrow_\psi Q_1'$ by a command $c$.

If $c$ is $take_\alpha$, then suppose it is applied with some actual arguments $s_1$, $s_2$ and $s_3$. If all these objects are initial then, because $c$ is also present in $C'$, we can apply it with the same actual arguments in $Q_2$ and obtain a configuration $Q_2'$ such that $B(Q_1', Q_2')$.

If not, we have two cases: whether or not $s_1$ and $s_3$ are both initial objects. If they are not both initial objects then, we can find $Q_2' = Q_2$ such that $Q_2 \rightarrow_{\psi_f}^* Q_2'$ and $B(Q_1', Q_2')$.

If $s_1$ and $s_3$ are both from $O_0$ then from the main result of [4] stated above, we have that there exists some initial objects $o_1, \cdots, o_i$, for some $i$ between 0 and $|O_0| - 2$, such that $connected(s_1, s_3, o_1, \cdots, o_i)$ is true and also, there exists some initial object $o$ such that $\alpha \in P_0(o, s_3)$. Since $\psi$ and $\psi_f$ are monotonic, these conditions are true also in $Q_2$ and thus, we can apply a command from $C'$ to add $\alpha$ in $[s_1, s_3]$. Consequently, we can obtain a configuration $Q_2'$ such that $Q_2 \rightarrow_{\psi_f}^* Q_2'$ and $B(Q_1', Q_2')$.

The case when $c$ is $grant_\alpha$ is similar.

If $c$ is a $create$ or $call$ command then, we can find $Q_2' = Q_2$ such that $Q_2 \rightarrow_{\psi_f}^* Q_2'$ and $B(Q_1', Q_2')$.

For the reverse, suppose that $Q_2 \rightarrow_{\psi_f} Q_2'$. Also, from the main result of [4], we can find a configuration $Q_1'$ such that $Q_1 \rightarrow_\psi^* Q_1'$ and $B(Q_1', Q_2')$.

The fact that $B(Q_0, Q_0)$ concludes our proof. $\qquad\square$

## 6  Conclusions

In this paper we have introduced two notions of simulation between protection systems. As a model for protection systems we have used the well-known access matrix model of Harrison, Ruzzo and Ullman ([2]). We have shown how we can use the resulting simulation relations to solve the safety problem for protection systems.

Then, we have used these relations to unify the proofs of decidability of the safety problem for several classes of protection systems from the literature: the mono-operational protection systems ([2]), the take-grant protection systems ([4]), and the monotonic typed access matrix systems with acyclic creation graphs ([9]). All these protection systems are infinite-state systems, but we have shown that they are simulated by some protection systems that do not create objects and consequently, are finite-state systems.

In future work, we will try to extend the results presented here and obtain new decidability results of the safety problem for protection systems. We will also try to consider other models for protection systems than the access matrix model used in this paper.

# References

1. Ammann, P.E., Sandhu, R.: Extending the creation operation in the schematic protection model. In Proc. of the 6th Annual Computer Security Applications Conference (1990) 304-348
2. Harrison, M.A., Ruzzo, W.L., Ullman, J.D: Protection in operating systems. Communications of ACM **19(8)** (1976) 461-471
3. Harrison, M.A., Ruzzo, W.L.: Monotonic protection systems. In DeMillo et al. (editors) "Foundations of Secure Computation", Academic Press 1978
4. Lipton, R.J., Snyder, L.: A linear time algorithm for deciding subject security. Journal of ACM **24(3)** (1977) 455-464
5. Lipton, R.J., Snyder, L.: On synchronization and security. In Demillo et al. (editors) "Foundations of Secure Computation" Academic Press 1978
6. Milner, R.: An algebraic definition of simulation between programs. In Proc. of the 2nd International Joint Conference on Artificial Intelligence (1971) 481-489
7. Park, D.: Concurrency and automata on infinite sequences. In Proc. of the 5th GI-Conference on Theoretical Computer Science (1981) 167-183
8. Sandhu, R.: The schematic protection model: its definition and analysis for acyclic attenuating schemes. Journal of ACM **35(2)** (1988) 404-432
9. Sandhu, R.: The typed access matrix model. In Proc. of the IEEE Symposium on Research in Security and Privacy (1992) 122-136

# Proof Obligations Preserving Compilation

## (Extended Abstract)

Gilles Barthe[1], Tamara Rezk[1], and Ando Saabas[2]

[1] INRIA Sophia Antipolis, France
{Gilles.Barthe, Tamara.Rezk}@sophia.inria.fr
[2] Institute of Cybernetics, Tallinn University of Technology, Estonia
ando@cs.ioc.ee

**Abstract.** The objective of this work is to study the interaction between program verification and program compilation, and to show that the proof that a source program meets its specification can be reused to show that the corresponding compiled program meets the same specification. More concretely, we introduce a core imperative language, and a bytecode language for a stack-based abstract machine, and a non-optimizing compiler. Then we consider for both languages verification condition generators that operate on programs annotated with loop invariants and procedure specifications. In such a setting, we show that compilation preserves proof obligations, in the sense that the proof obligations generated for the source annotated program are the same that those generated for the compiled annotated program (using the same loop invariants and procedure specifications). Furthermore, we discuss the relevance of our results to Proof Carrying Code.

## 1 Introduction

### 1.1 Background and Contribution

Interactive verification techniques provide a means to guarantee that programs are correct with respect to a formal specification, and are increasingly being supported by interactive verification environments that can be used to prove the correctness of safety critical or security sensitive software. For example, interactive verification environments are being used to certify the correctness of smartcard software, both for platforms and applications.

However interactive verification environments typically operate on source code programs whereas it is clearly desirable to obtain correctness guarantees for compiled programs, especially in the context of mobile code where code consumers may not have access to the source program. Therefore it seems natural to study the relation between interactive program verification and compilation.

In this paper, we focus on the interaction between compilation and verification condition generators (VC generators), which are used in many interactive verification environments to guarantee the correctness of source programs, and by several proof carrying code (PCC) architectures to check the correctness of compiled programs. Such VC generators operate on annotated programs that

T. Dimitrakos et al. (Eds.): FAST 2005, LNCS 3866, pp. 112–126, 2006.

carry loop invariants and procedure specifications expressed as preconditions and postconditions, and yield a set of proof obligations that must be discharged in order to establish the correctness of the program.

The main technical contribution of the paper is to show in a particular setting that compilation preserves proof obligations, in the sense that the set of proof obligations generated for an annotated source code program $P$ is equal to the set of proof obligations generated for the corresponding annotated compiled program $\mathcal{C}(P)$ (we let $\mathcal{C}(.)$ be some compilation function), where annotations for $\mathcal{C}(P)$ are directly inherited from annotations in $P$. The immediate practical consequence of the equivalence is that the results of interactive source program verification (i.e. the proofs that are built interactively) can be reused for checking compiled programs, and hence that it is possible to bring the benefits of interactive program verification (at source code level) to the code consumer.

One important question is whether preservation of proof obligations can be derived from the semantical correctness of the compiler (in the sense that compiled programs have the same semantics as their source counterpart), and thus can be established independently of the exact definition of the compiler. The answer is negative: our results hold for a specific compiler that does not perform any optimization, and simple program optimizations invalidate preservation of proof obligations. We return to this point in Section 5.

Another question is the choice of the source and target languages: our source and target languages are loosely inspired from Java (e.g. we handle procedure calls differently), as our main application scenario deals with Java-enabled mobile phones.

## 1.2   Application Scenarios

In this paragraph, we propose a scenario that exploits preservation of proof obligations to bring the benefits of interactive source program verification to the code consumer. The scenario may be viewed as an instance of Proof Carrying Code (PCC) [9], from which it inherits benefits including its robustness under the code/specification being modified while transiting from producer to consumer and/or under the assumption of a malicious producer, and issues including the difficulty of expressing security policies for applications, etc.

**Scenario.** Consider a mobile phone operator that is keen of offering its customers a new service and has the possibility to do so by deploying a program $\mathcal{C}(P)$ originating from an untrusted software company. The operator is worried about the negative impact on its business if the code is malicious or simply erroneous, and wants to be given guarantees for $\mathcal{C}(P)$. For liability reasons, the operator does not want to see the source code, and for intellectual property reasons, the software company does not want to disclose its source code nor does it authorize the operator to modify the compiled code to insert additional checks.

The equivalence of proof obligations can be used to justify the following scenario: the operator provides a partial specification of the program, e.g. a precondition $\phi$ and a postcondition $\psi$ for the program **main** procedure, and requires the company to show that the program meets this partial specification. There are two possibilities: either the software company verifies directly $\mathcal{C}(P)$, which is definitely a possibility but not the most comfortable one, or thanks to preservation of proof obligations, it can also set to verify $P$, and benefits from the structured nature of modern programming languages in which we assume that $P$ has been written. To verify $P$, the software company suitably annotates the program, leading to an annotated program $P'$. Then it generates the set of proof obligations for $P'$ and discharges each proof obligation using some verification tool that produces proofs. The compiled annotated program is sent to the operator, together with the set of proof obligations and their proofs. Upon reception, the operator checks that the compiled annotated program provided by the software company matches the partial specification it formulated in the first place (here it has to check that the precondition and postcondition are unchanged), and then run its own verification condition generator, and checks with the help of the proofs provided by the software company that these proof obligations can be discharged.

Our application scenario is being considered for specific application domains, such as midlets, where operators currently dispose of a large number of GSM applications that they do not want to distribute to their customers due to a lack of confidence in the code. Of course, we do not underestimate that our approach is costly, both by the infrastructure it requires, and by the effort involved in using it (notably by involving program verification). However, the pay-off is that our approach enables to prove precisely properties of programs, i.e. in particular correct programs will not be rejected because of some automatic method which is overly conservative (i.e. rejects correct programs).

Our approach can also be used in other mobile code scenarios. Consider for example a repository of certified algorithms; the algorithms have been written in different programming languages, but they are stored in the directory as compiled programs, e.g. as CLR programs. Prior to adding a new algorithm, say an efficient algorithm to verify square root, the maintainer of the repository asks for a certificate that the algorithm indeed computes the square root. The correctness of the algorithm must be established through interactive verification, say by the implementer of the algorithm. The implementer has the choice to write a proof using a program logic for the language in which the algorithm was developed, or using an appropriate bytecode logic. Once again, it seems likely that the first approach would be favored, and therefore that proof obligation preserving compilation would be useful.

## 1.3   Related Work

There are several lines of work concerned with establishing a relation between source programs and compiled programs. The most established line of work is undoubtedly compiler verification [7], which aims at showing that a compiler preserves the semantics of programs.

A more recent line of work is translation validation, proposed by A. Pnueli, M. Siegel and E. Singerman [11], and credible compilation, proposed by M. Rinard [13], aim at showing for each individual run of the compiler that the resulting target program implements correctly the source program, i.e. has the same semantics. This is achieved by the automatic generation of invariants for each program point in the source code that must be satisfied at the corresponding program points in the source code. This technique does not allow to verify that a given specification is satisfied. Related work has also been done by X. Rival [14, 15], who uses abstract interpretation techniques to infer invariants at the source level and compile these invariants for the target level.

Our work is complementary to approaches to Proof-Carrying Code based on certifying compilation. In [10], Necula and Lee propose to focus on safety properties which can be proved automatically through an extended compiler that synthesizes annotations from the information it gathers about a program, and a checker that discharges proof obligations generated by the verification condition generator. Certifying compilers are very important for the scalability of PCC, but of course the requirement of producing certificates automatically reduces the scope of properties it can handle.

There are also some recent works on program specification and verification that involve at source level and target levels: the Spec# project [3] has defined an extension of C# with annotations and type support for nullity discrimination. Such annotated programs are then compiled (with their specifications) to extended .NET files, which can be run using the .NET platform. Specifications are checked at run-time or verified using a static checker (called Boogie). This work does not consider explicitly the relationship between source and compiled program verification (but the Spec# methodology implicitly assumes some relation between the two, otherwise letting users to specify source code and have Boogie verifying the corresponding compiled program would be meaningless). In a similar line of work, L. Burdy and M. Pavlova [5] have extended the proof environment Jack, which provides a verification condition generator for JML-annotated sequential Java programs, with a verification condition generator for extended Java class files that accommodate compiled JML annotations. However, they do not establish any formal relation between the two VC generators. Independently of this work, F. Bannwart and P. Müller [2] have considered proof compilation for a substantial fragment of sequential Java, and have discuss the translation of proofs from source code to bytecode. However, their work does not discuss automatic proof verification, neither establishes the correctness of proof compilation in their setting. None of these works discusses optimizations.

For completeness, we also mention the existence of many Hoare-like logics and weakest precondition calculi for low-level languages such as the JVM or .NET or assembly languages, see e.g. [1, 4, 8, 12, 16]; many of these works have been proposed in the context of PCC.

*Contents.* The remaining of the paper is organized as follows. Section 2 introduces syntax and annotation language, and VC generators for the assembly and source languages. Preservation of proof obligations is addressed in Section 3. Section 4 illustrates how our approach can be applied to guarantee program correctness. Finally, we conclude in Section 5 with related work and directions for future research.

## 2   Language and Proof Systems Definitions

In the sequel, we let $V$ be the set of values that are manipulated by programs (here $V = \mathbb{Z}$), and assume given a set $\mathbb{A} \subseteq V \times V \to V$ of arithmetic operations and a set $\mathbb{C} \subseteq V \times V \to \{0, 1\}$ of comparison operators. Furthermore, we assume given a set $\mathcal{M}$ of procedure names and a set $\mathcal{X}$ of program variables.

### 2.1   The Assembly Language

The assembly language SAL is a stack-based language with conditional and unconditional jumps, procedure calls and exceptions. It is powerful enough to compile the core imperative language described in Section 2.2.

SAL programs are sets of procedures with a distinguished procedure **main**. Each procedure $m$ consists of a function from its set $\mathcal{P}_m$ of program points to instructions where the set of instructions is defined in Figure 1, and of a partial function $\mathsf{Handler}_m : \mathcal{P}_m \rightharpoonup \mathcal{P}_m$ which specifies for each program point its handler, if any. We write $\mathsf{Handler}_m(l) \uparrow$ if $\mathsf{Handler}_m(l)$ is undefined, and $\mathsf{Handler}_m(l) \downarrow$ otherwise. Program states are pairs consisting of a global register map, and a stack of frames, which correspond to the execution context of a procedure, and which consist of an operand stack, a program counter and the name of the procedure being executed. The operational semantics is standard (except for assert that does not change the state, i.e. it is like a no operation instruction). Note that upon a procedure invocation, a new frame is created with an empty operand stack and with the program pointer set to 1 (the initial instruction of a procedure). As to exception handling, the intuitive meaning is that if the execution at program point $l$ in procedure $m$ raises an exception and $\mathsf{Handler}_m(l) = t$, then control is transferred to $t$ with an empty operand stack. If on the contrary $\mathsf{Handler}_m(l)$ is not defined, then the top frame is popped from the stack and the exception is transferred to the next frame.

$$
\begin{array}{llll}
instr ::= & \mathsf{prim}\ op & \text{primitive arithmetic operation} \\
& | & \mathsf{push}\ n & \text{push } n \text{ on stack} \\
& | & \mathsf{load}\ x & \text{load value of } x \text{ on stack} \\
& | & \mathsf{store}\ x & \text{store top of stack in } x \\
& | & \mathsf{if}\ cmp\ j & \text{conditional jump} \\
& | & \mathsf{goto}\ j & \text{unconditional jump} \\
& | & \mathsf{assert}\ \Phi & \text{assertion } \Phi \\
& | & \mathsf{nop} & \text{no operation} \\
& | & \mathsf{invoke}\ m & \text{procedure invocation} \\
& | & \mathsf{throw} & \text{throw an exception} \\
& | & \mathsf{return} & \text{end of program}
\end{array}
$$

where $op : \mathbb{A}$, and $cmp : \mathbb{C}$, and $x : \mathcal{X}$, and $n : V$, $j : \mathbb{N}$, $m : \mathcal{M}$ and $\Phi$ is an assertion.

**Fig. 1.** Instruction set

In the sequel, we use the successor relation $\mapsto \subseteq \mathcal{P}_m \times \mathcal{P}_m$ which relates instruction to their successors. We assume that the successor of an assert instruction always belongs to the instructions of the procedure (we need this assumption for the sake of simplicity of definition of proof obligations further on).

**Assertion language.** The assertion language is a standard-first order language that contains comparison between arithmetic expressions as base assertions, and is closed under conjunction and implication. One unusual feature of arithmetic expressions is that there are two special constants $st$ and $top$ for reasoning about the stack. The constant $top$ represents the size of the stack in the current state, while the constant $st$ can be thought of as an array used for an abstract representation of the operand stack. Thus we can refer to the elements of an array via expressions of the form $st(top - i)$. The set of arithmetic expressions is defined inductively as follows:

$$
\begin{aligned}
se &::= top \mid se - 1 \\
aexpr &::= n \mid x \mid aexpr \; op \; aexpr \mid st(se)
\end{aligned}
$$

where $op : \mathbb{A}$.

The semantics of assertions is standard, except that assertions that refer to an undefined arithmetic expression, i.e. that contain a reference to an element outside the stack bounds, are considered to be false.

The definition of the VC generator relies extensively on substitution operators. Besides the rules for substituting variables, which are standard, we also have substitution rules for $top$ and for the non-atomic expressions, namely $st(top)$ and $top - 1$.

**Well-annotated programs.** Verification condition generators compute from partially annotated programs a fully annotated program, in which all program points of each procedure of the program have an explicit precondition attached to them. VCGens are partial functions that require programs to be sufficiently annotated in the first place. We call such programs well-annotated.

The property of being well-annotated can be formalized through an induction principle that is reminiscent of the accessible fragment of a binary relation: that is, given a procedure $P_m$, a predicate $R$ on $\mathcal{P}_m$, we define **ext** $R$ inductively by the clauses: i) if $i \in R$ then $i \in$ **ext** $R$; ii) if for all $j \in \mathcal{P}_m$ such that $i \mapsto j$, we have $j \in$ **ext** $R$, then $i \in$ **ext** $R$. Informally, **ext** $R$ is the set of points from which all paths eventually arrive at $R$.

**Definition 1 (Well-annotated program).**

1. *Let* $\mathcal{P}_m^{\text{assert}}$ *and* $\mathcal{P}_m^{\text{return}}$ *be the set of program points* $i$ *such that* $P_m[i]$ *is an* assert *instruction and* return *instruction respectively. Then* $P_m$ *is a well-annotated procedure code iff* **ext** $(\mathcal{P}_m^{\text{assert}} \cup \mathcal{P}_m^{\text{return}}) = \mathcal{P}_m$.
2. *A program is well-annotated if it comes equipped with functions* $EPost :$ $\mathcal{M} \to$ Assn *and* $NPost : \mathcal{M} \to$ Assn *that give the exceptional and normal postcondition of each procedure, and a function* $Pre : \mathcal{M} \to$ Assn *which gives*

*the precondition of a procedure, preconditions and postconditions assertions
do not contain st or top, and each procedure is well-annotated.*

Given a well-annotated program, one can generate a precondition for each program
point. Indeed, the assertion at any given program point can be computed from the
assertions for all its successors; the latter may either be given initially (as part of
the partially annotated program), or have been computed previously. Note that
the definition of well-annotated program does not require programs to have any
particular structure, e.g. unlike [12], they do not rule out overlapping loops.

**Verification condition generator.** The verification condition generator for
assembly programs, $vcg_a$, is defined as a function that takes as input a well-
annotated program $P$ and returns an assertion for each program point in $P$.
This assertion represents the weakest liberal precondition that an initial state
before the execution of the corresponding program point should satisfy for the
method to terminate in a state satisfying its postcondition, that is $NPost(m)$
in case of normal termination or $EPost(m)$ in case the method terminates with
an unhandled exception.

The computation of $vcg_a$ proceeds in a modular way, i.e. procedure by procedure, and uses annotations from the procedure under consideration, as well as
the preconditions and post-conditions of procedures called by $m$. Concretely for
each program point, $vcg_a$ is defined by a case analysis on the instruction $P_m[i]$.

Its definition is given in Figure 2. Notice that we use $-2$, that does not belong
to the assertion language, instead of $-1-1$ as syntactic sugar in the definition.
After calculating $vcg_a$ of the procedure $P_m$ (w.r.t. the annotations of $P_m$), we
define the set of proof obligations $PO_m$ as

$$PO_m(P_m, NPost(m), EPost(m))$$
$$= \{\Phi_i \Rightarrow vcg_a(i+1) \mid i \in \mathcal{P}_m^{assert}\}$$
$$\cup \{NPost(m') \Rightarrow vcg_a(i+1) \mid P_m[i] = \text{invoke } m'\}$$
$$\cup \{Pre(m) \Rightarrow vcg_a(1)\} \cup \mathcal{M}_h(m) \cup \mathcal{M}_{\bar{h}}(m)$$

where

$$\mathcal{M}_h(m) = \{EPost(m') \Rightarrow vcg_a(t) \mid \quad P_m[i] = \text{invoke } m' \wedge \text{Handler}_m(i) = t\}$$
$$\mathcal{M}_{\bar{h}}(m) = \{EPost(m') \Rightarrow EPost(m) \mid \quad P_m[i] = \text{invoke } m' \wedge \text{Handler}_m(i) \uparrow\}$$

Proof obligations fall in one of the following categories:

- proof obligations that correspond to assertions in code;
- proof obligations triggered by procedure calls, where one has to verify that
  the postcondition of the invoked procedure implies the normal precondition
  computed for the program point that corresponds to the program point of
  the procedure invocation;
- the proof obligation that establishes that the normal precondition computed
  for the first program point follows from the procedure precondition;

| | |
|---|---|
| push $n$ : | $\mathrm{vcg}_a(i) = \mathrm{vcg}_a(i+1)[n/st(top), top/top - 1]$ |
| prim $op$ : | $\mathrm{vcg}_a(i) = \mathrm{vcg}_a(i+1)[st(top - 1)\ op\ st(top)/st(top), top - 1/top]$ |
| load $x$ : | $\mathrm{vcg}_a(i) = \mathrm{vcg}_a(i+1)[x/st(top), top/top - 1]$ |
| store $x$ : | $\mathrm{vcg}_a(i) = \mathrm{vcg}_a(i+1)[top - 1/top, st(top)/x]$ |
| if $cmp$ $j$ : | $\mathrm{vcg}_a(i) = st(top - 1)\ cmp\ st(top) \Rightarrow \mathrm{vcg}_a(i+j)[top - 2/top]$ |
| | $\qquad\qquad \wedge\neg(st(top - 1)\ cmp\ st(top)) \Rightarrow \mathrm{vcg}_a(i+1)[top - 2/top]$ |
| goto $j$ : | $\mathrm{vcg}_a(i) = \mathrm{vcg}_a(i+j)$ |
| assert $\Phi$ : | $\mathrm{vcg}_a(i) = \Phi,$ |
| nop : | $\mathrm{vcg}_a(i) = \mathrm{vcg}_a(i+1)$ |
| throw : | $\mathrm{vcg}_a(i) = EPost(m)$ \quad if $\mathrm{Handler}_m(i) \uparrow$ |
| throw : | $\mathrm{vcg}_a(i) = \mathrm{vcg}_a(t)$ \quad\quad if $\mathrm{Handler}_m(i) = t$ |
| invoke $m'$ : | $\mathrm{vcg}_a(i) = Pre(m')$ |
| return : | $\mathrm{vcg}_a(i) = NPost(m)$ |

**Fig. 2.** Verification condition generator for SAL procedures

- proof obligations triggered by procedure calls for the case that such calls raise an exception that is handled by the procedure $m$. Here one has to verify that the exceptional postcondition of $m$ implies the normal precondition computed for the handler of the program point where procedure invocation occurs;
- proof obligations triggered by procedure calls for the case that such calls raise an exception that is not handled by the procedure $m$. Here one has to verify that the exceptional postcondition of the procedure called implies the exceptional postcondition of $m$.

We define the set of proof obligation of a program as the union of the proof obligations of all its methods:

$$PO(P) = \bigcup_{m \in \mathcal{M}} PO_m(P_m, NPost(m), EPost(m))$$

One can prove that the verification condition generator is sound, in the sense that if the program $P$ is called with registers set to values that verify the precondition of the procedure main, and $P$ terminates normally, then the final state will verify the normal postcondition of main. Likewise, if $P$ terminates abnormally, that is if an exception is thrown and there is no handler, then the final state will verify the exceptional postcondition of main. Soundness is proved first for one step of execution, and then extended to execution traces by induction on the length of the execution.

## 2.2 Source Language

The source language IMP is an imperative language with loops and conditionals, procedures and exceptions.

**Definition 2.** *1. The set* AExpr *of arithmetic expressions, and* AProg$_{IMP}$ *of commands are given by the following syntaxes:*

*expr*      $::= x \mid n \mid expr \; op \; expr$
*cmpexpr* $::= expr \; cmp \; expr$
*comm*    $::=$ skip $\mid x := expr \mid comm; comm \mid$ while $\{I\}$ *cmpexpr* do *comm* $\mid$
            if *cmpexpr* then *comm* else *comm*$\mid$try *comm* catch *comm* $\mid$
            throw $\mid$ call $m$

*where op and cmp are as in Section 2.1 and I is an assertion as defined in Section 2.1, but without the constants top and st.*

2. *We define a program P in* IMP *as a set of procedures (we use m to name a procedure), and their corresponding bodies, which are a command from* AProg$_{IMP}$ *(we use P$_m$ to name a procedure code).*

We define a standard verification condition generator vcg, which takes as input a command and an assertion, and returns an assertion. The function is implicitly parameterized by assertions; concretely, we assume that all procedures are annotated with a precondition, a normal postcondition, and an exceptional postcondition.

$$
\begin{aligned}
&\mathsf{vcg}(\mathsf{skip}, Q, R) = Q \\
&\mathsf{vcg}(x := e, Q, R) = Q[e/x] \\
&\mathsf{vcg}(c_1; c_2, Q, R) = \mathsf{vcg}(c_1, \mathsf{vcg}(c_2, Q, R), R) \\
&\mathsf{vcg}(\mathsf{while} \; \{I\} \; e \; \mathsf{do} \; c_1, Q, R) = I \\
&\mathsf{vcg}(\mathsf{if} \; e_1 \; cmp \; e_2 \; \mathsf{then} \; c_1 \; \mathsf{else} \; c_2, Q, R) = \\
&\hspace{4cm} (e_1 \; cmp \; e_2) \Rightarrow \mathsf{vcg}(c_1, Q, R) \wedge \\
&\hspace{4cm} \neg(e_1 \; cmp \; e_2) \Rightarrow \mathsf{vcg}(c_2, Q, R) \\
&\mathsf{vcg}(\mathsf{try} \; c \; \mathsf{catch} \; c', Q, R) = \mathsf{vcg}(c, Q, \mathsf{vcg}(c', Q, R)) \\
&\mathsf{vcg}(\mathsf{throw}, Q, R) = R \\
&\mathsf{vcg}(\mathsf{call} \; m', Q, R) = Pre(m')
\end{aligned}
$$

**Fig. 3.** Verification condition generator for *IMP* procedures

We also define inductively the set $PO_c$ of proof obligations for a command as follows:

$$
\begin{aligned}
&PO_c(\mathsf{skip}, Q, R) = \emptyset \\
&PO_c(x := e, Q, R) = \emptyset \\
&PO_c(c_1; c_2, Q, R) = PO_c(c_1, \mathsf{vcg}(c_2, Q, R), R) \cup PO_c(c_2, Q, R) \\
&PO_c(\mathsf{while} \; \{I\} \; e \; \mathsf{do} \; c_1, Q, R) = \\
&\hspace{2cm} PO_c(c_1, Q, R) \cup \{I \Rightarrow (e \Rightarrow \mathsf{vcg}(c_1, I, R) \wedge \neg e \Rightarrow Q)\} \\
&PO_c(\mathsf{if} \; e_1 \; cmp \; e_2 \; \mathsf{then} \; c_1 \; \mathsf{else} \; c_2, Q, R) = \\
&\hspace{4cm} PO_c(c_1, Q, R) \cup PO_c(c_2, Q, R) \\
&PO_c(\mathsf{throw}, Q, R) = \emptyset \\
&PO_c(\mathsf{call} \; m', Q, R) = \{EPost(m') \Rightarrow R\} \cup \{NPost(m') \Rightarrow Q\} \\
&PO_c(\mathsf{try} \; c \; \mathsf{catch} \; c', Q, R) = PO_c(c, Q, \mathsf{vcg}(c', Q, R)) \cup PO_c(c', Q, R)
\end{aligned}
$$

As in SAL, proof obligations fall in one of the following categories:

- proof obligations that correspond to annotations in while loops;
- proof obligations triggered by procedure calls,
- proof obligations triggered by procedure calls for the case that such calls raise an exception that is handled by the procedure $m$.

We define for every procedure $m$ with body $c$, the set of proof obligations $PO_m(c, NPost(m), EPost(m))$ as:

$$PO_c(c, NPost(m), EPost(m)) \cup$$
$$\{Pre(m) \Rightarrow \mathsf{vcg}(c, NPost(m), EPost(m))\}$$

That is, the proof obligations of a method are those generated by the body of the methods plus the proof obligation that establishes that the precondition computed for the body of the methods follows from the procedure precondition.

Finally, the set of proof obligation for a program $P$ is defined as the union of proof obligations for each method in $P$:

$$PO(P) = \bigcup_{m \in \mathcal{M}} PO_m(P_m, NPost(m), EPost(m))$$

## 3   Proof Obligations Preserving Compilation

This section shows that the sets of proof obligations are preserved by a standard non-optimizing compiler. The consequence of this result is that having annotations and proofs of proof obligations for the source code, the same evidence can be used to prove automatically the correctness of its corresponding compiled program.

**Definition 3.** *The compilation function $\mathcal{C}_p : \mathsf{AProg}_{IMP} \rightarrow \mathsf{AProg}_{SAL}$ is defined in Figure 4, using an auxiliary function $\mathcal{C}_e : \mathsf{AExpr} \rightarrow \mathsf{AProg}_{SAL}$ (also defined in Figure 4), and another auxiliary function to define exception tables (defined in Figure 5).*

The compilation of exception tables defines handlers for program points of instructions enclose in the "try" part of try-catch commands as the first program point of the code enclose in their "catch" part.

Throughout this section, we use $\mathsf{vcg}(p, Q, R)$ to denote both verification condition generator at source code and bytecode. For the bytecode, $\mathsf{vcg}(p, Q, R)$ is $\mathsf{vcg}_a(i)$ where the normal and exceptional postconditions are $Q$ and $R$ resp. and where $i$ is the first program point in $p$.

We begin with an auxiliary lemma about expressions. Given a list $P$ of instructions, we use the notation $P[i...j]$ to denote the list of instructions from instruction at $i$ up to $j$.

**Lemma 1.** *Let $e$ be an arithmetic expression in $\mathsf{AExpr}$ which appears in program $P$, and suppose that we have that $\mathcal{C}_e(e) = \mathcal{C}_c(P)[i...j]$. Let $Q$ be an assertion in $\mathsf{Assn}$ that includes an arithmetic expression $st(top)$. Assume $\mathsf{vcg}_a(j+1) = Q$. Then $\mathsf{vcg}(i) = Q[e/st(top), top/top-1]$.*

$$\mathcal{C}_e(x) = \text{load } x$$
$$\mathcal{C}_e(n) = \text{push } n$$
$$\mathcal{C}_e(e \text{ } op \text{ } e') = \mathcal{C}_e(e) :: \mathcal{C}_e(e') :: \text{prim } op$$
$$\mathcal{C}_c(\text{skip}) = \text{nop}$$
$$\mathcal{C}_c(x := e) = \mathcal{C}_e(e) :: \text{store } x$$
$$\mathcal{C}_c(c_1; \text{ } c_2) = \mathcal{C}_c(c_1) :: \mathcal{C}_c(c_2)$$
$$\mathcal{C}_c(\text{while } \{I\} \text{ } e_1 \text{ } cmp \text{ } e_2 \text{ do } c) = \text{let } \text{ } l_1 = \mathcal{C}_e(e_1); l_2 = \mathcal{C}_e(e_2); l_3 = \mathcal{C}_c(c); x = \#l_3;$$
$$y = \#l_1 + \#l_2 \text{ in goto } (\#l_3 + 1) :: l_3 ::$$
$$\text{assert } I :: l_2 :: l_1 :: \text{if } cmp \text{ } (pc - x - y)$$
$$\mathcal{C}_c(\text{if } e_1 \text{ } cmp \text{ } e_2 \text{ then } c_1 \text{ else } c_2) = \text{let } \text{ } l_e = \mathcal{C}_e(e_1) :: \mathcal{C}_e(e_2); lc_1 = \mathcal{C}_c(c_1); lc_2 = \mathcal{C}_c(c_2);$$
$$x = \#lc_2; y = \#lc_1 \text{ in } l_e :: \text{if } cmp \text{ } (pc + x + 2) :: lc_2$$
$$:: \text{goto } (y + 1) :: lc_1$$
$$\mathcal{C}_c(\text{call } m'((e))) = \mathcal{C}_e((e)) :: \text{invoke } m'$$
$$\mathcal{C}_c(\text{throw}) = \text{throw}$$

$$\mathcal{C}_c(\text{try } c_1 \text{ catch } c_2) = \text{let } lc_1 = \mathcal{C}_c(c_1); lc_2 = \mathcal{C}_c(c_2);$$
$$x = \#lc_2; \text{ in}$$
$$lc_1 :: \text{goto } (x + 1) :: lc_2$$

**Fig. 4.** Compiling IMP to SAL

$$\mathcal{X}(c_1; \text{ } c_2) = \mathcal{X}(c_1) :: \mathcal{X}(c_2)$$

$$\mathcal{X}(\text{while } e \text{ do } c) = \mathcal{X}(c)$$

$$\mathcal{X}(\text{if } e \text{ then } c_1 \text{ else } c_2) = \mathcal{X}(c_1) :: \mathcal{X}(c_2);$$

$$\mathcal{X}(\text{try } c_1 \text{ catch } c_2) = \text{let } \text{ } lc_1 = \mathcal{C}_c(c_1); lc_2 = \mathcal{C}_c(c_2);$$
$$x = \#lc_1; \text{ in}$$
$$\mathcal{X}(c_1) :: \mathcal{X}(c_2) :: \langle 1, x + 1, x + 2 \rangle$$

$$\mathcal{X}(\_) = \epsilon$$

**Fig. 5.** Definition of exception tables

The following lemma states that if there exists a handler $c'$ at source level for a command $c$, then any exception thrown in the compilation of $c$ will have a handler that corresponds to the compilation of $c'$.

**Lemma 2 (Handler Preserving Compiler).** *Let command* try $c$ catch $c'$ *s.t. it is the inner-most try-catch command enclosing $c$ and let $P_m[i \ldots j] = \mathcal{C}_c(c)$ and $P_m[i' \ldots j'] = \mathcal{C}_c(c')$ be compilations of $c$ and $c'$. Then for any $h \in \{i \ldots j\}$ that can throw an exception in $P_m$, $\text{Handler}_m(h) = i'$ and if $c$ is not enclosed in a try-catch command $\text{Handler}_m(h) \uparrow$.*

The following proposition establishes that compilation "commutes" with verification condition generation.

**Proposition 1.** $\mathsf{vcg}(\mathcal{C}_c(c), Q, R) = \mathsf{vcg}(c, Q, R)$

The following theorem claims that the set of proof obligations of the original program are the same of the proof obligations generated after compilation.

**Theorem 1 (Proof Obligation Preserving Compilation).**

$$PO_m(\mathcal{C}_c(c), Q, R) = PO_m(c, Q, R)$$

## 4 Example

The purpose of this section is to illustrate how the application scenario from the introduction can be applied to guarantee that compiled applications meet high-level security properties, such as the absence of uncaught exceptions, as well as specific security properties, such as non-interference; the latter is encoded in our language using self-composition as described in [6]. Here the operator will determine which program variables (in a more realistic language one would focus on method parameters) of the program $P$ to be certified are to be considered confidential. In turn, this choice sets the precondition and the postcondition, namely $\boldsymbol{x} = \boldsymbol{x}'$, where $\boldsymbol{x}$ are the low variables of $P$, and $\boldsymbol{x}'$ is a renaming of the low variables of $P$. Suppose in addition that the operator does not want the program to raise uncaught exceptions. Then the code producer must establish

$$\{\boldsymbol{x} = \boldsymbol{x}'\}P; P'\{\boldsymbol{x} = \boldsymbol{x}', \texttt{false}\}$$

where $P'$ is a renaming of $P$ with fresh variables $\boldsymbol{x}'$ for low variables, and $\boldsymbol{y}'$ for high-variables. False as the exceptional postcondition denotes that an exception should not be thrown. To make matter precise, consider that $P$ is the program constituted of two procedures main and aux that take one public parameter $x$ and one private parameter $y$, with main and aux defined as

$$\begin{aligned} \mathsf{main} &== x := y; \ \mathsf{call} \ \mathsf{aux} \\ \mathsf{aux} &== x := 3; \ \mathsf{while} \ x \geq 1 \ \mathsf{do} \ y := y * x; x := x - 1 \end{aligned}$$

(Note that the program is non-interfering, since it always return with $x = 0$. However, the program is typically rejected by a type system.)

In order to prove the required properties, the software company must provide appropriate precondition and postcondition for the method aux, as well as appropriate loop invariants, and discharge the resulting proof obligations for the program **verif** defined as

$$\mathsf{verif} == x := y; \ \mathsf{call} \ \mathsf{aux}; \ x' := y'; \ \mathsf{call} \ \mathsf{aux}'$$

The annotated program is given in Figure 6, where we use red to denote the specification provided by the operator, and green to denote the specification provided by the software company. We denote with blue the set of proof obligations. In Figure 7, we show the annotated compiled program.

$\{x = x'\}$verif $== x := y;$ call aux; $x' := y';$ call aux$'$
$\{x = x', false\}$

$\{true\}$
aux $== x := 3;$ while $\{0 \leq x\}$ $x \geq 1$ do $y := y * x; x := x - 1$
$\{x = 0, false\}$

$\{x = 0\}$
aux$'$ $== x' := 3;$ while $\{0 \leq x' \wedge x = 0\}x' \geq 1$ do $y' := y' * x'; x' := x' - 1$
$\{x = 0 \wedge x' = 0, false\}$

Proof Obligations for main:
$x = x' \Rightarrow true$
$false \Rightarrow false, \ x = 0 \Rightarrow x = 0$
$false \Rightarrow false \ x = 0 \wedge x' = 0 \Rightarrow x = x'$

Proof Obligations for aux:
$true \Rightarrow 0 \leq 3$
$0 \leq x \Rightarrow (x \geq 1 \Rightarrow 0 \leq x - 1 \wedge x < 1 \Rightarrow x = 0)$

Proof Obligations for aux':
$x = 0 \Rightarrow 0 \leq 3 \wedge x = 0$
$0 \leq x' \wedge x = 0 \Rightarrow (x' \geq 1 \Rightarrow 0 \leq x' - 1 \wedge x = 0 \wedge x < 1 \Rightarrow x = 0 \wedge x' = 0)$

**Fig. 6.** Example: Program with specification of Non-Interference

Precondition $x = x'$

| $i$ | $P[i]$ | $vcg_a(i)$ |
|---|---|---|
| 1 | load y | true |
| 2 | store x | true |
| 3 | invoke aux | true |
| 4 | load y' | x =0 |
| 5 | store x' | x = 0 |
| 6 | invoke aux' | x =0 |
| 7 | return | x =x' |

$PO_{main}$ :
$x = x' \Rightarrow true$
$false \Rightarrow false, \ x = 0 \Rightarrow x = 0$
$false \Rightarrow false \ x = 0 \wedge x' = 0 \Rightarrow x = x'$

Posts    $x = x', false$

**Fig. 7.** Compilation of the Example (main procedure)

# 5    Concluding Remarks

This paper shows, in a simple context, that it is possible to transfer evidence of program correctness from a source program to its compiled counterpart. Furthermore, we have shown on simple examples the possible uses of our results, and discussed some possible application domains. Although not reported here, we have also implemented a small prototype compiler and proof obligation generators to experiment our approach small examples.

We now intend to extend our results to (non-optimizing compilers for) programming languages such as Java and C#. Furthermore, we intend to extend our results to optimizing compilers. However, preservation of proof obligations may be destroyed by simple program optimizations. If we allow optimizations, it is necessary to focus on a more general property that involves an explicit representation of proofs.

*Property of Proof Compilation.* For every annotated program $P$, a proof compiler is given by:

- a function $f$ that gives for every proof obligation at the assembly level a corresponding proof obligation at the source level;
- a function that transforms, for every proof obligation $\xi$ at the assembly level, proofs of $f(\xi)$ into proofs of $\xi$.

Proof compilation is a generalization of preservation of proof obligations and allows to bring the benefits of source code verification to code consumers. Like preservation of proof obligations, it is tied to a specific compiler; additionally, it is tied to a representation of proofs (although some degree of generality is possible here).

Preliminary investigations indicate that proof compilation is feasible for most common program optimizations. These results will be reported elsewhere.

Furthermore, we would like to explore further scenarios in which proof compilation could be used advantageously. We only mention two particularly interesting scenarios: the compilation of aspect-oriented programming, and the compilation of domain-specific languages DSLs into general purpose programs. The latter application domain seems particularly relevant since one could hope to exploit the features of DSLs to achieve easy proofs at the source code level.

Another item for future work is an evaluation of the usefulness of preservation of proof obligations and proof compilation on larger case studies. In the short term, the most promising application of our technique concerns high-level security properties that are often found in security policies for mobile applications; many of such properties are either recommended internally by the security experts to developers, or by external companies with strong security expertise (e.g. some certification authority) to solution providers (e.g. our telecom operator in the scenario of Subsection 1.2). In the longer term, it would be interesting to investigate the applicability of our method to the problem of performing dynamic updates of mobile devices infrastructures; indeed, such a scenario will probably require to establish that components behave according to their specification.

*Acknowledgments.* We thank Benjamin Grégoire, César Kunz, Dante Zanarini and the anonymous referees for valuable comments on a preliminary version of this paper. This work was partially supported by the Estonian-French cooperation program Parrot, the EU projects APPSEM II, eVikings II, and INSPIRED, the Estonian Science Foundation grant no 5567, and the French ACI Sécurité SPOPS.

# References

1. D. Aspinall, S. Gilmore, M. Hofmann, D. Sannella, and I. Stark. Mobile Resource Guarantees for Smart Devices. In G. Barthe, L. Burdy, M. Huisman, J.-L. Lanet, and T. Muntean, editors, *Proceedings of CASSIS'04*, volume 3362 of *Lecture Notes in Computer Science*, pages 1–27, 2005.
2. F. Bannwart and P. Müller. A program logic for bytecode. In F. Spoto, editor, *Proceedings of Bytecode'05*, Electronic Notes in Theoretical Computer Science. Elsevier Publishing, 2005.
3. M. Barnett, K.R.M. Leino, and W. Schulte. The spec# programming system: An overview. In G. Barthe, L. Burdy, M. Huisman, J.-L. Lanet, and T. Muntean, editors, *Proceeings of CASSIS'04*, volume 3362 of *Lecture Notes in Computer Science*, pages 50–71. Springer-Verlag, 2005.
4. N. Benton. A typed logic for stacks and jumps. Manuscript, 2004.
5. L. Burdy and M. Pavlova. Java bytecode specification and verification. In *Proceedings of SAC'06*, 2006. To appear.
6. P. D'Argenio G. Barthe and T. Rezk. Secure information flow by self-composition. In R. Foccardi, editor, *Proceedings of CSFW'04*, pages 100–114. IEEE Press, 2004.
7. Joshua D. Guttman and Mitchell Wand. Special issue on VLISP. *Lisp and Symbolic Computation*, 8(1/2), March 1995.
8. N.A. Hamid and Z. Shao. Interfacing hoare logic and type systems for foundational proof-carrying code. In K. Slind, A. Bunker, and G. Gopalakrishnan, editors, *Proceedings of TPHOLs'04*, volume 3223 of *Lecture Notes in Computer Science*, pages 118–135. Springer-Verlag, 2004.
9. G.C. Necula. Proof-Carrying Code. In *Proceedings of POPL'97*, pages 106–119. ACM Press, 1997.
10. G.C. Necula and P. Lee. The Design and Implementation of a Certifying Compiler. In *Proceedings of PLDI'98*, pages 333–344, 1998.
11. A. Pnueli, E. Singerman, and M. Siegel. Translation validation. In B. Steffen, editor, *Proceedings of TACAS'98*, volume 1384 of *Lecture Notes in Computer Science*, pages 151–166. Springer-Verlag, 1998.
12. C.L. Quigley. A Programming Logic for Java Bytecode Programs. In D. Basin and B. Wolff, editors, *Proceedings of TPHOLs'03*, volume 2758, pages 41–54, 2003.
13. M. Rinard. Credible compilation. Manuscript, 1999.
14. X. Rival. Abstract Interpretation-Based Certification of Assembly Code. In L.D. Zuck, P.C. Attie, A.Cortesi, and S. Mukhopadhyay, editors, *Proceedings of VM-CAI'03*, volume 2575 of *Lecture Notes in Computer Science*, pages 41–55, 2003.
15. X. Rival. Symbolic Transfer Functions-based Approaches to Certified Compilation. In *Proceedings of POPL'04*, pages 1–13. ACM Press, 2004.
16. M. Wildmoser and T. Nipkow. Asserting bytecode safety. In S. Sagiv, editor, *Proceedings of ESOP'05*, volume 1210 of *Lecture Notes in Computer Science*. Springer-Verlag, 2005.

# A Logic for Analysing Subterfuge in Delegation Chains

Hongbin Zhou and Simon N. Foley

Department of Computer Science,
University College Cork, Ireland
{zhou, s.foley}@cs.ucc.ie

**Abstract.** Trust Management is an approach to construct and interpret the trust relationships among public-keys that are used to mediate security-critical actions. Cryptographic credentials are used to specify delegation of authorisation among public keys. Existing trust management schemes are operational in nature, defining security in terms of specific controls such as delegation chains, threshold schemes, and so forth. However, they tend not to consider whether a particular authorisation policy is well designed in the sense that a principle cannot somehow bypass the intent of a complex series of authorisation delegations via some unexpected circuitous route.

In this paper we consider the problem of *authorisation subterfuge*, whereby, in a poorly designed system, delegation chains that are used by principals to prove authorisation may not actually reflect the original intention of all of the participants in the chain. A logic is proposed that provides a systematic way of determining whether a particular delegation scheme using particular authorisation is sufficiently robust to be able to withstand attempts at subterfuge. This logic provides a new characterisation of certificate reduction that, we argue, is more appropriate to open systems.

## 1 Introduction

Many commercial access control systems are closed and tend to rely on centralised authorisation policy/servers. An access control decision corresponds to determining whether some authenticated user has been authorised for the requested operation. This strategy of first determining who the user is and then whether that user is authorised has its critics, citing, for instance, single point of failure, scalability issues and excessive administrative overhead. A perhaps overlooked advantage of this approach is that administrators exercise tight control when granting access. The administrators are familiar with all of the resources that are available and they make sure that the user gets the appropriate permissions; no more and no less. The opportunity to subvert the intentions of a good administrator is usually small.

Cryptographic authorisation certificates bind authorisations to public keys and facilitate a decentralised approach to access control in open systems. Trust

T. Dimitrakos et al. (Eds.): FAST 2005, LNCS 3866, pp. 127–141, 2006.

Management [15, 5, 9, 16, 1, 6] is an approach to constructing and interpreting the trust relationships among public-keys that are used to mediate access control. Authorisation certificates are used to specify delegation of authorisation among public keys. Determining authorisation in these systems typically involves determining whether the available certificates can prove that the key that signed a request is authorised for the requested action.

However, these approaches do not consider how the authorisation was obtained. They do not consider whether a principal can somehow bypass the intent of a complex series of authorisation delegations via some unexpected circuitous but authorised route. In an open system no individual has a complete picture of all the resources and services that are available. Unlike the administrator of the closed system, the principals of an open system are often ordinary users and are open to confusion and subterfuge when interacting with resources and services. These users may inadvertently delegate un-intended authorisation to recipients.

In this paper, we further explore the problem of *authorisation subterfuge* [14], whereby, in a poorly designed system, delegation chains that are used by principals to prove authorisation may not actually reflect the original intention of all of the participants in the chain. For example, the intermediate principals of a delegation chain may inadvertently issue incorrect certificates, when the intended resource owner is unclear to intermediate participants in the chain. Existing Trust Management approaches such as [1, 9, 16] avoid this issue by assuming that all certificates are correctly in place, well understood by principals, and may not be improperly used.

However, we argue that subterfuge is a realistic problem that should addressed in a certificate scheme. For example, the payment systems [2, 3, 12] are vulnerable to authorisation subterfuge (leading to a breakdown in authorisation accountability) if care is not taken to properly identify the 'permissions' indicating the payment authorisations when multiple banks and/or provisioning agents are possible. In open systems, a permission for a resource should be uniquely related back to the resource owner, and this relationship should be understood by all related principals. If it is not well understood, then it may be subject to authorisation subterfuge. Therefore, authorisation in open systems should involve determining whether the available certificates can prove that the key that signed a request was intentionally authorised for the service.

In this paper we propose the Subterfuge Logic (SL) which can be used for analysing authorisation subterfuge. The logic is used to determine whether an authorisation through a delegation chain can be uniquely related to its intended resource and the resource owner.

The paper is organised as follows. In Section 2 we describe a series of subterfuge attacks that can be carried out on certificate chains. Section 3 explores similarities between these attacks on certificates and replay attacks on authentication protocols. Analysing a collection of certificates for potential subterfuge is not unlike checking whether it is possible for an 'intruder' to interfere with a certificate chain. Section 4 proposes the Subterfuge logic which can be used to determine whether performing a delegation operation might leave the delegator open to subterfuge. Examples from Section 2 are analysed in Section 5 and Section 6 illustrates how subterfuge can also arise in local naming. Finally, we conclude in Section 7.

## 2    Authorisation Subterfuge

### 2.1    SPKI/SDSI Authorisation

SPKI/SDSI [9] relies on the cryptographic argument that a public key provides a globally unique identifier that can be used to refer to its owner in some way. However, public keys are not particularly meaningful to users and, therefore, SPKI/SDSI provides local names which provide a consistent scheme for naming keys relative to one another. For example, the local name that Alice uses for Bob is (Alice's Verisign's Bob), which refers to Bob's public key as certified by the Versign that Alice knows. By binding local names to public keys with name certificates, principals may delegate their authorisation to others beyond their locality through a chain of local relationships.

A SPKI/SDSI name certificate is denoted as (K, A, S), where: K specifies the certificate issuer's signature key, and identifier A is defined as the local name for the subject S. For example, $(K_B, \text{Alice}, K_A)$ indicates that $K_B$ refers to $K_A$ using the local name Alice. A SPKI/SDSI authorisation certificate is denoted as (K, S, d, T), where: K specifies the certificate issuer's signature key; tag T is the authorisation delegated to subject S (by K) and d is the delegation bit (0/1). For example, $K_B$ delegates authorisation $T$ to Alice by signing $(K_B, \text{Alice}, 0, T)$, where 0 indicates no further delegation. Note that for the sake of simplicity, in this paper, we do not include a validity period V in certificates.

Authorisation tags are specified as s-expressions. For example, Example 2.6 in [10] specifies tag T1= tag (purchase(*range le <amount>),(*set <<items>>)) such that it

> "[...] might indicate permission to issue a purchase order. The amount of the purchase order is limited by the second element of the (purchase) S-expression and, optionally, a list of purchasable items is given as the third element. The company whose purchase orders are permitted to be signed here will appear in the certificate permission chain leading to the final purchase order. Specifically, that company's key will be the issuer at the head of the (purchase). [...]" [10]

### 2.2    Authorisation Examples

A company *ComA* permits its manager *Emily* to issue purchase orders, and *Emily* may also delegate this right to others. Having received a certificate from *ComA*, *Emily* delegates this right (issuing a purchase order) to an employee *Bob* via *Alice*. We have the following certificates: $C_1=(K_{ComA}, K_{Emily}, 1, T1)$; $C_2=(K_{Emily}, K_{Alice}, 1, T1)$, and $C_3=(K_{Alice}, K_{Bob}, 0, T1)$ (*Alice* delegates this right to employee *Bob*, But *Bob* may not delegate this right to others).

$$CC_1 : K_{ComA} \xrightarrow{C_1} K_{Emily} \xrightarrow{C_2} K_{Alice} \xrightarrow{C_3} K_{Bob}$$

$$CC_2 : K_{ComB} \xrightarrow{C_4} K_{Clark} \xrightarrow{C_5} K_{Alice} \xrightarrow{C_6} K_{David}$$

(a) certificate chain $CC_1$ and $CC_2$

(b) delegation graph for T1

**Fig. 1.** Certificates in a Scenario

Suppose that there is another company $ComB$ which also uses the tag T1 to issue purchase orders. Suppose that Alice also works for $ComB$. Clark, a senior manager in $ComB$, holds the right to issue purchase orders, and delegates this right to Alice. $ComB$ employee David accepts authority from Alice to issue purchase orders. We have certificates: $C_4=(K_{ComB}, K_{Clark}, 1, T1)$; $C_5=(K_{Clark}, K_{Alice}, 1, T1)$, and $C_6=(K_{Alice}, K_{David}, 0, T1)$. Figure 1 depicts the certificate chains $CC_1$ and $CC_2$ that Bob and David respectively use to prove authority to issue purchase orders.

## 2.3   Authorisation Subterfuge

The examples above are effective when separate chains $CC_1$ and $CC_2$ are used to prove authorisation. However, their combination, depicted in Figure 1(b), result in further delegation chains $CC_3$ and $CC_4$ and these lead to some surprising interpretations of how the authorisation was acquired.

$$CC_3 : K_{ComA} \xrightarrow{C_1} K_{Emily} \xrightarrow{C_2} K_{Alice} \xrightarrow{C_6} K_{David}$$

$$CC_4 : K_{ComB} \xrightarrow{C_3} K_{Clark} \xrightarrow{C_4} K_{Alice} \xrightarrow{C_5} K_{Bob}$$

**Subterfuge 1: passive attack.** Alice's intention, when she signed $C_6$, was that David should use chain $CC_2$ as proof of authorisation when making purchases. However, unknown to Alice, dishonest David collects all other certificates and uses the chain $CC_3$ as his proof of authorisation.

This confusion may introduce problems if the certificate chains that are used to prove authorisation are also used to provide evidence of who should be billed for the transaction. In delegating, Alice believes that chain $CC_2$ (from $ComB$) provides the appropriate accountability for Clark's authorisation.

**Subterfuge 2: outer-active attack.** The above passive attack can be transformed into a more active attack. David sets up a shelf company $ComB$ with

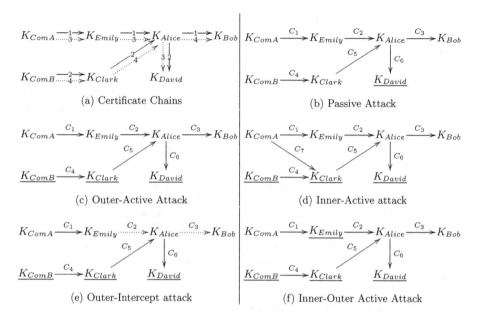

**Fig. 2.** Attack graphs

fictitious employee Clark. Using attractive benefits, David masquerading as Clark, lures Alice to join *ComB*. Clark delegates authorisations (T1) to Alice that correspond to authorisation already held by Alice. However, Alice does not realize this and, in the confusion, further delegates the authorisation to David; an authorisation from *ComA* that normally he would not be expected to hold.

In both of these cases we think of Alice as more *confused* in her delegation actions rather than incompetent; the permission naming scheme influences her local beliefs and it was the inadequacy of this scheme that led to her confusion. Perhaps Alice has too many certificates to manage and in the confusion looses track of which permissions should be associated with which keys.

*ComA* may attack *ComB* in the same way to get the money back by $CC_4$. However, if *ComB* updates its certificate, then Alice does not hold the right for *ComB* and *ComA* cannot get its money back.

**Subterfuge 3: inner-active attack.** Clark is a manager in *ComA* and *ComB* and colludes with David (*ComB* employee). Clark delegates authorisation T1 legitimately obtained from *ComB* to Alice. However, suppose that unknown to Alice, Clark is coincidentally authorised to do T1 by *ComA* (via $C_7$) and Clark intercepts the issuing of credential $C_1$ and conceals it. Alice delegates what she believes to be T1 from *ComB* to David via $C_6$. However, David can present chain $[C_7; C_5; C_6]$ as proof that his authorisation originated from *ComA*.

The above authorisation subterfuge may be avoided if Alice is very careful about how she delegates. However the following attacks are a bit more difficult for Alice to avoid.

**Subterfuge 4: (outer-intercept attack).** Clark intercepts certificate $C_2$ and conceals it. When delegating authorisation to David, Alice believes that the chain is $[C_4; C_5; C_6]$ from $ComB$, however David knowingly or unknowingly uses a different chain $[C_1; C_2; C_6]$.

**Subterfuge 5: (inner-outer active attack).** Alice has a legitimate expectation that so long as she delegates competently then she should not be liable for any confusion that is a result of poor system/permission design. Alice can use this view to act dishonestly. In signing a certificate she can always deny knowledge of the existence of other certificates and the inadequacy of permission naming in order to avoid accountability. While Alice secretly owns company $ComB$, she claims that he cannot be held accountable for the 'confusion' when Bob (an employee of $ComA$) uses the delegation chain $[C_4; C_5; C_3]$ to place an order for Alice.

## 2.4   Avoiding Subterfuge: Accounting for Authorisation

The underlying problem with the examples in the previous section is that the permission T1 is not sufficiently precise to permit Alice to distinguish the authorisations that are issued by different principals. An ad-hoc strategy to avoid this problem would be to ensure that each permission is sufficiently detailed to avoid any ambiguity in the sense that it is clear from whom the authorisation originated. This provides a form of accountability for the authorisation. For example, including a company name as part of the permission may help avoid the vulnerabilities in the particular example above.

However, at what point can a principal be absolutely sure that an ad-hoc reference to a permission is sufficiently complete? Achieving this requires an ability to be able to fix a permission within a global context, that is, to have some form of global identifier and/or reference for the permission.

Public keys provide globally unique identifiers that are tied to the owner of the key. These can also be used to avoid permission ambiguity within delegation chains. For example, given authorisation certificate $(K_{ComA}, K_E, 1, [T1.K_{ComA}])$, there can be no possibility of subterfuge when Emily delegates to Alice with $(K_E, K_A, 1, [T1.K_{ComA}])$. In this case the authorisation $[T1.K_{ComA}]$ is globally unique and the certificate makes the intention of the delegation and where it came from (authorisation accountability) very clear.

SPKI [9] characterises the checking of authorisation as *"is principal X authorised to do Y?"*. However, the examples above illustrate that this is not sufficient; we argue that checking *"is principal X authorised to do Y by Y's owner Z?"* would be more appropriate.

Needless to say that this strategy does assume a high degree of competence on Alice's part to be able to properly distinguish between permissions $[T1.K_{ComA}]$ and $[T1.K_{ComB}]$, where, for instance, each public key could be 342 characters long (using a common ASCII encoding for a 2048 bit RSA key). One might be tempted to use SDSI-like local names to make this task more manageable for Alice. However, in order to prevent subterfuge, permissions require a name that is unique across all name spaces where it will be used, not just the local name space of Alice. In Alice's local name space the permission [T1.*(Emily's ComA)*] may refer to a different *ComA* to the *ComA* that Alice knows.

Another possible source of suitable identifiers is a global X500-style naming service (if it could be built) that would tie global identities to real world entities, which would in turn be used within permissions. However, X500-style naming approaches suffer from a variety of practical problems [7] when used to keep track of the identities of principals. In the context of subterfuge, a principal might easily be confused between the (non-unique) common name and the global distinguished name contained within a permission that used such identifiers.

Certificate chains have been used in the literature to support degrees of accountability of authorisation, for example, [3, 12, 2]. The micro-billing scheme [3] uses KeyNote to help determine whether a micro-check (a KeyNote credential, signed by a customer) should be trusted and accepted as payment by a merchant. The originator of the chain is the provisioning agent, who is effectively responsible for ensuring that the transaction is paid for. In [12], delegation credentials are used to manage the transfer of micro-payment contracts between public keys; delegation chains provide evidence of contract transfer and ensure accountability for double-spending. These systems are vulnerable to authorisation subterfuge (leading to a breakdown in authorisation accountability) if care is not taken to properly identify the 'permissions' indicating the payment authorisations when multiple banks and/or provisioning agents are possible.

## 3    Subterfuge in Satan's Computer

Authorisation subterfuge is possible when one cannot precisely account for how an authorisation is held. In signing a certificate, we assume that the signer is in some way willing to account for the authorisation that they are delegating. The authorisation provided by a certificate chain that is not vulnerable to subterfuge can be accounted for by each signer in the chain. A principal who is concerned about subterfuge will want to check that the permission that is about to be delegated can also be accounted for by others earlier in the chain: the accountability 'buck' should preferably stop at the head of the chain!

We are interested in determining whether, given a collection of known certificates, it is safe for a principal to delegate some held authorisation to another principal. By safe we mean that subterfuge is not possible. In simple terms, this requires determining if it is possible for a malicious outsider to interfere with a certificate chain with a view to influencing the authorisation accountability. In order to help understand this we draw comparisons between subterfuge attacks and attacks on authentication protocols. Our hypothesis is that techniques for analysing one can be used to analyse the other (as we shall see in the next section when we use a BAN-like logic to analyse subterfuge in delegation chains).

A certificate is a signed message that is exchanged between principals; an authentication protocol step can be an encrypted message that is exchanged between principals. A certificate chain is an ordering of certificates exchanged between principals. An authentication protocol is an ordering of encrypted messages exchanged between principals. For example, the chain $CC_1$ could be represented by the following protocol.

$$msg1 \quad ComA \rightarrow E \quad : \{K_{ComA}, K_E, 1, T1\}_{K_{ComA}}$$
$$msg2 \quad E \rightarrow A \quad : \{K_E, K_A, 1, T1\}_{K_E}$$
$$msg3 \quad A \rightarrow B \quad : \{K_A, K_B, 0, T1\}_{K_A}$$

There are differences between authentication protocols and certificate chains. A round of a typical authentication protocol has a fixed and small number of predefined messages, while the number of participants and messages in a certificate chain are unlimited and, sometimes, it may not be predetermined.

An attack from Section 2 is represented as follows.

$$msg2'. \quad I(CA) \rightarrow A \quad : \{K_I, K_A, 1, T1\}_{K_I}$$
$$msg3'. \quad A \rightarrow D \quad : \{K_A, K_D, 0, T1\}_{K_A}$$

Subterfuge attacks involve a malicious user (the intruder $I$) removing/hiding and replaying certificates between different certificate chains. These actions are comparable to a combination of the replay attacks [4]:

**Freshness attack.** "When a message (or message component) from a previous run of a protocol is recorded by an intruder and replayed as a message component in the current run of the protocol."

**Parallel session attack.** "When two or more protocol runs are executed concurrently and messages from one are used to form messages in another."

The analysis of an authentication protocol typically centres around an analysis of nonce properties: *if one may correctly respond to the nonce challenge in a round of an authentication protocol, it is the regular responder.*

**Freshness.** A nonce is a number used once in a message. Message freshness fixes a message as unique and ties it to a particular protocol run.

**Relevancy to originator.** A nonce is related to its originator. The nonce verifier is also the nonce provider (originator). The nonce originator generates the nonce and this means that it can recognise and understand its relationship with the nonce.

**Relevance of message.** In a two-party mutual authentication protocol, each principal generates its own nonce. A principal uses its own nonce and the other principal's nonce to relate its own message to the other's message.

There are some similarities between these nonce properties and the permission properties that rely on unique permissions.

**Uniqueness.** is required in a permission string to account for its originator within a particular certificate chain.

**Relevancy to originator.** A permission should be related to its originator and it should be possible for others along the chain to recognise this relationship.

**Relevance of certificates.** Certificates can be used to delegate combinations of permissions that originated from different sources. These new certificates should be account for the authorisation of the originators.

Lowe [17] defines the correctness of authentication as:

> "*A protocol guarantees agreement to a participant B (say, as the responder) for certain data items x if: each time a principal B completes a run of the protocol as responder using x, which to B appears to be a run with A, then there is a unique run of the protocol with the principal A as initiator using x, which to A appears to be a run with B.*"

We characterise accountability of authorisation within a certificate chain as follows.

> *A certificate chain guarantees the principal A's accountability of authorisation to a participant B (say, as the delegatee) for certain permission R if: each time a principal B is delegated a right R, which to B appears to be a certificate chain with A, then there is a unique certificate chain with the principal A as initial delegator authorising R.*

We use a BAN-style logic to reason about this notion of accountability of authorisation.

## 4   A Logic for Analysing Certificate Chains

In the last thirty years, a variety of techniques for analysing authentication protocols have been proposed. The previous section demonstrated similarities between (freshness) vulnerabilities in authentication protocols and (subterfuge) vulnerabilities in delegation chains. In this section we develop the Subterfuge Logic (SL) which draws on some of the techniques from BAN-like logics to analyse subterfuge in certificate chains.

### 4.1   The Language

The logic uses the following basic formulae. $P$, $Q$,$R$ and $S$ range over principals; $X$ represents a message, which can be data or formulae or both; $\phi$ will be used to denote a formula. The basic formulae are the following:

- $\sharp(X)$: Formula $X$ is a globally unique identifier. For example, this is typically taken as true for X.500 distinguished names and for public keys.
- $X \mid P$: represents the message $X$, as guaranteed/accounted for by principal $P$; this means that $P$ is willing to be held accountable for the consequences of action $X$. For example, it is in Alice's interest to delegate $T1 \mid K_{ComA}$ to Bob, as opposed to just $T1$.

- $X \rightsquigarrow P$: Principal $P$ is an originator of formula $X$. In the examples above, we write $\mathsf{T1}|K_{ComA}$ to mean that permission $\mathsf{T1}$ was first uttered by $K_{ComA}$ in some chain. Note that we assume that the same global unique formula (permission) cannot originate from two different principals, that is, if $X \rightsquigarrow P$, $X \rightsquigarrow Q$ and $\sharp(X)$ then $P = Q$.
- $P \ni X$: $P$ is authorised for the action $X$.
- $P \succ X$: $P$ is authorised to delegate $X$ to others.
- $P \parallel\!\!\sim X$: $P$ directly says $X$. This represents a credential that is directly exchanged between principals.
- $P \mathrel{\mid\!\sim} X$: $P$ says $X$. $P$ directly says $X$ or others say $X$ (who have been delegated to speak on $X$ by $P$).

Further formulae can be derived by using propositional logic. If $\phi_1$ and $\phi_2$ are formulae, then $\phi_1 \wedge \phi_2$ ($\phi_1$ and $\phi_2$), $\phi_1 \vee \phi_2$ ($\phi_1$ or $\phi_2$), and $\phi_1 \rightarrow \phi_2$ are formulae.

SPKI/SDSI credentials can be encoded within the logic as follows. An authorisation credential $(\mathsf{K}, \mathsf{S}, 0, \mathsf{T})$ is represented as $\mathsf{K} \parallel\!\!\sim (\mathsf{S} \ni \mathsf{T})$, and credential $(\mathsf{K}, \mathsf{S}, 1, \mathsf{T})$ represented as $\mathsf{K} \parallel\!\!\sim (\mathsf{S} \ni \mathsf{T} \wedge \mathsf{S} \succ \mathsf{T})$. The purpose of the logic is to permit a principal decide whether it would be safe for it to delegate an authorisation based on the collection of credentials that it currently holds. For the examples above, Alice would like to be able to test whether it is safe for her to write a credential corresponding to $K_{Alice} \parallel\!\!\sim (K_{David} \ni \mathsf{T1})$. That is, she wishes that someone further back on the chain will accept accountability for the action, that is, $K_{Alice} \succ \mathsf{T1}|K_{ComA}$ can be deduced (which is not possible for the examples in Section 2). Note that in signing the credential, Alice is also accepting accountability for the authorisation.

## 4.2   Inference Rules

### Gaining Rules

**G1.** If $P$ holds authorisation for $X$, for which $Q$ can be held accountable, and $Q$ may delegate $X$ then $P$ is also authorised for $X$.

$$\frac{P \ni X \,|\, Q, Q \succ X}{P \ni X}$$

**G2.** We have a similar rule for authorisation to delegate.

$$\frac{P \succ X \,|\, Q, Q \succ X}{P \succ X}$$

### Direct Delegation

**D1.** Direct delegation of authority assumes that the delegator accepts responsibility for the action.

$$\frac{P \parallel\!\!\sim (Q \ni X)}{P \mathrel{\mid\!\sim} (Q \ni X \,|\, P), Q \ni X \,|\, P}$$

**D2.** We have a similar rule for authorisation to delegate.

$$\frac{P \parallel\!\!\sim (Q \succ X)}{P \mid\!\!\sim (Q \succ X \mid P), Q \succ X \mid P}$$

**D3.** The usual conjunction rules apply.

$$\frac{P \parallel\!\!\sim (\phi_1 \wedge \phi_2)}{P \parallel\!\!\sim \phi_1, P \parallel\!\!\sim \phi_2}$$

## Indirect Delegation

**I1.** If principal $P$ says that $Q$ is authorised to perform an action $X$ (with $R$ accountable), and $P$ is authorised to delegate $X$ (with $R$ accountable), then $Q$ is authorised to perform $X$ (with $R$ accountable).

$$\frac{P \mid\!\!\sim (Q \ni X \mid R), P \succ X \mid R}{Q \ni X \mid R}$$

**I2.** We have a similar rule for authorisation to delegate.

$$\frac{P \mid\!\!\sim (Q \succ X \mid R), P \succ X \mid R}{Q \succ X \mid R}$$

**I3.** If principal $P$ says that $Q$ is authorised to perform action $X$ by $P$, then $P$ says that $Q$ is authorised to perform $X$.

$$\frac{P \mid\!\!\sim (Q \ni X \mid P)}{P \mid\!\!\sim (Q \ni X)}$$

**I4.** Accountability can be stripped from an authorisation. Note, however, that stripping accountability does not refute the existence of the accountability.

$$\frac{P \mid\!\!\sim (Q \succ X \mid P)}{P \mid\!\!\sim (Q \succ X)}$$

**I5.** Accountability is transitive along certificate chains.

$$\frac{P \mid\!\!\sim (Q \succ X \mid R), R \mid\!\!\sim (P \succ X \mid S)}{R \mid\!\!\sim (Q \succ X \mid S)}$$

**I6.** We have a similar rule for authorisation.

$$\frac{P \mid\!\!\sim (Q \ni X \mid R), R \mid\!\!\sim (P \succ X \mid S)}{R \mid\!\!\sim (Q \ni X \mid S)}$$

## Unique Origin Rules

**U1.** If $Q$ is authorised for unique $X$ that originated from $P$ then $P$ can be held accountable for $X$.

$$\frac{\sharp(X), X \rightsquigarrow P, Q \ni X}{Q \ni X \mid P}$$

**U2.** We have a similar rule for authorisation to delegate.

$$\frac{\sharp(X), X \rightsquigarrow P, Q \succ X}{Q \succ X \mid P}$$

## 5    Analysing Authorisation Subterfuge

The example from Section 2 is analysed using the Subterfuge Logic as follows. Certificates $C_1$ and $C_2$ are encoded by the following formulae. Note that principal names are abbreviated to their first initial if no ambiguity can arise.

$$K_{ComA} \parallel\!\sim ((K_E \ni \mathsf{T1}) \wedge (K_E \succ \mathsf{T1}))$$
$$K_E \parallel\!\sim ((K_A \ni \mathsf{T1}) \wedge (K_A \succ \mathsf{T1}))$$

Assumptions regarding uniqueness include the following.

$$\sharp(K_{ComA}), \sharp(K_{ComB}), \sharp(K_A), \sharp(K_B), \sharp(K_C), \sharp(K_E)$$

Principal $ComA$ is assumed authorised to delegate and accept accountability for the authorisations $\mathsf{T1}$ that it originates.

$$K_{ComA} \succ (\mathsf{T1} | K_{ComA})$$

Before delegating authority for $\mathsf{T1}$ to Bob, Alice wishes to test whether it is safe to do so. Alice tests whether $ComA$ accepts accountability for this action, that is she attempts to deduce $K_A \succ \mathsf{T1} | K_{ComA}$ using the above assumptions within the logic. This is not possible since no assumption is made regarding uniqueness of $\mathsf{T1}$, and, therefore, we cannot deduce $K_E \mathrel{\stackrel{\cdot}{\sim}} (K_A \succ T_1 | K_{ComA})$; thus Alice refrains from the delegation.

In Trust Management public keys provide globally unique identifiers that are tied to the owner of the key. These can also be used to avoid authorisation ambiguity within delegation chains. For example, given SPKI certificate $(\mathsf{K}_{ComA}, \mathsf{K}_E, 1, [\mathsf{T1.K}_{ComA}])$, there can be no possibility of subterfuge when Emily delegates to Alice by signing the certificate $(\mathsf{K}_E, \mathsf{K}_A, 1, [\mathsf{T1.K}_{ComA}])$. In this case the authorisation $[\mathsf{T1.K}_{ComA}]$ is globally unique, that is $\sharp(\mathsf{T1}|K_{ComA})$ and the certificate makes the intention of the delegation and accountability very clear.

The revised certificates are represented in the logic as follows.

$$K_{ComA} \parallel\!\sim ((K_E \ni T_1 | K_{ComA}) \wedge (K_E \succ T_1 | K_{ComA}))$$
$$K_E \parallel\!\sim ((K_A \ni T_1 | K_{ComA}) \wedge (K_A \succ T_1 | K_{ComA}))$$

Given these certificates then Alice can deduce

$$K_A \succ \mathsf{T1} | K_{ComA}$$

and can safely delegate to Bob as

$$K_A \parallel\!\sim (K_B \ni T_1 | K_{ComA})$$

and we can deduce that $K_B \ni T_1 \mid K_{ComA}$. Considering other certificates, including

$$K_{ComB} \parallel\!\sim ((K_C \ni T_1 | K_{ComB}) \wedge (K_C \succ T_1 | K_{ComB}))$$
$$K_C \parallel\!\sim ((K_A \ni T_1 | K_{ComB}) \wedge (K_A \succ T_1 | K_{ComB}))$$
$$K_A \parallel\!\sim (K_D \ni T_1 | K_{ComB})$$

we can deduce $K_D \ni T_1 | K_{ComB}$, the expected authorisation.

Suppose that $ComB$ issues confusing certificates to Clark, who in turn delegates the incorrect authorisation to Alice.

$$K_{ComB} \mathrel{\|\!\!\sim} ((K_C \ni T_1 \,|\, K_{ComA}) \wedge (K_C \succ T_1 \,|\, K_{ComA}))$$
$$K_C \mathrel{\|\!\!\sim} ((K_A \ni T_1 \,|\, K_{ComA}) \wedge (K_A \succ T_1 \,|\, K_{ComA}))$$

In this case we can deduce $K_{ComB} \mathrel{\|\!\sim} (K_A \succ T_1 \,|\, K_{ComA})$ and thus and $K_A \succ T_1 \,|\, K_{ComB}$. However, before $A$ delegates this right for $K_{ComA}$, she needs (but cannot hold) the following formulae $K_{ComB} \succ T_1 \,|\, K_{ComA}$, or $K_C \succ T_1 \,|\, K_{ComA}s$. Thus, she should not delegate and therefore resists the subterfuge attack.

The conventional SPKI/SDSI authorisation certificate reduction rule can be described as

$$P \mathrel{\|\!\sim} (Q \succ X) \wedge Q \mathrel{\|\!\sim} (R \succ X) \rightarrow P \mathrel{\|\!\sim} (R \succ X)$$

in the SL logic (with a similar relationship for delegation of authorisation). Such relationship does not facilitate the tracking of accountability during certificate reduction.

## 6    Subterfuge in Local Names

Subterfuge is also possible when using local name certificates. Ellison and Dohrmann [8] describe a model based on SPKI/SDSI name certificates for access control in mobile computing platforms. A group leader controls all rights of a group. A group leader may delegate the right "admitting members" to other principals. For example, $K_G$ is a group leader; $K_G$ admits $K_A$ as its group member by certificate $C_1$. $K_G$ defines a large random number $n$, which will be used as $K_A$'s local name for $K_G$'s member. Then, $K_G$ issues certificate $C_2$ to $K_A$ which means that if $K_A$ accepts a principal as ($K_A$'s $n$), then the principal also becomes $K_G$'s group $G$'s member. $K_A$ admits $K_B$ as $K_A$'s $n$ by $C_3$. Together with $C_2$, $K_B$ also becomes a member of $K_G$'s $G$ as presented in $C_4$. The certificates are as follows.

$$C_1 = (\mathsf{K_G}, \mathsf{G}, \mathsf{K_A}); \qquad C_2 = (\mathsf{K_G}, \mathsf{G}, (\mathsf{K_A'\, s}\ n)); \qquad C_3 = (\mathsf{K_A}, \mathsf{n}, \mathsf{K_B})$$

From these we can deduce $(\mathsf{K_G}, \mathsf{G}, \mathsf{K_B})$, that is, $\mathsf{K_B}$ is now a member of group $\mathsf{G}$.

The scheme works in a decentralised manner and thus no single member will hold the entire membership list. This means that there is no easy way to prove non-membership. The strategy described in the paper is sufficiently robust as it relies on face-to-face verification of certificate $C_2$ when a member joins.

However, the nonce is large and there may be potential for confusion during the face-to-face verification and this can lead to subterfuge. Consider the following certificates.

$$C_1' = (\mathsf{K_I}, \mathsf{G_I}, \mathsf{K_A}); \qquad C_2' = (\mathsf{K_I}, \mathsf{G_I}, (\mathsf{K_A'\, s}\ n)); \qquad C_3' = (\mathsf{K_A}, \mathsf{n}, \mathsf{K_I})$$

Suppose that the intruder $K_I$ wants to join $K_G$'s group $\mathsf{G}$. $K_I$ intercepts $C_2$ and issues $C_2'$ by using the number in $C_2$. In the confusion, $K_A$ issues $C_3'$ which corresponds to admitting $K_C$ (which the intruder controls) as a member of $K_I$'s $G_I$ for $K_A$. In this case, $K_C$ may use $C_2$ and $C'_3$ to prove its membership in $K_G$'s group $G$.

## 7    Conclusions

In this paper we described how poorly characterised permissions within cryptographic credentials can lead to authorisation subterfuge during delegation operations. This subterfuge results in a vulnerability concerning the accountability of the authorisation provided by a delegation chain: does the delegation operations in the chain reflect the true intent of the participants?

The challenge here is to ensure that permissions can be referred to in a manner that properly reflects their context. Since permissions are intended to be shared across local name spaces then their references must be global. In the paper we discuss some ad-hoc strategies to ensure globalisation of permissions. In particular, we consider the use of global name services and public keys as the sources of global identifiers.

The Subterfuge Logic proposed in this paper provides a systematic way of determining whether a particular delegation scheme using particular ad-hoc permissions is sufficiently robust to be able to withstand attempts at subterfuge. This logic provides a new characterisation of certificate reduction that, we argue, is more appropriate to open systems. We believe that it will be straightforward to extend the Subterfuge Logic to consider subterfuge in SDSI-like local names (as considered in Section 6).

Trust Management, like many other protection techniques, provide operations that are used to control access. As with any protection mechanism the challenge is to make sure that the mechanisms are configured in such a way that they ensure some useful and consistent notion of security. Subterfuge logic helps to provide assurance that a principal cannot bypass security via some unexpected but authorised route. This general goal of analysing unexpected but authorised access is not limited to just certificate schemes. Formal techniques that analyse whether a particular configuration of access controls is effective is considered in [11, 13]; strategies such as well formed transactions, separation of duties and protection domains help to ensure that a system is sufficiently robust to a malicious principle. We are currently exploring how the subterfuge logic can be extended to include such robustness building strategies.

## Acknowledgements

This work is supported by the UCC Centre for Unified Computing under the Science Foundation Ireland WebComG project and by Enterprise Ireland Basic Research Grant Scheme (SC/2003/007).

# References

1. M. Blaze, J. Feigenbaum, J. Ioannidis, and A. D. Keromytis. The keynote trust-management system, version 2, September 1999. IETF RFC 2704.
2. M. Blaze, J. Ioannidis, S. Ioannidis, A. Keromytis, P. Nikander, and V. Prevelakis. Tapi: Transactions for accessing public infrastructure. In *Proceedings of the 8th IFIP Personal Wireless Communications (PWC) Conference*, 2003.
3. M. Blaze, J. Ioannidis, and A. D. Keromytis. Offline micro-payments without trusted hardware. In *Financial Cryptography*, Grand Cayman, February 2001.
4. J. A. Clark and J. L. Jacob. A survey of authentication protocol literature, version 1.0. In *http://www.cs.york.ac.uk/jac/*, 1997.
5. D. Clarke, J.-E. Elien, C. Ellison, M. Fredette, A. Morcos, and R. L. Rivest. Certificate chain discovery in spki/sdsi. *Journal of Computer Security*, 9(4):285–322, 2001.
6. J. DeTreville. Binder, a logic-based security language. In *Proceedings of the 2002 IEEE Symposium on Research in Security and Privacy*, pages 105–113. IEEE Computer Society Press, 2002.
7. C. Ellison. The nature of a usable PKI. *Computer Networks*, 31:823–830, 1999.
8. C. Ellison and S. Dohrmann. Public-key support for group collaboration. *ACM Transactions on Information and System Security (TISSEC)*, 6(4):547–565, 2003.
9. C. Ellison, B. Frantz, B. Lampson, R. L. Rivest, B. Thomas, and T. Ylonen. Spki certificate theory, September 1999. IETF RFC 2693.
10. C. M. Ellison, B. Frantz, B. Lampson, R. Rivest, B. M. Thomas, and T. Ylonen. Spki examples, September 1998.
11. S. Foley. A non-functional approach to system integrity. *IEEE Journal on Selected Areas in Communications*, 21(1), Jan 2003.
12. S. Foley. Using trust management to support transferable hash-based micropayments. In *Proceedings of the 7th International Financial Cryptography Conference*, Gosier, Guadeloupe, FWI, January 2003.
13. S. Foley. Believing in the integrity of a system. In *IJCAR Workshop on Automated Reasoning for Security Protocol Analysis*. Springer Verlag Electronic Notes in Computer Science, 2004.
14. S. N. Foley and H. Zhou. Authorisation subterfuge by delegation in decentralised networks. In *International Security Protocols Workshop*, Cambridge, UK, April 2005.
15. R. Housley, W. Polk, W. Ford, and D. Solo. Internet x.509 public key infrastructure certificate and certificate revocation list (crl) profile, April 2002.
16. N. Li et al. Beyond proof-of-compliance: Safety and availability analysis in trust management. In *Proceedings of 2003 IEEE Symposium on Security and Privacy*. IEEE, 2003.
17. G. Lowe. A hierarchy of authentication specifications. In *PCSFW: Proceedings of The 10th Computer Security Foundations Workshop*. IEEE Computer Society Press, 1997.

# Probable Innocence Revisited[*]

Konstantinos Chatzikokolakis and Catuscia Palamidessi

INRIA Futurs and LIX, École Polytechnique
{kostas, catuscia}@lix.polytechnique.fr

**Abstract.** In this paper we study probable innocence, a notion of probabilistic anonymity provided by protocols such as Crowds. The authors of Crowds, Reiter and Rubin, gave a definition of probable innocence which later has been interpreted by other authors in terms of the probability of the users from the point of view of the observer. This formalization however does not seem to correspond exactly to the property that Reiter and Rubin have shown for Crowds, the latter, in fact, is independent from the probability of the users.

We take the point of view that anonymity should be a concept depending only on the protocol, and should abstract from the probabilities of the users. For strong anonymity, this abstraction leads to a concept known as conditional anonymity. The main goal of this paper is to establish a notion which is to probable innocence as conditional anonymity is to strong anonymity. We show that our definition, while being more general, corresponds exactly to the property that Reiter and Rubin have shown for Crowds, under specific conditions. We also show that in the particular case that the users have uniform probabilities we obtain a property similar to the definition of probable innocence given by Halpern and O'Neill.

## 1 Introduction

Often we wish to ensure that the identity of the user performing a certain action is maintained secret. This property is called *anonymity*. Examples of situations in which we may wish to provide anonymity include: publishing on the web, retrieving information from the web, sending a message, etc. Many protocols have been designed for this purpose, for example, Crowds [1], Onion Routing [2], the Free Haven [3], Web MIX [4] and Freenet [5].

Most of the protocols providing anonymity use random mechanisms. Consequently, it is natural to think of anonymity in probabilistic terms. Various notions of probabilistic anonymity have been proposed in the literature, at different levels of strength. The notion of anonymity in [6], called conditional anonymity in [7, 8], and investigated also in [9], describes the ideal situation in which the protocol does not leak any information concerning the identity of the user. This property is satisfied for instance by the Dining Cryptographers with fair coins [6]. Protocols used in practice, however, especially in presence of attackers or corrupted users, are only able to provide a weaker notion of anonymity.

In [1] Reiter and Rubin have proposed an hierarchy of notions of probabilistic anonymity in the context of Crowds. We recall that Crowds is a system for anonymous

---

[*] This work has been partially supported by the Project Rossignol of the ACI Sécurité Informatique (Ministère de la recherche et nouvelles technologies).

T. Dimitrakos et al. (Eds.): FAST 2005, LNCS 3866, pp. 142–157, 2006.

web surfing aimed at protecting the identity of the users when sending (originating) messages. This is achieved by forwarding the message to another user selected randomly, which in turn forwards the message, and so on, until the message reaches its destination. Part of the users may be corrupted (attackers), and one of the main purposes of the protocol is to protect the identity of the originator of the message from those attackers.

Quoting from [1], the hierarchy is described as follows. Here the *sender* stands for the user that forwards the message to the attacker.

*Beyond suspicion.* From the attacker's point of view, the sender appears no more likely to be the originator of the message than any other potential sender in the system.

*Probable innocence.* From the attacker's point of view, the sender appears no more likely to be the originator of the message than to not be the originator.

*Possible innocence.* From the attacker's point of view, there is a nontrivial probability that the real sender is someone else.

In [1] probable innocence was also expressed with a precise mathematical formula and proved to hold for Crowds under certain conditions. Also, Halpern and O'Neill have proposed a formal interpretation of the notions above in [8]. In particular, the definition they give for probable innocence is that, if a user $i$ has been the originator, then the probability for the attacker that $i$ is the originator is smaller than 1/2. However, the property of probable innocence that Reiter and Rubin express formally and prove for the system Crowds in [1] does not mention the user's probability of being the originator, but only the probability of the event observed by the attacker. More precisely, the property proved for Crowds is that the probability that the originator forwards the message to an attacker (given that an attacker receives eventually the message) is smaller than $1/2$.

The property proved for Crowds in [1] depends only on the way the protocol works, and on the number of the attackers. It is totally independent from the probability of each user to be the originator. This is of course a very desirable property, since we do not want the correctness of a protocol to depend on the users' intentions of originating a message. For stronger notions of anonymity, this abstraction from the users' probabilities leads to the notion of probabilistic anonymity defined in [9], which is equivalent to the conditional anonymity defined in [7, 8]. Note that this definition is different from the notion of *strong probabilistic anonymity* given in [7, 8]: the latter depends, again, on the probabilities of the users.

Another intended feature of our notion of probable innocence is the abstraction from the specific characteristics of Crowds. In Crowds, there are certain symmetries that derive from the assumption that the probability that user $i$ forwards the message to user $j$ is the same for all $i$ and $j$. The property of probable innocence proved for Crowds depends strongly on this assumption. We want a general notion that has the possibility to hold even in protocols which do not satisfy the Crowds' symmetries.

## 1.1   Contribution

The main goal of this paper is to establish a general notion of probable innocence which, like probabilistic anonymity, is independent from the probabilities of the users. We show that our definition, while being more general, corresponds exactly to the property that Reiter and Rubin have proved for Crowds, under the specific symmetry conditions which are satisfied by Crowds. We also show that in the particular case that the users have uniform probability of being the originator, we obtain a property similar to the definition of probable innocence given by Halpern and O'Neill.

## 1.2  Plan of the Paper

In next section we recall some notions which are used in the rest of the paper: the Probabilistic Automata, the framework for anonymity developed in [9], and the definition of (strong) probabilistic anonymity given in [9]. In Section 3 we illustrate the Crowds protocol, we recall the property proved for Crowds and the definition of probable innocence by Halpern and O'Neill, and we discuss them. In Section 4 we propose our notion of probable innocence and we compare with those of Section 3. The full version of this paper, including the proofs of all propositions, can be found in [10].

# 2  Preliminaries

## 2.1  Probabilistic Automata

In our approach we consider systems that can perform both probabilistic and nondeterministic choice. Intuitively, a probabilistic choice represents a set of alternative transitions, each of them associated to a certain probability of being selected. The sum of all probabilities on the alternatives of the choice must be 1, i.e. they form a *probability distribution*. Nondeterministic choice is also a set of alternatives, but we have no information on how likely one alternative is selected.

There have been many models proposed in literature that combine both nondeterministic and probabilistic choice. One of the most general is the formalism of *probabilistic automata* proposed in [11]. In this work we use this formalism to model anonymity protocols. We give here a brief description of it.

A probabilistic automaton consists in a set of states, and labeled transitions between them. For each node, the outgoing transitions are partitioned in groups called *steps*. Each step represents a probabilistic choice, while the choice between the steps is nondeterministic.

Figure 1 illustrates some examples of probabilistic automata. We represent a step by putting an arc across the member transitions. For instance, in (a), state $s_1$ has two steps, the first is a probabilistic choice between two transitions with labels $a$ and $b$, each with probability $1/2$. When there is only a transition in a step, like the one from state $s_3$ to state $s_6$, the probability is of course 1 and we omit it.

In this paper, we use only a simplified kind of automaton, in which from each node we have either a probabilistic choice or a nondeterministic choice (more precisely, either one step or a set of singleton steps), like in (b). In the particular case that the choices are all probabilistic, like in (c), the automaton is called *fully probabilistic*.

Given an automaton $M$, we denote by $etree(M)$ its unfolding, i.e. the tree of all possible executions of $M$ (in Figure 1 the automata coincide with their unfolding because there is no loop). If $M$ is fully probabilistic, then each execution (maximal branch) of $etree(M)$ has a probability obtained as the product of the probability of the edges along

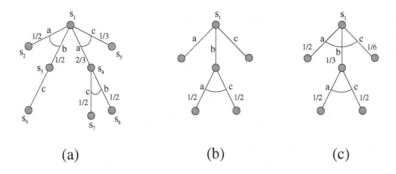

(a)                    (b)                    (c)

**Fig. 1.** Examples of probabilistic automata

the branch. In the finite case, we can define a probability measure for each set of executions, called *event*, by summing up the probabilities of the elements[1]. Given an event $x$, we will denote by $p(x)$ the probability of $x$. For instance, let the event $c$ be the set of all computations in which $c$ occurs. In (c) its probability is $p(c) = 1/3 \times 1/2 + 1/6 = 1/3$.

When nondeterminism is present, the probability can vary, depending on how we *resolve* the nondeterminism. In other words we need to consider a function $\varsigma$ that, each time there is a choice between different steps, selects one of them. By pruning the non-selected steps, we obtain a fully probabilistic execution tree $etree(M, \varsigma)$ on which we can define the probability as before. For historical reasons (i.e. since nondeterminism typically arises from the parallel operator), the function $\varsigma$ is called *scheduler*.

It should then be clear that the probability of an event is relative to the particular scheduler. We will denote by $p_\varsigma(x)$ the probability of the event $x$ under the scheduler $\varsigma$. For example, consider (a). We have two possible schedulers determined by the choice of the step in $s_1$. Under one scheduler, the probability of $c$ is $1/2$. Under the other, it is $2/3 \times 1/2 + 1/3 = 2/3$. In (b) we have three possible schedulers under which the probability of $c$ is $0$, $1/2$ and $1$, respectively.

## 2.2   Anonymity Systems

The concept of anonymity is relative to the set of anonymous users and to what is visible to the observer. Hence, following [12, 13] we classify the actions of the automaton into the three sets $A$, $B$ and $C$ as follows:

- $A$ is the set of the anonymous actions $A = \{a(i) \mid i \in I\}$ where $I$ is the set of the identities of the anonymous users and $a$ is an injective function from $I$ to the set of actions, which we call *abstract action*. We also call the pair $(I, a)$ *anonymous action generator*.
- $B$ is the set of the observable actions. We will use $b$, $b'$, ... to denote the elements of this set.
- $C$ is the set of the remaining actions (which are unobservable).

---

[1] In the infinite case things are more complicated: we cannot define a probability measure for all sets of execution, and we need to consider as event space the $\sigma$-field generated by the *cones* of $etree(M)$. However, in this paper, we consider only the finite case.

Note that the actions in $A$ normally are not visible to the observer, or at least, not for the part that depends on the identity $i$. However, for the purpose of defining and verifying anonymity we model the elements of $A$ as visible outcomes of the system.

**Definition 1.** *An anonymity system is a tuple* $(M, I, a, B, Z, p)$, *where* $M$ *is a probabilistic automaton,* $(I, a)$. *is an anonymous action generator,* $B$ *is a set of observable actions,* $Z$ *is the set of all possible schedulers for* $M$, *and for every* $\varsigma \in Z$, $p_\varsigma$ *is the probability measure on the event space generated by* $etree(M, \varsigma)$.

*For simplicity, we assume the users to be the only possible source of nondeterminism in the system. If they are probabilistic, then the system is fully probabilistic, hence* $Z$ *is a singleton and we omit it.*

We introduce the following notation to represent the events of interest:

- $a(i)$ : all the executions in $etree(M, \varsigma)$ containing the action $a(i)$;
- $a$ : all the executions in $etree(M, \varsigma)$ containing an action $a(i)$ for an arbitrary $i$;
- $o$ : all the executions in $etree(M, \varsigma)$ containing as their maximal sequence of observable actions the sequence $o$ (where $o$ is of the form $b_1 b_2 \ldots b_n$ for some $b_1$, $b_2, \ldots, b_n \in B$). We denote by $O$ (*observables*) the set of all such $o$'s.

We use the symbols $\cup, \cap$ and $\neg$ to represent the union, the intersection, and the complement of events, respectively.

We wish to keep the notion of observables as general as possible, but we still need to make some assumptions on them. First, we want the observables to be disjoint events. Second, they must cover all possible outcomes. Third, an observable $o$ must indicate unambiguously whether $a$ has taken place or not, i.e. it either implies $a$, or it implies $\neg a$. In set-theoretic terms it means that either $o$ is a subset of $a$ or of the complement of $a$. Formally[2]:

*Assumption 1 (on the observables)*

1. $\forall \varsigma \in Z. \forall o_1, o_2 \in O.\ o_1 \neq o_2 \Rightarrow p_\varsigma(o_1 \cup o_2) = p_\varsigma(o_1) + p_\varsigma(o_2)$
2. $\forall \varsigma \in Z.\ p_\varsigma(O) = 1$
3. $\forall \varsigma \in Z. \forall o \in O.\ (p_\varsigma(o \cap a) = p_\varsigma(o))\ \lor\ p_\varsigma(o \cap \neg a) = p_\varsigma(o)$

Analogously, we need to make some assumption on the anonymous actions. We consider first the conditions tailored for the nondeterministic users: each scheduler determines completely whether an action of the form $a(i)$ takes place or not, and in the positive case, there is only one such $i$. Formally:

*Assumption 2 (on the anonymous actions, for nondeterministic users)*

$$\forall \varsigma \in Z.\ p_\varsigma(a) = 0 \lor (\exists i \in I.\ (p_\varsigma(a(i)) = 1 \ \land\ \forall j \in I.\ j \neq i \Rightarrow p_\varsigma(a(j)) = 0))$$

---

[2] Note that the intuitive explanations here are stronger than the corresponding formal assumptions because, in the infinite case, there could be non-trivial sets of measure 0. However in the case of anonymity we usually deal with finite scenarios. In any case, these formal assumptions are enough for the ensuring the properties of the anonymity notions that we need in this paper.

We now consider the case in which the users are fully probabilistic. The assumption on the anonymous actions in this case is much weaker: we only require that there be at most one user that performs $a$, i.e. $a(i)$ and $a(j)$ must be disjoint for $i \neq j$. Formally:

*Assumption 3 (on the anonymous actions, for probabilistic users)*

$$\forall i, j \in I. \ i \neq j \ \Rightarrow \ p(a(i) \cup a(j)) = p(a(i)) + p(a(j))$$

### 2.3  Strong Probabilistic Anonymity

In this section we recall the notion of strong anonymity proposed in [9].

Let us first assume that the users are nondeterministic. Intuitively, a system is strongly anonymous if, given two schedulers $\varsigma$ and $\vartheta$ that both choose $a$ (say $a(i)$ and $a(j)$, respectively), it is not possible to detect from the probabilistic measure of the observables whether the scheduler has been $\varsigma$ or $\vartheta$ (i.e. whether the selected user was $i$ or $j$).

**Definition 2.** *A system* $(M, I, a, B, Z, p)$ *with nondeterministic users is anonymous if*

$$\forall \varsigma, \vartheta \in Z. \ \forall o \in O. \ p_\varsigma(a) = p_\vartheta(a) = 1 \ \Rightarrow \ p_\varsigma(o) = p_\vartheta(o)$$

The probabilistic counterpart of Definition 2 can be formalized using the concept of *conditional probability*. Recall that, given two events $x$ and $y$ with $p(y) > 0$, the conditional probability of $x$ given $y$, denoted by $p(x \mid y)$, is equal to $p(x \cap y)/p(y)$.

**Definition 3.** *A system* $(M, I, a, B, p)$ *with probabilistic users is anonymous if*

$$\forall i, j \in I. \ \forall o \in O. \ (p(a(i)) > 0 \wedge p(a(j)) > 0) \Rightarrow p(o \mid a(i)) = p(o \mid a(j))$$

The notions of anonymity illustrated so far focus on the probability of the observables. More precisely, it requires the probability of the observables to be independent from the selected user. In [9] it was shown that Definition 3 is equivalent to the notion adopted implicitly in [6], and called *conditional anonymity* in [7]. As illustrated in the introduction, the idea of this notion is that a system is anonymous if the observations do not change the probability of the $a(i)$'s. In other words, we may know the probability of $a(i)$ by some means external to the system, but the system should not increase our knowledge about it.

**Proposition 1 ([9]).** *A system* $(M, I, a, B, p)$ *with probabilistic users is anonymous iff*

$$\forall i \in I. \ \forall o \in O. \ p(o \cap a) > 0 \ \Rightarrow \ p(a(i) \mid o) = p(a(i) \mid a)$$

*Note 1.* To be precise, the probabilistic counterpart of Definition 2 should be stronger than that given in Definition 3, in fact it should be independent from the probabilities of the users, like Definition 2 is. We could achieve this by assuming the system to be parametric with respect to the probability distribution of the users, and then require the formula to hold for every possible distribution. Proposition 1 should be modified accordingly.

*Note 2.* The large number of anonymity definitions often leads to confusion. In the rest of the paper we will refer to Definition 3 as *(strong) probabilistic anonymity*. By *conditional anonymity* we will refer to the condition in Proposition 1 which corresponds to the definition of Halpern and O'Neill ([7]). Finally by *strong anonymity* we will refer to the corresponding definition in [7] which can be expressed as:

$$\forall i, j \in I. \ \forall o \in O : p(a(i) \mid o) = p(a(j) \mid o) \tag{1}$$

## 3  Probable Innocence

Strong and conditional anonymity are notions which are usually difficult to achieve in practice. For instance, in the case of protocols like Crowds, the originator needs to take some initiative, thus revealing himself to the attacker with greater probability than the rest of the users. As a result, more relaxed levels of anonymity, such as probable innocence, are provided by real protocols.

### 3.1  The Crowds Protocol

This protocol, presented in [1], allows Internet users to perform web transactions without revealing their identity. The idea is to randomly route the request through a crowd of users. Thus when the web server receives the request he does not know who is the originator since the user who sent the request to the server is simply forwarding it. The more interesting case, however, is when an attacker is a member of the crowd and participates in the protocol. In this case the originator is exposed with higher probability than any other user and strong anonymity cannot be achieved. However, it can be proved that Crowds provides probable innocence under certain conditions.

More specifically a crowd is a group of $m$ users who participate in the protocol. Some of the users may be corrupted which means they can collaborate in order to reveal the identity of the originator. Let $c$ be the number of such users and $p_f$ a parameter of the protocol, explained below. When a user, called the *initiator* or *originator*, wants to request a web page he must create a *path* between him and the server. This is achieved by the following process:

- The initiator selects randomly a member of the crowd (possibly himself) and forwards the request to him. We will refer to this latter user as the *forwarder*.
- A forwarder, upon receiving a request, flips a biased coin. With probability $1 - p_f$ he delivers the request directly to the server. With probability $p_f$ he selects randomly, with uniform probability, a new forwarder (possibly himself) and forwards the request to him. The new forwarder repeats the same procedure.

The response from the server follows the same route in the opposite direction to return to the initiator. It must be mentioned that all communication in the path is encrypted using a *path key*, mainly to defend against local eavesdroppers (see [1] for more details). In this paper we are interested in attacks performed by corrupted members of the crowd to reveal the initiator's identity. Each member is considered to have only access to the traffic routed through him, so he cannot intercept messages addressed to other members.

## 3.2  Definition of Probable Innocence

Probable innocence is verbally defined by Reiter and Rubin ([1]) as "the sender (the user who forwards the message to the attacker) appears no more likely to be the originator than not to be the originator". Two different approaches to formalize this notion exist, the first focuses on the probability of the observables and the second on the probability of the users.

**First approach (focus on the probability of the observables):** Reiter and Rubin ([1]) give a definition which considers the probability of the originator being observed by a corrupted member, that is being directly before him in the path. Let $I$ denote the event "the originator is observed by a corrupted member" and $H_{1+}$ the event "at least one corrupted member appears in the path". Then probable innocence can be defined as

$$p(I \mid H_{1+}) \leq 1/2 \tag{2}$$

In [1] it is proved that this property is satisfied by Crowds if $n \geq \frac{p_f}{p_f - 1/2}(c + 1)$.

For simplicity, we suppose that a corrupted user will not forward a request to other crowd members, so at most one user can be observed. This approach is also followed in [1, 14, 15] and the reason is that by forwarding the request the corrupted users cannot gain any new information since forwarders are chosen randomly.

We now express the above definition in the framework of this paper (Section 2.2). Since $I \Rightarrow H_{1+}$ we have $p(I \mid H_{1+}) = p(I)/p(H_{1+})$. If $A_i$ denotes that "user $i$ is the originator" and $D_i$ is the event "the user $i$ was observed by a corrupted member (appears in the path right before the corrupter member)" then $p(I) = \sum_i p(D_i \wedge A_i) = \sum_i p(D_i \mid A_i)p(A_i)$. Since $p(D_i \mid A_i)$ is the same for all $i$ then the definition (2) can be written $\forall i : p(D_i \mid A_i)/P(H_{1+}) \leq 1/2$.

Let $A$ be the set of all crowd members and $O = \{o_i \mid i \in A\}$ the set of observables. Essentially $a(i)$ denotes $A_i$ and $o_i$ denotes $D_i$. Note that $D_i$ is an observable since it can be observed by a corrupted user (remember that corrupted users share their information). Also let $h = \bigvee_{i \in A} o_i$, meaning that some user was observed. The definition (2) can now be written:

$$\forall i \in A : p(o_i \mid a(i)) \leq \frac{1}{2}p(h) \tag{3}$$

This is indeed an intuitive definition for Crowds. However there are many questions raised by this approach. For example, we are only interested in the probability of one specific event, what about other events that might reveal the identity of the initiator? For example the event $\neg o_i$ will have probability greater than $p(h)/2$, is this important? Moreover, consider the case where the probability of $o_i$ under a different initiator $j$ is negligible. Then, if we observe $o_i$, isn't it more probable that user $i$ sent the message, even if $p(o_i \mid a(i))$ is less than $p(h)/2$?

If we consider arbitrary protocols, then there are cases where the condition (3) does not express the expected properties of probable innocence. We give two examples of such systems in 2 and we explain them below.

*Example 1.* On the left-hand side of figure 2, $m$ users are participating in a Crowds-like protocol. The only difference, with respect to the standard Crowds, is that user

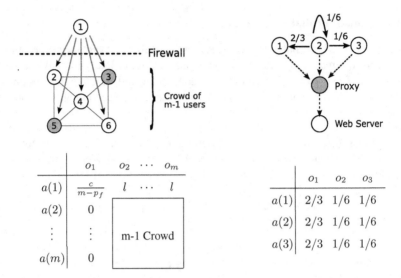

**Fig. 2.** Examples of arbitrary (non symmetric) protocols. The value at position $i, j$ represents $p(o_j \mid a(i))$ for user $i$ and observable $o_j$.

1 is behind a firewall, which means that he can send messages to any other user but he cannot receive messages from any of them. In the corresponding table we give the conditional probabilities $p(o_j \mid a(i))$, where we recall that $o_j$ means that $j$ is the user who sends the message to the corrupted member, and $a(i)$ means that $i$ is the initiator. When user 1 is the initiator the probability of observing him is $\frac{c}{m-p_f}$ (there is a $c/m$ chance that user 1 sends the message to a corrupted user and there is also a chance that he forwards it to himself and sends it to a corrupted user in the next round). All other users can be observed with the same probability $l$. When any other user is the initiator, however, the probability of observing user 1 is 0, since he will never receive the message. In fact, the protocol will behave exactly like a Crowd of $m - 1$ users as it is shown in the table.

Note that Reiter and Rubin's definition (3) requires the diagonal of this table to be less than $p(h)/2$. In this example the definition holds provided that $m - 1 \geq \frac{p_f}{p_f - 1/2}$ $(c + 1)$. In fact, for all users $i \neq 1$, $p(o_i \mid a(i))$ is the same as in the original Crowds (which satisfies the definition) and for user 1 it is even smaller. However, probable innocence is violated. If a corrupted member observes user 1 he can be sure that he is the initiator since no other initiator leads to the observation of user 1. Indeed $p(a(1) \mid o_1) = 1$. But this is against our intuition of probable innocence.

*Example 2.* On the left-hand side we have an opposite counter-example. Three users want to communicate with a web server, but they can only access it through a proxy. We suppose that all users are honest but they do not trust the proxy so they do not want to reveal their identity to him. So they use the following protocol: the initiator first forwards the message to one of the users 1, 2 and 3 with probabilities $2/3, 1/6$ and $1/6$ respectively, regardless of which is the initiator. The user who receives the message forwards it to the proxy. The probabilities of observing each user are shown in the corresponding table. Regardless of which is the initiator, user 1 will be observed with probability $2/3$ and the others with probability $1/6$ each.

In this example Reiter and Rubin's definition does not hold since $p(o_1 \mid a(1)) > 1/2$. However all users produce the same observables with the same probabilities hence we cannot distinguish between them. Indeed the system is strongly anonymous (Definition 3 holds)! Thus, in the general case, we cannot adopt (3) as the definition of probable innocence since we want such a notion to be implied by strong anonymity.

However, it should be noted that in the case of Crowds the definition of Reiter and Rubin is correct, because of a special symmetry property of the protocol. This is discussed in detail in Section 4.1.

Finally, note that the above definition does not mention the probability of any user. We are only interested in the probability of the event $o_i$ *given the fact* that $i$ is the initiator. The user itself might have a very small or very big probability of initiating the message. This is a major difference with respect to the next approach.

**Second approach (focus on the probability of the users):** Halpern and O'Neill propose in [7] a general framework for defining anonymity properties. We give a very abstract idea of this framework, detailed information is available in [7]. In this framework a system consists of a group of agents, each having a local state at each point of the execution. The local state contains all information that the user may have and does not need to be explicitly defined. At each point $(r, m)$ user $i$ can only have access to his local state $r_i(m)$. So he does not know the actual point $(r, m)$ but at least he knows that it must be a point $(r', m')$ such that $r'_i(m') = r'_i(m')$. Let $K_i(r, m)$ be the set of all these points. If a formula $\phi$ is true in all points of $K_i(r, m)$ then we say that $i$ knows $\phi$. In the probabilistic setting it is possible to create a measure on $K_i(r, m)$ and draw conclusions of the form "formula $\phi$ is true with probability $p$".

To define probable innocence we first define a formula $\theta(i, a)$ meaning "user $i$ performed the event $a$". We then say that a system has probable innocence if for all points $(r, m)$, the probability of $\theta(i, a)$ in this point for all users $j$ (that is, the probability that arises by measuring $K_j(r, m)$) is less that one half.

This definition can be expressed in the framework of Section 2.2. The probability of a formula $\phi$ for user $j$ at the point $(r, m)$ depends only on the set $K_j(r, m)$ which itself depends only on $r_j(m)$. The latter is the local state of the user, that is the only things that he can observe. In our framework this corresponds to the observables of the probabilistic automaton. Thus, we can reformulate the definition of Halpern and O'Neill as:

$$\forall i \in I, \forall o \in O : p(a(i) \mid o) \leq 1/2 \tag{4}$$

This definition is similar to the one of Reiter and Rubin but not the same. The difference is that it considers the probability of the user given an observation, not the opposite. If this probability is less that one half then intuitively $i$ appear less likely to have performed $o$ than not to.

The problem with this definition is that the probabilities of the users are not part of the system and we can make no assumptions about them. Consider for example the case where we know that user $i$ visits very often a specific web site, so even if we have 100 users, the probability that he performed a request to this site is 0.99. Then we cannot expect this probability to become less than one half under all observations. A similar remark about strong anonymity led Halpern and O'Neill to define conditional anonymity. If a user $i$ has higher probability of performing an action than user $j$ then we cannot expect this to change because of the system. Instead we can request that the system does not provide any new information about the originator of the action.

## 4    A New Definition of Probable Innocence

In this section we give a new definition of probable innocence that generalizes the existing ones by abstracting from the probabilities of the users. These probabilities, although they affect the probability measure $p$ of the anonymity system, are not part of the protocol and can vary in different executions. To model this fact, let $u$ be a probability measure on the set $I$ of anonymous users. Then, we suppose that the anonymity system is equipped with a probability measure $p_u$, which depends on $u$, satisfying the following conditions:

$$p_u(a(i)) = u(i) \tag{5}$$
$$p_u(o \mid a(i)) = p_{u'}(o \mid a(i)) \tag{6}$$

for all users $i$, observables $o$ and user distributions $u, u'$ such that $u(i) > 0, u'(i) > 0$. Condition (5) requires that the selection of user is made using the distribution $u$. Condition (6) requires that, having selected a user, the distribution $u$ does not affect the probability of any observable $o$. In other words $u$ is used to select a user and only for that. This is typical in anonymity protocols where a user is selected in the beginning (this models the user's decision to send a message) and then some observables are produced that depend on the selected user. We will denote by $p(o \mid a(i))$ the probability $p_u(o \mid a(i))$ under some $u$ such that $u(i) > 0$.

In general we would like our anonymity definitions to range over all possible values of $u$ since we cannot assume anything about the probabilities of the users. Thus, Halpern and O'Neill's definition (4) should be written: $\forall u \forall i \forall o : p_u(a(i) \mid o) \leq 1/2$ which makes even more clear the fact that it cannot hold for all $u$, for example if we take $u(i)$ to be very close to 1. On the other hand, Reiter and Rubin's definition contains only probabilities of the form $p(o \mid a(i))$. Crowds satisfies condition (6) so these probabilities are independent from $u$.

In [7], where they define conditional anonymity, Halpern and O'Neill make the following remark about strong anonymity. Since the probabilities of the users are generally unknown we cannot expect that all users appear with the same probability. All that we can ensure is that the system does not reveal any information, that is that the probability of every user before and after making an observation should be the same. In other words, the fraction between the probabilities of any couple of users should not be one, but should at least remain the same before and after the observation.

We apply the same idea to probable innocence. We start by rewriting relation (4) as

$$\forall i \in A, \forall o \in O : 1 \geq \frac{p_u(a(i) \mid o)}{p_u(\bigvee_{j \neq i} a(j) \mid o)} \tag{7}$$

As we already explained, if $u(i)$ is very high then we cannot expect this fraction to be less than 1. Instead, we could require that it does not surpass the corresponding fraction of the probabilities before the execution of the protocol. So we generalize condition (7) in the following definition.

**Definition 4.** *A system* $(M, I, a, B, p_u)$ *has probable innocence if for all user distributions* $u$, *users* $i \in I$ *and observables* $o \in O$, *the following holds:*

$$(n - 1)\frac{p_u(a(i))}{p_u(\bigvee_{j \neq i} a(j))} \geq \frac{p_u(a(i) \mid o)}{p_u(\bigvee_{j \neq i} a(j) \mid o)}$$

*where* $n = |I|$ *is the number of anonymous users.*

In probable innocence we consider the probability of a user compared to the probability of all the other users together. Definition 4 requires that the fraction of these probabilities after the execution of the protocol should be no bigger than $n - 1$ times the same fraction before the execution. The $n - 1$ factor comes from the fact that in probable innocence *some* information about the sender's identity is leaked. For example, if users are uniformly distributed, each of them has probability $1/n$ before the protocol and the sender could appear with probability $1/2$ afterwards. In this case, the fraction between the sender and all other users is $\frac{1}{n-1}$ before the protocol and becomes 1 after. Definition 4 states that this fraction can be increased, thus leaking some information, but no more than $n - 1$ times.

Definition 4 generalizes relation (4) and can be applied in cases where the distribution of users is not uniform. However it still involves the probabilities of the users, which are not a part of the system. What we would like is a definition similar to Def. 3 which involves only probabilities of events that are part of the system. To achieve this we rewrite Definition 4 using the following transformations. For all users we assume that $u(i) > 0$. Users with zero probability could be removed from Definition 4 before proceeding.

$$(n - 1)\frac{p_u(a(i))}{\sum_{j \neq i} p_u(a(j))} \geq \frac{p_u(a(i) \mid o)}{\sum_{j \neq i} p_u(a(j) \mid o)} \Leftrightarrow$$

$$(n - 1)\frac{p_u(a(i))}{\sum_{j \neq i} p_u(a(j))} \geq \frac{\frac{p_u(o \mid a(i)) p_u(a(i))}{p_u(o)}}{\sum_{j \neq i} \frac{p_u(o \mid a(j)) p_u(a(j))}{p_u(o)}} \Leftrightarrow$$

$$(n - 1) \sum_{j \neq i} p_u(o \mid a(j)) p_u(a(j)) \geq p_u(o \mid a(i)) \sum_{j \neq i} p_u(a(j))$$

We obtain a lower bound of the left clause by replacing all $p_u(o \mid a(j))$ with their minimum. So we require that

$$(n - 1) \min_{j \neq i}\{p_u(o \mid a(j))\} \sum_{j \neq i} p_u(a(j)) \geq p_u(o \mid a(i)) \sum_{j \neq i} p_u(a(j)) \Leftrightarrow \qquad (8)$$

$$(n - 1) \min_{j \neq i} p_u(o \mid a(j)) \geq p_u(o \mid a(i)) \qquad (9)$$

Condition (9) can be interpreted as follows: for each observable, the probability that user $i$ produces it should be balanced by the corresponding probabilities of the other users. It would be more natural to have the sum of all $p_u(o\,|\,a(j))$ at the left side, in fact the left side of (9) is a lower bound of this sum. However, since the probabilities of the users are unknown, we have to consider the "worst" case where the user with the minimum $p_u(o\,|\,a(j))$ has the greatest probability of appearing.

Finally, condition (9) is equivalent to the following definition that we propose as a general definition of probable innocence.

**Definition 5.** *A system* $(M, I, a, B, p_u)$ *has probable innocence if for all observables* $o \in O$ *and for all users* $i, j \in I$:[3]

$$(n - 1)p(o\,|\,a(j)) \geq p(o\,|\,a(i))$$

The meaning of this definition is that in order for $p_u(a(i))/p_u(\bigvee_{j \neq i} a(j))$ to increase at most by $n - 1$ times (Def. 4), the corresponding fraction between the probabilities of the observables must be at most $n - 1$. Note that in probabilistic anonymity (Def. 3) $p(o\,|\,a(i))$ and $p(o\,|\,a(j))$ are required to be equal. In probable innocence we allow $p(o\,|\,a(i))$ to be bigger, thus losing some anonymity, but no more than $n - 1$ times.

Definition 5 has the advantage of including only the probabilities of the observables and not those of the users, similarly to the Definition 3 of probabilistic anonymity. It is clear that Definition 5 implies Definition 4 since we strengthened the first to obtain the second. Since Definition 4 considers all possible distributions of the users, the inverse implication also holds. The proof of all propositions can be found in [10].

**Proposition 2.** *Definitions 4 and 5 are equivalent.*

*Examples.* Recall now the two examples of figure 2. If we apply Definition 5 to the first one we see that it doesn't hold since $(n - 1)p(o_1\,|\,a(2)) = 0 \ngeq \frac{c}{n - p_f} = p(o_1\,|\,a(1))$. This agree with our intuition of probable innocence being violated when user 1 is observed. In the second example the definition holds since $\forall i, j\ :\ p(o_i\,|\,a(i)) = p(o_j\,|\,a(j))$. Thus, we see that in these two examples our definition reflects correctly the notion of probable innocence.

## 4.1   Relation to Other Definitions

**Definition by Reiter and Rubin.** Reiter and Rubin's definition can be expressed by the condition (3). It considers the probabilities of the observables (not the users) and it requires that for each user, a special observable, meaning that the user is observed by a corrupted member, has probability less than $p(h)/2$. As we saw at the examples of figure 2 what is important is not the actual probability of an observable under a specific user, but its relation with the corresponding probabilities under the other users.

However in Crowds there are some important symmetries. First of all the number of the observables is the same as the number of users. For each user $i$ there is an observable $o_i$ meaning that the user $i$ is observed. When $i$ is the initiator, $o_i$ has clearly a higher probability than the other observables. However, since forwarders are randomly

---

[3] Remember that $p_u(o\,|\,a(i))$ is independent from $u$ so we can take any distribution such that $u(i) > 0$, for example a uniform one.

selected, the probability of $o_j$ is the same for all $j \neq i$. The same holds for the observables. $o_i$ is more likely to have been performed by $i$. However all other users $j \neq i$ have the same probability of producing it. These symmetries can be expressed as:

$$\forall i \in I, \forall k, l \neq i : p(o_k \mid a(i)) = p(o_l \mid a(i)) \tag{10}$$

$$p(o_i \mid a(k)) = p(o_i \mid a(l)) \tag{11}$$

Because of these symmetries, we cannot have a situation similar to the ones of Figure 2. On the left-hand side, for example, the probability $p(o_1 \mid a(2)) = 0$ should be the same as $p(o_3 \mid a(2))$. To keep the value 0 (which is the reason why probable innocence is not satisfied) we should have 0 everywhere in the row (except $p(o_2 \mid a(2))$) which is impossible since the sum of the row should be $p(h)$ and $p(o_2 \mid a(2)) \leq p(h)/2$.

So the reason why probable innocence is satisfied in Crowds is not the fact that observing the initiator has low probability (what definition (2) ensures) by itself, but the fact that definition (2), because of the symmetry, forces the probability of observing any of the other users to be high enough.

**Proposition 3.** *Under the symmetry requirements (10) and (11), Definition 5 is equivalent to the one of Reiter and Rubin.*

Note that the number of anonymous users $n$ is not the same as the number of users $m$ in Crowds, in fact $n = m - c$ where $c$ is the number of corrupted users.

**Definition of Halpern and O'Neill.** One of the motivations behind the new definition of probable innocence is that it should make no assumptions about the probabilities of the users. If we assume a uniform distribution of users then it can be shown that our definition becomes the same as the one of Halpern and O'Neill.

**Proposition 4.** *The definition of Halpern and O'Neill can be obtained by Definition 4 if we consider a uniform distribution of users, that is a distribution $u$ such that $\forall i, j \in I : u(i) = u(j) = 1/n$.*

Note that the equivalence of Def. 4 and Def. 5 is based on the fact that the former ranges over all possible distributions $u$ (details about the proof can be found in [10]). Thus Def. 5 is strictly stronger than the one of Halpern and O'Neill.

**Probabilistic anonymity.** It is easy to see that strong anonymity (equation (1)) implies Halpern and O'Neill's definition of probable innocence. Definition 5 preserves the same implication in the case of probabilistic anonymity.

**Proposition 5.** *Probabilistic anonymity implies probable innocence (Definition 5).*

The relation between the various definitions of anonymity is summarized in Figure 3. The classification in columns is based on the type of probabilities that are considered. The first column considers the probability of different users, the second the probability of the same user before and after an observation and the third the probability of the observables. Concerning the lines, the first corresponds to the strong case and the second to probable innocence. It is clear from the table that the new definition is to probable innocence as conditional anonymity is to strong anonymity.

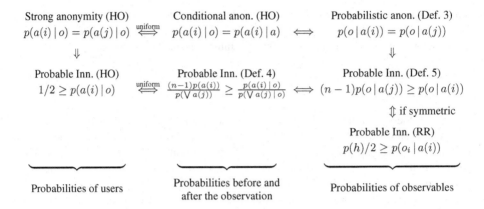

**Fig. 3.** Relation between the various anonymity definitions

## 5   Conclusion

In this paper we consider probable innocence, a weak notion of anonymity provided by real-world systems such as Crowds. We analyze the definitions of probable innocence existing in literature, in particular: the one by Reiter and Rubin which is suitable for systems which, like Crowds, satisfy certain symmetries, and the one given by Halpern and O'Neill, which expresses a condition on the probability of the users.

Our contribution is a definition of probable innocence which is (intuitively) adequate for a general class of protocols, abstracts from the probabilities of the users and involves only the probabilities that depend solely on the system. The new definition is shown to be equivalent to the existing ones under symmetry conditions (Reiter and Rubin) or uniform distribution of the users (Halpern and O'Neill).

## References

1. Reiter, M.K., Rubin, A.D.: Crowds: anonymity for Web transactions. ACM Transactions on Information and System Security **1** (1998) 66–92
2. Syverson, P., Goldschlag, D., Reed, M.: Anonymous connections and onion routing. In: IEEE Symposium on Security and Privacy, Oakland, California (1997) 44–54
3. Dingledine, R., Freedman, M.J., Molnar, D.: The free haven project: Distributed anonymous storage service. In: Designing Privacy Enhancing Technologies, International Workshop on Design Issues in Anonymity and Unobservability. Volume 2009 of LNCS., Springer (2000) 67–95
4. Berthold, O., Federrath, H., Köpsell, S.: Web mixes: A system for anonymous and unobservable internet access. In: Designing Privacy Enhancing Technologies, International Workshop on Design Issues in Anonymity and Unobservability. Volume 2009 of LNCS., Springer (2000) 115–129
5. Clarke, I., Sandberg, O., Wiley, B., Hong, T.W.: Freenet: A distributed anonymous information storage and retrieval system. In: Designing Privacy Enhancing Technologies, International Workshop on Design Issues in Anonymity and Unobservability. Volume 2009 of LNCS., Springer (2000) 44–66

6.  Chaum, D.: The dining cryptographers problem: Unconditional sender and recipient untrace-ability. Journal of Cryptology **1** (1988) 65–75
7.  Halpern, J.Y., O'Neill, K.R.: Anonymity and information hiding in multiagent systems. In: Proc. of the 16th IEEE Computer Security Foundations Workshop. (2003) 75–88
8.  Halpern, J.Y., O'Neill, K.R.: Anonymity and information hiding in multiagent systems. Journal of Computer Security (2005) To appear.
9.  Bhargava, M., Palamidessi, C.: Probabilistic anonymity. In: Proceedings of CONCUR 2005. LNCS, Springer-Verlag (2005) To appear. Report version available at `http://www.lix.polytechnique.fr/~catuscia/papers/Anonymity/report.ps`.
10. Chatzikokolakis, K., Palamidessi, C.: Probable innocence revisited. Technical report, INRIA Futurs and LIX (2005) Available at `http://www.lix.polytechnique.fr/~catuscia/papers/Anonymity/reportPI.pdf`.
11. Segala, R., Lynch, N.: Probabilistic simulations for probabilistic processes. Nordic Journal of Computing **2** (1995) 250–273 An extended abstract appeared in *Proceedings of CONCUR '94*, LNCS 836: 481-496.
12. Schneider, S., Sidiropoulos, A.: CSP and anonymity. In: Proc. of the European Symposium on Research in Computer Security (ESORICS). Volume 1146 of LNCS., Springer-Verlag (1996) 198–218
13. Ryan, P.Y., Schneider, S.: Modelling and Analysis of Security Protocols. Addison-Wesley (2001)
14. Shmatikov, V.: Probabilistic analysis of anonymity. In: IEEE Computer Security Foundations Workshop (CSFW). (2002) 119–128
15. Wright, M., Adler, M., Levine, B., Shields, C.: An analysis of the degradation of anonymous protocols. In: ISOC Network and Distributed System Security Symposium (NDSS). (2002)

# Relative Trustworthiness

Johan W. Klüwer[1] and Arild Waaler[2]

[1] Dep. of Philosophy, University of Oslo
johanw@filosofi.uio.no
[2] Finnmark College and Dep. of Informatics,
University of Oslo
arild@ifi.uio.no

**Abstract.** We present a method for trust scenarios with more than one trustee, where sets of trustees are ordered in a relation of relative trustworthiness. We show how a priority structure implicit in a trust relation can be made fully explicit by means of a lattice and how a system of default expectations arises from a systematic interpretation. The default structure lends itself to formal interpretation, but is independent of a particular logical language. The theory is designed to directly extend the analysis of the concept of trust given by Andrew Jones.

## 1 Introduction

In this paper, we present a method for representing and reasoning about attitudes of trust with regard to a base set of trustees. We have two primary aims. First, we want to clarify issues of *relative* trust: of a subject that trusts a variety of entities, but with different degrees of confidence. Second, we make a distinction between trust *by default* and unconditional, full trust, and provide a structured way from the former to the latter. An outcome of the analysis is that the trusting subject's expectations about relative trustworthiness may need to be corrected once the consequences of default attitudes have been worked out.

We do not attempt to give an account of what constitutes trust in itself. Instead, we have designed the relative-trust framework to be directly applicable, as a compatible extension, to the conceptual analysis of trust given by Andrew Jones [2]. Jones provides a minimal characterization, designed to be valid for every kind of trust, from trust in mere regularities to trust in the operations of complex normative structures. Quite appropriately for the fundamental analysis, he does not discuss the complexities involved in trusting more than one entity. In scenarios involving multiple trustees, distinctions between different degrees of trust are however quite essential. Conflicts or violations of trust may have systematic impact, and a proper and efficient way of handling the relational structures involved is important for the conception of trust to have practical application. This paper provides a method for applying Jones' analysis to scenarios in which an arbitrary number of entities are trusted. We provide various examples, intended to demonstrate applicability in real cases.

T. Dimitrakos et al. (Eds.): FAST 2005, LNCS 3866, pp. 158–170, 2006.

## 2    The Notion of Trust

### 2.1    Trust as Rule- and Conformity-Belief

Our point of departure is to adopt the analysis of trust given by Jones [2]. According to that analysis, a trusting attitude essentially consists in having a pair of *beliefs*: a *rule-belief* and a *conformity-belief*.[1] Jones' exposition employs five different scenarios, which involve different types of trust but nevertheless are seen to satisfy the same pattern; we quote three of them [2, p. 226]:

*S1 (the regularity scenario). x* believes that there exists a regularity in *y*'s behavior, so that under particular kinds of circumstances *y* exhibits a particular kind of behavior ... In addition, *x* believes that this regularity will also be instantiated on some future occasion(s); that is to say, *x* believes that the future occasion(s) will not prove to be an exception.

*S2 (the obligation scenario). x* believes that there is a rule requiring *y* to do *Z*, and that *y*'s behavior will in fact comply with this rule.

*S4 (the informing scenario). x* believes that *y* is transmitting some information to him, and that the content of *y*'s message, or signal, is reliable.

A trusting subject believes a pair of propositions about a trusted entity: that a rule or regularity applies to the trustee (rule-belief), and that the rule or regularity is in fact followed or instantiated (conformity-belief). For brevity, we will use the letter $R$ to denote the trust rule constitutive of a given scenario, and the expression $R(a)$ to express the statement that the rule applies to an entity $a$. We will use the letter $C$ to denote the according predicate for conformity, with $C(a)$ meaning that $a$ does in fact conform. I.e.,

$$x \text{ is trusted iff } R(x) \text{ and } C(x) \text{ are both believed.}$$

As examples matching the scenarios quoted above, consider the following pairs (note that these are not intended to strictly match the presentation in [2]).

S1  $R(a)$: $a$ usually goes to the movies on Sunday; $C(a)$: $a$ will go the movies this Sunday.

S2  $R(a)$: $a$ ought to repay the €10 he borrowed; $C(a)$: $a$ will pay the €10.

S4  $R(a)$: $a$ ought to deliver only true information; $C(a)$: the information $a$ delivers is true.

We want to extend this analysis of trust with a structured approach to trust in *sets* of trustees, one that can handle trust that several people will be going to the movies, that several sources deliver true information, and so forth.

### 2.2    Relative Trustworthiness

When we are presented with a situation in which more than one agent is trusted according to the same criterion, we can always ask questions of *degrees* of trust. We often

---

[1] We will assume throughout that having such a pair of beliefs is not only necessary but also sufficient for trust, which is natural for present purposes. Note that Jones doesn't commit to this strong thesis.

need to consider trusting attitudes directed toward not single agents, but *sets* of agents
– such as, one may believe that some members of a set of agents will conform without
believing that every member of the set will. Is it more likely that *a* will conform than
that *b* will conform, or that only one of the two (*a* and *b*) will conform than that both
will? In general, when a rule *R* applies to every member in a set of agents *X*, we may
need to consider a range of trust attitudes, perhaps a distinct one for each subset of *X*.

In the following, talk about "what is believed" is assumed to apply to an implicit
doxastic subject that has beliefs at different *degrees of confidence*, abbreviated *doc*. We
will use the notion of degree of confidence informally here; cf. [5, section 3.5] for a
formal approach and discussion.

It is natural to say that a rule *R* establishes a *dimension* of trust according to which
agents, or sets of agents, can be trusted to greater or lesser degrees. Prioritized beliefs
about conformity with the rule establishes a relation between the trusted entities: The
degrees of confidence with which conformity-beliefs are held imply a structure of *relative trustworthiness*.

We consider the following to be guiding principles for what follows.

Given a set of trustees, that some member(s) will conform to the rule is at least
as plausible as that every member will conform. $\qquad(1)$

If some entity *x* is trusted, and *y* is at least as trustworthy as *x*, then rationality
demands that *y* should be trusted too. $\qquad(2)$

Accept that a trustee (set of trustees) will in fact conform, unless this is inconsistent with what you have already accepted. $\qquad(3)$

We will introduce a formal apparatus for representing the set of trustees, and the *trustworthiness relation* between subsets of the set of trustees. The definition of the
trustworthiness relation will be quite similar to the one introduced by John Cantwell [1].

There is a wide range of scenarios to which the relative-trust approach is relevant, as
we will try to illustrate this with examples following the formal exposition. Examples
in section 3.3 demonstrate simple applications to trust in information sources. In section 4, we describe the case of a legal jury, in which the majority vote is decisive, an
authentication scenario in which input from three different entities is considered, and a
debtors scenario.

### 2.3   The Basic Pre-order on Trustees

Given a trust scenario as defined by a general rule *R* and conformity criterion *C*, let $\mathfrak{S}$
be a (possibly empty) finite set of *trustees*. The members of $\mathfrak{S}$ are precisely those single
trustees that the implicit subject believes the rule *R* to apply to.[2]

Notation: Small Latin letters $a, b, c$ denote trustees, small variable letters $x, y, z$ range
over trustee units, capital Latin letters $A, B, C$ denote particular sets of trustee units,
and capital variable letters $X, Y, Z$ range over arbitrary sets of trustee units. We will

---

[2] We assume that the rule-beliefs of the subject are believed with full conviction (at a maximal
*doc*), although nothing will turn on this. In particular, we make no attempt at providing a
formalism for the rules *R*.

sometimes have to collect sets of trustee units, for which we shall use capital Greek letters $\Gamma, \Delta$.

The *trustworthiness relation* $\trianglelefteq$ is a relation between subsets of $\mathfrak{S}$; we will often refer to these subsets as *trustee units*. A trustee unit $x$ is an entity that is capable of being the subject of a conformity-belief that $C(x)$, as follows: A singleton unit $\{a\}$ represents a single trustee, and $C(\{a\})$ is the proposition that $a$ will conform. With a non-singleton unit $x$, conformity $C(x)$ is taken to mean that *some* member of $x$ will conform to the rule.

We assume that the trustworthiness relation is reflexive and transitive (a *pre-order*). Two trustee units $x$ and $y$ may be *trustworthiness-equivalent*, written $x \sim y$.

$$x \sim y \quad =_{\text{def}} \quad x \trianglelefteq y \text{ and } y \trianglelefteq x \tag{4}$$

We write $x \lhd y$ to express that $y$ is strictly more trustworthy than $x$.

$$x \lhd y \quad =_{\text{def}} \quad x \trianglelefteq y \text{ and not } x \sim y \tag{5}$$

Trustee units that are unrelated by $\trianglelefteq$ will be called *independent*, denoted $x \wr y$. If no two trustee units are independent, we say $\trianglelefteq$ is *connected*.

We interpret the trustworthiness relation in terms of belief, at different degrees of confidence, that trustee units will conform. If $x \lhd y$, the subject has a stronger belief that $y$ will conform than that $x$ will. $x \sim y$ means that belief in conformity for $x$ is just as strong as that for $y$.[3] Independence $x \wr y$ obtains when the strength of belief that $x$ will conform is not comparable to that which which $y$ is believed to conform (neither stronger than, weaker than, or the same). If we allow for the trusting subject to reflect on its own degrees of conviction, we may say that independence is a consequence of lack of belief, where neither of $x \rhd y$, $x \lhd y$, and $x \sim y$ is believed to obtain.

Principle (1) implies that enlargement of a trustee unit with new members may never yield a unit that is less likely to conform. Hence, a unit will be at least as trustworthy as every unit that it contains as a subset. This motivates taking the following principle, which we will occasionally refer to as *monotonicity*, to be valid.

$$x \trianglelefteq x \cup y. \tag{6}$$

It follows that for each source unit $x$, the following hold.

$$x \trianglelefteq \mathfrak{S}, \tag{7}$$

$$\emptyset \trianglelefteq x. \tag{8}$$

To see why (7) is valid, note that conformity by $\mathfrak{S}$ is secured as long as just one trustee conforms. At the other extreme, we stipulate that the empty set is a limit case that never conforms, motivating (8).

The framework we present is general, because it is is not sensitive to the type of members of $\mathfrak{S}$, but therefore also weak on assumptions. Consider some likely applications and according kinds of trustees: Sources of information are a prominent type, and could include sensors taking measurements, newspapers, or witnesses; for these, trust

---

[3] To be precise, let the expression "$\varphi$ is believed more strongly than $\psi$" mean (i) that $\varphi$ is believed at some *doc*, and (ii) that every *doc* at which $\psi$ is believed is inferior to a *doc* at which $\varphi$ is believed. For equally strong belief, (ii) is, $\psi$ is believed at every *doc* at which $\varphi$ is believed.

will typically be of the S1 "regularity" or S4 "information" kinds. Agents, artificial and human, are another major class, and typically subject to rules in the sense of obligations S2. For instance, in a "debtors" scenario, $\mathfrak{S}$ may consist of individuals that owe money, and the subject believes each of them to be under obligation to make appropriate repayments. Surely, in many concrete cases it will be reasonable to adopt domain-specific constraints that strengthen the trustworthiness relation.

## 2.4   The Poset of Trust-Equivalent Trustee Units

To have an *attitude* of trust, given some $\mathfrak{S}$, is to trust a (possibly empty) set of trustee units. In terms of belief in conformity, having an attitude of trust toward a set of trustee units $A$ amounts to believing that at least one member of each trustee unit in $A$ will conform. For example, a trust attitude that is directed toward the trustee units $x$, $y$, and $z$ involves conformity beliefs $C(x), C(y), C(z)$ – for each unit $x$, $y$, and $z$, *some* member of the unit is expected to conform to the relevant trust rule.

In the following, we will allow ourselves to talk about attitudes as being nothing more than sets of trustee units, and to say that a trustee unit is "included" in an attitude of trust, meaning that it is among those trusted. The empty set represents the minimal attitude of placing trust in none of the trustee units; it will be denoted by the symbol $\wedge$.

Given a trust relation $\lhd$, we can distinguish those trust attitudes that respect the relation. The relevant principle is expressed in rule (2), that $x$ may only be trusted if every $y \unrhd x$ is trusted as well. In this section and the next, we identify the *permissible* trust attitudes according to this principle.

We use the following standard terminology. In a *poset* $(S, \leq)$ the $\leq$-relation is reflexive, transitive and anti-symmetric. The poset has a unique cover relation $\prec$, defined as $x \prec y$ iff $x < y$ and $x \leq z < y$ implies $z = x$. $C \subseteq S$ is an *antichain* if every two distinct elements in $C$ are incomparable by $\leq$. Note in particular that $\emptyset$ is an antichain. Every subset of $S$ has $\leq$-minimal elements, and the set of these elements is an antichain. $\uparrow C$ denotes an *up-set*, defined as $\{x \mid (\exists y \in C)(y \leq x)\}$. The set of antichains in a poset is isomorphic to the set of up-sets under set inclusion.

If an attitude of trust includes a trustee unit $x$, but not an equivalently trustworthy trustee unit $y$, then the attitude is not permissible.[4] This motivates a focus on the equivalence classes of $\mathfrak{S}$ modulo $\sim$. Where $x \subseteq \mathfrak{S}$,

$$[x] \quad =_{\text{def}} \quad \{y : x \sim y\} \tag{9}$$

Let $\hat{\mathfrak{S}}$ be the set of all equivalence classes of $\mathfrak{S}$ modulo $\sim$. We will say a set of trustees $x$ is *vacuous* with regard to trustworthiness if $x \in [\emptyset]$ (cf. (8)). In the extreme case that every trustee unit is a member of $[\emptyset]$, the only permissible attitudes are $\wedge$ and $[\emptyset]$, and the trustworthiness relation itself is said to be vacuous.

Where $X$ and $Y$ are in $\hat{\mathfrak{S}}$, define a relation $\dot{\lhd}$ of relative strength between them as follows.

$$X \dot{\lhd} Y \quad =_{\text{def}} \quad (\exists x \in X)(\exists y \in Y)(x \lhd y) \tag{10}$$

Let $X \dot{\unlhd} Y$ designate $X \dot{\lhd} Y$ or $X = Y$. $X \wr Y$ designates independence.

---

[4] Note that this is implied by the interpretation of trustworthiness-equivalence in terms of equally strong beliefs in conformity.

**Lemma 1.** $(\dot{\mathfrak{S}}, \dot{\trianglelefteq})$ *is a poset in which* $[\emptyset]$ *is the unique minimum and* $[\mathfrak{S}]$ *the unique maximum.* $(\dot{\mathfrak{S}}, \dot{\trianglelefteq})$ *is a linear order iff* $(\wp\,\mathfrak{S}, \trianglelefteq)$ *is connected.*

*Proof.* Monotonicity entails the unique minimum and maximum. The other properties follow easily from the construction of $(\dot{\mathfrak{S}}, \dot{\trianglelefteq})$.

## 2.5   A Lattice of Trust Levels

We know from Lemma 1 that $(\dot{\mathfrak{S}}, \dot{\trianglelefteq})$ is a poset, one that orders sets of equivalent trustee units according to strength. Given this poset, it straightforward to identify the permissible trust attitudes: a trust attitude is permissible if it is an up-set in $(\dot{\mathfrak{S}}, \dot{\trianglelefteq})$. Technically, we will represent an attitude by its set of minima, or equivalently, by an antichain in the partial order $(\dot{\mathfrak{S}}, \dot{\trianglelefteq})$. We define the set $\mathfrak{T}$ of permissible trust attitudes as follows,

$$\mathfrak{T} = \{\cup\Gamma \mid \Gamma \text{ is an antichain in } (\dot{\mathfrak{S}}, \dot{\trianglelefteq})\}.$$

There is a natural relation of strength between permissible trust attitudes. Having a weak trust attitude means trusting only that few trustee units will conform, or perhaps none; a strong attitude means trusting many trustee units, or perhaps all, will conform to the relevant trust rule. Let $\Gamma$ and $\varDelta$ be antichains in $(\dot{\mathfrak{S}}, \dot{\trianglelefteq})$. We define the relation $\leq$ between permissible attitudes by

$$\cup\Gamma \leq \cup\varDelta \text{ iff } \uparrow\!\varDelta \subseteq \uparrow\!\Gamma.$$

The attitude $\wedge$ of trusting no trustee unit, $\cup\emptyset$, is $\leq$-maximal in $\mathfrak{T}$. This is natural, as the corresponding attitude of trusting no trustee unit will always have a maximal degree of reliability. Ordered by $\leq$, the members of $\mathfrak{T}$ form a lattice in which lesser nodes represent stronger trust attitudes. It is natural to talk about the permissible trust attitudes as corresponding to a hierarchy of degrees of trust. We shall hence occasionally refer to $\mathfrak{T}$ as the set of *trust levels*.[5]

In the lattice $(\mathfrak{T}, \leq)$, $A < B$ intuitively means that $B$ is a level of trustworthiness that is genuinely greater than $A$. Let $\sqcap$ denote meet and $\sqcup$ denote join. Then $A \sqcap B$ is the weakest trust level that is at least as strong as both $A$ and $B$; if $A$ and $B$ are comparable by $\leq$, it is equal to the stronger of the two, but if not, it is stronger than both and refers to the level that combines the two. $A \sqcup B$ is the strongest trust level that is at least as weak as both $A$ and $B$. (In terms of attitudes, $A \sqcap B$ refers to the attitude of believing all units in $A$ and all units in $B$ to conform, and $A \sqcup B$ to the attitude that some unit in $A$ or in $B$ will conform.)

The lattice of trust levels makes explicit what the permissible trust attitudes are and how they are related with regard to strength. This makes it suitable as a frame of reference for choosing, in a given scenario, a *threshold* of trust: a level that is deemed sufficiently trustworthy. The lattice lays out the rational options – it presents us with the set of trusting attitudes that are permissible, given the initial trustworthiness relation,

---

[5] The strength of levels of trustworthiness varies inversely with strength of the requisite attitudes. For instance, consider the attitude $\wedge$ of not trusting any trustee unit. This represents a maximally weak attitude that does not require any belief in conformity. $\wedge$ is however maximal as a level of trustworthiness, as the empty set of trustee units can never fail to conform.

and properly relates them according to reliability. Setting a threshold may also be described in terms of *risk*. If $A < B$, then to choose $A$ as the threshold of trust is to take a greater risk with regard to trusting than if $B$ is chosen. A level of trustworthiness can be used to specify a "limit" of risk, to draw a line between what is trusted, and not trusted, in the non-relative sense of the word. For example, with a threshold at $A \sqcup B$, if $A$ and $B$ are comparable, risk is limited to the more trustworthy of the two; if incomparable, then to the closest level that represents comparably less risk than both $A$ and $B$. To say that $A \sqcap B$ lies within the risk limit means that $A$ and $B$ are both considered reliable (i.e., that all trustee units in both $A$ and $B$ are trustworthy).

Using the lattice notation, a threshold of trust can be conveniently specified by direct reference to trustee units. Observe that each member of $\dot{\mathfrak{S}}$ is a member of $\mathfrak{T}$. Therefore, any expression using members of $\dot{\mathfrak{S}}$ (i.e., equivalence classes of source units), $\sqcap$ and $\sqcup$ denotes a unique level of trust.

# 3   Default, Expected Trust vs. Actual Trust

## 3.1   A Tree of *fallbacks* for Broken Trust

The core of a *default* conception of relative trust is the default rule (3) to assume trustees to conform, unless this is in conflict with what you already know. We presently interpret this rule with respect to relative trust. Let us consider a trusting subject that has only permissible trust attitudes. In the non-relative sense of "trust", $\wedge$ is always trustworthy, and an attitude $X$ is adopted, on condition that every $Y \geq X$ is also adopted, by default.

Now, if adopting an attitude $X$ should be inconsistent with adopting a weaker attitude $Y$, then $X$ is not an acceptable trust level, and we say that trust at $X$ is *broken*. Trust at $X$ is broken if conformity by the trustee units at $X$ has implications that are inconsistent with the consequences of conformity accepted at a superior level. If we allow for the trusting subject to have antecedent beliefs, such beliefs may also be inconsistent with trusting at level $X$.

When blocking occurs, the significance of trusting at $X$ should be identified with the adoption of some weaker, acceptable trust attitude. We will call this the *fallback* of $X$. The fallback, as the value of a blocked default, is the key notion that allows us to view relative trust as a default attitude.

Let $X$ be an element of $\mathfrak{T}$ different from $\wedge$, and let $\Gamma$ be the $\leq$-cover of $X$. Given that $\Gamma$ is singleton, we straightforwardly identify $\bigcup \Gamma$ as the appropriate fallback of $X$. Where not, note that by construction of the lattice, $X$ is a level composed of a set of simpler levels, the members of $\Gamma$. That trust is broken at $X$ means some of these levels are not trustable. In this case, the fallback of $X$ should be identified as a level with greater trustworthiness than every $Y$ immediately superior to $X$. Let the fallback $\mathfrak{f}(X)$ of $X$ be defined as

$$\mathfrak{f}(X) = \text{lub}(\Gamma) \text{ in } (\mathfrak{T}, \leq).$$

The fallback function is undefined for $\wedge$; otherwise every node has a unique fallback. $\wedge$, representing the trust level of antecedent knowledge (if any), is always the fallback of $[\mathfrak{S}]$. Note that every path from the lattice maximum $\wedge$ to a trust level $X$ must go through $\mathfrak{f}(X)$, and that $\mathfrak{f}(X)$ is the $\leq$-minimal node with this property.

The *fallback tree* $(\mathfrak{T}, \prec)$ is defined as the weakest relation such that for all $X \in \mathfrak{T}$, $\mathfrak{f}(X) \prec X$. It is easy to show that the fallback tree is indeed a tree with root $\wedge$.

## 3.2   Formal Representation of Trust Scenarios

The fallback tree of a given trust scenario has been described informally in terms of default inference. For the representation of a fallback tree in the language of a default *logic*, we require a target language with sufficient expressive power. For certain simple kinds of scenarios, a translation has been provided in [4], namely, for the case of trusted sources of information whose conformity propositions can be expressed as formulae of propositional logic, or in a restricted multi-modal doxastic language. In these cases, various default logics can be chosen for expression of the default structure.

There are however prominent cases of trust that would require a more complex formalism. One case in point is where conformity consists in *action*, as might be expressed in a modal language with "praxeological" operators. (For instance, conformity for the rule "*a* ought to see to it that *p* is true" could be expressed, using a notation of currency, as $E_a p$.) In such scenarios, agents are typically trusted to bring about or secure that states of affairs obtain. For a formal representation of such scenarios, we would need a language capable of expressing both default attitudes and action statements.

In the following, we will assume that a *knowledge base* of statements is believed at the trust level $\wedge$. We represent the knowledge base by the symbol $\kappa$. Different applications of the theory might require different implementations with regard to the content of $\kappa$. In particular, if it is desired that *rule-beliefs* are made formally explicit, it may be natural to let $\kappa$ contain formulae of a greater complexity than those expressing conformity-beliefs (for illustration, cf. [3, section 3.4.3], where rule- and conformity-beliefs for a different types of scenarios are expressed in a formal, multi-modal language).

## 3.3   After the Default Evaluation: A New Trust Relation

If desired, we can interpret a trustworthiness relation as representing the subject's *default expectation* about which trustees will conform to the general trust rule $R$. We then say that belief in conformity is by default only, as opposed to full belief.

After evaluation of a set of defaults, in sequences as given by the fallback tree, we do however have a situation in which conformity-propositions are believed *not* by default, but unconditionally (although typically still at a variety of degrees of confidence). The outcome of evaluation of the default structure is a (prioritized) belief state in which unconditional conformity-beliefs are held at every non-blocked level where trust is not broken. For each trustee unit $x$ s.t. $C(x)$ is believed (at whatever degree of confidence), there is trust; where not, the lack of conformity-belief implies that $x$ is not trusted. A *new* trustworthiness relation arises from this resulting belief state, as can be determined from the fallback tree in the following way.

1. Where $x$ is not trusted at any level, say $x$ is vacuous: $x \sim \emptyset$.
2. Where $x$ and $y$ are trusted, interpret the trust levels as levels of confidence to determine relative trustworthiness.
3. Apply *monotonicity* to get a proper trustworthiness relation.

Such a "consequent", post-evaluation relation may be seen as expressing explicitly the subject's trust attitudes, as a result of a reasoned working out of the consequences of initial expectations of trustworthiness. It is natural to see this in a dynamic perspective: the initial, "antecedent" trust relation expresses the subject's expectation of trustworthiness. Evaluation of the default structure amounts to working out the consequences of this expected order, and the result is a possible modification of the trustworthiness relation. Some trustee units may be demoted as vacuous, while others may be promoted to greater trustworthiness.

We intend to address the dynamics of evolving trust relations in future work. For now, we simply give some examples to illustrate how a new trustworthiness relation can be determined from the outcome of the evaluation of defaults. In these examples, $a$ and $b$ are assumed to be information sources delivering propositional formulae. We display the fallback trees, decorated with post-evaluation formulae at each node. (The nodes $\wedge$ and $\emptyset$ have been omitted from the graphs to save space.) Where a level has obtained its value $\varphi$ from a fallback, we indicate this as "$\perp/\varphi$".

In referring to particular trustee units in examples we will consistently simplify notation by omitting brackets: $a \lhd bc$ is, e.g., shorthand for $\{a\} \lhd \{b, c\}$. Likewise, the set $\{\{a\}, \{a, b\}\}$ will be denoted $a, ab$. Observe that the symbol $a$ should, depending on the context, either be taken as a reference to the trustee $a$ or to the singleton trustee set $\{a\}$ or to the singleton trustee set collection $\{\{a\}\}$.

*Example 1 (No relation change).* Let $\kappa$ be empty, and assign information as $\kappa : \top$, $a : p \wedge q$, $b : q \wedge r$. We assume a linear relation where $ab \rhd a \rhd b \rhd \emptyset$. The decorated fallback tree shows that no trust is broken – all trust expectations are met. In this case, there is no reason to revise the trust relation post-evaluation; the consequent relation is the same as the expected relation.

$$ab \; : q \wedge (p \vee r)$$
$$|$$
$$a \; : p \wedge q$$
$$|$$
$$b \; : p \wedge q \wedge r$$

*Example 2 (Modification of trust relation).* Here is a case in which the composite $ab$ is trusted (intuitively, what $a$ and $b$ agree on is acceptable), while $a$ and $b$ both turn out to be untrustable. This will typically arise in cases where $a$ and $b$ are equivalently trustworthy, but provide incompatible information, so let $ab \rhd a \sim b \rhd \emptyset$. Assign information as $\kappa : \top$, $a : p \wedge q$, $b : p \wedge \neg q$. Note that $C(ab)$ is $p$, $C(a)$ is $p \wedge q$, $C(b)$ is $p \wedge \neg q$.

$$ab \; : p$$
$$|$$
$$a, b \; : \perp/p$$

Here, the belief $p$ at level $ab$ means $ab$ is trusted. Neither $a$ nor $b$ is trusted, because the requisite conformity-beliefs are missing: this means both $a$ and $b$ should be considered vacuous post-evaluation. The antecedent and consequent trust relations are the following.

*Example 3 (Independent levels, no change).* Another example in which no revision of the trustworthiness relation is called for. Let *a* and *b* be independent, non-vacuous, and less trustworthy than *ab*. Assign information as $\kappa : \top, a : p \wedge q, b : p \wedge \neg q$.

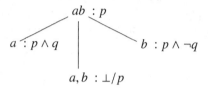

## 4   Examples

*Example 4 (Jury).* We consider a simplified characterization of trust attitudes toward a legal jury. Each juror is required to deliver a statement that a defendant is guilty ($p$) or not guilty ($\neg p$). The jurors are subject to various norms about exercising their best judgment, honesty, and so forth. Our aim is only to characterize the notion of "the" statement made by the jury, as typically given by a *majority* vote (in the case of a tie, no statement is made). Trust in the jury's judgment is therefore trust that what the majority agrees on is correct.

The jurors are most naturally considered to be equally trustworthy: The judgment of one is as good as that of any other, and furthermore, every set of *n* jurors is equivalently trustworthy to any other set with the same number of members. Majority rule means each set of jurors that has less than half of the jury's members is considered vacuous. (Where, e.g., agreement of five out of seven members is required for a valid decision, four-member trustee units also need to be considered vacuous.)

Posets of the trust relations for two-, three-, and four-member juries, according to these requirements, will be as follows; let $\mathfrak{S}$ be, respectively, $\{a, b\}$, $\{a, b, c\}$, and $\{a, b, c, d\}$.

$$ab \qquad abc \qquad abcd$$
$$| \qquad\qquad | \qquad\qquad\qquad |$$
$$a, b, \emptyset \qquad ab, ac, bc \qquad abc, abc, acd, bcd$$
$$| \qquad\qquad\qquad |$$
$$a, b, c, \emptyset \qquad ab, ac, ad, bc, bd$$
$$|$$
$$a, b, c, d, \emptyset$$

Because conformity by each juror requires only a "yes" or "no" statement, we can simplify these relations to having only two levels: Any statement agreed to by at least the majority of trustees will be sufficient for a majority vote, and any statement by smaller trustee units will then be overruled. The simplified relations are the following.

$$ab \qquad abc, ab, ac, bc \qquad abcd, abc, abc, acd, bcd$$
$$| \qquad\qquad | \qquad\qquad\qquad |$$
$$a, b, \emptyset \qquad a, b, c, \emptyset \qquad ab, ac, ad, bc, bd, a, b, c, d, \emptyset$$

*Example 5 (Authentication).* For this example, we wish to represent an authentication or admission test, in which three trustees $a$, $b$, and $c$ each deliver a statement $p$ for "admit" or $\neg p$ for "don't admit". Concrete scenarios matching this may be admissions procedures for entering an education, or a security clearance system.

For the trust relation, we assume that $abc \rhd ab \rhd ac$ and $abc \rhd bc$, and that $bc$ is incomparable to $ab$ and $ac$ ($bc \wr ab$ and $bc \wr ac$). Because conformity consists only in a simple "yes" or "no" reply, the singleton trustee units are all vacuous (as in example 4). The following drawings illustrate the trust relation, the lattice of trust levels, and the fallback tree.

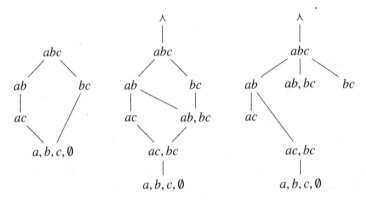

*Example 6 (Debtors).* Assume the trusting subject has lent money to three agents: €20 to agent $a$, €30 to $b$, and €10 to $c$. The agents are under obligation to repay their debts, but the subject is not convinced that they will all in fact conform: his knowledge of background circumstances inform him that at most €50 will be returned to him.

For the trust relation, assume it is rather certain that either $a$ or $b$ will be paying and less so that $c$ will. $c$ on his own is however more trustworthy than each of $a$ and $b$; furthermore, $a$ and $b$ are equivalent with regard to trustworthiness (so must be considered in tandem). Making no further assumptions, we obtain the following trust relation.

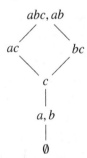

The conformity propositions of this scenario are always logically independent, so any contradiction leading to broken trust will be with the prior knowledge $\kappa$. If we let the subject's expected return be given as a minimal possible outcome at a given trust level, we can decorate the fallback tree with numerical values. (Note that the node $ac, bc$, corresponding to conformity by either $c$, or both $a$ and $b$, is introduced as a "new" level of trust in the lattice construction.) Consider $abc, ab$ as an example of how minimal expected value at a trust level can be computed: conformity by $a$ is sufficient for conformity of this node, implying a yield of €20.

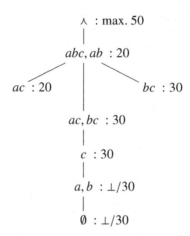

Assume the subject's threshold of trustworthiness is the level $c$. The minimal expected return will then be €30: The minimum yield of conformity at $abc, ab$ is given if $a$ conforms and pays €20. Add to this minimal yield at $ac, bc$, which means $a$ (already secured from $abc, ab$) and $c$ conform, giving €30. The level $c$ requires conformity by $c$, which is already secured.

With a threshold of trust set to $a, b$, matching an expectation that $a$ and $b$ will both pay their debts, the expected yield would also be €30. Prior knowledge $\kappa$ is not consistent with of all three debtors conforming, and the post-evaluation yield is then given by the fallback level $c$ of $a, b$.

## 5    Conclusion and Future Work

In this paper we have presented a theory about trust in cases where there is more than one trustee, assuming that a relation, according to a dimension given by a rule or regularity, between trustee units is given. We have shown how the priority structure implicit in a trust relation can be made fully explicit by means of a lattice, and how a system of default expectations arises as an interpretation of the fallback tree corresponding to the lattice.

As the examples illustrate, the theory is adaptable to a wide range of situations and is not tied to a particular logical language. In future work we want to study more closely the dynamics of trust revisions, i.e., rational attitudes towards trust that agents should form in response to observations of the trustees' actual conformity to expectations. We also want to study representations of the default structure that arises from fallback trees within a variety of logical languages, in particular with respect to different language constructs for modalities.

# References

1. John Cantwell. Resolving conflicting information. *Journal of Logic, Language, and Information*, 7:191–220, 1998.
2. Andrew J. I. Jones. On the concept of trust. *Decision Support Systems*, 33:225–232, 2002.
3. Andrew J. I. Jones. A logical framework. In Jeremy Pitt, editor, *The Open Agent Society*. John Wiley & Sons, Chichester, UK, 2005. To be published.
4. Johan W. Klüwer and Arild Waaler. Trustworthiness by default. In *Computational Logic in Multi-Agent Systems (CLIMA) VI*, 2005.
5. Arild Waaler, Johan W. Klüwer, Tore Langholm, and Espen H. Lian. Only knowing with degrees of confidence. *Journal of Applied Logic*, 2005. To appear.

# Secure Untrusted Binaries — Provably!

Simon Winwood[1,2] and Manuel M.T. Chakravarty[1]

[1] University of New South Wales,
School of Computer Science & Engineering,
Sydney, Australia
[2] National ICT Australia, ERTOS
{sjw, chak}@cse.unsw.edu.au

**Abstract.** A standard method for securing untrusted code is code *rewriting*, whereby operations that might compromise a safety policy are secured by additional dynamic checks. In this paper, we propose a novel approach to sandboxing that is based on a combination of code rewriting and hardware-based memory protection. In contrast to previous work, we perform rewriting on raw binary code and provide a machine-checkable proof of safety that includes the interaction of the untrusted binary with the operating system. This proof constitutes a crucial step towards the use of rewritten binaries with proof-carrying code.

## 1  Introduction

Consider the following common scenario: A computer user has obtained a program or program component in binary form and wishes to execute it without the risk of compromising a given security policy; for example, certain files may not be altered. Typically, the user will not have access to the source code and often will not trust the code producer, either due to fear of malicious intent or because of software bugs. Hence, the user needs to *sandbox* the binary, such that the rest of the system is shielded from security violations of the untrusted code.

Sandboxing can either be achieved by operating system abstractions based on *memory protection hardware* or by *software-based fault isolation (SFI)* [1]. SFI is based on *code rewriting*, whereby all potentially dangerous instructions are secured by dynamic checks. This rewriting process is typically performed in the compiler backend [1] or on an assembly representation of the code [2,3,4,5] with some additional constraints, including reserved (sometimes globally so) registers for sandboxing.

In this paper, we propose a novel *hybrid* approach that combines binary rewriting with hardware-based memory protection. Our approach works for raw binary code, where no symbolic information of the source program is available. In contrast to traditional sandboxing by operating systems, we can support fine-grained security policies with standard kernels. Moreover, we provide a machine-checkable proof of safety that includes the interaction of the untrusted binary with the operating system, formalised using Isabelle/HOL. The interaction with the operating system includes memory protection domains as well as fine-grained

T. Dimitrakos et al. (Eds.): FAST 2005, LNCS 3866, pp. 171–186, 2006.
© Springer-Verlag Berlin Heidelberg 2006

constraints on permissible system calls. The only other work known to us that includes a machine-checkable proof of safety for sandboxed binaries is McCamant & Morrisett's [5] recent result. Their work extends the original SFI work of Wahbe et al. to CISC processors.

Proof carrying code (PCC) [6] addresses the same scenario by placing the onus of proof on the code producer: Each binary, when being distributed, must be accompanied by a machine-checkable proof of safety. The binary is executed only if this proof is found to be valid.

In practice, few code producers supply the required proofs. Our approach addresses this problem by allowing uncertified components, without requiring the rewriting tool in the trusted computing base. Using our proof of safety for the rewritten binary, the binaries' conformance can be checked without any knowledge of the rewriting process. Alternatively, our methods enable code producers to generate proofs of safety without special compiler support.

Our formalisation is based on a low-level machine model characterising a subset of the Alpha architecture [7], complete with memory protection and an operating system abstraction. On the basis of this machine model, we have formalised the effect of a binary rewriting strategy that introduces reference monitors enforcing control flow and intercepting all system calls. In particular, we show that the reference monitors in rewritten binaries cannot be compromised and that they detect all security violations; i.e., that the rewritten binary conforms to the security policy enforced by the monitor.

The proof and related lemmas are all machine-checked using the Isabelle/HOL proof assistant. All formal definitions and lemmas in this paper were generated by Isabelle: what you see is what we proved. The proofs are available online at http://www.cse.unsw.edu.au/~sjw/proofs/rewrite.html.

In summary, we claim the following contributions:

- A rewriting technique to enforce security policies involving constraints on system calls in raw binary-only code (Sect. 2).
- A formal machine-model of a subset of the Alpha architecture, complete with memory protection and an operating system abstraction (Sect. 3).
- A machine-checkable proof of safety of rewritten binaries (Sect. 4).

In particular, we do not know of any other hybrid approach that combines OS-mediated hardware protection with binary rewriting, nor do we know of any proof of safety that includes reasoning about protection domains and system calls. We believe that our approach is practical, as most untrusted binaries are distributed as plain machine code and because all modern operating systems—with the exception of some embedded systems—support memory protection. We discuss related work in detail in Sect. 5.

## 2    Rewriting, Reference Monitors and Proofs

Continuing the scenario from the previous section, let us suppose that the security policy of our computer user asserts that untrusted binaries can only alter

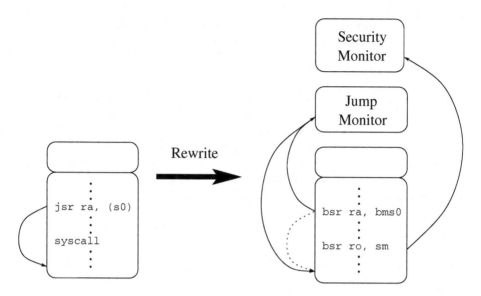

**Fig. 1.** After rewriting, jumps become branches into the jump monitor, system calls become branches into the security monitor

files in the directory /tmp and, in addition, write to the special stream stdout. As all access to files and streams is via system calls, we need to monitor all system calls issued by the untrusted code.

The operating system (OS) kernel itself already checks that arguments to system calls are within certain limits. However, standard OS kernels support only coarse-grain checks; for example, file access depends on user and group permissions and is not easily changed on a process by process basis for a single user. The arguments of other system calls, for example process creation, are even more difficult to monitor. Hence, fine-grained security policies require reference monitors [8] outside of the operating system.

The obvious place for such monitors is within the process that executes the untrusted code. The problem is then to ensure that even malicious untrusted code cannot circumvent the monitor. As usual, we ensure this by tracking aspects of the untrusted code's control flow in addition to its system calls.

## 2.1   Securing the Binary

We add two out-of-line reference monitors, which we call the *jump monitor* and *security monitor*, respectively. All jump instructions within the untrusted code, whose destination we cannot statically determine, are replaced by a branch into the jump monitor. The jump monitor ensures that control is not transferred to an illicit target address and then transfers control to that target. Moreover, all system calls are replaced by branches into the security monitor, which performs the system call if it is admissible. The effect of the rewriting process is illustrated in Fig. 1.

**Table 1.** Increase of runtime in rewritten binaries for a subset of the SPEC CPU2000 benchmark suite on a 600MHz Alpha 21264. Missing are those benchmarks which would not compile on our test system. The benchmarks were run using the `runspec` command; the results are based on the average of the 3 times reported.

| gzip | 0.09% | wupwise | 9.71% | swim | 1.38% | mgrid | 1.32% | applu | 3.75% |
|---|---|---|---|---|---|---|---|---|---|
| vpr | 1.88% | mesa | 9.71% | art | -0.10% | mcf | 0.18% | equake | 4.06% |
| crafty | 18.24% | ammp | -1.35% | parser | 8.98% | sixtrack | 0.34% | eon | 20.41% |
| gap | 17.26% | twolf | 7.26% | apsi | 0.81% | | | | |

The rewriting process simply inspects all instructions and alters indirect jumps (`jsr` instructions on the Alpha) and systems calls as follows:

```
foreach instruction I in binary            jmon (r):
   case I in
        syscall    -> bsr  t0, smon              sll    r, BITS, r
        jsr r, r'  -> bsr  r, jmon(r')           srl    r, BITS, r
        _          -> I                          jsr    (r)
```

Here $jmon(r)$ is the portion of the jump monitor dealing with jumps via register $r$. Furthermore, register `t0` is chosen to be a register which may be corrupted by the OS under the calling convention in effect.

*Integrity of monitors.* The actual enforcement of the security policy is performed by the security monitor. The jump monitor is required so untrusted code cannot circumvent the checks of the security monitor by simply jumping into the middle of it. In other words, the jump monitor ensures that entry to the security monitor is only possible through well-defined entry points.

We use hardware-based memory protection to prevent the untrusted code from dynamically altering its own or a monitors code; i.e., all code pages are write-protected. Moreover, we prevent the untrusted code from generating code on the fly in other areas, by using hardware-based memory protection to ensure that only the untrusted code and the monitors are on executable memory pages.

*Performance.* Rewriting obviously does not come for free, but usually increases the runtime of the untrusted code. However, the benchmarks displayed in Table 1, on the basis of the SPEC CPU2000 benchmark suite, show that these increases are, on average, fairly small for our system.

A restriction of our rewriting method on the Alpha architecture is that the maximum branch displacement is 2MB in either direction, thus limiting the maximum code size.

## 2.2   Protection Domains

The integrity of our method obviously depends on the availability of hardware-based memory protection. Moreover, in contrast to other approaches to sandboxing, we do not attempt to restrict the targets of load and store instructions of untrusted binaries. Hence, an untrusted binary with its jump and security monitor needs to be placed into its own protection domain.

This is contrary to the purely software-based fault isolation as first popularised by Wahbe et al. [1]. However, three practical considerations support our hybrid approach:

1. In current computing environments, users often need to execute untrusted binaries that are largely standalone programs; i.e., they do not cross protection domains frequently.
2. Recent advances in systems research has demonstrated cross-domain calls with very little overhead [9].
3. Pure software-based approaches often need to rewrite assembly code, whereas binaries are typically distributed as raw binaries that include no symbolic information (not even debugging symbols).

Consequently, we believe that our approach is practical.

### 2.3  Verifier

Binary code rewriting tools are complex. Hence, they should remain outside of the trusted computing base. However, this requires a verifier that checks at load time that a binary has been appropriately rewritten. In our case, this is simple. The verifier checks that the untrusted code does not contain any `jsr` and `syscall` instructions. Furthermore, all branch targets (of `bsr` instructions) must be within the untrusted code or at appropriate entry points of the jump or security monitor. These checks together are sufficient for the proof of safety (c.f., Sect. 4.4).

## 3  The Machine Model

To define a notion of secure program execution, we need a formal semantics of the *instruction set architecture (ISA)* of the processor executing these programs. We achieve this by formalising the relevant parts of the informal definition of the Alpha architecture [7]. Our formal semantics is organised in two stages: Firstly, we define the semantics of each instruction with respect to a simple machine state; secondly, we lift these semantics to a more realistic system state which includes memory protection, exceptions, and an abstract model of the operating system. The following two subsection cover each of these stages, respectively.

### 3.1  The Base Machine

The *basic machine state* comprises a heap $h$, a register file $rf$, and a program counter $pc$. The data type used to represent instructions is shown in Fig. 2; the *Decode* function decodes 32bit words into instructions. This function is lifted to machine states by the $SDecode_1$ and $ADecode_1$ functions ($ADecode_1$ decodes at an arbitrary address rather than the pc).

**datatype** SpecialInstruction = Illegal Word | SystemCall
**datatype** AOp = AOaddq | AOsubq | AOsll | AOsrl | AOcmpeq | AOcmplt
**datatype** BOp = BOlt | BOeq

**datatype** Instruction
    = AOp AOp Reg Reg-Or-Lit Reg  *Arithmetic or logical instruction*
    | BOp BOp Reg Word           *Conditional branch*
    | Br  Reg Word              *Branch to address*
    | Lda Reg Reg Word           *Load address (add immediate)*
    | Ldq Reg Reg Word           *Load word*
    | Stq Reg Reg Word           *Store word*
    | Jsr Reg Reg              *Jump to address in register*
    | Special SpecialInstruction    *System call or illegal instruction*

**Fig. 2.** The Instruction datatype and auxiliary types

$$S = (h,\ rf,\ pc)$$

$$\frac{SDecode_1\ S = AOp\ aop\ r_1\ ri\ r_d \quad v = liftimm\text{-}u\ (bv\text{-}op64\text{-}uu\ (aop\text{-}semantics\ aop)\ (rf\ r_1))\ rf\ ri}{S \longmapsto^1 (h,\ update\text{-}rf\ rf\ r_d\ v,\ update\text{-}pc\ pc)}$$

$$\frac{SDecode_1\ S = Lda\ r_d\ r_s\ off}{S \longmapsto^1 (h,\ update\text{-}rf\ rf\ r_d\ (rf\ r_s \oplus off),\ update\text{-}pc\ pc)}$$

$$\frac{SDecode_1\ S = Ldq\ r_d\ r_s\ off \quad v = mem\text{-}to\text{-}word\ h\ (rf\ r_s \oplus off)\ 8}{S \longmapsto^1 (h,\ update\text{-}rf\ rf\ r_d\ v,\ update\text{-}pc\ pc)}$$

$$\frac{SDecode_1\ S = Stq\ r_s\ r_d\ off \quad h' = word\text{-}to\text{-}mem\ h\ (rf\ r_d \oplus off)\ (rf\ r_s)}{S \longmapsto^1 (h',\ rf,\ update\text{-}pc\ pc)}$$

$$\frac{SDecode_1\ S = BOp\ bop\ r\ disp \quad pc' = (\text{if}\ bop\text{-}semantics\ bop\ (rf\ r)\ \textbf{then}\ mkbranchpc\ pc\ disp\ \textbf{else}\ update\text{-}pc\ pc)}{S \longmapsto^1 (h,\ rf,\ pc')}$$

$$\frac{SDecode_1\ S = Br\ r_r\ disp \quad v = update\text{-}pc\ pc \quad pc' = mkbranchpc\ pc\ disp}{S \longmapsto^1 (h,\ update\text{-}rf\ rf\ r_r\ v,\ pc')}$$

$$\frac{SDecode_1\ S = Jsr\ r_r\ r_d \quad v = update\text{-}pc\ pc}{S \longmapsto^1 (h,\ update\text{-}rf\ rf\ r_r\ v,\ bv\text{-}align\ (rf\ r_d)\ 2)}$$

**Fig. 3.** The transition relation representing the semantics of the base machine. The term $w \oplus w'$ represents unsigned word addition modulo $2^{64}$; *liftimm-u f rf ri* lifts $f$ to the value of *ri*, which may be an immediate or a register; and *bv-op64-uu* returns the result of the given function modulo $2^{64}$.

The evaluation relation is shown in Fig. 3. Evaluation is a partial function: For all states $s$, except those where the current instruction is *Special*, there is one and only one next state $t$ such that $s \longmapsto^1 t$.

**Lemma 1 (Simple evaluation is partial).**

*1.* If $s \longmapsto^1 t$ and $s \longmapsto^1 t'$ then $t = t'$.
*2.* If $\forall X.\ SDecode_1\ s \neq Special\ X$ then $\exists t.\ s \longmapsto^1 t$.

We also define a set of well-formed states $WfState_1$, containing only those states which reflect possible Alpha machine states. Evaluation preserves well-formedness.

## 3.2   Protection, OS Models, and Exceptions

The base system defines an idealised processor: Apart from illegal instructions and system calls, the base system can always transition (Lemma 1). A realistic system imposes additional constraints; for example, valid memory addresses must be aligned. We model this more realistic system state, shown in Fig. 4, by lifting the base machine state to include protection domains and operating system state. We also lift the $WfState_1$ relation to include the additional state; to favour conciseness, we omit the definition and references to the notion of well-formed states.

Note that the presented system is more general than required for the reasoning in this paper, as it includes multiple protection domains. We plan to exploit this generality in future work, where we study the interaction between multiple protection domains.

**Modelling Operating System Properties.** To formalise security policies including constraints on permissible system calls, such as file system access, we need to encode properties of the underlying operating system. However, we would like to do this such that our formal model is not tied to a specific operating system.

**datatype** Capability = Read | Write | Exec
**types**
   PD = Domain $\Rightarrow$ Addr $\Rightarrow$ Capability $\Rightarrow$ bool
   Exception = Domain $\Rightarrow$ Addr

**record** $'a$ State =
   sheap :: Heap               *Memory heap*
   spd :: PD                   *Protection domain (per domain)*
   srf :: Domain $\Rightarrow$ Regfile  *Register file (per domain)*
   spc :: Domain $\Rightarrow$ Addr     *Program counter (per domain)*
   sos :: $'a$                 *Operating system state*

**Fig. 4.** The lifted machine state. Note that it is parameterised by the type of the operating system state.

We achieve this using Isabelle's *axiomatic type classes*, which support reasoning about the members of a collection of abstract types. An axiomatic type class specifies properties that hold for all instance types of that class. Hence, these properties may be used in proofs about any type of the collection. In other words, these proofs are parametric with respect to the instance type.

$$\frac{\neg \; spd \; S \models spc \; S \; d \; \uparrow_d \; Exec}{(S, \; d) \; bad} \qquad \frac{SDecode \; d \; S = Special \; (Illegal \; w)}{(S, \; d) \; bad}$$

$$\frac{\begin{array}{c} SDecode \; d \; S = Ldq \; r_1 \; r_2 \; off \\ \neg \; spd \; S \models srf \; S \; d \; r_2 \oplus off \uparrow_d \; Read \end{array}}{(S, \; d) \; bad} \qquad \frac{\begin{array}{c} SDecode \; d \; S = Ldq \; r_1 \; r_2 \; off \\ \neg \; bv\text{-}aligned \; (srf \; S \; d \; r_2 \oplus off) \; 3 \end{array}}{(S, \; d) \; bad}$$

$$\frac{\begin{array}{c} SDecode \; d \; S = Stq \; r_1 \; r_2 \; off \\ \neg \; spd \; S \models srf \; S \; d \; r_2 \oplus off \uparrow_d \; Write \end{array}}{(S, \; d) \; bad} \qquad \frac{\begin{array}{c} SDecode \; d \; S = Stq \; r_1 \; r_2 \; off \\ \neg \; bv\text{-}aligned \; (srf \; S \; d \; r_2 \oplus off) \; 3 \end{array}}{(S, \; d) \; bad}$$

**Fig. 5.** Rules for determining whether a state will raise an exception. There are 3 main causes: illegal instructions, insufficient permissions, and misaligned memory addresses.

System calls are modelled with the *osstep* function and exceptions with the *osexception* function[1]; the operating system type class assumes both functions preserve well-formedness.

**Modelling Protection and Exceptions.** Protection and exceptions are interdependent; hence, we need to handle them together. We define a judgement on states $(S, \; d)$ *bad*, shown in Fig. 5, which holds when execution of state $S$ should raise an exception. This may be due to protection errors, alignment errors, or illegal instructions.

We model memory protection by a function from protection domains and addresses onto a set of capabilities. We use the judgement $pd \models addr \uparrow_d cap$ to denote domain $d$ has permission $cap$ to address $addr$ in the protection domain $pd$. The effects of memory protection are shown in Fig. 5: Any attempt at executing an instruction at a non-executable address will result in an exception, as will reading or writing memory without the required permissions.

**The Evaluation Relation.** Figure 6 shows the lifted evaluation relation; cases for exceptions and system calls are added, in addition to the basic evaluation relation. Evaluation is total.

**Lemma 2 (Evaluation total).**

*1.* $\exists S'. \; S \longmapsto_d S' \wedge S' \in WfState$
*2.* If $S \longmapsto_d S'$ and $S \longmapsto_d S''$ then $S' = S''$.

Memory protection allows us to show that values at non-writable addresses will not change across evaluation.

**Lemma 3 (Heap value preservation).**

If $S \longmapsto_d S'$ and $\neg \; (S, \; d) \; bad$ and $\neg \; spd \; S \models a \uparrow_d Write$ and $SDecode \; d \; S \neq Special \; SystemCall$ then $sheap \; S' \; a = sheap \; S \; a$.

---

[1] By modelling system calls and exceptions with functions rather than relations we are assuming a deterministic system.

$$\frac{(S,\ d)\ bad}{S \longmapsto_d\ osexception\ d\ S} \qquad \text{(BAD)}$$

$$\frac{\neg\ (S,\ d)\ bad \qquad state\text{-}to\text{-}state_1\ d\ S \longmapsto^1 t}{S \longmapsto_d\ lift_1\ d\ t\ S} \qquad \text{(GOOD)}$$

$$\frac{\neg\ (S,\ d)\ bad \qquad SDecode\ d\ S = Special\ SystemCall}{S \longmapsto_d\ osstep\ S\ d} \qquad \text{(SYSCALL)}$$

**Fig. 6.** The semantics of the lifted machine. The $lift_1$ function lifts from base states, and $state\text{-}to\text{-}state_1$ does the inverse.

## 4 A Proof of Security

On the basis of the formal machine model, we now outline the proof of safety of rewritten binaries. More precisely, we show that all executions of a program that has been re-written, as described in Sect. 2, satisfy the security policy enforced by the security monitor.

### 4.1 A Compositional Theory of Modules

After rewriting, a program has three components: (1) the untrusted code, (2) the jump monitor, and (3) the security monitor. We wish to show properties of each component in isolation; indeed, for this proof, we do not know the details of the security and jump monitors, only that they enforce some security policy. In addition, the security monitor can enforce this security policy only when entered at known addresses, and only for states over which it has control; i.e., those inside the monitor.

We thus introduce the concept of a *module*, a datatype with a membership predicate on states and a set of entry points. The intuition is that a program is composed of a number of modules, and the module predicate determines whether a state is within that particular module. In our proofs each component (the jump monitor, the security monitor, and the untrusted code) corresponds to a module.

Execution traces are treated as sequences of *super-states*, each super-state corresponding to execution within a single module. The formalisation is as follows: We split the execution trace into *P-sequences*, where each element in a P-sequence satisfies some membership predicate. The judgement $\sigma \models_P T \rightarrow_d T'$ asserts that each state in the P-sequence $\sigma$ (the trace from $T$ to $T'$ in domain $d$) satisfies the predicate $P$. A P-sequence represents a super-state.

P-sequences compose into *super-sequences* as shown in Figure 7; the judgement $Z \models_\Pi T \Rightarrow_d T'$ states that the super-sequence $Z$ (from state $T$ to state $T'$ in domain $d$) consists of P-sequences each of which satisfies a predicate in $\Pi$. Moreover, all but the last P-sequence must be *maximal*. A maximal P-sequence is one in which the following state does *not* satisfy the predicate. From a super-sequence one may derive the reflexive-transitive closure, and visa-versa.

$$\frac{S \in \mathit{WfState} \qquad P\ S}{[S] \models_P S \rightarrow_d S} \qquad \text{(P-SINGLE)}$$

$$\frac{S \in \mathit{WfState} \qquad P\ S \qquad S \longmapsto_d S' \qquad \sigma \models_P S' \rightarrow_d S''}{S{\cdot}\sigma \models_P S \rightarrow_d S''} \qquad \text{(P-STEP)}$$

$$\frac{P \in \Pi \qquad \sigma \models_P S \rightarrow_d S'}{[\sigma] \models_\Pi S \Rightarrow_d S'} \qquad \text{(S-SINGLE)}$$

$$\frac{P \in \Pi \qquad \sigma \models_P S \rightarrow_d^! S' \qquad S' \longmapsto_d T \qquad Z \models_\Pi T \Rightarrow_d T'}{\sigma{\cdot}Z \models_\Pi S \Rightarrow_d T'} \qquad \text{(S-STEP)}$$

**Fig. 7.** Judgements relating P-sequences and super-sequences

*module-pseq-prop M P I d* ≡
∀ *S S′ σ.*
  *spc S d* ∈ *entry-points M* ∧ *I S* ∧ *σ* $\models_{in\text{-}module\text{-}pred\ M}$ *S* →$_d$ *S′* ⟶ *P S′*

*module-pseq-inv M I d* ≡
∀ *S S′ σ.*
  *spc S d* ∈ *entry-points M* ∧ *I S* ∧ *σ* $\models_{in\text{-}module\text{-}pred\ M}$ *S* →$_d^!$ *S′* ⟶
  *I* (*eval-next S′ d*)

*module-set-ok P I modules d* ≡
∀ *S*∈*WfState.*
  (∃!*M. M* ∈ *modules* ∧ *in-module-pred M S*) ∧
  (∀ *M*∈*modules.*
    (*I S* ∧ *in-module-pred M S* ⟶ *spc S d* ∈ *entry-points M*) ∧
    *module-pseq-prop M P I d* ∧ *module-pseq-inv M I d*)

**Fig. 8.** Proof obligations for a set of modules

## Lemma 4 (Equivalence between super-sequences and $\longmapsto_d^*$).

1. If $Z \models_\Pi S \Rightarrow_d S'$ then $S \longmapsto_d^* S'$.
2. If ∀ $S$∈*WfState*. ∃!$P.\ P \in \Pi \wedge P\ S$ and $S \longmapsto_d^* S'$ then ∃$Z.\ Z \models_\Pi S \Rightarrow_d S'$.

Finally, we define the concept of a valid module set (*module-set-ok P I modules d*), shown in Fig. 8, relative to some invariant *I* and property *P*. A valid module set must cover all possible states with one and only one module. The invariant *I* must at least imply that modules transfer control to other modules via the entry points; in general, this invariant will also relate the given state to the initial state. If each module preserves the invariant and has the required property, then the composition of the modules into a program has that property.

## Rule 1 (Compositional rule for modules).

If $Z \models_{in\text{-}module\text{-}pred\ '\ modules} S \Rightarrow_d S'$ and *module-set-ok P I modules d* and *I S* then *P S′*.

$S \sim_d S' \equiv$
$weak\text{-}eqv\text{-}heaps \ (spd \ S) \ d \ (sheap \ S) \ (sheap \ S') \wedge$
$spd \ S \ d \ = \ spd \ S' \ d \wedge exceptos\text{-}entry \ (sos \ S) \ d \ = \ exceptos\text{-}entry \ (sos \ S') \ d$

$weak\text{-}eqv\text{-}heaps \ pd \ d \ h1 \ h2 \ \equiv$
$\forall \ addr.$
$\quad |addr| = 64 \ \wedge$
$\quad \neg \ pd \models addr \uparrow_d Write \wedge (pd \models addr \uparrow_d Read \vee pd \models addr \uparrow_d Exec) \longrightarrow$
$\quad h1 \ addr = h2 \ addr$

**Fig. 9.** Definition of weak state equivalence

## 4.2 Exceptions

Next, we discuss the richer exception model required to reason about program behaviour. We have settled on modelling exceptions as a control flow to some address in the program[2]. This address is obtained from the operating system state component by the *exceptos-entry* function.

An alternative model could define exceptions to terminate the program, either using an additional distinguished machine state, or by looping in the same state and so constantly generating exceptions. The approach taken, however, has the advantage of being closer to that is typically implemented by an operating system.

## 4.3 Weak State Equivalence

We define an equivalence relations on states, shown in Fig. 9. This definition reflects the consequences of memory protection.

Two states are *weakly equivalent* ($S \sim_d S'$), with respect to a particular domain, if they have weakly equivalent *heaps*, the protection domains are the same (i.e., memory permissions are the same), and the exception entry point is the same. Two *heaps* are *weakly equivalent* (*weak-eqv-heaps pd d h h'*), with respect to a particular domain and protection domain, if each memory location without write permissions but with read or execute permission is identical.

Under normal execution, each state will be weakly equivalent to the following state: Changes to protection domains and exception entry points are only possible via system calls, and memory protection ensures that memory locations without write permissions are preserved.

**Lemma 5 (Equivalence preservation).**

If $S_0 \sim_d S$ and $S \longmapsto_d S'$ and $\neg \ (S, d) \ bad$ and $SDecode \ d \ S \neq Special \ SystemCall$ then $S_0 \sim_d S'$.

The following lemma is the main use of memory protection. If two states are weakly equivalent, and an address is executable, then the same instruction will be executed in both states.

---

[2] This models the behaviour of some UNIX systems on a signal, for example.

**Lemma 6 (Decode equality).**

If $S \sim_d S'$ and $bv$-$aligned$ $a$ $2$ and $\neg$ $spd$ $S \models a \uparrow_d Write$ and $spd$ $S \models a \uparrow_d Exec$
then $ADecode$ $d$ $S$ $a = ADecode$ $d$ $S'$ $a$.

## 4.4   The Proof Environment

The initial state of the program is assumed to contain three modules: the untrusted code which has been rewritten, the jump monitor, and the security monitor. The predicates for each monitor are based on the program counter address:
We assume some watermark '$ut$-$top$' between the untrusted code and the jump
monitor, and some '$bm$-$top$' between the jump monitor and the security monitor.

The entry points set for the untrusted module is defined to be all addresses
below $ut$-$top$. The entry points for the other modules are fixed but not defined.

We define an invariant $I$ as

$$I = (\lambda S.\ S_0 \sim_D S \wedge spc\ S\ D \in \bigcup entry\text{-}points \ ' \ modules)$$

This is the strongest statement we can make about the machine state after
executing untrusted code: Memory protection allows us weak state equivalence,
and control-flow rewriting gives us known entry points.

We also fix some policy $syscall$-$policy$ which is a predicate on states that must
hold immediately before a system call. The property which must be shown to
hold for each module is the following.

$$Pred =$$
$$(\lambda S.\ can\text{-}exec\ S\ D\ (spc\ S\ D) \wedge SDecode\ D\ S = Special\ SystemCall \longrightarrow$$
$$syscall\text{-}policy\ S)$$

That is, if executing the instruction at that address[3] will not cause an exception, then the security policy must hold for that state.

We assume that the initial protection domain does not allow both $Write$ and
$Exec$ permissions for an address, and that both the exception entry point and
initial entry point are within the security monitor. The former is required to
handle exceptions in a manner which can be reasoned about, the latter is to
allow the security to set up any private state.

The following assumptions about the untrusted code model the effects of the
binary rewriting:

– No indirect jumps.

$$\forall addr\ r_r\ r_d.$$
$$addr <_B ut\text{-}top \wedge can\text{-}exec\ S_0\ D\ addr \longrightarrow ADecode\ D\ S_0\ addr \neq Jsr\ r_r\ r_d$$

---

[3] $can$-$exec$ predicate holds when a particular address (the program counter in this
case) is executable.

– No system calls.

$\forall\ addr.$
  $addr <_B\ ut\text{-}top\ \wedge\ can\text{-}exec\ S_0\ D\ addr\ \longrightarrow$
  $ADecode\ D\ S_0\ addr\ \neq\ Special\ SystemCall$

– All branches are within the untrusted code or are to a monitor entry point.

$\forall\ addr\ disp.$
  $addr <_B\ ut\text{-}top\ \wedge$
  $can\text{-}exec\ S_0\ D\ addr\ \wedge$
  $((\exists\ bop\ r.\ ADecode\ D\ S_0\ addr\ =\ BOp\ bop\ r\ disp)\ \vee$
  $(\exists\ r.\ ADecode\ D\ S_0\ addr\ =\ Br\ r\ disp))\ \longrightarrow$
  $mkbranchpc\ addr\ disp\ \in\ \bigcup entry\text{-}points\ `\ modules$

We also assume that the final instruction in the program is a branch. This is required only when the next address after the program isn't a module entry point (or isn't executable).

Finally, we assume that both monitors satisfy the invariant and security properties.

## 4.5   The Proof of Security

The following lemma is a consequence of the Decode equality lemma (Lemma 6), and one of the principal reasons for our use of protection domains: The value of an instruction in a state reached from the initial state is the same as at the initial state. This implies that properties about the untrusted program assumed in Sect. 4.4 hold in subsequent states.

**Lemma 7 (Decode preservation).**

If $\neg\ (S,\ D)\ bad$ and $S_0 \sim_D S$ and $S \in WfState$ then $ADecode\ D\ S_0\ (spc\ S\ D)\ =$ $SDecode\ D\ S$.

The compositional rule for modules requires us to show that the untrusted component preserves the invariant and has the *Pred* property.

**Lemma 8 (Invariant preservation).**

If $\sigma \models_{in\text{-}module\text{-}pred\ ut\text{-}module}\ S \to^!_D S'$ and $spc\ S\ D \in entry\text{-}points\ ut\text{-}module$ and $I\ S$ then $I\ (eval\text{-}next\ S'\ D)$.

The proof is by induction over the structure of the P-sequence. There are two cases:

**P-SINGLE.** We are then looking at the last state in current module: by assumption, the next state is in another module. We then need to show that the next state is weakly equivalent to the current state, and that the program counter in the next state is in the set of entry points for the next module. These obligations are shown by case analysis over the next evaluation step (evaluation is total, so the next state is always defined).

**BAD.** The next state is an exception, which causes control to be transfered to an entry point in the security monitor.

**GOOD.** From Lemma 3 we have weak equivalence; from the properties of rewritten binaries in Sect. 4.4 we have that the current instruction must be a branch, and thus is to some module entry point.

**SYSCALL.** It is not possible for untrusted code to perform a system call, so this case is trivially true.

**P-STEP.** In the step case, we have as the induction hypothesis that the invariant holds at the last state. We then need only show that the current state is weakly equivalent to the next state. This is true by Lemma 3.

The next statement asserts that the security policy is respected.

**Lemma 9 (Security policy).**

If $\sigma \models_{in\text{-}module\text{-}pred\ ut\text{-}module} S \rightarrow_D S'$ and $I\ S$ then $Pred\ S'$.

This proof is similar to the previous proof, and also proceeds by induction over the P-sequence. With Lemma 7 it is essentially trivial as no system call can occur.

Having shown that the untrusted code preserves the invariant and has the security property, we can now show that the system is secure.

**Lemma 10 (Safety of rewritten binaries).**

If $S_0 \longmapsto_D^* S'$ then $Pred\ S'$.

The proof is by Rule 1 using the assumptions about the jump and security monitors from Sect. 4.4 and Lemmas 8 and 9.

## 5   Related Work

A number of approaches rewrite at the assembly level, for example Software-based Fault Isolation (SFI) [1] and PittSFIeld [5]. The Naccio system [10] rewrites binaries so that high level resource policies may be enforced. The Gleipnir project [11,12] uses binary rewriting to ensure control safety. Finally, Prasad and Chiueh [4] present a system based on binary rewriting for preventing buffer overflow attacks.

In the SFI approach, assembly programs are modified so that the address of register-indirect jumps and memory operations are forced to be within a region of the address space. This is done by setting and clearing bits in the top of the address.

An important aspect of the SFI approach is that verifying that a program has been rewritten is separate from the transformation process itself. This results in a smaller trusted computing base.

Although SFI claims to work on binaries, in practice it inserts extra instructions into the program binary, and hence requires symbol information so that the binary can be re-linked. The implementation discussed in Wahbe et. al. [1] uses a modified version of the gcc compiler. In addition, SFI restricts components to a single region, and thus disallows (safe) sharing.

Of the related work listed above, the PittSFIeld and Gleipnir projects are of particular relevance to the work presented in this paper, as both verify the soundness of their approaches. Both projects examine SFI-like systems on the IA-32 platform, a particularly tricky endeavour due to the variable length instruction format; unlike RISC systems, it is possible to jump into the middle of an instruction, and hence execute a different instruction than was statically checked.

The Gleipnir project aims to enforce Control-Flow Integrity (CFI), that is, ensuring that the control flow of a program is not tampered with by an external attacker. In their approach, a binary's control flow graph extracted by the Vulcan tool [13] is used to generate a set of equivalence classes based on branch targets. These equivalence classes are then assigned unique identifiers, which are inserted before the target code. Whenever a jump is to be taken, the program checks the identifier at the target address contains the correct identifier. If this check fails, then the contents of that register have been tampered with, and thus the attacker can be denied. One point to note is that the Vulcan tool requires a significant amount of information about the binary in order to construct the CFG.

The formal analysis [12] of this approach is a human-checked proof based on a simplified RISC-like processor. The proof assumes that code memory and data memory are disjoint, and that branches into instructions are impossible. They make the interesting assumption that an attacker has control over the heap and then show that CFI holds.

The PittSFIeld project aims to enforce memory and control safety. The basic approach is similar to SFI, however the problem of variable length instructions is addressed by forming instruction groups, each aligned to a $k$-byte boundary. By ensuring that the bottom $k$ bits of a jump value are cleared (using the SFI technique), this approach removes the threat of jumping into the middle of an instruction at the cost of inserting nop instructions into the binary, and hence requiring linking information.

The formal analysis uses the ACL2 theorem prover to model a subset of the IA-32 architecture. A proof of safety is then shown. Their simpler security property (i.e. memory and control safety) is reflected in their proofs: because they do not model a security monitor, they are able to directly induct over evaluation.

# 6   Concluding Remarks

We introduced a novel hybrid sandboxing technique that combines hardware-based memory protection with binary rewriting. We can support fine-grained security policies with standard operating system kernels and provide a machine-checkable proof of safety that includes the interaction of the untrusted binary with the operating system. The formalisation is based on a machine model that includes protection domains and system calls, which to our knowledge is a first.

The main limitation of the presented work is that we so far only demonstrated its feasibility for RISC architectures. CISC architectures, and in particular the IA32 ISA, poses new challenges due to its variable-length instructions. We plan to address these challenges in future work.

## Acknowledgements

We wish to thank Gerwin Klein for his help on using the Isabelle/HOL theorem prover.

## References

1. Wahbe, R., Lucco, S., Anderson, T.E., Graham, S.L.: Efficient software-based fault isolation. ACM SIGOPS Operating Systems Review **27** (1993) 203–216
2. Small, C., Seltzer, M.I.: MiSFIT: Constructing safe extensible systems. IEEE Concurrency **6** (1998) 34–41
3. Úlfar Erlingsson, Schneider, F.B.: SASI enforcement of security policies: A retrospective. In: New Security Paradigms Workshop, Caledon Hills, Ontario, Canada, ACM SIGSAC, ACM Press (1999) 87–95
4. Prasad, M., cker Chiueh, T.: A binary rewriting defense against stack based buffer overflow attacks. In: USENIX Annual Technical Conference, General Track. (2003) 211–224
5. McCamant, S., Morrisett, G.: Efficient, verifiable binary sandboxing for a CISC architecture. Technical report, MIT LCS (2005)
6. Necula, G.C., Lee, P.: Safe, untrusted agents using proof-carrying code. In Vigna, G., ed.: Mobile Agents and Security. Volume 1419 of Lecture Notes in Computer Science., Springer-Verlag, Berlin Germany (1998) 61–91
7. Sites, R.L., Witek, R.L.: Alpha architecture reference manual. Digital Press. Third edn. (1998)
8. Schneider, F.B.: Enforceable security policies. Information and System Security **3** (2000) 30–50
9. Liedtke, J., Elphinstone, K., Schönberg, S., Härtig, H., Heiser, G., Islam, N., Jaeger, T.: Achieved IPC performance (still the foundation for extensibility). In: Proc. 6th HotOS, Cape Cod, MA, USA (1997) 28–31
10. Evans, D., Twyman, A.: Flexible policy-directed code safety. In: Proceedings of the IEEE Symposium on Research in Security and Privacy, Oakland, CA, IEEE Computer Society, Technical Committee on Security and Privacy, IEEE Computer Society Press (1999) 32–45
11. Abadi, M., Budiu, M., Úlfar Erlingsson, Ligatti, J.: Control-flow integrity. Technical Report MSR-TR-05-18, Microsoft Research (2005)
12. Abadi, M., Budiu, M., Úlfar Erlingsson, Ligatti, J.: A theory of secure control flow. Technical Report MSR-TR-05-17, Microsoft Research (2005)
13. Srivastava, A., Edwards, A., Vo, H.: Vulcan: Binary transformation in a distributed environment. Technical Report MSR-TR-2001-50, Microsoft Research (2001)

# Normative Specification:
# A Tool for Trust and Security

Olga Pacheco

CCTC/Department of Informatics,
University of Minho, Portugal
omp@di.uminho.pt

**Abstract.** Many software systems can be viewed as organizational systems, where the different components are seen as autonomous entities, interacting with each other, collaborating toward system's aims.In such systems we may not have full control over the behavior of all its components. Normative specification of an organizational system, provides a way of describing the norms that regulate the behavior of a system and of its components, stating how they are expected to behave, assuming however, that they may deviate from that ideal behavior. In this paper we use an action and deontic modal logic for the normative specification of organizational systems. This logical framework allows us to describe expected behavior of agents, detect non-ideal behavior and identify the agents that, direct or indirectly, are responsible for it. We argue that normative specification can be an useful tool to increase trust and security in complex computational systems and propose a responsibility-based trust concept.

## 1 Introduction

Computer systems interact with humans by rending services or solving problems. People trust them if they don't fail, or, if they do, by believing that someone will be *responsible* by any damage caused. But we cannot attribute responsibilities to a computer system (computers don't go to prison, they don't own goods, ...). In the end, there must always be some person (human or artificial[1]) responsible. Even in some network, where you interact with "faceless" software agents, you know that, indirectly, you are interacting with some person, company, university, or some other institution, with some legal statute. And if this link to persons does not exist, or it is not possible to trace it, there are trust and security problems. Cases abound in the Internet context.

So, how should we establish this link between software agents and persons? Before trying to answer this question, lets notice that a software system is part of the organization where it is used. Moreover, many software systems can be viewed, themselves, as organizational systems, where the different components are seen as autonomous entities, interacting with each other, collaborating toward system's aims. This view suggests that the components of a computer

---

[1] Artificial person in the legal sense.

T. Dimitrakos et al. (Eds.): FAST 2005, LNCS 3866, pp. 187–202, 2006.

system must, somehow, be integrated in the organization structure. In this paper we suggest an unifying and integrating model, where software agents are specified at the same level as human agents: they are just entities acting and interacting in some society or organization.

In complex computational systems we may not have full control over the behavior of all its components, because we might not have complete information, because it might be too complex or expensive, because humans are involved (with their intrinsic unpredictability), or for some other reason. But, at least, we must know how each component is *expected to behave*, otherwise the result of combining them to form the system would be useless. Normative specification of an organizational system, provides a way of describing the norms that regulate the behavior of a system and of its components, stating how they are expected to behave, assuming however, that they may deviate from that ideal behavior, and being prepared to react to that. In this paper, for simplicity reasons, we refer to norms just as the set of obligations and permissions that result from them[2].

Lets state some language conventions that will be used through the paper. We will adopt the designation "agent" for any entity capable to act (human, software/hardware component or even some organization). Following this anthropomorphic convention, we will say that a software/hardware component can "occupy" positions in an organization and say that it can "act" and bring about some state of affairs.

In this paper we use an action and deontic modal logic for the normative specification of organizational systems and of interaction between agents. This logical framework allows us to describe expected behavior of agents, detect nonideal behavior and identify the agents that, direct or indirectly, are responsible for it. Based on the possibility to trace responsibility, a trust notion is suggested. We argue that normative specification can be an useful tool to increase trust and security in complex computational systems.

**Structure of the Paper.** We start by briefly presenting the multi-modal logic that will be used in this paper to formally specify and reason about organizational systems and interaction. In section 3 it is presented the model we adopt for organizational systems and for interaction between agents, which is based on the legal concepts of artificial person and contract. A concept of trust is then suggested. In section 4 we specify an example and reason about it. We conclude with section 5, where we synthesize the main contributions of the paper and mention some research directions.

## 2    An Action and Deontic Logic: $\mathcal{L_{DA}}$

In this paper we will use logic as a tool to formally specify concepts relevant to the problem we are addressing (e.g. action in a role, representation, responsibility, etc.), to express relations between them and to characterize their properties. This logical framework will be used to specify contract-based interactions in

---

[2] For a more detailed and realistic view of norms see, for example, [21], [15].

some society of agents (including human agents, software/hardware agents, institutional agents), and reason about them.

## 2.1   Roles and Action in a Role

S. Kanger, I. Pörn and L. Lindahl, have combined deontic and action logics and used them to describe social interaction and complex normative concepts (see e.g. [11], [18],[9] [12]). They introduce a relativized modal action operator, $E_i$, being expressions like $E_i\psi$ read: *agent i brings about that $\psi$*. This approach has been followed by many researchers (e.g. [1] ,[7], [10], [19], [20]).

Following this tradition, in [4] it was proposed a new action operator that tries to capture the notion of *action of an agent in a role*. Informally, roles are properties or qualifications of agents, which are relevant for action and usually correspond to positions in an organization or in contracts (e.g. president of the board, representative). [3]

To know the role an agent is playing when he acts is crucial to analyze the deontic classification of the action (e.g. is it a permitted action?) and the effects of the action (e.g on other agents actions or legal effects – obligations resultant from the action). For example, when an agent $x$ acts as president of a company $y$ bringing about a state of affairs $\psi$, he also acts as representative of that company, and as a result, his action will count as an action of company $y$. And if he does something wrong when acting in the role of president of $y$, the company will, most probably, be also responsible for $x$'s actions. But if $x$ does the same action in another role, his action will not count as an action of company $y$.

In [4] it was proposed a new action operator of the form $E_{a:r}$ (for $a$ an agent and $r$ a role), being expressions of the form $E_{a:r}\psi$ read as: *agent a, playing the role r, brings it about that $\psi$*. The modal operator $E_{a:r}\psi$ relates an agent playing a role with the state of affairs he brings about, omitting details about the specific actions that have been performed (and setting aside temporal aspects). It has an adequate abstraction level to be used in high-level models of specification, where we want to describe agent's behavior without wanting to enter in details about the specific actions and tasks.

These action operators were combined with personal deontic operators in order to express obligations and permissions of agents in roles ($O_{a:r}\psi$ – read as *agent a is obliged to bring about $\psi$ by acting in role r*;  $P_{a:r}\psi$ – read as *agent a is permitted to bring about $\psi$ when acting in role r*).

Next, we will present the main features of the logic $\mathcal{L}_{\mathcal{DA}}$ proposed in [4] and [17], in a simplified and very brief way. Due to space limitations, we will omit details about semantics.

## 2.2   The Formal Language of $\mathcal{L}_{\mathcal{DA}}$

$\mathcal{L}_{\mathcal{DA}}$ is a multi-modal (with deontic and action modal operators) first-order many-sorted language. The non-modal component of $\mathcal{L}_{\mathcal{DA}}$ is used to express

---

[3] Many other researchers use the concept of role and try to formalize it, for purposes similar to ours (e.g. [2], [6], [13], [22]).

factual descriptions, and properties and relationships between agents. It contains a finite number of sorts, not related with agents or roles, and three special sorts: $Ag$ (the agent sort), $R$ (the role sort) and $AgR$ (the agent in a role sort). In this paper we will decompose the agent sort $Ag$ in three distinct agents sorts: $iAg$ - the institutional agent sort, $sAg$ - the software agent sort, $hAg$ - the human agent sort. When it is not relevant to distinguish the kind of agent we will just use $Ag$.

As usual, for each of these sorts we assume an infinite number of variables, and possibly some constants. (We are not considering variables of the sort $AgR$). There may be functions between these sorts, but we do not consider any function with $Ag$ as co-domain (the terms of sort $Ag$ are either variables or constants). The terms of each of these sorts are defined as usual.

The terms of the sort $AgR$ are built as follows:

(i) If $t$ is a term of sort $Ag$ and $r$ is a term of sort $R$, then   $t : r$   is a term of sort $AgR$.

For each role $r$, there exists a predicate (qualification predicate), denoted by *is-r* of sort $(Ag)$. $qual(a : r)$ is an abbreviation of *is-r*$(a)$, and intuitively means that agent $a$ is qualified to play the role $r$.

The formulas of $\mathcal{L}_{\mathcal{DA}}$ are inductively defined as follows:

(i) if $p$ is a predicate symbol of sort $(s_1, \ldots, s_n)$ and $t_1, \ldots, t_n$ are terms of sort $s_1, \ldots, s_n$, then $p(t_1, \ldots, t_n)$ is a formula (an atomic formula);

(ii) if $\phi$ is a formula, then $\neg\phi$ is a formula;

(iii) if $\phi_1$ and $\phi_2$ are formulas, then $(\phi_1 \wedge \phi_2)$ is a formula;

(iv) if $\phi$ is a formula and $x^s$ is a variable of sort $s$, then $(\forall_{x^s})\phi$ is a formula;

(v) if $\phi$ is a formula and $a : r$ is a term of sort AgR, then $E_{a:r}\phi$, $O_{a:r}\phi$ and $P_{a:r}\phi$ are formulas.

The other standard logical connectives ($\vee$, $\rightarrow$ and $\leftrightarrow$) and the existential quantifiers are introduced through the usual abbreviation rules.

## 2.3   Some Logical Principles of $\mathcal{L}_{\mathcal{DA}}$

The logical principles satisfied by the proposed operators have been discussed and presented in [4] and [17]. Here, we just list some of those principles, related with the action and deontic modal operators, to give some intuition about them.[4]

The formal properties of the action operator $E_{a:r}$ are described bellow:

|  | **Axioms:** |  |
|---|---|---|
| $(T_E)$ | $E_{a:r}B \rightarrow B$ | success operator |
| $(C_E)$ | $E_{a:r}A \wedge E_{a:r}B \rightarrow E_{a:r}(A \wedge B)$ |  |
| (Qual) | $E_{a:r}B \rightarrow qual(a : r)$ | agents that act in roles are qualified |
| (Itself) | $(\forall_x)qual(x : itself)$ | every agent is qualified to act as itself |
|  | **Proof rule:** |  |
| $(RE_E)$ | If $\vdash A \leftrightarrow B$ then $\vdash E_{a:r}A \leftrightarrow E_{a:r}B$ |  |

---

[4] Naturally, we assume that all tautologies are axioms of our logic, and the set of theorems of our logic is closed under Modus Ponens. With respect to the first-order component, we have the usual properties of quantifiers.

With respect to the formal properties of the deontic operators, and of the relationships between each other and with the action operator, we consider the following axioms and proof-rules:

| **Axioms:** | |
| --- | --- |
| $(C_O)$ | $O_{a:r}A \wedge O_{a:r}B \rightarrow O_{a:r}(A \wedge B)$ |
| $(O \rightarrow P)$ | $O_{a:r}B \rightarrow P_{a:r}B$ |
| $(O \rightarrow \neg P\neg)$ | $O_{a:r}B \rightarrow \neg P_{a:r}\neg B$ |
| $(O \wedge P)$ | $O_{a:r}A \wedge P_{a:r}B \rightarrow P_{a:r}(A \wedge B)$ |
| **Proof rules:** | |
| $(RE_O)$ | If $\vdash A \leftrightarrow B$ then $\vdash O_{a:r}A \leftrightarrow O_{a:r}B$ |
| $(RM_P)$ | if $\vdash A \rightarrow B$ then $\vdash P_{a:r}A \rightarrow P_{a:r}B$ |
| $(RM_{EP})$ | If $\vdash E_{a_1:r_1}A \rightarrow E_{a_2:r_2}B$ then $\vdash P_{a_1:r_1}A \rightarrow P_{a_2:r_2}B$ |

More details can be found in the above referred papers.

# 3   A Role Based Model for Organizations and Interaction

## 3.1   Artificial Person's Classification: A Safety Mechanism

When a set of persons decide to create a company, with some purpose in mind, the company must be classified in legal terms as an artificial person (e.g. as an association, as a foundation, as a liability society,...). This classification implies a formal description of the structure of the company (a set of positions that the members of the company will occupy) and a set of norms describing how the holders of each position are expected to behave (what they are obliged to do, or not to do, what are their powers, ...). The structure of the company and the norms regulating it, are described in the statutes of the company. The statutes are public and are determined, at least in general terms, by the legal classification of the company. The statutes describe the company's aims and how they will be achieved.

Any artificial person has *juridical personality* (i.e. it may be the subject of obligations, rights,...) and *legal qualification* (i.e. it can exercise their rights and be responsible for the unfulfillment of obligations)[5]. Law imposes the legal classification of a company as an artificial person, for *security reasons*: people that will interact with the company must know how they should expect the company to behave and who is going to be responsible when things go wrong. For more details about this issue see [16] and [17].

We think that a similar characterization, legal or not, should be transposed to virtual organizations, because, although they exist and act in a virtual environment, they, directly or indirectly, interact with people, and so, the same security issues are present.

## 3.2   A Role-Based Model

Based on the legal concept of artificial person presented above, in [17] we have proposed a model of organizations (human or virtual), that we called *institutional*

---

[5] This fact allow us to say that a company may be seen as an agent.

*agent*. An institutional agent is an abstract entity, having a structure described by a set of roles and a set of norms defining what should be done in each role (a set of obligations or permissions[6] – the deontic characterization of the role). In this context, roles are positions in an organization (e.g. president of the board of directors, associate, secretary, ...). The roles of an institutional agent are represented by a set of predicates $is - role(r, i)$ of sort $(R, Ag)$, meaning that role $r$ is part of the structure of institutional agent $i$.

Those roles are occupied by agents (human agents $(hAg)$, software/hardware agents $(sAg)$ or other institutional agents $(iAg)$).This information is expressed in our model by a set of predicates of the form $qual(a : r)$ of sort $AgR$, meaning that agent $a$ is qualified to act in role $r$. These agents may change through time, without affecting the identity of the institutional agent. The deontic characterization of a role in an organization is part of the identity of the organization and does not depend on the agent that holds that role in a particular moment. To capture this idea, deontic notions will be attached to roles, but they are actually interpreted as applied to the holders of such roles, when acting in such roles (deontic notions are only meaningful when applied to agents). To capture this we introduce the following abbreviations:

$$O_r\psi \stackrel{abv}{=} (\forall_x)(qual(x : r) \rightarrow O_{x:r}\psi)$$
$$P_r\psi \stackrel{abv}{=} (\forall_x)(qual(x : r) \rightarrow P_{x:r}\psi)$$

When we have multiple agents holding a role, all of them "inherit" the deontic characterization of the role. For instance, if there is some obligation associated to a role (e.g. associates are obliged to pay a fee), all of its holders will be under that obligation and all of them will have to fulfill it [7].

An institutional agent is an agent that interacts in society like any other agent: it can establish contracts or other kind of relationships with other agents, it can occupy roles and act on that roles, it may be the subject of obligations or other normative concepts, and may be responsible for the unfulfillment of obligations or other non-ideal situations. But an institutional agent, being an abstract entity, is not capable to act directly. So, how can it fulfill obligations? It acts through the agents that occupy the roles of its structure. The actions of the agents that hold roles in the structure of an institutional agent, count as actions of the institutional agent, through representation mechanisms, that can be captured as follows:

$$r1 : REP(a : r2, \psi) \stackrel{abv}{=} (\forall_x)(E_{x:r1}\psi \rightarrow E_{a:r2}\psi)$$

---

[6] Other normative concepts can be used to characterize roles. For simplicity reasons, we only use the two just mentioned.

[7] As argued in [17] a role is different from the set of its holders. We cannot attribute an obligation to the set of the holders (e.g. directors of a company), as a whole, and assume that one of its members may fulfill the obligation on behalf of the others, without knowing who that agent was, because it would not be possible to attribute responsibilities for that action. If we feel the need for that, we probably need to consider another institutional agent (e.g. the board of directors) and characterize its internal structure, defining how the obligation of this new agent may be fulfilled by its members.

$r1 : REP(a : r2, \psi)$ means that the role $r1$ is a representative role of $a$, for $\psi$.

Thus, any agent that holds role $r1$ and brings it about that $\psi$ when acting in that role, produces $\psi$ on behalf of $a$ (acting in role $r2$). $\psi$ is the scope of representation.

It must be clearly defined in the structure of an institutional agent what are the representative roles (see below) and the respective scope of representation. Only the agents that hold those roles can act on behalf of the institutional agent.

Moreover, it must be also defined how the obligations of an institutional agent are transmitted to the roles of its structure, stating who will be responsible for fulfilling each of those obligations. To express the transmission of obligations of an organization to specific roles of its structure (and indirectly, to the holders of those roles), we can use formulas like the following ones:

$$O_{x:itself}\psi \rightarrow O_r\psi \quad \text{(for } r \text{ a role of the structure of organization } x\text{)}.$$

### 3.3   Contracts as a Safety Mechanism

When two agents[8] establish a contract between each other, they commit themselves to act in accordance with what is stated in that contract. Usually, in a contract the agents involved attribute obligations, permissions, powers, to each other, and establish the sanctions that should be applied when the parts violate what as been formally agreed. In this sense, contracts are a safety mechanism. That is why people use them. We suggest to use them also in virtual environments.

When two agents establish a contract between each other, they may attribute roles to each other (e.g. *mandatory* and *manager* in a mandate contract) and deontically characterize those roles. One of the agents may be representative of the other agent. In that case, it must be also defined in the contract the scope of representation for that role. To express this representation notion associated to an agent in a role, we introduce a new abbreviation:

$$(x : r_1) : REP(y : r2, \psi) \overset{abv}{=} (E_{x:r1}\psi \rightarrow E_{y:r2}\psi)$$

Sometimes we may want to say that an agent $x$ is representative of another agent $y$, for everything, in the sense that, everything $x$ does is done on behalf of $y$. To express this situation we will use the following abbreviation:

$$(x : r_1) : REP(y : r2, *) \overset{abv}{=} (E_{x:r1}\psi \rightarrow E_{y:r2}\psi)$$

Using $C(x, y)$ to denote (the content of) a contract between agents $x$ and $y$, we may say that a contract $C(x, y)$ is a formula similar to the following one:

$qual(x : r1) \wedge qual(y : r2) \wedge$     *Attribution of roles to agents*
$P_{x:r_1} A_1 \wedge O_{x:r_1} A_2 \wedge \ldots$     *Deontic characterization of $r_1$*
$P_{y:r_2} B_1 \wedge O_{y:r_2} B_2 \wedge \ldots$     *Deontic characterization of $r_2$*
$x : r_1 : REP(y : r2, C_1) \wedge \ldots$   *Scope of representation of $r_1$*

---

[8] For simplicity reasons we only consider contracts between two agents.

$$y : r_2 : REP(x : r1, D_1) \land \ldots \quad \textit{Scope of representation of } r_2$$
$$E_{x:r_1} E_1 \rightarrow O_{y:r_2} G_1 \qquad\qquad \textit{Conditional obligation}$$
$$E_{x:r_1} \neg L_1 \rightarrow O_{x:r_1} M_1 \qquad\quad \textit{Sanction to violations of } O_{x:r_1} L_1$$
$$\ldots$$

The formalization of conditional obligations or of the sanctions resultant from violations of norms will not be addressed it in this paper (see, e.g. [3] about dyadic logics and contrary-to-duties).

An example of a contract between $a$ and $b$:

$$C(a, b) = \quad qual(a{:}r1) \quad \land \quad qual(b{:}r2)$$
$$P_{a:r1} B \quad \land \quad P_{a:r1} C \quad \land O_{b:r2} D \quad \land$$
$$(a : r1) : REP(b : r2, B) \quad \land \quad (a : r1) : REP(b : r2, C)$$

In this contract, the qualifications of $r1$ and $r2$ are assigned to $a$ and $b$, respectively. It is given permission to $a$ to act on behalf of $b$ for $B$ and $C$. Agent $b$ becomes under obligation $D$.

Another example is a contract, where agent $a$ accepts to hold role $r$ in the organization $i$, is:

$$C(a, i) = \quad qual(a{:}r) \quad \land$$
$$O_{a:r} B \quad \land \quad P_{a:r} C \quad \land \quad O_{i:itself} D$$
$$E_{a:r} \neg B \rightarrow O_{a:r} F$$

In this contract, specific obligations and permissions are attributed to agent $a$ when acting in role $r$. These specific obligations and permissions will be added to the deontic characterization of role $r$ (defined in the organization's structure independently of any agent) which will be inherited by agent $a$ because he will become holder of $r$. Sanctions for unfulfilled obligations are also stated.

### 3.4   Computer Systems and Organizations

A software system is part of the organization where it is used. Moreover, many software systems can be viewed, themselves, as organizational systems, where the different components are seen as autonomous entities, interacting with each other, collaborating toward system's aims. This view suggests that the components of a computer system must, somehow, be *integrated in the organization structure*.

Some tasks may be done either by a human agent or by a software system. And it may be irrelevant for those who interact with that system if those tasks are done by human or software agents (e.g to buy a ticket to a machine or to an human employee; to submit a conference paper to a cyber chair or to a human chair). According to this, we may consider that software components may play roles in an organization as any human agent, and be themselves classified as agents[9]. By doing that, it will be clarified what the software component is expected to do (through role characterization: if a software agent occupies a role, it should behave as described in that role). Moreover, when it fails it will be possible to identify who will be *responsible for*

---

[9] Of course not all software programs should be classified as agent. Only those rendering services that may correspond to some role.

*that failure.* Lets discuss this responsibility issue, trying to understand what are the differences between a software agent and a human agent with respect to responsibility.

As we said before, we cannot attribute responsibilities to a computer system. There must always be some person (human or artificial) responsible for it. When I interact with an ATM machine and something goes wrong, I complain to the bank responsible for it. Another example: when I interact with a cyber chair trying to submit a paper to a conference, and I don't succeed, I try to contact the member of the organizing committee responsible for it.

We may identify different persons that may be responsible for a software failure:

- *the developer of the software* – if the software fails because it is not well done (some technical or conceptual problem).
- *the user of the software* – if he does not follow the use instructions of the software.
- *the company where the software is used* – if there is no bad use, the company that owns the software and provides the service, must be responsible for any damage caused; the company may transmit that responsibility to other agents: the builder of the software or the agent of the company that maintains the software.

How can we make sure that it is possible to trace responsibilities from software agents to persons? First of all, a software agent must always act as *representative* of some other agent (the institutional agent or some other agent member of the institutional agent). To capture that, we must define a "contract" between the organization and the software agent, stating the role it plays in the organization, and defining that it always will act as representative. Secondly, there must exist (formal or informal) contracts between the persons involved: a contract between the company and the software developer (to assure maintenance of the software), a contract between the software user and the company (securing user's rights, in one side; securing the company against bad use, on the other side).

## 3.5   A Trust Concept

Lets return to our initial statement: people trust a software system if it does not fail or, when it does, if it is possible to determine who is responsible for that failure (in order to repair any damage caused). Based on this very restricted notion of trust, we propose the concept of *trusty institutional agent*: an institutional agent is trusty with respect to its software components if it is possible to determine the persons (human or artificial) responsible for the actions of the software components that play roles in its structure. We will now try to formalize this concept in the logic.

We will start by defining what we mean by *responsibility*.[10] We will consider (in a very simplistic way) only *responsibility for action in a role*:

$$RESP(x:r,\phi) \stackrel{def}{=} E_{x:r}\phi$$

If we combine this responsibility concept with the representation concept presented before, we can trace responsibilities for action and infer:

$$E_{x:r}\phi \ \wedge \ (x:r):REP(y:r1,\phi) \rightarrow RESP(y:r1,\phi)$$

Thus, we say that an agent $x$ acting in role $r$ is responsible for $\phi$, if he acted in that role to bring about $\phi$, or if we can infer, through representation mechanisms, that he brought about $\phi$ (indirectly).

We can now use this responsibility concept to define different levels of trust:

**T-SAR:** *a software agent in a role is trusty for some action* if, when it produces that action in that role, it is possible to find some non-software agent responsible for that action:

$$T-SAR(sa:r,\phi) \stackrel{def}{=} E_{sa:r}\phi \rightarrow \exists_y \exists_{r1}(RESP(y:r1,\phi) \wedge \neg(is-sAg(y)))$$

where   $is-sAg(y)$ is a predicate meaning that $y$ is a software agent.

**T-SA:** *a software agent is trusty for some action*:

$$T-SA(sa,\phi) \stackrel{def}{=} \forall_r((qual(sa:r) \wedge P_r\phi) \rightarrow T-SAR(sa:r,\phi))$$

**T-I:** *an institutional agent is trusty for some action*:

$$T-I(i,\phi) \stackrel{def}{=} \forall_{sa}((is-sAg(sa) \wedge member(sa,i)) \rightarrow T-SA(sa,\phi))$$

where   $member(a,i) \stackrel{def}{=} \exists_r(is-role(r,i) \wedge qual(a:r))$ and $is-role(r,i)$ means that $r$ is a role of the structure of $i$.

## 4   An Example

We are going to synthesize the information presented above, specifying the institutional agent of Fig.1, the agents that support its structure and the contracts established between them. Fig.1 represents part of the structure of a railway company $(i)$, having two software agents playing roles in it: a ticket machine

---

[10] A first and natural attempt would be simply to use the representation notion presented before as a way of transmission of responsibilities. But there is a problem: representation is not transitive. We cannot say that:

$$(x:r):REP(y:r1,\phi) \wedge (y:r1):REP(z:r2,\phi) \rightarrow (x:r):REP(z:r2,\phi)$$

Representation is a relationship between agents. There might exist a relationship between $x$ and $y$ where it is stated $(x:r):REP(y:r1,\phi)$; there might exit another relationship between $y$ and $z$ where it is stated $(y:r1):REP(z:r2,\phi)$. But from those two relationships we cannot infer that there is a relationship between $x$ and $z$. For example, $x$ may be representative of a company $k$ for $\phi$, and the company $k$ may hold the role of single auditor of company $i$, being representative of $i$ for $\phi$. From that we cannot conclude that $x$ is representative of $i$ for $\phi$ (there is no relationship between them).

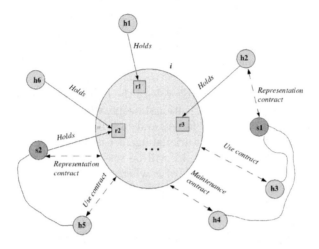

**Legend:**
Human agents: $h_1..h_6$;
Software agents: $s1$ - *railway time-table database*, $s2$ - *ticket machine* ;
Roles: $r1$ - *railway manager*, $r2$ - *ticket seller*, $r3$ - *schedule manager*

**Fig. 1.** Software agents in an institutional agent

($s2$) that plays the role of ticket seller ($r2$), which is also played by a human agent ($h6$); a railway time-table database ($s1$) that helps ($h2$) the schedule manager ($r3$) to tell information about the railway time-table. $h3$ is a user that will consult railway time-table, using $s1$. $h5$ is a user that will buy tickets using $s2$. $h1$ is the railway manager ($r1$) and $h4$ supplies the software $s1$ for the company $i$.

The specification of an institutional agent involves a name, $i$, and a structure $ST_i$:    $ST_i = < R_i, DCR_i, TO_i, RER_i >$.

$ST_i$, the *structure* of the organization $i$, is formed by a set of roles $R_i$, the deontic characterization of each role $DCR_i$, the transmission of obligations from the organization to specific roles of its structure $TO_i$ and the representative roles $RER_i$ [11].

$$
\begin{aligned}
ST_i &= \; < R_i, DCR_i, TO_i, RER_i > \\
R_i &= \{ \, is-role(r1,i), is-role(r2,i), is-role(r3,i), ...\} \\
DCR_i &= \{ \, O_{r1}A1, P_{r1}B1, \\
&\qquad O_{r2}A2, O_{r2}B2, \\
&\qquad O_{r3}A3, ...\} \\
TO_i &= \{ \, O_{i:itself}A1 \rightarrow O_{r1}A1, O_{i:itself}A2 \rightarrow O_{r2}A2, O_{i:itself}A3 \rightarrow O_{r3}A3, ...\} \\
RER_i &= \{ \, r1 : REP(i : itself, A1), r2 : REP(i : itself, A2), r3 : REP(i : itself, A3), ...\}
\end{aligned}
$$

---

[11] The specification of an organization includes other components, not considered here for simplicity reasons.

where:

$A1$ - Define trains' schedule; $B1$ - Change ticket prices; $A2$ - Collect the appropriate ticket prices; $B2$ - Inform users to use the exact amount of money, when there is no change; $A3$ - Inform about train schedule.

Notice that $r1$ is a representative role of the institutional agent for $A1$ (so, its holder, acts on behalf of the institutional agent, when bringing about $A1$ in role $r1$), $r2$ a representative role of $i$ for $A2$ and $r3$ is a representative role of $i$ for $A3$. Another remark: when the institutional agent $i$ is under the obligation to bring about $A1$, the holder of the role $r1$ will be responsible for bringing about $A1$, fulfilling that obligation on behalf of $i$; when the institutional agent $i$ is under the obligation to bring about $A2$ or $A3$ they will be transmitted to the holders of $r2$ or $r3$, respectively.

A society of agents will be characterized by a set of contracts between the agents of the society, regulating their interactions. The society of agents of Fig. 1 may be specified by a tuple with the following components:

$$SA =< iAg, sAg, hAg, CONT >$$

where $iAg$ is the specification of each institutional agent of the society (it is formed by a set of pairs $< i, ST_i >$, as explained above); $sAg$ contains the identification of the software agents of the society; $hAg$ contains the identification of the human agents of the society; and $CONT$ contains the contracts that the agents established between each other.

$$
\begin{aligned}
SA &= \ < iAg, sAg, hAg, CONT > \\
iAg &= \{\ is - iAg(i)\} \\
sAg &= \{\ is - sAg(s1), is - sAg(s2)\} \\
hAg &= \{\ is - hAg(h1), is - hAg(h2), is - hAg(h3), is - hAg(h4), \\
&\quad\ is - hAg(h5), is - hAg(h6)\} \\
CONT &= \{\ Cont1(h1, i), Cont2(h2, i), Cont3(h6, i), \\
&\quad\ Cont4(s2, i), Cont5(s1, h2) \\
&\quad\ Cont6(h4, i), Cont7(h3, i), Cont8(h5, i)\} \\
Cont1(h1, i) &= \ qual(h1 : r1) \\
Cont2(h2, i) &= \ qual(h2 : r3) \\
Cont3(h6, i) &= \ qual(h6 : r2) \\
Cont4(s2, i) &= \ qual(s2 : r2) \wedge (s2 : r2) : REP(i : itself, *) \\
Cont5(s1, h2) &= \ qual(s1 : r) \wedge (s1 : r) : REP(h2 : r3, *) \\
Cont6(h4, i) &= \ qual(h4 : r4) \wedge qual(i : r5) \wedge O_{i:r5}A4 \wedge O_{h4:r4}B4 \\
Cont7(h3, i) &= \ qual(h3 : r6) \wedge O_{h3:r6}A5 \wedge O_{i:itself}B5 \\
Cont8(h5, i) &= \ qual(h5 : r8) \wedge O_{h5:r8}A6 \wedge O_{i:itself}B6
\end{aligned}
$$

Contracts $Cont1(h1, i), Cont2(h2, i), Cont3(h6, i)$ formalize the relationship established between $i$ and $h1$, $h2$ and $h3$ respectively, assigning to $h1$, $h2$ and $h3$ the roles $r1$, $r2$ and $r3$, respectively. In contract $Cont4(s2, i)$ role $r2$ is assigned to software agent $s2$. This agent will act as representative of the institutional agent $i$. In contract $Cont5(s1, h2)$ role $r$ is assigned to the software agent $s1$, that will represent agent $h2 : r3$. Contract $Cont6(h4, i)$ represents a maintenance contract: $h4$ is responsible for the software $s1$. Contract $Cont7(h3, i)$ and

$Cont8(h5, i)$ represents user contracts: it formalizes the norms that agents interacting with the software should respect.

The specification of this society of agents can now be analyzed in order to see if it obeys to the safety requirements discussed above.

It is easy to prove that the railway company is trusty with respect to its software components, i.e., all the software agents of the company have persons responsible for their actions: $h2$ is responsible for $s1$, and $i$ is responsible for $s2$.

Lets now analyze the chain of responsibilities for action.

### 4.1 Chain of Responsibilities

The logic $\mathcal{L}_{\mathcal{DA}}$ can be used to trace responsibilities for action. Assuming that an action of an agent in a role occurred, we want to analyze its deontic effects or its effects on actions of other agents. Our aim is to verify if the action was valid $(E_{a:r}\psi \wedge P_{a:r}\psi)$, if there was a fulfillment of some obligation $(E_{a:r}\psi \wedge O_{a:r}\psi)$ or if there was a violation of some obligation $(E_{a:r}\neg\psi \wedge O_{a:r}\psi)$. In this latter case, we want to be able to identify the agents that are (directly and indirectly) responsible for the violation.

A specification of a society of agents $SA$ defines a particular language and a set of formulas of that language. If we add this set of formulas to the logic $\mathcal{L}_{\mathcal{DA}}$ as new axioms, we obtain a new logic that we call the theory defined by $SA$, denoted by $\mathcal{T}(\mathcal{SA})$. Then, we can prove if some formula $\psi$ can be deduced from $\Delta$ in $\mathcal{T}(\mathcal{SA})$, being$\Delta$ some set of formulas (typically action or deontic formulas)[12]:

$$\Delta \vdash_{\mathcal{T}(SA)} \psi$$

Lets now present examples of inferences that can be done from the specification presented above. Due to space limitations, we will not present the formal proofs, but just sketch them.

**Case 1:** *The railway time-table database s1 gives the user h3 correct information about trains'schedule (A3), which is an obligation of i.*

$\Delta = \{E_{s1:r}A3, O_{i:itself}A3\}$
$\psi = (E_{h2:r3}A3 \wedge O_{h2:r3}A3) \wedge (E_{i:itself}A3 \wedge O_{i:itself}A3)$

From $E_{s1:r}A3$ and $(s1 : r) : REP(h2 : r3, *)$ we can infer $E_{h2:r3}A3$.

As we have $O_{r3}A3 \wedge qual(h2 : r3)$ we may conclude that h2 has fulfilled his obligation $E_{h2:r3}A3 \wedge O_{h2:r3}A3$.

But we also have $r2 : REP(i : itself, A3)$ and from that and $E_{h2:r3}A3$ infer $E_{i:itself}A3$.

Thus we have $(E_{i:itself}A3 \wedge O_{i:itself}A3)$ meaning that $i$ has fulfilled his obligation.

---

[12] Notions of theorem, and deduction from hypothesis are defined as in [5], for example.

**Case 2:** *The railway time-table database* $s1$ *gives the user* $h3$ *incorrect informa-tion about trains' schedule* $(\neg A3)$. *This failure is due to a technical problem* $\neg B4$ *of the responsibility of* $h4$ *(we will represent this causality by an implication).*

$$\Delta = \{E_{h4:r4}\neg B4, E_{h4:r4}\neg B4 \rightarrow E_{s1:r}\neg A3, O_{i:itself}A3\}$$
$$\psi = (E_{h4:r4}\neg B4 \wedge O_{h4:r4}B4) \wedge (E_{h2:r3}\neg A3 \wedge O_{h2:r3}A3) \wedge (E_{i:itself}\neg A3 \wedge O_{i:itself}A3)$$

From $E_{h4:r4}\neg B4$ and contract $Cont6$ we have the violation $E_{h4:r4}\neg B4 \wedge O_{h4:r4}B4)$.

From $E_{h4:r4}\neg B4$ and $E_{h4:r4}\neg B4 \rightarrow E_{s1:r}\neg A3$ we can infer $E_{s1:r}\neg A3$.

As we have $(s1:r): REP(h2:r3,*)$ and $E_{s1:r}\neg A3$, we can infer $E_{h2:r3}\neg A3$.

From $O_{r3}A3 \wedge qual(h2:r3)$ we can infer $O_{h2:r3}A3$, and we detect another violation $E_{h2:r3}\neg A3 \wedge O_{h2:r3}A3$.

As we have $.r3: REP(i:itself, A3)$ and $E_{h2:r3}\neg A3$, we can infer $E_{i:itself}\neg A3$ and detect yet another violation $(E_{i:itself}\neg A3 \wedge O_{i:itself}A3)$.

**Case 3:** *The ticket machine (s2) has no change and tells the users to use the exact amount of money (B2).* $h5$ *wants to buy a ticket but uses an amount of money superior than the ticket price* $(\neg A6)$, *misusing* $s2$. *This causes* $s2$ *not to collect the appropriate ticket price* $(\neg A2)$, *because it has no change.*

$$\Delta = \{E_{s2:r2}B2, E_{h5:r7}\neg A6, (E_{h5:r7}\neg A6 \rightarrow E_{s2:r2}\neg A2), O_{i:itself}A2\}$$

$$\psi = (E_{s2:r2}B2 \wedge O_{s2:r2}B2) \wedge (E_{h5:r7}\neg A6 \wedge O_{h5:r7}A6) \wedge (E_{s2:r2}\neg A2 \wedge O_{s2:r2}A2) \wedge$$
$$(E_{i:itself}\neg A2 \wedge O_{i:itself}A2)$$

From $Cont4(s2, i)$ we have $qual(s2, r2)$ and $(s2:r2): REP(i:itself, *)$. From $qual(s2, r2)$ and $O_{r2}B2$ we infer $O_{s2:r2}B2$, and detect a fulfillment of an obliga-tion $E_{s2:r2}B2 \wedge O_{s2:r2}B2$.

From $Cont8(h5, i)$ we have $O_{h5:r7}A6$. Thus we detect a violation $E_{h5:r7}\neg A6 \wedge O_{h5:r7}A6$.

From $E_{h5:r7}\neg A6$ and $E_{h5:r7}\neg A6 \rightarrow E_{s2:r2}\neg A2$ we infer $E_{s2:r2}\neg A2$.

From $qual(s2, r2)$ and $O_{r2}A2$ we infer $O_{s2:r2}A2$, and detect a violation of an obligation $E_{s2:r2}\neg A2 \wedge O_{s2:r2}A2$.

As we have $E_{s2:r2}\neg A2$ and $(s2:r2): REP(i:itself, *)$ we infer $E_{i:itself}\neg A2$, and we detect another violation $E_{i:itself}\neg A2 \wedge O_{i:itself}A2$.

## 5    Conclusions and Future Work

In this paper we proposed a model for the normative specification of organiza-tional systems (human or virtual) based on the concept of role and on the legal concepts of artificial person and contract. In that model we explicitly describe the norms that regulate the systems and their components, stating how they should behave, assuming however that they may deviate from what is expected of them. The proposed model is supported by a multi-modal action and deontic logic. With that logical framework we can describe expected behavior of agents, verify if agents actions in a role are valid, if they correspond to the fulfillment of obligations or, on the contrary, if they correspond to a violation of some obligation. When non-ideal situations, like the latter, occur, it is possible to identify the agents that, directly or indirectly, are responsible for them.

We argued that the integration of computer systems in organizational structure helps to clarify what is expected of software/hardware components, and helps to identify who will be responsible for failure.

We also defended that the use of the model proposed can be useful in the formalization of virtual organizations, or in other virtual environments. The security issues that lead to this kind of models are also present in virtual contexts. Adopting them may contribute to increase trust in the interactions between agents.

These models are suited to high-level specification and may be useful to a first level of specification of systems, giving a normative view of them.

There are many open problems in this approach. The notion of trust presented is very specific and needs further research. We have to refine this high-level model relating states of affairs with actions (possibly using event calculus, following the work of M. Sergot). We also have to detail contracts and norms, possibly including contrary-to-duties(c.f. the work of A.Jones and J. Carmo) and/or using defeasible logic (c.f. the work of G. Governatori, A. Rotolo and G. Sartor). Another research direction is to use the different kinds of action (direct action, indirect action, attempted action) proposed by F. Santos, A. Jones and J. Carmo, to distinguish different levels of responsibility. We are also addressing issues related with the dynamics of this logics, and with their automation. Those issues are crucial to make this approach interesting to model real cases.

# References

1. Belnap, N. and Perloff, M.: "Seeing To It That: A Canonical Form for Agentives", *Theoria*, **54**, 1989, 175–199.
2. Bertino, E. and Ferrari, E. and Atluri, V.: "A Flexible Model for the Specification and Enforcement of Authorizations in Workflow Management Systems",*Proceedings of 2nd ACM Workshop on Role Based Access Control*, 1997, 1–12.
3. Carmo, J. and Jones, A.:"Deontic Logic and Contrary-to-Duties". D. Gabbay and F. Guenthner (eds.) *Handbook of Philosophical Logic*, volume 8, 265–343, Kluwer Academic Publishers, 2nd edition, 2002.
4. Carmo, J and Pacheco, O.: "Deontic and action logics for organized collective agency, modeled through institutionalized agents and roles", *Fundamenta Informaticae*, Vol.48 (No. 2,3), pp. 129-163, IOS Press, November, 2001, .
5. B. J. Chellas: *Modal Logic - an Introduction*, Cambridge University Press, 1980.
6. Cuppens, F.: "Roles and Deontic Logic".A.J.I. Jones and M. Sergot (eds.),*Proceedings of Second International Workshop on Deontic Logic in Computer Science (DEON'94)*, Complex 1/94 NRCCL, Oslo, 1994, 86–106.
7. Elgesem, D.: *Action Theory and Modal Logic*, PhD thesis, Department of Philosophy, University of Oslo, 1993.

8. G. Governatori, J. Gelati, A. Rotolo and G. Sartor: "Actions, Institutions, Powers. Preliminary Notes", *International Workshop on Regulated Agent-Based Social Systems (RASTA'02)*, Fachbereich Informatik, Universität Hamburg, pp. 131-147, 2002.

9. R. Hilpinen (ed.), *Deontic Logic: Introductory and Sistematic Readings*,Dordrecht: D.Reidel, 1971.

10. A. J. I. Jones and M. J. Sergot: "A Formal Characterization of Institutionalized Power", *Journal of the IGPL* , **4(3)**, pp.429-445, 1996. Reprinted in E. Garzón Valdés, W. Krawietz, G. H. von Wright and R. Zimmerling (eds.), *Normative Systems in Legal and Moral Theory*, (Festschrift for Carlos E. Alchourrón and Eugenio Bulygin), Berlin: Duncker & Humblot, pp.349-369, 1997.

11. S. Kanger: "Law and Logic", *Theoria*, **38**, 1972.

12. L. Lindahl: *Position and Change - A Study in Law and Logic*, Synthese Library **112**, Dordrecht:D. Reidel, 1977.

13. Massacci, F.: "Reasoning about Security: a Logic and a Decision Method for Role-Based Access Control". D. Gabbay et al. (eds.), *Proc. of the Int. Joint Conference on Qualitative and Quantitative Practical Reasoning*, LNAI, **1244**, Springer Verlag, 1997, 421–435.

14. Meyer, J.-J. Ch. and Wieringa, R. J.: "Deontic Logic: A Concise Overview". J.-J.CH. Meyer and R.J. Wieringa (eds), *Deontic Logic in Computer Science: Normative System Specification*, John Wiley & Sons, 1993, 3–16.

15. Minsky, N., Ungureanu, V.: "Law-Governed Interaction: A Coordination and Control Mechanism for Heterogeneous Distributed Systems". in *ACM Transactions on Software Engineering and Methodology (TOSEM)*, (Vol 9, No 3, pages: 273-305) July 2000.

16. O. Pacheco and J. Carmo: "Collective Agents: from Law to AI", Proceedings of 2nd French-American Conference on Law and Artificial Intelligence, Nice, 1998.

17. O. Pacheco and J. Carmo: " A Role Based Model for the Normative Specification of Organized Collective Agency and Agents Interaction", *Journal of Autonomous Agents and Multi-Agent Systems*, Vol. 6, Issue 2, pp.145-184, Kluwer, March 2003.

18. I. Pörn: *Action Theory and Social Science: Some Formal Models*, Synthese Library, **120**, Dordrecht : D. Reidel, 1977.

19. Santos, F. and Jones, A.J.I. and Carmo, J.: "Responsibility for Action in Organizations: a Formal Model". G. Holmstrom-Hintikka and R. Tuomela (eds.), *Contemporary Action Theory*, **II** (Social Action), Synthese Library, **267**, Kluwer, 1997, 333–350.

20. Santos, F. and Carmo, J.: " Indirect Action, Influence and Responsibility", in M. Brown and J.Carmo (eds.), *Deontic Logic, Agency and Normative Systems*, Springer, Workshops in Computing Series, 194-215, 1996.

21. Sergot, M.:"Modelling unreliable and untrustworthy agent behavior". In *Proc.Workshop on Monitoring, Security and Rescue Techniques in Multiagent Systems (MSRAS'04)*, Poland, Advances in Soft Computing. Springer-Verlag, 2004.

22. Skarmeas, N.:"Modeling Organizations using Roles and Agents", *Proceedings of 5h Hellenic Conference on Informatics*, Athens, 1995.

# Type-Based Distributed Access Control
## vs. Untyped Attackers

Tom Chothia[1] and Dominic Duggan[2]

[1] Laboratoire d'Informatique (LIX), École Polytechnique (CNRS),
91128 Palaiseau Cedex, France
tomc@lix.polytechnique.fr
[2] Department of Computer Science, Stevens Institute of Technology,
Hoboken, NJ 07030, USA
dduggan@cs.stevens-tech.edu

**Abstract.** This paper considers what happens when a system erroneously places trust in an attacker. More precisely we consider untyped attackers inside a distributed system in which security is enforced by the type system. Our *Key-Based Decentralised Label Model* for distributed access control combines a weak form of information flow control with cryptographic type casts. We extend our model to allow inside attackers by using three sets of type rules. The first set is for honest principals. The second set is for attackers; these rules require that only communication channels can be used to communicate and express our correctness conditions. The third set of type rules are used to type processes that have become corrupted by the attackers. We show that the untyped attackers can leak their own data and disrupt the communication of any principals that place direct trust in an attacker, but no matter what the attackers try, they cannot obtain data that does not include at least one attacker in its access control policy.

## 1 Introduction

Type systems can provide a lightweight method to ensure security properties of a given piece of code. Once checked, the program can be run, with few restrictions, in the knowledge that the guarantees of the type system will still hold. These guarantees can be extended to distributed processes communicating across an untrusted network, as long as each trusted process is well-typed. This paper addresses the question of what happens when a number of these "trusted" processes ignore the security types with the aim of acquiring sensitive data and disrupting other principals.

In previous work [CDV03], we introduce the *Key-Based Decentralised Label Model* (KDLM) for distributed access control. It combines a weak form of information flow control with typed cryptographic operations. The motivation is to have a type system that ensures access control while giving the application the responsibility to secure network communications, and to do this safely. This removes the need to force the user into a "one size fits all" security solution, which would have to be implemented in the trusted computing base. The original system included primitives for the declassification and packaging of data, including these in our system would obstruct the explanation of our method for dealing with untyped attackers. So, we show how safety in the face of untyped attackers can be proved for a cut-down version of our previous system, which

T. Dimitrakos et al. (Eds.): FAST 2005, LNCS 3866, pp. 203–216, 2006.

we refer to as mini-KDLM. This calculus is simple enough to illustrate the ideas of our system, while still capturing the salient features of KDLM.

We show that the untyped attackers can leak their own data and disrupt the communication of any other principals that place direct trust in an attacker. However, no matter what the attackers try, they cannot obtain data that does not include an attacker in its access control policy. We achieve this result by using a type system with three sets of type rules. The first set allows principals to be well-typed in the KDLM style. Attackers have their own type rules that allow them to ignore the access control types. That attackers have type rules at all is down to the need to maintain the separation between base types and channel types (pretending that an integer has a channel type won't make it into a communication channel). The final set of type rules allow for names that have been misplaced in honest principals; we refer to processes that have been interfered with in this way as corrupt. These rules allow for one name to take the place of another name, with a different type, as long as both names originally included at least one attacker in their access control policy.

Our rules for attackers and corrupt processes require data not to be misplaced, unless it includes an attacker in its access control policy. So, we show the correctness of our system by showing that well-typed systems always reduce to well-typed systems. To assist us, we first prove a lemma: in a well-typed system, we may substitute one type for another and the system will remain well-typed as long as both types originally included an attacker in their access control policy. We prove this lemma by showing that we can use the type rules for corrupt processes to type any sub-processes affected by the type change.

The contributions of this work are:

- The simplified, distributed, access control system mini-KDLM
- A model of untyped attackers and a correctness proof for systems under attack in mini-KDLM.
- Showing how distributed, untyped attackers can be dealt with using a different set of type rules for honest principals, attackers and principals corrupted by the attackers.

In Section 2, we review the KDLM type system for distributed access control and introduce the simplified version, mini-KDLM. Next, in Section 3 we introduce the model of untyped attackers. In Section 4, we show how type rules can be used to characterize principals that have been corrupted by an attacker. Section 5 proves the correctness of our system by way of a subject reduction result. Section 6 discusses related work and finally, Section 7 concludes and briefly discusses further work.

## 2   Mini-KDLM

The Decentralized Label Model (DLM) [ML97] is a model of information flow control that was introduced by Myers and Liskov. This model avoids one undesirable aspect of classical information flow control - the need for some centrally defined lattice of information levels - by implicitly defining a lattice based on access control.

More recently we combined ideas from DLM and cryptographic APIs [Dug03] to make the Key-based Decentralized Label Model (KDLM). This system provides

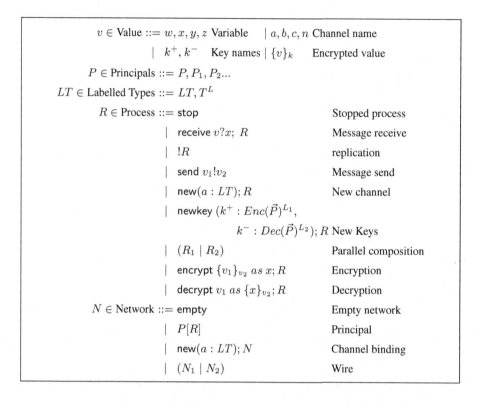

**Fig. 1.** Syntax of mini-KDLM

distributed access control and forms the basis for mini-KDLM. The argument for our approach is the usual end-to-end argument in system design: it is ultimately unrealistic to expect there to be a single "one size fits all" solution to network security in the runtime. The application must be able to build its own network security stack for any approach to scale, so the type system prevents the application from violating the access control policy while leaving it free to establish network security however it sees fit.

The syntax of mini-KDLM is given in Figure 1. Most of this is similar to the spi-calculus [AG99]. The new term $P[R]$ is the process $R$ running under the control of the principal $P$. It should be noted that this does not represent a location. It is possible to have two threads running for different principals on the same computer, just as it is possible for processes running for the same principal to run in two different places. We reduce and type each process running for a principal on its own, using the structural equivalence rule:

$$P[\,R_1 \mid R_2\,] \equiv P[\,R_1\,] \mid P[\,R_2\,]$$

The calculus is monadic, meaning that channels only pass a single name at a time. We could extend the calculus to pass multiple channels at a time by repeating the type checks for each name passed, or by packaging up a number of names into a single

$$P_1[\text{ send } a!b\,]\mid P_2[\text{ receive } a?x;\,R\,]\rightarrow P_2[\,R[b/x]\,]$$

$$P[\text{encrypt } \{v\}_{k+}\text{ as } x;\,R\,]\rightarrow P[\,R[\{v\}_k/x]\,]$$

$$P[\text{decrypt } \{v\}_k\text{ as } \{x\}_{k-};\,R\,]\rightarrow P[\,R[v/x]\,]$$

$$\frac{N_1\rightarrow N_1'}{N_1\mid N_2\rightarrow N_1'\mid N_2}$$

$$\frac{N\rightarrow N'}{\text{new }(a:LT);\,N\rightarrow\text{new }(a:LT);\,N'}$$

$$\frac{R\equiv R_1\quad R_1\rightarrow R_1'\quad R_1'\equiv R'}{R\rightarrow R'}$$

**Fig. 2.** The Semantics

$$!R\;\equiv\;R\mid!R\qquad\qquad \text{stop}\mid R\;\equiv\;R$$
$$R_1\mid R_2\;\equiv\;R_2\mid R_1\qquad R_1\mid(\,R_2\mid R_3\,)\;\equiv\;(\,R_1\mid R_2\,)\mid R_3$$
$$\text{new}(a:LT);\,R\;\equiv\;R\quad a\notin fn(R)\qquad P[\,R_1\mid R_2\,]\;\equiv\;P[\,R_1\,]\mid P[\,R_2\,]$$
$$(\,\text{new}(a:LT);\,R_1\,)\mid R_2\;\equiv\;\text{new}(a:LT);\,(\,R_1\mid R_2\,)\quad a\notin fn(R_2)$$
$$\text{new}(a_1:LT_1);\,\text{new}(a_2:LT_2);\,R\;\equiv\;\text{new}(a_2:LT_2);\,\text{new}(a_1:LT_1);\,R$$

plus the equivalent rules for Networks and newkey.

**Fig. 3.** Equivalence Rules

object and placing a policy on the object that is at least as restrictive as the policies on the names it contains.

The semantics of this calculus is given in Figure 2. This too is similar to the spi-calculus, in particular encrypting a name $a$ with a key $k$ results in the term $\{a\}_k$. This term cannot be identified as $a$, and cannot be used to communicate. The decrypt operation pattern matches the key name and will decrypt the data if the correct key is provided, otherwise it will halt. The new construct generates a new and unique name. The structural equivalence rules allow the scope of a new name to be expanded, as long as it does not capture any other names, using the rule:

$$(\text{new}(a:LT);\,R)\mid R'\equiv\text{new}(a:LT);\,(R\mid R')\quad\text{if }a\notin fn(Q)$$

where $fn(R')$ are the names in $R'$ that do not appear under a binder. The communication rule cannot be applied across a new name construct hence new and "old" names represented by the same symbol cannot communicate. The other structural equivalence rules are given in Figure 3.

$$
\begin{aligned}
T \in \text{Types} ::= \ & \text{Chan}(LT) && \text{Channel Type} \\
| \ & \langle \rangle && \text{Null Type} \\
| \ & Enc(\vec{P}) \mid Dec(\vec{P}) && \text{Key Type} \\
L \in \text{Label} ::= \ & \vec{P} \mid Public && \text{Access Control Policy} \\
LT \in \text{Labelled type} ::= \ & T^L && \text{Protected Data}
\end{aligned}
$$

**Fig. 4.** Syntax of Sensitivity Types

$$
\frac{\Gamma \vdash N_1 \quad \Gamma \vdash N_2}{\Gamma \vdash (N_1 \mid N_2)} \qquad \frac{\Gamma \cup \{(a : LT)\} \vdash N}{\Gamma \vdash \mathsf{new}(a : LT)N}
$$

$$
\frac{\Gamma \vdash P[R_1] \quad \Gamma \vdash P[R_2]}{\Gamma \vdash P[(R_1 \mid R_2)]} \qquad \frac{\Gamma \cup \{(a : T^L)\} \vdash P[R] \quad P \in L \quad \vdash T^L}{\Gamma \vdash P[\mathsf{new}(a : T^L); R]}
$$

$$
\frac{\Gamma \vdash v : \text{Chan}(T^L)^{L_0} \quad P \in L_0 \quad \Gamma \cup \{(x : T^L)\} \vdash P[R]}{\Gamma \vdash P[\mathsf{receive} \ v?x; \ R]}
$$

$$
\frac{\Gamma \vdash v_0 : \text{Chan}(T^L)^{L_0} \quad \Gamma \vdash v : T^L \quad P \in L_0}{\Gamma \vdash P[\mathsf{send} \ v_0!v]}
$$

$$
\frac{\vdash Enc(\vec{P})^{L_1} \quad \vdash Dec(\vec{P})^{L_2} \quad P \in L_1 \cap L_2 \quad \Gamma \cup \{k^+ : Enc(\vec{P})^{L_1}, k^- : Dec(\vec{P})^{L_2}\} \vdash P[R]}{\Gamma \vdash P[\mathsf{newkey} \ (k^+ : Enc(\vec{P})^{L_1}, k^- : Dec(\vec{P})^{L_2}); R]}
$$

$$
\frac{\Gamma \vdash v_0 : T^L \quad \Gamma \vdash v : Enc(L)^{L_k} \quad \Gamma \cup \{x : T^{Public}\} \vdash P[R] \quad P \in L_k}{\Gamma \vdash P[\mathsf{encrypt} \ \{v_0\}_v \ as \ x; R]}
$$

$$
\frac{\Gamma \vdash v_0 : T^{Public} \quad \Gamma \vdash v : Dec(L_p)^{L_k} \quad \Gamma \cup \{x : T^{L_p}\} \vdash P[R] \quad P \in L_k}{\Gamma \vdash P[\mathsf{decrypt} \ v_0 \ as \ \{x\}_v; R]}
$$

**Fig. 5.** Types for Networks

The access controls are enforced using the type system given in Figure 4 (syntax), Figure 5 (type rules) and Figure 6 (well-formed types). We do not enumerate the base types here, but they could include types such as *int* for integers, and *string* for strings. The channel type Chan($LT$) is the type of the communication channel that carries a value of type $LT$. A protected type adds a policy label to a channel or base type, for

$$\frac{v_0 : T^L \in \Gamma \qquad v : Enc(L)^{L_k} \in \Gamma \qquad \vdash T^L \qquad \vdash Enc(L)^{L_k}}{\Gamma \vdash \{v_0\}_v : T^{Public}}$$

$$\frac{\Gamma \vdash k^- : Dec(\vec{P})^{L'} \qquad k^+ : Enc(\vec{P})^L \in \Gamma \qquad \vdash Enc(\vec{P})^L}{\Gamma \vdash k^+ : Enc(\vec{P})^L}$$

$$\frac{\Gamma \vdash k^+ : Enc(\vec{P})^{L'} \qquad k^- : Dec(\vec{P})^L \in \Gamma \qquad \vdash Dec(\vec{P})^L}{\Gamma \vdash k^- : Dec(\vec{P})^L}$$

$$\frac{v : T^L \in \Gamma \quad \vdash T^L}{\Gamma \vdash v : T^L} \quad \frac{\vdash T^L \quad L_0 \subseteq L}{\vdash Chan(T^L)^{L_0}} \quad \frac{L \subseteq \vec{P}}{\vdash Dec(\vec{P})^L} \quad \frac{L \subseteq \vec{P}}{\vdash Enc(\vec{P})^L}$$

**Fig. 6.** Well-Formed Types and Names

instance $int^{\{Alice,Bob\}}$ is an integer that can only be used by the principals Alice and Bob. The aim of this type system is to ensure that names only ever reach principals that are mentioned in their policy, i.e., given a network which includes the sub-term $P[R]$, all names that occur in the process $R$ must name the principal $P$ in their policy.

In this section we direct the reader's attention to the basic calculus; we discuss encryption in the next section. We restrict the types given to names in Figure 6 and we restrict how a process can use those names in Figure 5. Our type judgement on networks takes the form $\Gamma \vdash P[R]$ where $\Gamma$ is a set of type bindings. The judgement on names $\Gamma \vdash a : LT$ means that $a$ has type $LT$ in $\Gamma$ and $LT$ is a well-formed type.

There are two fundamental restrictions imposed by the type system, the first is on channel types and the second is on the send action. Channels are required to have a policy that is more restrictive than the policy of the data they carry. This is enforced by the following rule from Figure 6.

$$\frac{\vdash T^L \quad L_0 \subseteq L}{\vdash Chan(T^L)^{L_0}}$$

Here $L_0$ is the set of principals that can access a channel of this type and $L$ is the set of principals that should be able to access the data sent across this channel. As a principal must possess a channel in order to be able to receive on it, the restriction $L_0 \subseteq L$ means that any restricted data can be sent over a correctly typed channel in the knowledge that any principal that can receive the data should be allowed to do so. The condition on the data type ($\vdash T^L$) ensures that this type is well-formed.

The type check on the send action, from Figure 5, ensures that only data of the correct type is sent over a channel, i.e., the type of $v$ matches the type that should be carried by $v_0$.

$$\frac{\Gamma \vdash v_0 : Chan(T^L)^{L_0} \quad \Gamma \vdash v : T^L \quad P \in L_0}{\Gamma \vdash P[send\ v_0!v]}$$

As with the other type rules, this rule also checks that the types are well-formed and that all of the names can be used by the current principal. In the case of the send rule we know that, as $v_0$ has a well-formed type, $L_0 \subseteq L$ and hence the condition $P \in L_0$ implies that $P$ is in the access control types for both $v$ and $v_0$.

## 2.1 Encryption and Types

The type system described so far is very restrictive. More over, it may not always be possible to have a secure channel between any two principals. To make this system more flexible we use encryption as a form of type downcasting. This allows us to send sensitive data over an insecure channel, in a way that is both secure and type safe.

We associate access control lists with cryptographic keys. Keys have the type $Enc(\vec{P})^L$ or $Dec(\vec{P})^L$ to represent an encryption or decryption key that enforces the policy $\vec{P}$ on data. These key types are in turn protected by a policy, in this case $L$. The type system ensures that encryption and decryption keys enforce the same policy and that the access control policy on the key is more restrictive than the policy it enforces.

When a piece of data needs to be sent over an insecure channel it is encrypted with a key that represents the list of principals that can access that data. Once encrypted, the type rules remove the access control policy from the data by setting it to $Public$. All principals can access public data so the test $P \in Public$ is true for any $P$. When public, encrypted data is decrypted the access control policy enforced by the decryption key is placed on the decrypted data.

We illustrate the process of sending data in Figure 7. In this picture, Alice wishes to send Bob some data, which is restricted to just the two of them. Lacking a secure channel she encrypts the data with a key that enforces the same policy as the one on the data, a type check ensures that these policies match. The encrypted data does not have any type restrictions and so can be sent to Bob over a public channel. Upon receiving the data, Bob decrypts it and replaces the access restrictions. Hence, as long as the key is restricted to just Alice and Bob, the data has safely passed from one principal to another and has arrived with the same type as it started with.

The type rule for encryption is given in Figure 5. This rule ensures that the right key is used to encrypt controlled data.

$$\frac{\Gamma \vdash v_0 : T^L \quad \Gamma \vdash v : Enc(L)^{L_k} \quad \Gamma \cup \{x : T^{Public}\} \vdash P[R] \quad P \in L_k}{\Gamma \vdash P[\text{encrypt } \{v_0\}_v \text{ as } x; R]}$$

We note that the policy on the data being encrypted ($L$) must match the policy that is enforced by the key. Once the name is encrypted the access control restrictions are removed, this is indicated by the $Public$ label on the encrypted data. The condition that requires the current principal to be included in the policy of the key ($P \in L_k$) and the well-formedness condition on the key type imply that well-typed principals will only try to encrypt data that they are allowed to use i.e., that $P \in L$.

The matching decryption rule takes a name, without any access restrictions, and tries to decrypt it. If the incorrect key is used the process halts. If the correct key is provided we decrypt the data and give it the access control policy that is enforced by the key. As

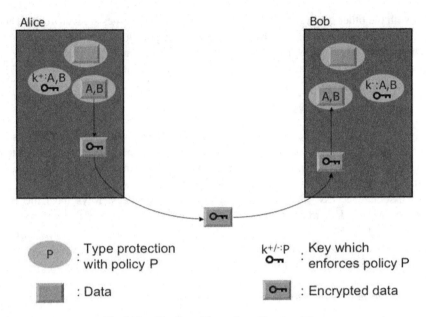

**Fig. 7.** Sending Data Through an Untrusted Area

the decryption and encryption part of a key must enforce the same policy, we know that the decrypted name has the same type as it had before it was encrypted.

Keys are restricted to a subset of the principals named in the access control policy they enforce, as seen in Figure 6. The well-formedness conditions on the key types also ensure that the encryption and decryption types for the same key enforce the same policy and that any encrypted terms in the initial network are also well-formed.

As an example, consider a system with two principals, a $PDA$ and a $Base$ computer. If the PDA uses data packets of type $data$, then a packet that was restricted to just the PDA and the owners base computer would have the type $data^{\{PDA, Base\}}$, whereas public data would have the type $data^{Public}$.

Imagine that the PDA has a cable that connects it to the base computer and a wireless connection. The socket for the cable connection on the PDA will securely connect the PDA and base computer, so it would have a type indicating that it is safe for restricted data, Cable_Socket : $\mathsf{Chan}(data^{\{PDA, Base\}})\{PDA\}$. The $PDA$ label on the socket indicates that the socket connection cannot be sent to another location. Data sent over the wireless connection, on the other hand, could easily be intercepted. It would be possible to use a secure transport layer to protect the data sent over this connection but this might be too great a burden for a the limited CPU and battery power of the PDA, or we might just want to keep the PDA software as simple as possible. So, we give the socket a type indicating that it is not safe for private data, Wireless_Socket : $\mathsf{Chan}(data^{Public})\{PDA\}$.

When the PDA software is compiled we will get a type error it the program might try to send any controlled data over the wireless connection without encrypting it. Once checked, the lightweight PDA program can run without any restrictions and without a cumbersome security transport layer.

# 3   Untyped Attackers

The aim of this paper is the correct integration of untyped attackers into our model. If an attacker is mentioned in the access control policy of a name it can acquire that name and send it on to anywhere it sees fit. So an untyped attacker can always leak some restricted data, but we can show that this abuse of trust is not transitive. If Alice restricts her data to just herself and to Bob, and excludes Eve, who does not respect the access control types, then the data should be safe from Eve, even if Bob trusts her with other data and channels.

We include attackers into our type system by adding two new sets of type rules and a new form of type judgement. We write $\Gamma \vdash_A N$ to mean that the network $N$ is well-typed given the fact that $A$ is a set of principals that can perform attacks by ignoring access control types. Processes can now be typed with the original "honest" type rules, or by a set of type rules for attackers, or by another set of type rules for processes that have been corrupted by misinformation from an attacker.

The type rules that the attackers must conform to are given in Figure 8. It may seem odd to have type rules for untyped attackers, however these rules place no restrictions on access control types. So, more accurately these are un-access-control-typed attackers. The type rules do force attackers to respect the basic nature of names. For instance, as

$$\frac{\Gamma \vdash_A N_1 \quad \Gamma \vdash_A N_2}{\Gamma \vdash_A (N_1 \mid N_2)} \qquad \frac{\Gamma \cup \{(a : LT)\} \vdash_A N}{\Gamma \vdash_A \mathsf{new}(a : LT)N}$$

$$\frac{\Gamma \vdash_A P[R_1] \quad \Gamma \vdash_A P[R_2]}{\Gamma \vdash_A P[(R_1 \mid R_2)]} \qquad \frac{\Gamma \cup \{(a : T^L)\} \vdash_A P[R] \quad P \in L \quad \vdash_A T^L}{\Gamma \vdash_A P[\mathsf{new}(a : T^L); R]}$$

$$\frac{\Gamma \vdash v : \mathsf{Chan}(T^L)^{L_0} \quad P \in A \quad L_0 \cap A \neq \{\} \quad \Gamma \cup \{x : T^L\} \vdash_A P[R]}{\Gamma \vdash_A P[\mathsf{receive} \ v?x; \ R]}$$

$$\frac{\Gamma \vdash v_0 : \mathsf{Chan}(T_1^{L_1})^{L_0} \quad \Gamma \vdash v : T_2^{L_2} \quad \lfloor T_1 \rfloor = \lfloor T_2 \rfloor}{\Gamma \vdash_A P[\mathsf{send} \ v_0!v]}$$

$$\frac{\Gamma \vdash v_0 : T^L \quad \Gamma \vdash v : Enc(L_p)^{L_v} \quad \Gamma \cup \{x : T^{Public}\} \vdash_A P[R]}{L_p \cap A \neq \{\} \quad L \cap A \neq \{\} \quad P \in A}{\Gamma \vdash_A P[\mathsf{encrypt} \ \{v_0\}_v \ as \ x; \ R]}$$

$$\frac{\Gamma \vdash v_0 : T^{Public} \quad \Gamma \vdash v : Dec(L_p)^{L_k} \quad \Gamma \cup \{x : T_p^L\} \vdash_A P[R]}{L_k \cap A \neq \{\} \quad P \in A}{\Gamma \vdash_A P[\mathsf{decrypt} \ v_0 \ as \ \{x\}_v; \ R]}$$

**Fig. 8.** Types for Attackers

communication channels must be supported by some kind of infrastructure, the attacker cannot turn an integer into a communication channel just by changing its type. We characterise the types the attacker can interchange by defining an erasure relation.

$$\lfloor \mathsf{Chan}(LT)^L \rfloor = \mathsf{Chan}(\lfloor LT \rfloor)^{Public} \qquad \lfloor \langle \rangle^L \rfloor = \langle \rangle^{Public}$$
$$\lfloor Enc(\vec{P})^L \rfloor = Enc(\vec{P})^{Public} \qquad \lfloor Dec(\vec{P})^L \rfloor = Dec(\vec{P})^{Public}$$

As long as the attackers only substitute names with the same erasure type, they can do what they like. In particular, the type of a name being sent over a channel does not have to match the type that should be carried by that channel. Also the policy enforced by the encryption key used to encode a name does not have to match the policy on that name. We cater for corruptly encrypted terms using the following additional type rule.

$$\frac{v_0 : T^L \in \Gamma \qquad v : Enc(L_p)^{L_k} \in \Gamma \qquad \vdash_A T^L \qquad \vdash_A Enc(L_p)^{L_k} \qquad L_p \cap A \neq \{\} \neq L \cap A}{\Gamma \vdash_A \{v_0\}_v : T^{Public}}$$

The attackers create "correct" types, this is because we do not consider attackers obtaining values created by other attackers as a security leak and if these names are passed to a genuine process then the real type of the name will not matter. The type rules also check that at least one attacker is named in each rule used. This is a correctness criterion that, in effect, states that the attackers have not been able to acquire any names that did not explicitly give access to an attacker. We show later that this correctness criterion is preserved by reduction.

## 4    Corrupted Principals

While the attackers cannot acquire sensitive data, they can cause their data to be misplaced. Hence, if you trust an untyped attacker you run the risk of becoming corrupted. We formalise this with the rules in Figure 9.

$$\frac{\Gamma \vdash v : \mathsf{Chan}(T^L)^{L_0} \qquad \Gamma \cup \{(x : T^L)\} \vdash_A P[R] \qquad A \cap L_0 \neq \{\}}{\Gamma \vdash_A P[\text{receive } v?x;\ R]}$$

$$\frac{\Gamma \vdash v_0 : \mathsf{Chan}(T_1^{L_1})^{L_0} \qquad \Gamma \vdash_A v : T_2^{L_2} \qquad \lfloor T_1 \rfloor = \lfloor T_2 \rfloor}{L_2 \cap A \neq \{\} \neq L_1 \cap A \qquad \textit{if } L_0 \cap A = \{\} \textit{ then } P \in L_0}{\Gamma \vdash_A P[\text{send } v_0!v]}$$

$$\frac{\Gamma \vdash v_0 : T^L \qquad \Gamma \vdash v : Enc(L_p)^{L_k} \qquad \Gamma \cup \{x : T^{Public}\} \vdash_A P[R]}{A \cap L \neq \{\} \neq L_p \cap A \qquad \textit{if } A \cap L_k = \{\} \textit{ then } P \in L_k}{\Gamma \vdash_A P[\text{encrypt } \{v_0\}_v \text{ as } x;\ R]}$$

$$\frac{\Gamma \vdash v_0 : T^{Public} \qquad \Gamma \vdash v : Dec(L_p)^{L_k} \qquad \Gamma \cup \{x : T^{L_p}\} \vdash_A P[R] \qquad A \cap L_k \neq \{\}}{\Gamma \vdash_A P[\text{decrypt } v_0 \text{ as } \{x\}_v;\ R]}$$

**Fig. 9.** Types for the Corrupt

We note that rather than having three separate sets of type rules, it would have been possible to have a single, complicated type rule for each piece of syntax. These rules would coalesce the conditions from each of the three type rules. For the sake of the reader's comfort, and our sanity, we decided to keep the rules simple.

The send rule may be corrupt in three ways: an attacker might have messed around with the communication channel that is being used to send the data, or the data that is being sent, or both. As the channel must have a well-formed type it is possible for an attacker to have access to the data being sent over the channel but not have access to the channel itself. This means that, if the send action is corrupt in any way, it must include an attacker in the payload type. We use an "if" statement to see if the communication channel may also be corrupt; if it cannot be, it must be in the right place, i.e., have the current principal in its policy. If an attacker has corrupted the data so the type of the channel's payload does not match the type of the name being sent then both must contain the name of an attacker.

In a similar way, if the attacker is named in any part of an encryption action it must be named in the policy enforced by the key and in the policy of the name being encoded. If an attacker is not named in the access control policy for the key then the attacker cannot interfere with the key and so the current principal must be mentioned. Of course, as the process has been corrupted, the policy enforced by the key does not have to match the policy on the data being encrypted.

## 5 Correctness

Our type system does not allow the attackers to possess data they are not supposed to have. For this reason, a well-typed system is one in which a leak has not yet occurred, as shown by the following lemma.

**Lemma 1.** *A well-typed network is correct, only names that explicitly allow access to an attacker appear outside their designated area:*

*If $\Gamma \vdash_A P[R]$ and $R = C[\text{send } v_1!v_2]$ or $R = C[\text{receive } v_1?x; R']$ or $R = C[\text{encrypt } \{v_1\}_{v_2} \text{ as } x; R']$ or $R = C[\text{decrypt } v_1 \text{ as } \{x\}_{v_2}; R']$ and $\Gamma' \vdash v_1 : T_1^{L_1}, v_2 : T_2^{L_2}$, where $\Gamma'$ is $\Gamma$ extended with the types defined by $C[\_]$ then $P \in L_1$ or $A \cap L_1 \neq \{\}$ and $P \in L_2$ or $A \cap L_2 \neq \{\}$.*

*Proof.* By induction on the syntax of $R$. We inspect the type rules for each piece of syntax, observe that the conditions are fulfilled and apply the induction hypothesis to type the remaining process.

The core of our correctness result takes the form of a subject reduction proof; we show that well-typed systems reduce to well-typed systems. The type system allows any given piece of syntax to be typed as an honest process, or an attacker, or a corrupted process. This leads to multiple cases to check when assuming a process is well-typed. A more interesting issue is that one type might have been used to type a name in a given process and then a name of a different type could be substituted into its place. This will happen when an attacker sends a wrongly typed name over a channel to an honest process. In which case the honest process will become corrupt and we will have to type the resulting process with the type rules for corrupt processes.

We use the following lemma to show that the substitution of one type for another is allowed by the type rules for corrupt processes, as long as there is an attacker in the policy of both names.

**Lemma 2.** *If* $\Gamma \cup \{x : T_1^{L_1}\} \vdash_A P[R]$ *then for all* $\vdash T_2^{L_2}$ *such that* $\lfloor T_1 \rfloor = \lfloor T_2 \rfloor$ *and* $A \cap L_1 \neq \{\}$ *and* $A \cap L_2 \neq \{\}$ *we have that* $\Gamma \cup \{x : T_2^{L_2}\} \vdash_A P[R]$.

*Proof.* By induction on the syntax of $R$. We give the receive case as an example.

- $R \equiv$ receive $x?y; \ R'$
  By the assumption that $P[R]$ is well-typed, with the original type for $x$, we know that there exists $T_3$ and $L_3$ such that $T_1 = \mathsf{Chan}(T_3^{L_3})$ and that $\Gamma \cup \{x : T_1^{L_1}, y : T_3^{L_3}\} \vdash_A P[R']$. As $\lfloor T_1 \rfloor = \lfloor T_2 \rfloor$ we know that $T_2 = \mathsf{Chan}(T_4^{L_4})$ for some $T_4$ such that $\lfloor T_3 \rfloor = \lfloor T_4 \rfloor$. By the well-formedness condition for channel types we know that $L_1 \subseteq L_3$ and $L_2 \subseteq L_4$ hence $A \cap L_3 \neq \{\}$ and $A \cap L_4 \neq \{\}$. So, we can apply the induction hypothesis to show that $\Gamma \cup \{x : T_2^{L_2}, y : T_4^{L_4}\} \vdash_A P[R']$. Noting that $A \cap L_2 \neq \{\}$ allows us to type $P[R]$ by the receive type rule for corrupt processes.

This lemma has proven the heart of our correctness result, however it remains to show that types only ever get mixed up when they include an attacker in their access control policy. We do this in our main theorem.

**Theorem 1 (Subject Reduction).** *If* $\Gamma \vdash_A N$ *and* $N \rightarrow N'$ *then* $\Gamma \vdash_A N'$.

*Proof.* By induction on the reduction $N \rightarrow N'$, for each reduction rule we consider each possible typing rule that could have been applied to type $N$. We then show that we can type $N'$, using Lemma 2 whenever the process becomes corrupted.

And finally, we restate this result as "correctness":

**Corollary 1.** *Given a well-typed honest network* $\Gamma \vdash N$, *for any set of attackers A and any network* $N_A$ *such that* $\Gamma \vdash_A N_A$ *the network* $N \mid N_A$ *cannot reduce to a state in which an attacker has a name that does not include an attacker in its access control policy.*

*Proof.* By Lemma 1 and Theorem 1.

## 6   Related Work

Mini-KDLM is designed to be simple enough to illustrate our correctness proof while still producing results that are relevant to full KDLM [CDV03]. So, naturally mini-KDLM is a cut down version of full KDLM. Both have policy types on data and keys that enforce policies, but full KDLM uses an abstraction of key names to represent policies, this allows for accountable declassification. In mini-KDLM we restrict both encryption and decryption keys, full KDLM splits the access control types into policies for security and authentication, meaning that encryption and signing keys can be made public. In other work we show how key names can be distributed and sketch how KDLM could be implemented as a type system for Java [CDV04].

Our work is partly inspired by the Distributed Label Model [ML97] this model was implemented as the language JFlow [Mye99]. The Jif/Split compiler [ZZNM02, ZCZM03] allows a program to be annotated with trust information, the code is then split into a number of programs that can be run on different hosts. The partitioning preserves the original semantics of the program and ensures that hosts that are not trusted to access certain data cannot receive that data. Hennessy and Riely [HR99, RH99], have developed a type system that controls attackers in the Dpi-calculus. They allow attackers to ignore the type rules, as we do here, but they use dynamic type checks to ensure that honest principals do not become corrupted.

Much of the work on wide-area languages has focused on security, for example providing abstractions of secure channels [AFG00, AFG99], controlling key distribution [CV99, CGG00], reasoning about security protocols [AG99, Aba97], etc. Abadi [Aba97] considers a type system for ensuring that secrecy is preserved in security protocols. Other work on security in programming languages has focused on ensuring and preventing unwanted security flows in programs [DD77, VS97, PC00]. Sabelfeld and Myers [SM02] provide an excellent overview of this work.

## 7    Conclusion and Further Work

We have extended the Key-Based Decentralised Label Model for access control to include inside, trusted attackers and proved that these attackers can cause only limited damage. The model works by having three sets of type rules: the first for honest processes, the second for attackers and the third for processes that have been corrupted by an attacker. The type rules also contain checks that ensure no data, which is not designated as accessible to an attacker, leaks outside its area. We prove the correctness of our system by showing subject reduction.

It may be interesting to introduce a sub-typing relation for labelled types. For instance, allowing data to be sent over channels that should carry a more restrictive data type, and effectively up grading the data's security restrictions. Modelling corrupted types as sub-types of the honest types may allow us to reduce the total number of type rules. However, this does not catch the different possible behaviours of honest participants and attackers and it may make the extension of the system more cumbersome.

We hope that this work will be a base from which to prove that an implementation of key-based decentralised access control in Java is safe from untyped attackers. We also hope that this method can be applied to other type systems for distributed security.

## References

[Aba97]    Martin Abadi. Secrecy by typing in security protocols. In *Theoretical Aspects of Computer Science*, pages 611–638, 1997.

[AFG99]    Martin Abadi, Cedric Fournet, and Georges Gonthier. Secure communications processing for distributed languages. In *IEEE Symposium on Security and Privacy*, 1999.

[AFG00]    Martin Abadi, Cedric Fournet, and Georges Gonthier. Authentication primitives and their compilation. In *Proceedings of ACM Symposium on Principles of Programming Languages*, 2000.

[AG99]    Martin Abadi and Andrew Gordon. A calculus for cryptographic protocols: The spi calculus. *Information and Computation*, 148(1):1–70, January 1999.

[CDV03]    Tom Chothia, Dominic Duggan, and Jan Vitek. Type-based distributed access control. In *Computer Security Foundations Workshop*, Asilomar, California, June 2003. IEEE.

[CDV04]    Tom Chothia, Dominic Duggan, and Jan Vitek. Principals, policies and keys in a secure distributed programming language. In *Foundations of Computer Security*, 2004.

[CGG00]    Luca Cardelli, Giorgio Ghelli, and Andrew D. Gordon. Secrecy and group creation. In *Concurrency Theory (CONCUR)*. Springer-Verlag, 2000.

[CV99]    Guiseppe Castagna and Jan Vitek. A calculus of secure mobile computations. In *Internet Programming Languages*, Lecture Notes in Computer Science. Springer-Verlag, 1999.

[DD77]    D. E. Denning and P. J. Denning. Certification of programs for secure information flow. *Communications of the ACM*, 1977.

[Dug03]    Dominic Duggan. Type-based cryptographic operations. *Journal of Computer Security*, 2003.

[HR99]    Matthew Hennessy and James Riely. Type-safe execution of mobile agents in anonymous networks. In *Secure Internet Programming: Security Issues for Distributed and Mobile Objects*, Lecture Notes in Computer Science. Springer-Verlag, 1999.

[ML97]    Andrew C. Myers and Barbara Liskov. A decentralized model for information flow control. In *Symposium on Operating Systems Principles*, 1997.

[Mye99]    Andrew C. Myers. Jflow: Practical mostly-static information flow control. In *Proceedings of ACM Symposium on Principles of Programming Languages*, pages 228–241, 1999.

[PC00]    Francois Pottier and Sylvain Conchon. Information flow inference for free. In *Proceedings of ACM International Conference on Functional Programming*, 2000.

[RH99]    James Riely and Matthew Hennessy. Trust and partial typing in open systems of mobile agents. In *Proceedings of ACM Symposium on Principles of Programming Languages*, 1999.

[SM02]    Andrei Sabelfeld and Andrew Myers. Language-based information-flow security. *IEEE Journal on Selected Areas in Communications*, 2002.

[VS97]    D. Volpano and G. Smith. A type-based approach to program security. In *Proceedings of the International Joint Conference on Theory and Practice of Software Development*. Springer-Verlag, 1997.

[ZCZM03]    Lantian Zheng, Stephen Chong, Steve Zdancewic, and Andrew C. Myers. Building secure distributed systems using replication and partitioning. In *IEEE Symposium on Security and Privacy*. IEEE Computer Society Press, 2003.

[ZZNM02]    Steve Zdancewic, Lantian Zheng, Nathaniel Nystrom, and Andrew C. Myers. Secure program partitioning. *Transactions on Computer Systems*, 20(3):283–328, 2002.

# A Security Management Information Model Derivation Framework: From Goals to Configurations

R. Laborde, F. Barrère, and A. Benzekri

Université Paul Sabatier - IRIT/SIERA,
118 Rte de Narbonne F31062 Toulouse Cedex04
Tel.: +33 (0) 5 61 55 60 86; Fax: +33 (0) 5 61 52 14 58
{laborde, barrere, benzekri}@irit.fr

**Abstract.** Security mechanisms enforcement consists in configuring devices with the aim that they cooperate and guarantee the defined security goals. In the network context, this task is complex due to the number, the nature, and the interdependencies of the devices to consider. We propose in this article a global and formal framework which models the network security management information from the security goals to the security mechanisms configurations. The process is divided into three steps. First, the security goals are specified and the specification consistency is checked. Secondly, the network security tactics are defined. An evaluation method guarantees the consistency and the correctness against the security goals. Finally, the framework verifies that the network security tactics can be enforced by the real security mechanisms.

## 1 Introduction

Basically, the security of distributed applications is supported by a set of security services. ISO defines the five following services [9]: access control, identification/ authentication, confidentiality, integrity, non-repudiation. These security services are implemented by means of security mechanisms such as security protocols (IPsec, SSL, SSH) or access control mechanisms (firewalls, Application Security Gateways, OS access control systems, antivirus). The security administrator should create his own security solution selecting the security services to use and the security mechanisms' configurations to apply.

But the distributed application security management is by nature a distributed function which implies the cooperation of different devices with different capabilities. In [11], we have pointed to different problems that can disturb this fragile co-ordination: the inconsistency and the non-correctness of the security mechanisms.

The security mechanisms inconsistency indicates that two or more security rules/configurations are contradictory. The atomic inconsistency problem indicates that two or more configuration rules for the same security mechanism and on the same device are incompatible. For example, one rule states that data flows with the source IP addresses in the range 10.0.0.0/8 can pass through the firewall and another rule on the same firewall states that the data flow with the source IP address 10.20.30.4 is denied. Several techniques [16] can be used to solve it, e.g. "negative authorizations take precedence", "the authorization that is most specific w.r.t. a partial order wins", etc. The distributed inconsistency concerns incompatible rules mapped

T. Dimitrakos et al. (Eds.): FAST 2005, LNCS 3866, pp. 217–234, 2006.
© Springer-Verlag Berlin Heidelberg 2006

on different security mechanisms or devices. Thus, the administrator should pay special attention to all dependency relations between rules applicable on different devices. For example, an IPsec tunnel is correctly configured between two VPN gateways and a firewall between them blocks their IPsec data flows. Some papers provide a partial solution considering only one kind of device, for example firewalls [2,5] or filtering IPsec gateways [7,8].

In addition to the inconsistency problem, security mechanisms implementation must guarantee the administrator's security objectives; this is the correctness problem. The approach followed by network management practitioners consists of using different abstraction levels of management information, from the goals to the configurations [14,17]. For example, policy based network management uses this approach in order to automate the management task [18]. Nevertheless, the refinement process, called in this context derivation, is not controlled yet.

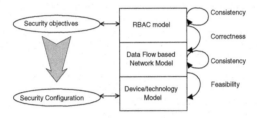

**Fig. 1.** The proposed framework process

In this article, we propose a global formal framework which includes an expression and a verification tool to control the network security management information. The correctness problem implies being able to specify the security goals, the security mechanisms and their configuration. The inconsistency problem depends only on the security mechanisms. Our framework is decomposed into three steps (fig. 1). The first one deals with the security goals specification and consistency evaluation using the RBAC model. The second part proposes the definition of a technology independent network security tactics which are evaluated against both inconsistency and correctness problems. The approach focuses on the data flows and the different applied treatments. The last part verifies that the security tactics can be enforced by the technologies used.

## 2   Network Security Goals Definition

When a user accesses a service, a set of data flow is exchanged between the device from which the user launches the service and the devices supporting the service execution (fig. 2). So, a relation between a network security policy and an application security policy can be distinguished. For example, if the application security policy states that user "$u_1$" can read object "$o_1$"- noted ($u_1$, $o_1$, +read), then it implies that a corresponding data flow $flow(o_1, +read)$ between the device of user "$u_1$" (noted device($u_1$)) and the device of "$o_1$" (noted device($o_1$)) can exist on the network. Consequently, the associated network security policy must allow the data flows $flow(o_1, +read)$ between these two devices – noted $\forall d_{u1} \in$ device($u_1$), $\forall d_{o1} \in$ device($o_1$),

$(d_{u1} \leftrightarrow d_{o1}, +\text{flow}(o_1, \text{read}))$. Conversely, if the application security policy states that user $u_2$ cannot read object $o_2$ noted $(u_2, o_2, -\text{read})$, there is no flow *flow($o_2$,read)* between the devices of $u_2$ and $o_2$. Therefore, the network security policy must forbid *flow($o_2$, read)* between the devices of $u_2$ and $o_2$, i.e., $\forall d_{u2} \in \text{device}(u_2)$, $\forall d_{o2} \in \text{device}(o_2)$, $(d_{u2} \leftrightarrow d_{o2}, - \text{flow}(o_2, \text{read}))$. We thus obtain the derivation relation noted "$\Rightarrow^d$" as $\forall\, u \in \text{USERS}, \forall\, o \in \text{OBJECTS}, \forall\, a \in \text{ACTIONS}, \forall d_u \in \text{device}(u)$, $\forall d_o \in \text{device}(o), (u, o, \pm a) \Rightarrow^d (d_u \leftrightarrow d_o, \pm \text{flow}(o, a))$.

Access control models [1,4] represent tools suited for application security modelling. First, they allow the expression that an entity (called user/subject) can perform or not given actions on another entity (called object). Moreover, each access control model is associated to a set of security validation techniques in order to guarantee the consistency of the defined rules.

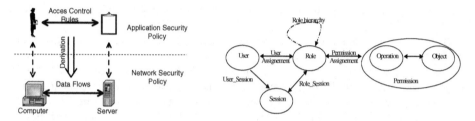

**Fig. 2.** Security policy derivation          **Fig. 3.** The NIST RBAC Model

The framework proposes the use of the NIST RBAC model [1] that brings the notion of role and hierarchy of roles (fig. 3). A role represents a group of users based on their competencies and responsibilities in a given organization [6], and role hierarchies [13] represents the organization considering its membership. An organizational structure is often specified in terms of organizational positions such as regional, site or departmental network manager, service administrator, service operator, company vice-president. Specifying organizational policies for people in terms of role-positions rather than persons, permits the assignment of a new person to the position without re-specifying the policies referring to the duties and authorizations of that position. Consequently, with RBAC, users are not directly granted permissions to perform an operation, but operations are associated with roles. Then, roles can be updated without having to update the privileges for every user which facilitates the users' management. RBAC also supports several well-known security principles including the specification of *competency to perform specific tasks*, the enforcement *of least privileges*, and the specification and enforcement of *conflicts of interest rules* [6]. Moreover, RBAC has the potential to support DAC or MAC policies and properties [15] such as the enforcement of the *simple security* and the *\*-properties* [3].

Thereafter, we consider that there is *no hierarchy* and that *roles have disjoint privileges* (if this is not the case then we may create a partition of this set): such a constraint will help us to group data flows based on the permissions assigned to one role and then identifying them by the role.

Users are considered in an RBAC system by their assigned role. Consequently, the derivation relation becomes: $\forall\, r \in \text{ROLES}, \forall\, o_i \in \text{OBJECTS}, \forall op_j \in \text{OPERATIONS}$,

$\forall u,u' \in$ USERS, $\forall d_u \in$ device(u), $\forall d_{u'} \in$ device(u'), $\forall\ d_{oi} \in$ device($o_i$) • (r, {($op_j$, $o_i$)}) $\in$ PA $\wedge$ (u,r) $\in$ UA $\wedge$ (u',r) $\notin$ UA $\Rightarrow^d \forall i,j$, ($d_u \leftrightarrow d_{oi}$, +flow($o_i$, $op_j$)) $\wedge$ ($d_{u'} \leftrightarrow d_{oi}$, - flow($o_i$, $op_j$)) where PA is the relation "Permission Assignment" and UA is relation "User Assignment".

Afterward, we note by the name of the role the set of flows corresponding to the permissions assigned to the role.

## 3   A Flow Oriented Modelling Language

The security application layer focuses on the end-to-end entities but intermediate systems (e.g. routers, switches, secure gateways, firewalls) are also involved in the security deployment. The problem consists in specifying the co-operation between different devices which demand different configurations based on the technologies implemented.

The notion of data flow is at the heart of the network security management problem. Data flows are not restricted to a set of IP addresses, application ports, etc. Here, data flows represent the data exchanged between the entities that perform given actions (the subjects in the RBAC model) and the entities that store information (the objects in the RBAC model). So our approach only considers the applicable treatments on data flows [12]. They can be brought together into four basic functionalities (fig. 4). Devices and networks are specified while interconnecting these basic functionalities:

- Mechanisms that *consume/produce* data flows such as end-systems - called end-flow functionalities,
- Mechanisms that *propagate* data flows such as physical supports and associated devices - called channel functionalities,
- Mechanisms that *transform* a data flow into another such as the security protocols or NAPT gateways - called transform functionalities,
- Mechanisms that *filter* data flows such as firewalls - called filter functionalities.

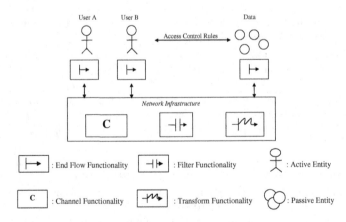

**Fig. 4.** The specification elements

Each basic functionality semantic is defined by means of Coloured Petri Nets (CPNs [10]) using "CPN tools" [19]. The colour of token specifies the data flow. The tuple $<ef_s,ef_d,role,transf\_list>$ defines a data flow where $ef_s$ is the end-flow that produced the data flow, $ef_d$ is the destination end-flow, *role* represents the data flow characteristics based on the access control rights associated to this role and *transf_list* is the list of transformations applied to the data flow.

The state of the system is represented by the tokens distribution in the places. In the CPN model, the state changes when a transition is fired. A boolean expression, called guard, can be associated to a transition as a fire condition. If tokens in places linked to the transition pre-arcs satisfy the guard, they are removed from the places and new ones are created into the places linked to the post-arcs. Functions on post-arcs allow the control of the colour and the number of the new tokens.

### 3.1 Active End-Flow Functionalities

Active end-flow functionalities (AEF) produce and consume data flows. They are connected to the RBAC model subjects. So, they constitute the first part of the association between the application security model and the network security model. Figure 5 specifies the formal semantic of the AEFs. The couple $ef_i^{em}/tef_i^{em}$ represents its production capacity. In the initial state, the place $ef_i^{em}$ contains one token for each data flow that it can send, i.e., the combination of the roles assigned to the subjects and the passive end-flows assigned to the same roles. The place $ef_i^{rec}$ corresponds to its data flows consuming capability.

### 3.2 Passive End-Flow Functionalities

Passive end-flow functionalities (PEFs) produce and consume data flows. Nevertheless, PEFs are connected to the objects of the RBAC model and form the other part of the link between the application and the network security model. Figure 6 specifies its formal semantic. We have modelled the couple AEF/PEF like the client/server interactions: PEFs reply to the data flows sent by the AEFs. Data flows are received in place $ef_i^{rec}$. If the data flow end-flow functionality destination is the same as one of its assigned roles and understandable (i.e. no transformation guaranteeing the confidentiality property is applied), the response is created (the OK_NOK_$ef_i$ post-arc, the place $ef_i^{em}$ and the transition $tef_i^{em}$).

### 3.3 Transform Functionalities

Transform functionalities represent the capability to modify the data flows. It can symbolize encryption protocols such as IPsec where one transform functionality adds some security services (e.g. confidentiality) and another removes it, or the Network Address Translation where only one transform functionality is concerned. We have defined the security group notion which characterizes everything that specifies a transformation. For example, one IPsec security association is specified by a specific security group with a set of associated security services. A LIFO (Last In First Out) structure represents the order of applied transformations. It naturally defines the encapsulations of transformations. The transform configurations are sets of $\{ef_s\},\{ef_d\},role \rightarrow group$ where $\{ef_s\}$ is the set of source end-flows, $\{ef_d\}$ is the set of

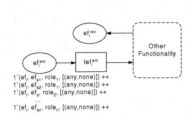

**Fig. 5.** The active end-flow functionality

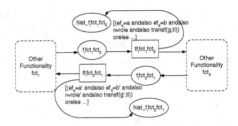

**Fig. 7.** The filter functionality

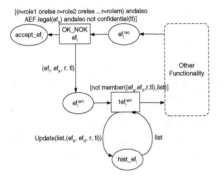

**Fig. 6.** The passive end-flow functionality

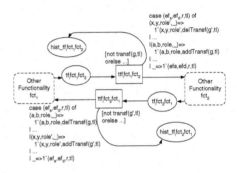

**Fig. 8.** The transform functionality

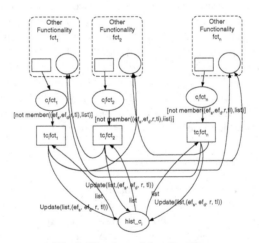

**Fig. 9.** The channel functionality

destination end-flows, *role* the used role and *group* the transformation to apply. The formal semantic is given in fig 8. The data flows are received in the place $f_i fct_j fct_k$. A transformation with a specific security group can be applied one time to a specific data flow (this constraint help us to obtain some interesting CPN properties). The guard on the transition $ttf_i fct_j fct_k$ guarantees it. If the token passes, it is stored in the place $hist\_tf_i fct_j fct_k$. Finally, the function on the post-arc removes (function delTransf) and/or adds (function addTransf) a transformation according to the configuration.

### 3.4  Filter Functionalities

The filter functionalities represent the capability to filter or let pass the data flows. They have a configuration which is a set of 4-tuples *{efs},{efd},role,group* where *{ef_s}* is the set of source end-flows, *{ef_d}* is the set of destination end-flows, *role* is the used role and *group* is the last secure group in the LIFO. The formal definition is given in fig 7. The filter capability is specified using guards on the transitions $tf_i fct_j fct_k$. If the token passes through the transition, it is stored in the place $hist\_f_i fct_j fct_k$.

### 3.5  Channel Functionalities

The channel functionalities represent the data flows propagation environment that can be material (e.g. wire or wireless) or an abstraction for the unknown systems (e.g. Internet). Figure 9 provides the formal semantic. A data flow is received from one of the connected functionalities $fct_j$ in place $c_i fct_j$ and is transmitted to all the other connected functionalities. A data flow can only be transmitted one time through a channel functionality thanks to the place $hist\_c_i$ whose colour domain is a list of flow. This constraint allows us to get some interesting CPN properties.

## 4  The Evaluation Method

The interactions between the specified atomic functionalities should be evaluated in order to prove that the security tactics involve no conflict and correspond to the required goal. The process allows the checking of the network security mechanisms consistency and their correctness against the RBAC policies. It is divided into five steps. First, a specification is transformed into the corresponding Colored Petri Net. It is produced by interconnecting each CPN sub-model of the basic functionalities in the specification. Then, the CPN model produces a reachability graph which can be analyzed thanks to the set of security properties defined in the Computational Tree Logic (CTL) such as classical properties (End-to-End properties, i.e., confidentiality and accessibility) and specific configuration properties (properties on intermediate functionalities) on the Kripke structure corresponding to the reachability graph. A theorem states that such an analysis is equivalent to the analysis of these properties without the CTL operators (i.e. in the first order logic) on the only one dead state of the Kripke structure which can be obtained by simulation. Finally, the model is checked, i.e. the dead state satisfies or not all the security properties. If it does not satisfy them then the mechanisms hence defined do not fulfill the requirements otherwise the specification is considered to be secure.

### 4.1  Network Security Properties Definition

We use the following notation:

– FUNCT, the set of functionalities,
– FILTER, the set of filter functionalities,

- ACTIVE, the set of AEFs and PASSIVE, the set of PEFs,
- ROLE, the set of roles,
- GROUP, the set security groups,
- Assigned :(ACTIVE∪ PASSIVE) $\rightarrow 2^{ROLE}$, the function defines the set of roles assigned to an end-flow functionality,
- TRANSF_LIST, the set of transformation LIFOs,
- FLOW, the set of colors in the CPN, and PLACE, the set of places in the CPN,
- Tokens: PLACE $\rightarrow$ Bag(FLOW), where Bag(FLOW) is the set of multi set on FLOW. It provides the set of tokens in a place,
- Confidential : TRANSF_LIST $\rightarrow$ Boolean, returns if a transform list contains a security group that provides the confidentiality property,
- $Path^k(fct_1, fct_n) = <fct_1, fct_2, ..., fct_i, ...fct_n>$ where $\forall i,j, i{\neq}j, fct_i \neq fct_j$, returns the $k^{th}$ path between $fct_1$ and $fct_n$.

For the simplification of properties writing, we use the special character "_" for indicating one of the possible values of the variable type. The expression "state $\models$ property" denotes that the state in the Kripke structure of the CPN reachability graph satisfies the property – $s_i$ is the initial state and $s_f$ is the dead sate.

In addition, we use the following CTL operators:

- $s \models AF(\phi)$ is true if for all the states sequences form "s", there is a state which satisfy $\phi$.
- $s \models AG(\phi)$ is true if for all the states sequences form "s", all the states satisfy $\phi$.

**Property of confidentiality**

Basically, the property of confidentiality protects the data from unauthorized disclosure. Thus, in our model, it prohibits an end-flow functionality from receiving at any time a untransformed data flow with any unassigned role.

$\forall ef \in ACTIVE, \forall <\_,\_,r,tl> \in FLOW, \neg Confidential(tl), r \notin Assigned(ef) \Rightarrow$
$s_i \models AG<\_,\_,r,tl> \notin Tokens(ef^{rec}).$

**Property of accessibility**

This property stipulates that all the granted services must be available to all the authorized entities. In the network environment, the data flows corresponding to this must be able to travel between both devices. Consequently, its translation in our model is that all active (resp. passive) end-flow functionalities must be able to consume all the data flows with an assigned role sent by every passive (resp. active) end-flow functionalities.

Let $ACTIVE_r = \{ef_a \in ACTIVE \mid r \in Assigned(ef_a)\}$
    $PASSIVE_r = \{ef_p \in PASSIVE \mid r \in Assigned(ef_p)\}$
$\forall r \in ROLE, \forall ef_a \in ACTIVE_r, \forall ef_p \in PASSIVE_r, \neg Confidential(tl),$
$s_i \models AF(<ef_p,ef_a,r,tl> \in Tokens(ef_a^{rec})) \wedge AF(<ef_a,ef_p,r,tl> \in Tokens(accept\_ef_p))$

As we intend to address devices configurations, we complete these classical security properties with new ones.

**Property of partitioning**
This is used to limit the propagation of data flows in order to respect the least privileges principle. It declares that a data flow can pass a filter functionality only if the latter is situated between the data flow source and an authorized destination. We apply this constraint to the filter functionalities, stating that a filter functionality allows a data flow to pass if it is situated between the data flow source and a possible authorized destination.

Let $ACTIVE_r = \{ef_a \in ACTIVE \mid r \in Assigned(ef_a)\}$
$\quad PASSIVE_r = \{ef_p \in PASSIVE \mid r \in Assigned(ef_p)\}$
$\forall f \in FILTER, \; \forall fct_1, fct_2 \in FUNCT, \; \forall r \in ROLE, \;\; \exists ef_a \in ACTIVE_r, \; \exists ef_p \in PASSIVE_r$, $s_i \; \models \forall k, \; f \notin Path_k(ef_a, ef_p) \Rightarrow AG(<ef_a, ef_p, r, \_> \notin Tokens(hist\_f\_fct_1 fct_2))$
$\wedge \; \forall k, \; f \notin Path_k(ef_p, ef_a) \Rightarrow AG(<ef_p, ef_a, r, \_> \notin Tokens(hist\_f\_fct_1 fct_2))$

The two following constraints aim to detect useless filtering or transform rules in the configurations.

**Non productive filtering rule**
This is used to eliminate unnecessary filtering rules. When f a filter functionality is connected to the functionalities $fct_1$ and $fct_2$, we say that the filtering rule $\{ef_s\}, \{ef_d\}, r, g$ from $fct_1$ to $fct_2$ is non productive if no data flow $<ef_s, ef_d, r, g.tl>$ tries to pass through the filter functionality.

Let the rule $FRL = fct_1 \rightarrow fct_2 \; \{ef_s\}, \{ef_d\}, r, g$ where $fct_1, fct_2 \in FUNCT$, $ef_s, ef_d \in ACTIVE \cup PASSIVE, r \in ROLE, g \in GROUP$ then FRL is non productive if and only if $s_i \models AG <ef_s, ef_d, r, g.tl> \notin Tokens(hist\_f\_fct_1 fct_2)$.

**Non productive transform rule**
When tf a transform functionality is connected to $fct_1$ and $fct_2$, we say that the transform rule $\{ef_s\}, \{ef_d\}, r \rightarrow g$ from $fct_1$ to $fct_2$ is non productive if any flow $<ef_s, ef_d, r, \_>$ passes through the transform functionality at any time.

Let $TRL = fct_1 \rightarrow fct_2 \; \{ef_s\}, \{ef_d\}, r \rightarrow g$ where $fct_1, fct_2 \in FUNCT, \; ef_s, ef_d \in ACTIVE \cup PASSIVE, r \in ROLE, g \in GROUP$ then TRL non productive if and only if $s_i \models AG <ef_s, ef_d, r, \_> \notin Tokens(hist\_f\_fct_1 fct_2) \vee AG <ef_d, ef_s, r, g.tl> \notin Tokens(hist\_f\_fct_2 fct_1)$.

## 4.2 State Graph Properties Definition

The state graph of a specification in our language has three important properties that make its analysis easier.

**Theorem 1:** All the state graphs of a specification in our language are finite.
*Demonstration*: See appendices (Section 9).

**Theorem 2:** All the state graphs of a specification in our language have a single dead state[1].
*Demonstration*: See appendices (Section 9).

---

[1] There is no transition from a dead state.

**Theorem 3:** The analysis of the dead state is necessary and sufficient for the properties defined in section 4.1
*Demonstration*: See appendices (Section 9).

Theorem 1 shows that it is possible to build all the states of a specification CPN reachability graph. Nevertheless, if the graph is sizeable, our method is vulnerable to the combinatorial explosion problem. Both theorem 1 and theorem 2 compensate for this problem because the single dead state is sufficient for the analysis and its uniqueness allows us to calculate it by simulation. Consequently, we don't have to build all the states. Therefore, our method does not suffer from the combinatorial state explosion and a sizeable specification can be analyzed. A Java-Based tool automates the calculation of the security tactic specifications CPN as well as the dead state of their reachability graphs. Also, it analyzes the dead state according to the previously described security properties.

## 5   A Specification Example

The following example explains how the language is used to implement an IPsec/VPN case study strategy definition (fig. 10). As in a traditional enterprise network, this example considers an edge router interconnecting a private network and a DMZ. The *App_Server* and the FTP servers are respectively installed in the private network and in the DMZ (fig. 6). The application level security policy is an RBAC one, without hierarchy, where two user groups *VPNmembers* and *Others* are defined. This organization is only based on the granted privileges. The *App_Server* server is dedicated only to the services usable by the *VPNmembers* group. The *FTP_Server* has two directories: /confidential and /pub. The directory "confidential" contains data only accessible to the *VPNmembers* users group. Data of the "pub" directory is accessible to everyone. $User_1$, $User_2$, $User_3$ and $User_4$ belong to *VPNmembers* and *Others* groups. $User_5$ is only member of the *Others* group.

The service management layer RBAC policy can be expressed as:

Permissions(VPNmembers)= {(+all_access,FTP_Server/confidential),
(+all_access, App_Server)}
Permissions(Others)= {(+all_access,FTP_Server/pub)}

The objective is to specify a VPN security strategy. The Private Network, the DMZ and the Internet interconnection infrastructures are specified thanks to channel functionalities because we use their transmission functionality. This approach of specification with large granularity only considers the minimum set of functionalities provided by these infrastructures: their interconnection capability.

On the contrary it is possible to refine a specification as the edge router shows it. It has obviously the interconnection functionality (the channel functionality), setting as a security gateway with filtering capabilities (the three filter functionalities) and encryption mechanisms (the transform functionality, for example an IPsec module is installed). The modelling of the routing is carried out by filtering rules on the filter functionalities.

The servers are specified by two PEF. The *App_Server* server (EF2) has the *VPNmembers* role because only the users with the *VPNmembers* role have the access

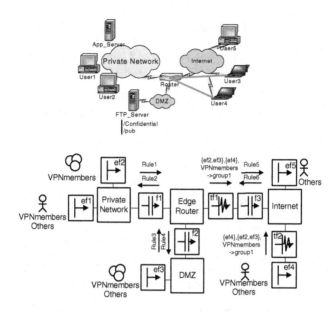

**Fig. 10.** Architecture and specification example

rights. The PEF corresponding to the FTP server (EF3) has the roles *Others* and *VPNmembers* because the permission (+all_access, FTP_Server/pub) is assigned to the *Others* role and (+all_access, FTP_Server/confidential) to the *VPNmembers* role.

The devices of user1 and user2 are represented by a single AEF (EF1) because user1 and user2 have the same roles (*Others* and *VPNmembers*) and are connected to the same channel functionality thanks to the concept of role which reduces the overall size of the specification. In the same way, the devices of user3 and user4 are specified by only one AEF (EF4). The device of user5 is specified by a different AEF (EF5) because the *VPNmembers* role is not assigned to him. Arbitrarily adding an AEF with roles which permissions are reduced makes it possible to define a degree of confidence that can be granted to a channel functionality. In this example, we do not specify the structure of the Internet network, but it is perceived as an interconnection environment where any connected user has at least the permission to access the /pub directory of the *FTP_Server*. This allows a great flexibility of specification according to the level of desired and/or known details.

Two transform configurations are defined on the transform functionalities $tf_1$ and $tf_2$ that add security properties - according to the group1 transform actions - to the communication between $ef_2$, $ef_3$ and $ef_4$ with the role *VPNmembers* (fig. 10). Moreover, the following filtering rules associated with the filter functionalities are specified:

- Rule1 = <{$ef_1$}, {$ef_3$}, VPNmembers, any>, <{$ef_2$}, {$ef_4$}, VPNmembers, any>,
        <{$ef_1$},{$ef_3$}, Others, any>
  ```
  This rule permits the untransformed data flows from ef₁ to ef₃
  with the roles VPNmembers and Others, and the untransformed
  data flows from ef₂ to ef₄ with the role VPNmembers.
  ```

- Rule2 = <{ef$_3$}, {ef$_1$}, VPNmembers, any>, <{ef$_4$}, {ef$_2$}, VPNmembers, any>
     <{ef$_3$},{ef$_1$}, Others, any>
  This rule grants the reverse data flows permitted by rule1 in
  order to enable bidirectional communications between the end-
  flows.
- Rule3 = <{ef$_3$},{ef$_1$, ef$_4$}, VPNmembers, any>, <{ef$_3$},{ef$_1$, ef$_4$, ef$_5$}, Others, any>
  This rule permits the untransformed data flows from ef3 to
  ef1 and ef4 with the roles VPNmembers and Others, and the
  untransformed data flows from ef3 to ef5 with the role
  Others.
- Rule4 = <{ef$_1$, ef$_4$}, {ef$_3$}, VPNmembers, any>,<{ef$_1$, ef$_4$, ef$_5$}, {ef$_3$}, Others, any>
  This rule grants the reverse data flows permitted by rule3.
- Rule5 = <{ef$_2$, ef$_3$}, {ef$_4$},VPNmembers, group1>, <{ef$_3$}, {ef$_4$, ef$_5$}, Others, any>
  This rule permits the data flows transformed according to
  group1 from ef2 and ef3 to ef4 with the role VPNmembers, and
  the untransformed data flows from ef3 to ef4 and ef5 with the
  role Others.
- Rule6 = <{ef$_4$}, {ef$_2$, ef$_3$},VPNmembers, group1>, <{ef$_4$, ef$_5$}, {ef$_3$}, Others, any>
  This rule grants the reverse data flows permitted by rule5.

This specification approach facilitates the security network management layer expression being technologies independent and aggregating management information with the concepts of basic functionalities and roles.

This specification respects all the previous properties (i.e. confidentiality, availability and partitioning) and contains no non productive filtering or transform rules. So, the functionalities' configurations are consistent and correct against the RBAC policy. Nevertheless, it does not imply that this network security tactics can be enforced by the underlying technologies.

## 6  Enforcement Validation

The language presented previously allows the expression of network security strategies using a data flow based approach and regardless of technology specifics. The language permits a high abstraction data flows definition. However, each technology used for enforcing the network security tactics has its own capabilities. A technology capability means:

1. the possible actions (i.e., the treatments that can be applied on the data flows),
2. and the possible discrimination criteria to differentiate the data flows (i.e., the set of data flow value types that the device/technology can perceive).

Examples of the discrimination criteria are:

- HTTP proxies can differentiate data flows based on keywords in HTML pages.
- Stateless firewalls can only differentiate data flows according to IP addresses, transport layer protocol and port numbers.
- Switches view data flows as MAC addresses, Source Service Access Points and Destination Service Access Points numbers.

## 6.1  Enforcement Formalisation

The problem of management refinement at this layer is to determine if the technologies are able to enforce the associated security tactics or not. By nature, the atomic functionalities represent the actions capabilities of the technologies. Then, the action part does not represent a possible refinement problem. Nevertheless, the language permits a high abstraction data flows definition. Consequently, a distinction between two data flows made at the network security tactics abstraction level by an atomic functionality does not imply that the corresponding technology is able to do it. This discrimination criteria problem is formalized as follows.

Let :
- D, the set of possible values characterizing data flows,
- T, the set of types of values (e.g., IP address, transport protocol, port number),
- $C_X \subseteq T$, the distinction capability of device X (e.g., routers perceive the IP addresses, transport protocol, port numbers, etc.). The distinction capability of a device is modelled as the set of types of values that it can distinguish.
- $f : T \rightarrow P(D_T)$ a technology layer data flow where $D_T$ is the set of values of type T. A data flow is modelled as a set of functions which return for each type of values a set of values of this type.
- F, the set of technology layer data flows,
- $\theta_G : 2^F \rightarrow 2^F$ , the function associated to the transform group G with $\theta_{any} = $ identity,
- $\delta : EF \times EF \times ROLE \rightarrow 2^F$, the function that creates the associated flows (i.e., the set of values) associated to an untransformed data flow in the Laborde et al model. .

**Definition 1.**
The derivation function between the network security tactics abstraction and device abstraction is defined as:
$$\Delta ((ef_1, ef2, role, <G_1 \bullet G_2 \bullet... G_n \bullet any>)) \equiv \theta_{G1} " \theta_{G2} "...\theta_{Gn} " \theta_{any} " \delta (ef_1, ef2, role)$$

**Definition 2.**
We call the technology X perception of the data flow f: $V_X(f) = f_{|C_X}$.

**Definition 3.**
We say that technology X confuses the data flows $f_1$ et $f_2$ if $V_X(\Delta(f_1)) \cap V_X(\Delta (f_2)) \neq \varnothing$ that we note $V_X(\Delta(f_1)) = V_X(\Delta (f_2))$.

**Definition 4 - Strict property of derivation capability.**
Technology X is said able to enforce a network security tactics:

1. if the strategy of functionality F associated to technology X states two different actions for two distinct data flows $f_1$ and $f_2$,
2. it implies $V_X(\Delta (f_1)) \neq V_X(\Delta (f_2))$

**Definition 5 - Loose property of derivation capability.**
Technology X is said able to enforce a network security tactics:

1. if the strategy of functionality F associated to technology X states two different actions for two distinct data flows $f_1$ and $f_2$, and (f_1 and f_2 pass through F)
2. it implies $V_X(\Delta (f_1)) \neq V_X(\Delta (f_2))$

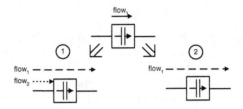

**Fig. 11.** Loose property of derivation capability example

The loose property of derivation capability, contrary to the strict property of derivation capability, considers that if X never sees $f_1$ and $f_2$, X can confuse both data flows and X is able to apply the network security tactics.

For example, the filter functionality tactics in fig 11 states that only the data flow $flow_1$ can pass. Implicitly, the other data flows such as $flow_2$ must be filtered. Then, two system behaviors are conceivable:

1. Both $flow_1$ and $flow_2$ try to pass through the filter functionality. In this case, $V_X(\Delta (flow_1))$ must be different from $V_X(\Delta (flow_2))$, where X is the technology that enforces the strategy.
2. Only $flow_1$ tries to pass through the filter functionality. In this case, $V_X(\Delta (flow_1))$ can be equal to $V_X(\Delta (flow_2))$ because X has never to distinguish $flow_1$ and $flow_2$.

## 6.2 Enforcement Analysis Example

In the example of fig. 10, the transform functionality $tf_2$ has the following configuration $\{ef_4\}$, $\{ef_2, ef_3\}$, VPNmembers $\rightarrow$ $group_1$. Both data flows $<ef_4, ef_3,$ VPNmembers, any> and $<ef_4, ef_3,$ Others, any> pass through $tf_2$. We recall that the directory "confidential" on *FTP_Server* contains data only accessible to the *VPNmembers* users group and the data of the "pub" directory is accessible to *Others*. We consider also that the security group $group_1$ represents an IPsec tunnel. The distinction capability of IPsec $C_{IPsec}$ is the set of types IP address, port number and transport protocol. Both *VPNmembers* and *Others* role use the same transport protocol TCP and protocol numbers 21 and upper than 1024.

**Case 1:** *The address space used for the VPN architecture is private.* So, the IP address of *FTP_Server* for the *VPNmembers* role is different from its IP address for the *Others* role. Consequently, $V_{IPsec}(\Delta(<ef_4, ef_3,$ VPNmembers, any>)) $\neq$ $V_{IPsec}(\Delta(<ef_4, ef_3,$ Others, any>)). Then, the tactics can be enforced by IPsec.

**Case 2:** *The address spaces used for the VPNmembers and Others roles are not different.* So, the IP address of *FTP_Server* for the *VPNmembers* role is the same as its IP address for the *Others* role. Consequently, $V_{IPsec}(\Delta(<ef_4, ef_3,$VPNmembers, any>)) = $V_{IPsec}(\Delta(<ef_4, ef_3,$ Others, any>)). Then, the tactics cannot be enforced by IPsec because IPsec confuses $\Delta(<ef_4, ef_3,$ VPNmembers, any>) and $\Delta(<ef_4, ef_3,$ Others, any>).

# 7   Conclusion

We have presented in this article a generic global framework that formalizes the network security information management derivation process from the goals to the configurations. The goals are specified via the RBAC model that allows us to use all the associated analysis works. We have defined a new model to specify the network security tactics using a data flow based approach. An analysis method has been described and its power has been discussed. Finally, we have defined a generic device configuration model and some derivation properties that ensure the network security tactics to be enforceable.

Our work guarantees that the network security goals are correctly enforced. Nevertheless, we do not consider the attackers in this framework. Consequently, our future work will focus on including this aspect (based on risk analysis methods and assurance evaluation methods) in order to prove a network assurance level.

**Acknowledgments.** We are grateful to G. Mackenzie Smith, D. Jones and B. Moore for their English writing comments, and L. Mehats for his modelling advices.

# References

1. ANSI, "Role-Based Access Control", ANSI/INCITS 359-2004, February 2004.
2. Y. Bartal., A. Mayer, K. Nissim and A. Wool. "Firmato: A Novel Firewall Management Toolkit". Proceedings of 1999 IEEE Symposiumon Security and Privacy, May 1999.
3. Bell, D. E., and L. J. LaPadula, "Secure Computer Systems: Mathematical Foundations and Model", Bedford, MA: The Mitre Corporation, 1973.
4. Bishop M., Computer Security: Art and Science, ISBN 0-201-44099-7, 2003.
5. Ehab Al-Shaer and Hazem Hamed, "Discovery of Policy Anomalies in Distributed Firewalls", in IEEE INFOCOMM'04, 2004.
6. D. F. Ferraiolo, D. R. Kuhn, R. Chandramouli, Role-Based Access Control, ISBN: 1-58053-370-1, 2003.
7. Z. Fu, F. Wu, H. Huang, K. Loh, F. Gong, I. Baldine and C. Xu. "IPSec/VPN Security Policy: Correctness, Conflict Detection and Resolution", In Policy'2001 Workshop, 2001.
8. Guttman J. D., Herzog A. M., "Rigorous automated network security management", International Journal of Information Security, Issue 3, Volume 4, 2004
9. ISO, "OSI Reference Model - Security Architecture", ISO 7498-2, 1988.
10. Jensen K., "An Introduction to the Theoretical Aspects of Coloured Petri Nets". In: A Decade of Concurrency, Lecture Notes in Computer Science vol. 803, 1994.
11. Laborde R., Nasser B., Grasset F., Barrère F., Benzekri A. "Network Security Management: A Formal Evaluation Tool based on RBAC Policies". IFIP NetCon'2004.
12. Laborde R., Nasser B., Grasset F., Barrère F., Benzékri A., "A formal approach for the evaluation of network security mechanisms based on RBAC policies", In ENTCS – proceedings of WISP'04, Vol. 121., Elsevier, 2005.
13. Moffett J. D., "Control Principle and Role Hierarchies", In Workshop on RBAC, 1998.
14. J. Moffet, M. Sloman: "Policy Hierarchies for Distributed Systems Management". IEEE Journal on Selected Areas in Communications, 11, 9, 1993.

15. Osborn, S., R. Sandhu, and Q. Munawer, "Configuring Role-Based Access Control To Enforce Mandatory and Discretionary Access Control Policies", ACM Transactions on Information and System Security, Vol. 3, No. 2, May 2002,pp. 85–106.
16. Samarati P., De Capitani di Vimercati S., "Access Control: Policies, Models and Mechanisms", Foundations of Security Analysis and Design, LNCS 2171, 2001.
17. Westerinen A., Schnizlein J., Strassner J., Scherling M., Quinn B., Herzog S., Huynh A., Carlson M., Perry J., Waldbusser S., "Terminology for Policy-Based Management", RFC 3198, November 2001.
18. Yavatkar R., Pendarakis D., Guerin R., "A Framework for Policy-based Admission Control", RFC 2753, 2000.
19. URL http://wiki.daimi.au.dk/cpntools/cpntools.wiki

# Appendices

We present here the demonstration of the three theorems.

## A  Demonstration of Theorem 1

In order to prove that the state graph is finite, we prove that the CPN is K-bounded. We use the following notation:

- $P$ is the finite set of places in the CPN that have the colour domain FLOW (i.e., all places excluding places $hist\_c_i$ and $hist\_ef_i$ that have the colour domain FLOW_LIST which is a data flow list. Data flows are ordered according to the colour domain FLOW ordering) ,
- $P_{HIST}$ is the finite set of places that have the colour domain FLOW_LIST,
- $Pre_P : P \rightarrow 2^P$, the relation that defines the set of places which have one of their post-arcs connected to the same transition as one of the pre-arcs of a place in the CPN,
- $P_{AEF} = \bigcup_{\forall i} \{ef_i^{em}\}$, the set of places $ef_i^{em}$ where $ef_i$ is an AEF,
- $nb\_tok : P \rightarrow N$, provides the number of tokens that have passed in one place,
- $<x_1, x_2, \ldots x_n>$ a path of places between $x_1$ and $x_n$ in the CPN where $\forall i > 0$, $x_i \in P$, $x_i \in Pre_p(x_{i+1})$,
- $[x_1 \nabla x_n]$ the set of path of places between $x_1$ and $x_n$.

By construction we have:

1. $\forall p \in P \backslash P_{AEF}, nb\_tok(p) \quad \displaystyle\sum_{x \in Pr\,ep(p)} nb\_tok(x)$

2. $\forall ef_i^{em} \in P_{AEF}, nb\_tok(ef_i^{em}) = k_i$ where $k_i$ is token number at the initial state,

3. $\forall p \in P_{HIST}, nb\_tok(p) \quad \displaystyle\sum_{x \in Pr\,e(p)} nb\_tok(x).$

Consequently,

$$\forall p \in P \backslash P_{EF}, nb\_tok(p) \quad \sum_{x \in Pr\,ep(p)} nb\_tok(x) \quad \sum_{x \in Pr\,ep(p)} \sum_{y \in Pr\,ep(x)} nb\_tok(y)$$

We note: $\forall p \in P \backslash P_{EF}$, $\forall y \in P$, $[y \, \nabla \, p]$, $nb\_tok(p) = \sum_{[y \nabla p]} nb\_tok(y)$

By recursion, we obtain:

$\forall p \in P \backslash P_{EF}$, $\forall ef_i^{em} \in P_{EF}$, $[ef_i^{em} \, \nabla \, p]$, $nb\_tok(p) \quad \sum_{[efiem \nabla p]} nb\_tok(ef_i^{em})$

If there is no cycle in the paths between two places $\sum_{[efiem \nabla p]} nb\_tok(ef_i^{em}) =$

$\sum_{[efiem \nabla p]} ki = K$

Else if there exist cycles in structural paths, for example $<x_2, x_3>$ is a cycle in the path $<x_1,\mathbf{x_2,x_3,x_2,x_3},x_4>$, then there is an infinite number of possible paths between $x_1$ and $x_4$, as $<x_1,x_2,x_3,x_2,x_3,x_2,x_3,x_4>$. So $\sum_{[efiem \nabla p]} ki \rightarrow \infty$

By construction a cycle in the CPN is produced by a cycle in the functionality specification in our language (i.e. there are several paths between two functionalities). Moreover, there are at least two channel functionalities and one or more filter and transform functionalities.

If there no transform functionality in the cycle. The tokens colours cannot change. A token with the same color can pass through a channel functionality once (place hits_$c_i$). So, the number of possible places path is finite.

If there is one or more transform functionalities, the tokens colours can change. However, the transform functionalities check if the transformation security group appear in the token transform list (guards on $ttf_i\_fct_jfct_k$). So, the number of tokens colours is finite according to the number of transform functionalities and also the number of possible places paths.

Consequently, $\forall p \in P \backslash P_{AEF}$, $nb\_tok(p) \quad \sum_{[efiem \nabla p]} nb\_tok(ef_i^{em}) \quad K'$.

In addition, there is only one token at each state in all the places $p \in P_{HIST}$. Nevertheless, this token can have an infinite number of possible values (the ordered list of flow length can be infinite). The number of token values being finite, the list of tokens that have passed through a channel or a PEF functionality is also finite.

To resume,     $\forall p \in P \backslash P_{AEF}$, $nb\_tok(p) \quad K'$
$\forall ef_i^{em} \in P_{AEF}$, $nb\_tok(ef_i^{em}) = k_i$
$\forall \, i$, $nb\_tok(c_i\_hist) \quad K''$

Then the CPN is structurally K-bounded and the state graph is finite.     ❑

## B  Demonstration of Theorem 2

Each token is consumed by an end-flow or stopped by a filter, transform or a channel functionality. They are also consumed by all the historic places. Then there is one or more dead state.

In addition, the CPN has a deterministic behaviour. There is no choice (i.e., a place with different post-arcs) in the produced CPN, and tokens are arranged in order in the flow list of the historical places. So the colour of the historical place does not take into account the incoming order. Consequently, there is only one dead state.    ❑

## C   Demonstration of Theorem 3

Let the function *post* that returns the post-arcs of a place. We can define the following simplification rules:

1. $\forall p \in PLACE$, $\forall f \in FLOW$, $post(p)=null$, $s_i \models AG(c \notin Tokens(p)) \Leftrightarrow s_f \models c \notin Tokens(p)$
   Proof:
   By definition $s_i \models AG(c \notin Tokens(p)) \Rightarrow s_f \models c \notin Tokens(p)$ because $s_f$ finishes all the traces. Moreover if $s_f \models c \notin Tokens(p)$ then $\forall s_j$, $<... s_j... s_f>$, $s_j \models c \notin Tokens(p)$ because $post(p)$ = null and then $s_i \models AG(c \notin Tokens(p))$

2. $\forall p \in PLACE$, $\forall f \in FLOW$, $post(p)=null$, $s_i \models AF(c \in Tokens(p)) \Leftrightarrow s_f \models c \in Tokens(p)$
   Proof:
   $s_i \models AF(c \in Tokens(p)) \Rightarrow \forall t = <s_i \ ... \ s_f>$, $\exists j \bullet < s_i...s_j...>$, $s_j \models c \in Tokens(p)$. But, $post(p)$ = null then $\forall k>j \bullet < s_i...s_j \ s_k...>$,$s_k \models c \in Tokens(p)$. Given that $s_f$ finishes all the sequences, $s_f \models c \in Tokens(p)$. Moreover, $s_f \models c \in Tokens(p) \Rightarrow \forall t = <s_i \ ... \ s_f>$, $\exists j \bullet <s_i...s_j...s_f>$, $s_j \models c \in Tokens(p)$. Then, $s_i \models AF \ c \in Tokens(p)$.

The application of these simplification rules allows rewriting of all the properties in section 4.1 without the CTL operators on the dead state.    ❑

# On Anonymity with Identity Escrow

Aybek Mukhamedov and Mark D. Ryan

School of Computer Science, University of Birmingham
{A.Mukhamedov, M.D.Ryan}@cs.bham.ac.uk

**Abstract.** *Anonymity with identity escrow* attempts to allow users of a service to remain anonymous, while providing the possibility that the service owner can break the anonymity in exceptional circumstances, such as to assist in a criminal investigation. A protocol for achieving anonymity with identity escrow has been presented by Marshall and Molina-Jiminez. In this paper, we show that that protocol suffers from some serious flaws. We also identify some other less significant weaknesses of the protocol, and we present an improved protocol which fixes these flaws. Our improved protocol guarantees anonymity even if all but one of the escrow holders are corrupt.

## 1 Introduction

Users of services such as opinion surveys or media downloads may wish to remain anonymous to the service provider. However, it may be important for service providers to be able to break anonymity in special circumstances – for example, to assist a criminal investigation. *Identity escrow* is designed to permit these two aims. The notion was first introduced by Kilian and Petrank in [2], which was motivated by the ideas from *key escrow encryption systems* (e.g. [3], [5]). It allows an agent $A$ to use services provided by $S$ without revealing her identity to $S$, while allowing $S$ to obtain it in pre-agreed special circumstances (e.g. in a misuse), thus offering a balance between privacy and monitoring/accountability. To achieve this, $A$ places her identity in an *escrowed certificate* generated with a trusted *issuer*, which she presents to $S$ when requesting its services. The certificate is *verifiable*, viz. $S$ is given a guarantee that the escrowed certificate is valid and that the identity is recoverable (with a help of *escrow agent*, which is the same as issuer in our exposition).

Clearly, this identity escrow system breaks down if issuer is dishonest, and to address this problem Marshall and Molina-Jiminez [4] proposed a protocol for anonymity with identity escrow, where escrowed certificate is generated by a set of issuers (named *identity token providers* in their paper). Neither $S$ nor any identity token provider are supposed to know the identity behind an escrowed certificate, but if it is proved necessary, all token providers can cooperate in order to reveal it.

In this paper, however, we show that their protocol suffers from serious flaws:

- **Service misuse.** Any token provider $T_i$ can misuse services of $S$ (or let someone else do that), and can implicate any entity (such as $A$) in such misuse.

T. Dimitrakos et al. (Eds.): FAST 2005, LNCS 3866, pp. 235–243, 2006.

- **Identity compromise.** For each escrowed certificate $\Phi$ that $S$ receives, there exists a token provider $T_i$ who in coalition with $S$ can recover the identity escrowed in $\Phi$.

  Additionally, if $S$ has successfully requested for a certain escrowed certificate to be uncovered, then it can discover the identity of any subsequent user of its services.

We also identify some other less significant weaknesses of the protocol in [4], and present an improved protocol which fixes these flaws. We beleive our protocol guarantees anonymity even if all but one of the token providers are corrupt.

The paper is organised as follows. In the next section, we present preliminaries, including the original protocol. Our analysis follows in section 3, and in section 4 we present our improved version of the protocol. Section 5 contains our conclusions.

## 2    Preliminaries

### 2.1    Notation

The following labeling conventions are used throughout the paper:

- $S$ denotes an anonymous service provider.
- $T = \{T_1, T_2, \ldots T_q\}$ is a set of *identity token providers*.
- $\Phi_i$ is an identity token issued by $T_{a_i}$. We also write $\Phi_A$ for the identity token obtained by $A$ by using the protocol.
- $E = \{E_1, \ldots, E_k\}$ is a set of *adjudicators*.
- $A$ is a service user. $\widehat{A}$ denotes the receiver $A$ of a message, when the identity of $A$ is not known to the message sender.
- $K_A$ is $A$'s public key. $\{m\}_K$ is the message $m$ deterministically encrypted with the public key $K$.
- $[m]_{K^-}$ is the message $m$ signed with the private key corresponding to the public $K$. We assume that $[\{m\}_K]_{K^-}$, $\{[m]_{K^-}\}_K$ and $m$ are all distinct (thus, in particular, the PKI algorithm is not simple use of RSA).

### 2.2    The Original Protocol

Marshall and Molina-Jiminez's protocol [4] consists of two parts:

- A *sign-up* protocol, which is the main protocol that is executed by $A$ to receive a token from the members of $T$. The token permits $A$ to use the service from $S$;
- and a *complaint resolution* protocol, which is executed by $S$ upon a misuse of its service, in order to reveal the identity of the offending anonymous user.

**Signup protocol.** In order for $A$ to use the services of $S$, she must place her identity in escrow with the elements of $T$ and obtain a token. She uses this token to prove to $S$ that she has placed her identity in escrow, and $S$ then provides the service.

The protocol works as follows. $A$ chooses a sequence $T_{a_1}, T_{a_2}, \ldots, T_{a_p}$ of elements of $T$ (possibly with duplications).

1)  $A \longrightarrow T_{a_1}$  :  $\{\, [\, \texttt{ITKReq}\, ]_{K_A^-} \,\}_{K_{T_{a_1}}}$

2)  $T_{a_1} \longrightarrow A$  :  $\{\, \Phi_1 \,\}_{K_A}$, where $\Phi_1 = [\, \{K_A\}_{K_{T_{a_1}}} \,]_{K_{T_{a_1}}^-}$

$\texttt{ITKReq}$ means "identity token request". Next, $A$ anonymises the token by getting $T_{a_2}, \ldots, T_{a_p}$ to encrypt and sign it:

$$
*\left\{
\begin{array}{l}
1a) \quad A \dashrightarrow T_{a_{i+1}} \; : \; \{\, \texttt{ITKSig}, \; \Phi_i \,\}_{K_{T_{a_{i+1}}}} \\
\qquad\qquad \text{where} \quad \Phi_i = [\, \{ \Phi_{i-1} \}_{K_{T_{a_i}}} \,]_{K_{T_{a_i}}^-} \\[2mm]
2a) \quad T_{a_{i+1}} \longrightarrow \widehat{A} \; : \; \{\, [\, \{ \Phi_i \}_{K_{T_{a_{i+1}}}} \,]_{K_{T_{a_{i+1}}}^-} \,\}_{K_{\widehat{A}}}
\end{array}
\right.
$$

Before signing the token, $T_{a+1}$ verifies that it has been signed by another token provider. $\texttt{ITKSig}$ indicates a signature request. $*$ indicates repeated application. The dashed arrow indicates that a message is sent anonymously, i.e. the receiver can not trace back the identity of the sender.

3)  $A \dashrightarrow S$  :  $\{\, \texttt{ServReq}, K_{\widehat{A}}, \Phi_A \,\}_{K_S}$

4)  $S \longrightarrow \widehat{A}$  :  $\{\, n, E \,\}_{K_{\widehat{A}}}$

5)  $A \dashrightarrow S$  :  $\{\, H \,\}_{K_S}$, where $H \subseteq E$ of cardinality $n$

6)  $S \longrightarrow \widehat{A}$  :  $\{\, \texttt{an\_id} \,\}_{K_{\widehat{A}}}$

$K_{\widehat{A}}$ is a new public key created by $A$ for use with the service. Obviously, only $A$ has the corresponding private key. In step 4, $S$ invites $A$ to choose a set $H \subseteq E$ of $n$ adjudicators, who will vote on whether $A$'s identity should be revealed in the case of a complaint. In step 6, $S$ sends an anonymous identifier for $A$ to use when using the services $S$ offers. In their paper [4], the authors stipulate that $S$ will divide the identity token into several parts and distribute them to adjudicators, using Rabin's information dispersal [7].

The authors assume that the identity token is uniquely tied to an entity, and adjudicators are trusted to provide a fair adjudication for complaints.

**Complaint resolution protocol.** When $S$ receives a complaint $\Psi$, the following protocol is executed, without $A$:

1)  $S \longrightarrow E_i$  :  $\{\, \texttt{AdjReq}, \Psi \,\}_{K_{E_i}}$

Message 1 is sent to each $E_i \in H$.

2)  $E_i \longrightarrow S$  :  $\{\, [\, V_i \,]_{K_{E_i}^-} \,\}_{K_S}$

The vote $V_i$ consists of a ballot (a decision by the adjudicator on the complaint $\Psi$, e.g yes/no) together with the complaint $\Psi$. If the votes are positive in the majority, $S$ presents the tuple of signed votes $V$ to $T_{a_p}$, the last token provider in the sequence chosen by $A$:

$$3) \quad S \quad \longrightarrow \quad T_{a_i} \quad : \quad \{\, \texttt{Reveal}, \Phi_i, \Psi, H, V \,\}_{K_{T_{a_i}}}$$

$$4) \quad T_{a_i} \quad \longrightarrow \quad S \quad : \quad \{\, \Phi_{i-1} \,\}_{K_S}$$

The last two steps are repeated several times, tracing backwards through the sequence $T_{a_1}, \ldots, T_{a_p}$ chosen by $A$, before finally obtaining $K_A$.

## 3   Analysis

The protocol is subject to the following serious vulnerabilities:

**Service Misuse.** *Any of the identity token providers can misuse services of $S$ (or let someone else to do that) and, furthermore, it can implicate any entity of its choice in such a misuse:*

Suppose $T_{a_i}$ is a dishonest token provider. He can present any intermediate token which he receives during the sign-up protocol to $S$, and obtain an identifier to use the service. He can misuse the service and in doing so implicate the user who initiated the creation of the intermediate token.

Moreover, since the identity token takes the form

$$[\,\{\, \ldots [\,\{K_A\}_{K_{T_{a_1}}}\,]_{K_{T_{a_1}}^-} \cdots \}_{K_{T_{a_p}}}\,]_{K_{T_{a_p}}^-}$$

and $T_{a_1}$ has access to $A$'s public key $K_A$, he can create $[\,\{K_A\}_{K_{T_{a_1}}}\,]_{K_{T_{a_1}}^-}$ and anonymously request the signature services from $T_{a_2}, \ldots, T_{a_p}$ in order to create the full token for $A$.

It is evident that such vulnerabilities are possible due to putting full trust on token providers and generating identity token $\Phi_A$ that is not tied to an anonymous key $K_{\hat{A}}$, i.e. whoever gets hold of the token can use it with a key of his own.

In addition, the authors of the protocol do not spell out assumptions they make on the anonymous channels. Thus, one could also claim that because a message anonymously sent by $A$ at step 1a does not include "reply instructions", e.g. a temporary public key $K_{\hat{A}}$, *any dishonest party $C$ that can eavesdrop on $A$'s outgoing messages of the protocol can acquire a valid identity token $\Phi_A$:* $C$ intercepts/copies messages, which are to be sent anonymously by $A$, and then, replays them anonymously to all $T_{a_i}$s in order to receive $\Phi_A$ which can be used to request services from $S$. Clearly, similar, but a weaker statement can be said of a dishonest entity that can eavesdrop on any of $T_{a_i}$s' connections.

Note that in any case, a dishonest $T_{a_i}$ or whoever misused the services of $S$ with $\Phi_A$, can not be shown to have cheated.

**Identity Compromise (1).** *Suppose $A$ has identified the sequence of token providers $T_{a_1}, T_{a_2}, \ldots, T_{a_p}$, and $T_{a_1}$ is dishonest. Then the service provider $S$ in a coalition with $T_{a_1}$ can identify the identity token that $A$ has submitted to $S$, viz. $\Phi_A$:*

Suppose $T_{a_1}$ is dishonest, i.e. it reveals to $S$ identity tickets it issues. Then it takes at most $n^{k-1}$ number of operations (`ITKSig` requests and encryptions), where $n$ is the total number of identity token providers and $k$ is the length of $A$'s requests chain, for the coalition to find out $\Phi_A$ - a straightforward brute-force search.

However, if we allow the coalition to eavesdrop on messages of other token providers $T_{a_i}$, then the number of operations they need to perform goes down to at most $n(k-1)$. This is done as follows:

- The coalition starts noting in a set $M$ all the messages that other token providers as well as $S$ receive from the moment $T_{a_1}$ sends $\Phi_1$.
- Upon reception of $\Phi_i$s check if any is in $M$, else wait until one of them is.
- Repeat the above steps until $\Phi_A$ is found.

So, it is now possible to find the corresponding token for the chosen identity within polynomial time in $k$ modulo the costs of eavesdropping.

**Identity Compromise (2).** *Suppose $S$ has successfully processed a complaint about a particular user. Then $S$ can reveal the identity of any subsequent user of the service.*

Once $S$ has successfully processed a complaint, he is in possession of the information $\Psi, H, V$ corresponding to the complaint. He can use this to make `Reveal` requests to any sequence of $T_i$'s corresponding to some other protocol session, and thereby break its anonymity.

**Other Weaknesses.** The protocol also has the following undesirable properties/glitches:

- Any third party can find out who misused the services of an anonymous service provider $S$.
- A dishonest service provider $S$ can adjust the set $H$ to include "convenient" adjudicators, when requesting to reveal the identity of an anonymous user in the complaint resolution protocol.
- Obviously, the last message in the complaint resolution protocol needs to be authenticated.

## 4   Improved Protocol

In order to present the protocol concisely, we omit details about $A$'s choice of the adjudicators $H \subseteq E$. We use just one adjudicator, which we note $E$.

## 4.1   The Protocol

It also consists of two parts - *signup* and *complaint resolution* - that have the same purpose as the previous ones, but with a different structure.

**Signup.** $A$ chooses a sequence $T_{a_1}, T_{a_2}, \ldots, T_{a_n}$ of elements of $T$ (possibly with duplications). In contrast with the previous protocol, we distinguish two temporary keys for $A$. $A$ creates a temporary service public key $K_{[A]}$ which she will use to identify herself to $S$. Additionally, she creates a public key $K_{\widehat{A}}$ which she will use in anonymous communication with token providers, to indicate who the reply needs to be sent to. The notation $A \longmapsto B$ means that $A$ anonymously sends a message to $B$. In this case, $B$ does not know $A$'s identity. Similarly, $A \longmapsfrom B$ means that $B$ receives a message anonymously, from $A$; $A$ does not know $B$'s identity.

$$1) \quad A \quad \longmapsto \quad T_{a_1} \quad : \quad \{ \text{ InitITKReq}, K_{[A]}, \ K_{\widehat{A}} \}_{K_{T_{a_1}}}$$

$$2) \quad T_{a_1} \quad \longmapsfrom \quad A \quad : \quad \{ \ \Phi_1 \ \}_{K_{\widehat{A}}},$$
$$\text{where } \Phi_1 = [ \ \{ \text{ InitITKReq}, K_{[A]} \ \}_{K_{T_{a_1}}} \ ]_{K_{T_{a_1}}^-}$$

By including the service key $K_{[A]}$ in the message of step 1, we will later have this key associated with $A$'s identity token in order avoid the Service Misuse attack, whereby anyone who acquires her token can use it to obtain a service on behalf of $A$ from $S$. Note that, in contrast with the previous protocol, $A$ has not revealed her identity to $T_{a_1}$.

For $i = 1$ to $n - 2$:

$$*\begin{cases} 1a) \quad A \quad \longmapsto \quad T_{a_{i+1}} \quad : \quad \{ \text{ ITKReq}, \ \Phi_i, \text{NT}_{a_{i+1}}, K_{\widehat{A}} \}_{K_{T_{a_{i+1}}}} \\ \qquad\qquad\qquad \text{where for } i > 1 \quad \Phi_i = [ \ \{ \ \Phi_{i-1}, \text{NT}_{a_i}, K_{\widehat{A}} \ \}_{K_{T_{a_i}}} ]_{K_{T_{a_i}}^-} \\ \\ 2a) \quad T_{a_{i+1}} \quad \longmapsfrom \quad A \quad : \quad \{ \ [ \ \{ \ \Phi_i, \text{NT}_{a_{i+1}}, \ K_{\widehat{A}} \ \}_{K_{T_{a_{i+1}}}} \ ]_{K_{T_{a_{i+1}}}^-} \}_{K_{\widehat{A}}} \end{cases}$$

Each time $A$ sends a message to $T_{a_i}$ containing $\Phi_{i-1}, \text{NT}_{a_i}, K_{\widehat{A}}$ and receives back from it a message with $\Phi_i = [ \ X \ ]_{K_{T_{a_i}}^-}$, she checks that $X = \{ \ \Phi_{i-1}, \text{NT}_{a_i}, K_{\widehat{A}} \ \}_{K_{T_{a_i}}}$, by reconstructing the encryption. By the end of the sequence of messages (1a, 2a) ($n - 2$ times), $A$ has obtained the token $\Phi_{n-1}$:

$$[\{ \ [\{ \cdots$$
$$[\{ \ [\{ \text{InitITKReq}, K_{[A]}\}_{K_{T_{a_1}}}]_{K_{T_{a_1}}^-}, \text{NT}_{a_2}, \ K_{\widehat{A}}\}_{K_{T_{a_2}}}]_{K_{T_{a_2}}^-}$$
$$\cdots \}_{K_{T_{a_{n-2}}}}]_{K_{T_{a_{n-2}}}^-}, \text{NT}_{a_{n-1}}\}_{K_{T_{a_{n-1}}}}]_{K_{T_{a_{n-1}}}^-}$$

which serves as a disguise of her key $K_{[A]}$. Note the nonces $\text{NT}_{a_i}$ in the above steps, generated by $A$. They are necessary in order to preclude the Identity Compromise (1) attack (see Analysis section).

We assume that all agents receiving a signed message verify the signature. Thus, on receiving message (1a), $T_{a+1}$ verifies that the token has been signed by another token provider before he signs it and sends it on.

Next, $A$ reveals her identity to $T_{a_n}$, by signing the token $\Phi_{n-1}$. Steps 3, 4, 3a, 4a reverse this sequence of encryptions, and at the same time they build up the identity token $\widetilde{\Phi}_{n-1}$.

$$3) \quad A \quad \longmapsto \quad T_{a_n} \quad : \quad \{\,[\,\texttt{ITKSig},\, \Phi_{n-1},\, A\,]_{K_A^-}\,\}_{K_{T_{a_n}}}$$

$$4) \quad T_{a_n} \quad \longrightarrow\!\!\!| \quad A \quad : \quad \{\,\widetilde{\Phi}_1\,\}_{K_A},$$
$$\text{where } \widetilde{\Phi}_1 = [\,\{\,[\,\texttt{ITKSig},\, \Phi_{n-1},\, A\,]_{K_A^-}\,\}_{K_{T_{a_n}}},\, \Phi_{n-1}\,]_{K_{T_{a_n}}^-}$$

After step 3a, before sending out a response, token provider $T_{a_{n-i}}$ checks that the key $K_{\widehat{A}}$ supplied in the ITKReq request matches the one embedded in $\Phi_{n-i}$ (cf. step 2a above). The same rule applies to $T_{a_1}$ at step 5. (Both token providers also check that $\widetilde{\Phi}$ contained in the ITKReq request was signed by some token provider.)

For $i = 1$ to $n - 2$:

$$* \begin{cases} 3a) \quad A \quad \longmapsto \quad T_{a_{n-i}} \quad : \quad \{\,\texttt{ITKSig},\, \widetilde{\Phi}_i, \texttt{NT}'_{a_{n-i}},\, K_{\widehat{A}}\,\}_{K_{T_{a_{n-i}}}} \\[2mm] \qquad \text{where for } i > 1 \quad \widetilde{\Phi}_i = [\,\{\,\widetilde{\Phi}_{i-1}, \texttt{NT}'_{a_{n-i+1}}\,\}_{K_{T_{a_{n+1-i}}}},\, \Phi_{n-i}\,]_{K_{T_{a_{n+1-i}}}^-} \\[4mm] 4a) \quad T_{a_{n-i}} \quad \longrightarrow\!\!\!| \quad A \quad : \quad \{\,[\,\{\,\widetilde{\Phi}_i, \texttt{NT}'_{a_{n-i}}\,\}_{K_{T_{a_{n-i}}}},\, \Phi_{n-i-1}\,]_{K_{T_{a_{n-i}}}^-}\,\}_{K_{\widehat{A}}} \end{cases}$$

$$5) \quad A \quad \longmapsto \quad T_{a_1} \quad : \quad \{\,\texttt{ITKSig}, \widetilde{\Phi}_{n-1}, \texttt{NT}'_{a_1}, K_{\widehat{A}}\,\}_{K_{T_{a_1}}}$$

$$6) \quad T_{a_1} \quad \longrightarrow\!\!\!| \quad A \quad : \quad \{\,[\,\{\,\widetilde{\Phi}_{n-1}, \texttt{NT}'_{a_1}\,\}_{K_{T_{a_1}}}, K_{[A]}\,]_{K_{T_{a_1}}^-}\,\}_{K_{\widehat{A}}}$$

Upon reaching $T_{a_1}$ we have the identity token for $A$:

$$\widetilde{\Phi}_A = [\,\{\,\cdots\,[\,\{\widetilde{\Phi}_1,\, \texttt{NT}'_{a_{n-1}}\}_{K_{T_{a_{n-1}}}},\, \Phi_{n-2}\,]_{K_{T_{a_{n-1}}}^-}\, \cdots \texttt{NT}'_{a_1}\}_{K_{T_{a_1}}},\, K_{[A]}\,]_{K_{T_{a_1}}^-}$$

The token $\widetilde{\Phi}_A$ associates the $K_{[A]}$ with $A$, and therefore can only be used by an entity which knows the private key corresponding to $K_{[A]}$.

$$7) \quad A \quad \longmapsto \quad S \quad : \quad \{\,\widetilde{\Phi}_A,\, K_{[A]}\,\}_{K_S}$$

$A$ presents the token to $S$ and initiates the service. $S$ checks that the key $K_{[A]}$ that $A$ provided is contained inside the token which is signed by one of the providers.

**Complaint Resolution.** We assume that a complaint $\Psi_{K_{[A]}}$ is uniquely associated with $A$'s service key $K_{[A]}$. It must be verifiable by an adjudicator $E$ and not forgeable by $S$. If the adjudicator agrees with the complaint he signs it and then sends it back to $S$.

$$1) \quad S \quad \longrightarrow \quad E \quad : \quad \{\, \texttt{AdjReq}, \Psi_{K_{[A]}}, S \,\}_{K_E}$$

$$2) \quad E \quad \longrightarrow \quad S \quad : \quad \{\, [\Psi_{K_{[A]}}]_{K_E^-} \,\}_{K_S}$$

$$3) \quad S \quad \longrightarrow \quad T_{a_1} \quad : \quad \{\, \texttt{Reveal}, \widetilde{\Phi}_A, \widetilde{\Psi}, S \,\}_{K_{T_{a_1}}}$$
$$\text{where } \widetilde{\Psi} = [\Psi_{K_{[A]}}]_{K_E^-}$$

$$4) \quad T_{a_1} \quad \longrightarrow \quad S \quad : \quad \{\, \widetilde{\Phi}_{n-1}, \texttt{NT}'_{a_1}, \widetilde{\Psi} \,\}_{K_S}$$

For $i = 1$ to $n - 2$:

$$* \begin{cases} 3a) \quad S \quad \longrightarrow \quad T_{a_{i+1}} \quad : \quad \{\, \texttt{Reveal}, ((\widetilde{\Phi}_{n-i}, \texttt{NT}_{a_i}, \texttt{NT}'_{a_i}), \ldots, \\ \qquad\qquad\qquad\qquad\qquad (\widetilde{\Phi}_{n-1}, \texttt{NT}'_{a_1}), \widetilde{\Phi}_n), \widetilde{\Psi}, S \,\}_{K_{T_{a_{i+1}}}} \\[2mm] 4a) \quad T_{a_{i+1}} \quad \longrightarrow \quad S \quad : \quad \{\, \widetilde{\Phi}_{n-i-1}, \texttt{NT}_{a_{i+1}}, \texttt{NT}'_{a_{i+1}}, \widetilde{\Psi} \,\}_{K_S} \end{cases}$$

$$5) \quad S \quad \longrightarrow \quad T_{a_n} \quad : \quad \{\, \texttt{Reveal}, ((\widetilde{\Phi}_1, \texttt{NT}_{a_{n-1}}, \texttt{NT}'_{a_{n-1}}), \ldots, \widetilde{\Phi}_n), \widetilde{\Psi} \,\}_{K_{T_{a_n}}}$$

$$6) \quad T_{a_n} \quad \longrightarrow \quad S \quad : \quad \{\, [\, \texttt{ITKSig}, \Phi_{n-1}, A \,]_{K_A^-}, \widetilde{\Psi} \}_{K_S}$$

In message 3a, the tuple of $\widetilde{\Phi}_i$s serves to prevent complaint resolution messages in one session being used in another. Each $T_{a_i}$ checks that the sequence he receives is correct, using the nonces $\texttt{NT}'_{a_i}$, and that the last element of the sequence is the token that the complaint $\Psi_{K_{[A]}}$ is uniquely associated with.

At the $n$th iteration $S$ reveals the identity of the user when it receives $[\, \texttt{ITKSig},$ $break\Phi_{n-1}, A \,]_{K_A^-}$ from $T_{a_n}$. Importantly, in the sequence of unfoldings of $\widetilde{\Phi}_{a_i}$s, $S$ also keeps track of $\Phi_{a_i}$s inside them, using the nonces $\texttt{NT}_{a_i}$, in order to make sure that $\Phi_{n-1}$ is formed from the key she was given in the service request step, viz. it is $K_{\widehat{A}}$. If there is a mismatch, she finds out which $T_{a_i}$ cheated, and, furthermore, has evidence to prove that to any other party.

## 4.2   Properties of the Protocol

If the token providers try to generate tokens by themselves, they can be shown to have cheated. Also the token created for $A$ is unusable by any other entity that acquires it.

If at least one of the token providers in the sequence $T_{a_1}, T_{a_2}, \ldots, T_{a_n}$ is honest, then $A$'s identity is not revealed without valid complaint. Thus, the protocol avoids the identity compromise attacks of section 3.

## 5   Conclusions

The protocol for anonymity with identity escrow in [4] is shown to have some serious flaws. We have presented an improved protocol to achieve the same aim, and in the future work we will verify the protocol using appropriate tools, such as Proverif [1] or Isabelle [6].

# References

1. B. Blanchet. An efficient cryptographic protocol verifier based on prolog rules. In S. Schneider, editor, *14th IEEE Computer Security Foundations Workshop*, pages 82–96, Cape Breton, Nova Scotia, Canada, June 2001. IEEE Computer Society Press.
2. J. Kilian and E. Petrank. Identity escrow. In *Advances in Cryptology (CRYPTO'98)*, number 1462 in LNCS, pages 169–187. Springer Verlag, 1998.
3. F. Leighton. Failsafe key escrow systems. Technical Memo 483, MIT Laboratory for Computer Science, 1994.
4. L. Marshall and C. Molina-Jiminez. Anonymity with identity escrow. In T. Dimitrakos and F. Martinelli, editors, *Proceedings of the 1st International Workshop on Formal Aspects in Security and Trust*, pages 121–129, Istituto di Informatica e Telematica, Pisa, 2003.
5. S. Micali. Fair public-key cryptosystems. In *Advances in Cryptology (CRYPTO'92)*, number 740 in LNCS. Springer Verlag, 1993.
6. L. C. Paulson. The inductive approach to verifying cryptographic protocols. *J. Computer Security*, 6:85–128, 1998.
7. M. O. Rabin. Efficient dispersal of information for security, load balancing and fault tolerance. *Journal of the ACM*, 36(2):335–348, 1989.

# Towards Verification of Timed Non-repudiation Protocols

Kun Wei and James Heather

Department of Computing, University of Surrey, Guildford,
Surrey GU2 7XH, UK
{k.wei, j.heather}@surrey.ac.uk

**Abstract.** Fairness of non-repudiation is naturally expressed as a liveness specification, as in [Sch98]; to formalize this idea, we apply the process algebra CSP to analyze the well-known Zhou-Gollmann protocol. We here model and verify a variant of the ZG protocol that includes a deadline (timestamp) for completion of the protocol, after which an agent can no longer initiate the recovery protocol with the TTP to get hold of the non-repudiation evidence. The verification itself is performed by the FDR model-checker.

## 1 Introduction

Security protocols are often complex because they represent concurrent systems in which various entities can run independently and simultaneously. Consequently, constructing proofs of correctness by hand can be arduous and error-prone.

Over the past decade, formal methods have been remarkably successful in their application to the analysis of security protocols. For example, the combination of CSP and FDR has proved to be an excellent tool for modelling and verifying safety properties such as authentication and confidentiality. However, non-repudiation properties have not yet been mastered to the same degree since they must often be expressed as liveness properties and the vast bulk of work to date has been concerned only with safety properties.

Schneider shows in [Sch98] how to extend the CSP approach to analyze non-repudiation protocols. His proofs of correctness, based on the traces and the stable failures models of CSP as well as on rank functions, are constructed by hand. For safety properties, one usually assumes that one honest party wishes to communicate with another honest party, and one asks whether a dishonest intruder can disrupt the communications so as to effect breach of security. When considering non-repudiation, however, we are concerned with protecting one honest party against possible cheating by his or her interlocutor. Thus a non-repudiation protocol enables parties such as a sender Alice and a responder Bob to send and receive messages, and provides them with evidence so that neither of them can deny having sent or received these messages when they later resort to a judge for resolving a dispute.

There are two basic types of non-repudiation: *Non-repudiation of Origin (NRO)* provides Bob with evidence of origin that unambiguously shows that

T. Dimitrakos et al. (Eds.): FAST 2005, LNCS 3866, pp. 244–257, 2006.

Alice has previously sent a particular message, and *Non-repudiation of Receipt (NRR)* provides Alice with evidence of receipt that unambiguously shows that Bob has received the message. Unforgeable digital signatures are usually the mechanism by which NRO and NRR can be obtained.

However, a major problem often arises: there may come a point during the run at which either Alice or Bob reaches an advantageous position; for example, Alice may have collected all the evidence she needs before Bob has collected his, and Alice may then deliberately abandon the protocol to keep her advantageous position. Usually we will want to ensure that the protocol is *fair*.

- *Fairness* guarantees that neither Alice nor Bob can reach a point where he or she has obtained non-repudiation evidence, but where the other party is prevented from retrieving any required evidence that has not already been obtained.

Obviously, fairness is the most difficult property to achieve in the design of such protocols, and several different solutions have been proposed. Two kinds of approach are discussed in [KMZ02], classified according to whether or not the protocol uses a trusted third party (TTP). The first kind of approach providing fairness in exchange protocols is based on either a *gradual exchange* [Ted83] or *probabilistic protocol* [MR99]. Without the involvement of a TTP, a sender Alice gradually releases messages to a responder Bob over many rounds of a protocol, with the number of rounds chosen by Alice and unknown to Bob. Bob is supposed to respond for every message, and any failure to respond may cause Alice to stop the protocol. However, such protocols require that all parties have the same computational power, and a large number of messages must be exchanged. The other kind of approach uses a TTP to handle some of the evidence. Many fair non-repudiation protocols use the TTP as a delivery authority to establish and transmit some key evidence. The efficiency of such protocols depends on how much a TTP is involved in the communication, since heavy involvement of the TTP may become a bottleneck of communication and computation.

In this paper, we will verify fairness of the timed Zhou-Gollmann protocol [ZG97] with an off-line TTP—that is, a TTP that is involved in the protocol only when parties are in dispute. To model such a protocol, we build a model of all of the entities involved in the network: a spy, a TTP, an honest party and so on. The factor of time is also considered in such a protocol; for example, it is reasonable that the responder should know when the evidence is available from the TTP, so that it does not have to poll the server at regular intervals, causing unnecessary network traffic.

In the CSP model, fairness is naturally described as a liveness property. It is impossible for fairness to guarantee that both Alice and Bob can collect the required evidence simultaneously, since we are dealing with an asynchronous network, but it does guarantee that either of them must be able to access the evidence as long as the other party has obtained it.

Fairness in the Zhou-Gollman protocol relies on the assumption that the communication channels between a TTP and all parties are *resilient*. A resilient channel may delay a message for a finite, unknown amount of time, but will eventually deliver it to its destination. Communication between parties, however, goes across *unreliable* channels that allow a message to be lost, delayed, or even delivered to the wrong destination.

The paper is organised as follows: the CSP notation is briefly introduced, and the timed Zhou-Gollmann protocol is described. We give details of the CSP modelling for every entity involved in a run, and its associated FDR encoding. Finally, we discuss the implications of the successful verification, and talk about future work.

## 2   CSP Notation

CSP is an event-orientated language for describing concurrent systems and their interactions. A security protocol is a concurrent system in which a series of messages are exchanged among the various parties involved. CSP is therefore well suited to the modelling and analysis of security protocols.

In CSP, a system can be considered as a process that might be hierarchically composed of many smaller processes. An individual process can be combined with events or other processes by operators such as prefixing, choice, parallel composition, and so on. For safety properties, the traces model of CSP is enough. In this paper, we use the stable failures model of CSP to verify fairness in the ZG protocol. We will briefly illustrate the CSP language and the semantic models; for a fuller introduction, the reader is referred to [Ros98, Sch99].

*Stop* is a stable deadlocked process that never performs any events. The process $c \rightarrow P$ behaves like $P$ after performing the event $c$. A event like $c$ may be compounded; for example, one often used patten of events is $c.i.j.m$ consisting of a channel $c$, a sender $i$, a receiver $j$ and a message $m$.

The external choice $P_1 \square P_2$ may behave either like $P_1$ or like $P_2$, depending on what events its environment initially offers it. The traces of internal choice $P_1 \sqcap P_2$ are the same as those of $P_1 \square P_2$, but the choice in this case is non-deterministic.

The process $P_1 \ _A\|_B \ P_2$ is the process where all events in the intersection of $A$ and $B$ must be synchronized, and other events within $A$ and $B$ can be performed independently by $P_1$ and $P_2$ respectively. An interleaving $P_1 \ ||| \ P_2$ executes each part entirely independently and is equivalent with $P_1 \ \|_\emptyset \ P_2$.

The process $P \setminus A$ will pass through the same events as P, but events in the set $A$ become be invisible. The renamed process $P[a \leftarrow b]$ means that the event $a$ is completely replaced by $b$ in the process $P$. In addition, processes may also be described recursively whenever such descriptions are well defined.

A trace is defined to be a sequence of finite events. A refusal set is a set of events from which a process can fail to accept anything no matter how long it is offered; $refusals(P/t)$ is the set of $P$'s refusals after the trace $t$; then $(t, X)$ is a failure in which $X$ denotes $refusals(P/t)$. If the trace $t$ can make no internal progress, this failure is called a *stable failure*.

Liveness is concerned with behaviour that a process is guaranteed to make available, and can be inferred from stable failures; for example, if, for a fixed trace $t$, we have $a \notin X$ for all stable failures of $P$ of the form $(t, X)$, then $a$ must be available after $P$ has performed $t$.

Verification in FDR is done by means of determining whether one process refines another. In the stable failures model, this equates to checking whether the traces and failures of one process are subsets of the traces and failures of the other:

$$P \sqsubseteq_F Q \equiv traces(P) \supseteq traces(Q) \wedge failures(P) \supseteq failures(Q)$$

For the properties we are considering, if $P$ meets the properties we are verifying, then $Q$ also meets them if $Q$ refines $P$.

## 3   The Timed Zhou-Gollmann Protocol

Zhou and Gollmann present a basic fair non-repudiation protocol using a lightweight TTP in [ZG96], which supports non-repudiation of origin and non-repudiation of receipt as well as fairness. They then propose an improved protocol in [ZG97], with an off-line TTP that is more efficient in environments in which the two parties usually play fair in a protocol run, and want to resort to the TTP only when they are in dispute. In addition, it is possible (and, indeed, desirable) to include a timeout in the protocol, so that the responder will know at what point he will be able to recover evidence from the TTP.

The main idea of all Zhou-Gollmann protocols is that a sender Alice delivers the ciphertext and the message key to Bob separately; the ciphertext is sent from the originator Alice to the recipient Bob, Alice then sends the message key encrypted with her secret key to Bob or the TTP. Finally Alice and Bob may get the evidence or confirmation messages from the TTP to establish the required non-repudiation. The notation below is used in the protocol description.

- $M$: message to be sent from $A$ to $B$.
- $K$: symmetric key defined by $A$.
- $C$: commitment (ciphertext) for message $M$ encrypted with $K$.
- $L$: a unique label used to identify a particular protocol run.
- $f_{NRO}, f_{NRR}, f_{EOO}, f_{EOR}, f_{SUB}, f_{CON}$: flags indicating the purpose of a signed message.
- $T$: the deadline by which the TTP must have been asked to make the evidence available to the public.
- $s_i$: an asymmetric key used to generate $i$'s digital signature.

After cutting down the plaintext part, the simplified protocol can be divided into a main protocol and a recovery protocol. In the normal case, the sender Alice and the responder Bob will exchange messages and non-repudiation evidence directly, described as follows:

1. $A \rightarrow B :$ $s_A(f_{NRO}, B, L, T, C)$
2. $B \rightarrow A :$ $s_B(f_{NRR}, A, L, T, C)$

3. $A \rightarrow B :$ $s_A(f_{EOO}, B, L, K)$

4. $B \rightarrow A :$ $s_B(f_{EOR}, A, L, K)$

And if Alice does not get message 4 from Bob after sending message 3, she then launches the recovery protocol to get the associated evidence from the TTP.

1. $A \rightarrow TTP :$ $s_A(f_{SUB}, B, L, T, K)$

2. $B \leftrightarrow TTP :$ $s_T(f_{CON}, A, B, L, T, K)$

3. $A \leftrightarrow TTP :$ $s_T(f_{CON}, A, B, L, T, K)$

We briefly examine the protocol step by step to see how it works. Firstly, Alice composes a message including a flag, a unique label $L$, the receiver's name $B$ and a ciphertext $C = K(M)$, along with a chosen deadline $T$ (which is to be interpreted according to the TTP's clock); Alice then signs the message with her private key and sends it to Bob. Secondly, Bob collects the message as one piece of evidence in which the label $L$ identifies the run of the protocol, and then Bob responds with his signed message to provide A with evidence that B really has received $C$ in this run. Bob can also refuse to respond to Alice if he is not satisfied with the deadline $T$.

After she has got a response, Alice directly sends the encrypted message key $K$ to Bob, and Bob then sends the associated evidence back again. The protocol is now successfully completed if no dispute occurs; however, if Alice does not get her evidence at step 3 of the main protocol, she can launch the recovery protocol and submit a message to the TTP to retrieve the evidence. The TTP will check the deadline $T$ first to determine whether or not to accept the request. If the request comes in before the deadline, the TTP will generate the evidence and make it available to Alice and Bob. The advantage of this deadline is that if Bob does not receive message 3 from Alice, he does not have to poll the TTP indefinitely to see if Alice has initiated the recovery protocol and thus made the key and the evidence available to him. He can simply wait until time $T$ and then poll the TTP. If Alice has already initiated the recovery protocol then he will be able to get the key $K$ and the non-repudiation evidence; if she has not done so then he will not be able to get the key or the evidence, but he will know that Alice cannot get the non-repudiation evidence either, since the deadline has now passed.

The guarantee of fairness of such a protocol comes from an assumption that the channels between TTP and the parties are resilient; that is, messages may be delayed, but will be eventually arrive in a finite amount of time. However, the channels between Alice and Bob can be unreliable; that is, the medium may delay, lose or misdirect messages.

Although Bob in the execution of the protocol can be temporarily in an advantageous position, Alice and Bob should be in a fair position at the end of the protocol. The introduction of the deadline $T$ does in principle compromise the fairness of the protocol; for instance, Alice may not get the evidence from Bob at step 4 in the main protocol, but the submission of Alice's request to initiate the recovery protocol may be so severely delayed that the deadline has passed by the time it arrives and the TTP refuses to respond to it. Alice will in this instance not get all the required evidence, even though Bob has obtained his. As suggested in [ZG97], Alice has to choose $T$ to be large enough that this issue will not arise in practice.

# 4   CSP Modelling

Fairness says that if either A or B has got full evidence, the other party cannot be prevented from retrieving the evidence indefinitely. We cannot assert for verifying fairness that once A has obtained the evidence then B must have obtained the evidence as well, because there may be a delay between A's reception and B's reception. However, we can ensure that the evidence must be available to B, or that a specific action must be about to happen to enable B to get the evidence in the future.

To check a protocol like this one with CSP, we have to build models of the parties, the TTP and the medium and see how they can interfere with each other. Since the protocol is used to protect parties that do not trust each other, we do not need to model a special intruder party. However, fairness is only guaranteed to the party who runs in accordance with the protocol; for example, if A releases the symmetric key $K$ before B responds, A will certainly place herself in a disadvantageous position.

In our model, we directly formalize the outcome of the TTP's test for whether the deadline has passed, without modelling specific values of $T$; in other words, we model the deadline $T$ as a boolean variable. When the TTP judges whether $T$ has expired, the outcome will be either true or false, and the TTP will accordingly either accept or refuse the request. The deadline test can be modelled within the TTP using internal choice.

## 4.1   Data Types

The above description of the protocol indicates that the message space contains flags, labels, various keys, names of parties, text messages, the deadline and combinations of these. Encryption, as is typical in these situations, are treated symbolically.

Like other model checkers, FDR can only verify systems with a reasonable number of states. Therefore, we assume that only two parties are communicating, and we restrict the number of possible messages of each data type.

```
datatype fact = Sq.Seq(fact) |
               SK.(fact,fact)| Encrypt.(fact,fact) |
               Alice | Bob | TTP |
               pkA | pkB | pkT | skA | skB | skT |
               fNRO | fNRR | fEOO | fEOR | fSUB | fCON |
               La | Lb | Ka | Kb | T | AtoB | BtoA
```

where the type fact is a collection of all constants, and it can be used to represent any message appearing in the protocol.

We also define some sets, functions and definitions to represent legitimate messages, symbolic encryption and mapping of labels, keys and messages with the identities of parties.

We assume that no party is able to forge other parties' digital signatures; that is, parties never release their private keys. In our scenario, we will treat A as a dishonest party, or a spy, and B is an honest party who always performs in accordance with the protocol; A and B may behave either as a sender or as a responder. A and B may run the protocol many times, and A may make use of the information deduced from B's messages to initiate a new run.

## 4.2    Defining Honest Parties

We now represent the behaviour of an honest party in the timed ZG protocol. The protocol specification assumes that the channel between parties is unreliable, whereas the channel between the TTP and parties is resilient. We define, as follows, the transmission of messages using CSP channels.

```
channel trans,rec:agents.agents.Umessages
channel send,get:allagents.allagents.Rmessages
channel evidence:agents.messages
```

where **trans** and **rec** are for unreliable channels, **send** and **get** are for resilient channels; the channel **evidence** represents announcement of parties' obtained evidence; **Umessages** and **Rmessages** include messages in unreliable channels and resilient channels respectively.

A party can act either as a sender or as a responder; once its labels have run out, it acts only as a responder.

```
User(id,ls) =   ls!=<> & Send(id,ls)
              [] Resp(id,ls)
```

When acting as a sender, the party chooses the facts from its own knowledge to construct and transmit the messages in turn. In order to keep the size of all parties' message spaces fairly small, the parties A and B have only one value for labels, message keys and plaintext, but A may get some of information from B such as the message key $Kb$ during the execution of the protocol and use it in later runs.

We integrate all behaviour of a party in the main protocol and the recovery protocol into one process. After A sends the message to B at step 3 in the main protocol, she may wait for a response from B and finish the protocol, or initiate the recovery protocol to retrieve the evidence from the TTP.

```
Send(id,ls) = |~|a:diff(agents,{id})@ (|~|l:label(id)@
                    (|~|k:symkeys(id)@ (|~|m:text(id)@
    trans.id.a.ske(sk(id),Sq.<fNRO,a,l,T,encrypt(k,m)>) ->
    rec.id.a.ske(sk(a),Sq.<fNRR,id,l,T,encrypt(k,m)>) ->
    trans.id.a.ske(sk(id),Sq.<fEOO,a,l,k>) ->
```

```
((rec.id.a.ske(sk(a),Sq.<fEOR,id,l,k>) -> User(id,tail(ls)))
 []
 (send.id.TTP.ske(sk(id),Sq.<fSUB,a,l,T,k>) ->
get.id.TTP.ske(skT,Sq.<fCON,id,a,l,T,k>)->User(id,tail(ls)))))))
```

The responder process performs the protocol from the opposite perspective. Note that we assume the responder can refuse to accept messages including its own labels, since the labels are usually generated associated with the plaintexts and the message keys; therefore, it is reasonable to suppose that the receiver is vigilant enough to spot such abuses.

```
Resp(id,ls) = []a:diff(agents,{id})@ ([]l:diff(labels,label(id))
                              @([]k:symmetrickey@([]m:plaintext@
  rec.id.a.ske(sk(a),Sq.<fNRO,id,l,T,encrypt(k,m)>)->
  trans.id.a.ske(sk(id),Sq.<fNRR,a,l,T,encrypt(k,m)>)->
((rec.id.a.ske(sk(a),Sq.<fEOO,id,l,k>) ->
  trans.id.a.ske(sk(id),Sq.<fEOR,a,l,k>)-> User(id,ls))
  []
 (get.id.TTP.ske(skT,Sq.<fCON,a,id,l,T,k>) ->User(id,ls))))))
```

The responder does accept any commitment because it does not know what the commitment means until the end of the run. In addition, A may not send message 3 to B at all; B must thus be able to check whether the evidence is available from the TTP.

For the purpose of verification, we define a process Show(id) to show the evidence that a party has obtained. This process may show the evidence to the network as long as the relevant party has got the evidence. Finally, a well-behaved party is described as:

```
Party(id,ls) = User(id,ls) [|{|rec,get|}|] Show(id)
```

## 4.3   Creating a Spy

In the modelling of the non-repudiation protocol, we do not define a special party, a spy, as different from the legitimate parties. On the contrary, we assume that one of two communicating parties is a spy who may be able to deduce something of value from the messages it has received. The non-repudiation protocol is supposed to provide fairness for an honest party even if the other party is a spy. Our spy model roughly corresponds to Roscoe's lazy spy model [Ros98], but slightly modified to suit our case. We here represent some key parts of the model; more details may be found in [Ros98].

A spy first has a set of deductive rules; for example, if it knows all members of a sequence, then it can build the sequence. A deduction is a pair (X,f) where X is a finite set of facts and f is an individual fact. Thus, anyone in possession of X can construct f as well. In our spy model, three types of deduction are built based on constructing and extracting sequences, symmetric-key encryption and public-key encryption.

The spy has an initial basic knowledge, such as public keys, labels and so on, and can further close up such basic facts by means of the `Close` function to construct a number of legitimate messages before the start of the protocol. The full initial knowledge of the spy is constructed by closing up the initial basic knowledge under deduction rules. In this case we chose Alice as a spy, what she initially knows may then be represented as follows:

```
IK= {Alice,Bob,TTP,pkA,pkB,pkT,skA,T,
     fNRO,fNRR,fEOO,fEOR,fSUB,fCON,La,Ka,AtoB}
Known = Close(IK)
```

In order to restrict the state space to a manageable size, we define a new set of deductions whose conclusion is something that the spy does not know yet, but that it will learn. In other words, the spy can never deduce anything it already knows. Additionally, to reduce the size of state space further and to ensure efficient compilation by the model checker, we define a parallel network which has one process for every fact inside the spy's `LearnableFacts`.

```
ignorantof(f) = member(f, messages)& learn.f -> knows(f)
     [] infer?t:{(X,f')|(X,f')<-Deductions,f==f'}->knows(f)


knows(f) = member(f,messages)&say.f -> knows(f)
     [] member(f,messages)&learn.f->knows(f)
     [] infer?t:{(X,f')|(X,f')<-Deductions,member(f,X)}->knows(f)
```

where `Deductions` is a collection of all possible deductive rules only for learnable facts.

Finally, the spy is then constructed by putting all these processes in parallel, hiding the inferences, and applying the *chase* operator[1].

```
Spy = chase((||f:LearnableFacts@[AlphaL(f)]ignorantof(f))
              \{|infer|}) ||| SayKnown
```

where `SayKnown` makes the spy say or learn legitimate messages in its `Known` facts.

To make the spy useful in a real network, we rename it so that it may communicate with other parties. Also, we provide the spy with the capability to show its evidence.

```
RenSpy(id) =((Spy[[say.f<-trans.a.b.f,learn.f<-rec.a.b.f|
                     a.b.f<-Ucomm,a==id]]
             [[say.f<-send.a.b.f,learn.f<-get.a.b.f|
                     a.b.f<-Rcomm,a==id]])
             [|{|rec,get|}|] Show(id))
```

where `Ucomm` and `Rcomm` are used to reduce unnecessary states; for example, `Rcomm` may restrict that one of agents must be the TTP and `f` must be the messages circulating in the resilient channel.

---

[1] The *chase* operator is designed specifically for this purpose; the reader is invited to consult [For97] for more information.

## 4.4   TTP and Medium

The trusted third party is supposed to act in accordance with its role in the protocol; that is, the TTP accepts signed messages, generates new evidence and makes them available to associated parties. The TTP also refuses to respond the parties whenever the deadline $T$ has expired. The test for expiry of the deadline $T$ is modelled by an internal choice in CSP. It is therefore modelled as follows:

```
Tnot(m)=send?a:agents!TTP!m->(Tnot(m) |~| Tknows(Gen(m)))
Tknows(S)=get?m:S->Tknows(S)[]idle-> Tknows(S)

TrustTP = (|||m:mess_SUB@ Tnot(m))
```

where, obviously, the TTP will not confirm the party's submission after $T$ in the Tnot(m); if the TTP accepts it, the message will go into the process Tknows where the evidence will be available to both parties. Note that we implement the possibility of delays in the resilient channels by introducing an action *idle* in the Tknows(S). When the TTP receives a message, it then can hold the message in a finite amount of time, but will send it out eventually. The TTP only accepts messages with the label $f_{SUB}$. Also, we define a function Gen(m) to transform submitted messages to confirmed messages for involved parties.

The medium provides two types of message delivery service: one is an unreliable channel where messages might be lost, delayed and sent to any address; another one is a resilient channel where messages might be delayed, but will eventually arrive, and also be guaranteed not to arrive at the wrong address. Since the resilient channel has been modelled in the definition of the TTP, the model of the medium here is defined only for the unreliable channel:

```
Hears(m) = member(m,Umessages)&
           trans?a?b:diff(agents,{a})!m -> Middle(m)
Middle(m) =  idle -> Middle(m)
          []lost -> Hears(m)
          []rec?a?b:diff(agents,{a})!m -> Hears(m)

Medium = |||m:Umessages@Hears(m)
```

The medium is modelled exactly in terms of its description in the protocol. We define two channels idle and lost to represent messages being delayed or lost.

## 4.5   Specification and Verification

The two parties and the TTP transmit messages via unreliable channels and resilient channels in the medium as shown in Figure 1. It would be desirable to allow more potential protocol participants, since the protocol is expected to be

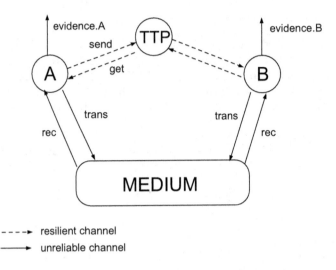

**Fig. 1.** Network for a non-repudiation protocol

correct even in the presence of other parties of the network. However, a bigger network would quickly give rise to state space explosion.

The entire network is the parallel combination of these components:

```
Network = ((RenSpy(Alice) ||| Party(Bob,<Lb>)
           [|{|send,get|}|]  TrustTP)
          [|{|trans,rec|}|]  Medium
```

We can then test for attacks on the protocol by checking whether this network satisfies a specification encapsulating the fairness property.

Fairness is naturally specified by Schneider [Sch98] in the stable failures model of CSP. The essence of his idea is that if one of the two parties has obtained full evidence, then the other party either is already in possession of it or is able to access it. We have slightly changed the above specification to meet the timed Zhou-Gollmann non-repudiation protocol, and we give here two specifications according to the different role of B.

First, we deal with the case where B acts as a responder. In the normal case, if A has got evidence of receipt then B must be in a position to obtain evidence of origin.

$$
\begin{aligned}
FAIR1(tr, X) \;\widehat{=}\; & evidence.A.s_B(f_{EOR}, A, La, T, Ka) \text{ in } tr \\
& \wedge\; evidence.A.s_B(f_{NRR}, A, La, C) \text{ in } tr \\
& \Rightarrow \\
& (evidence.B.s_A(f_{NRO}, B, La, Ka) \notin X \\
& \wedge\; evidence.B.s_A(f_{EOO}, B, La, T, Ka) \notin X)
\end{aligned}
$$

When a dispute arises, the specification is defined as follows:

$$FAIR2(tr, X) \triangleq evidence.A.s_T(f_{CON}, A, B, La, T, Ka) \text{ in } tr$$
$$\wedge \; evidence.A.s_B(f_{NRR}, A, La, T, C) \text{ in } tr$$
$$\Rightarrow$$
$$get.B.TTP.s_T(f_{CON}, A, B, La, T, Ka) \notin X \vee$$
$$(evidence.B.s_A(f_{NRO}, B, La, T, Ka) \notin X$$
$$\wedge \; evidence.B.s_T(f_{CON}, A, B, La, T, Ka) \notin X)$$

The above specification shows that if A holds the full evidence, then B must either be able to get the evidence or have already obtained such evidence.

Secondly, we deal with the case in which B acts as a sender. For this case, the specification is different from the above one, since a sender is in a weaker position in the protocol. If no dispute arises:

$$FAIR3(tr, X) \triangleq evidence.A.s_B(f_{EOO}.A.Lb.Kb) \text{ in } tr$$
$$\wedge \; evidence.A.s_B(f_{NRO}.A.Lb.T.C) \text{ in } tr$$
$$\Rightarrow$$
$$send.B.TTP.s_B(f_{SUB}.B.Lb.T.Kb) \text{ in } tr \vee$$
$$send.B.TTP.s_B(f_{SUB}.B.Lb.T.Kb) \notin X$$

Because of the unreliable channel between A and B, B may not obtain the evidence, but he can not be prevented from initiating the recovery protocol. Furthermore, if B has launched the recovery protocol, he then must be able to get the evidence from the TTP.

$$FAIR4(tr, X) \triangleq send.B.TTP.s_B(f_{SUB}, A, Lb, T, Kb) \text{ in } tr$$
$$\Rightarrow$$
$$get.B.TTP.s_T(f_{CON}, B, A, Lb, T, Kb) \notin X$$

To meet the fairness property of the timed Zhou-Gollmann protocol, the process Network must satisfy the $FAIR1$–$FAIR4$ in the stable failures model of CSP.

The formal verification shows there is no more fault in the timed ZG protocol under the assumptions described in this paper, other than the compromise caused by the introduction of the deadline $T$. As the designers say, the deadline $T$ may result in the sender not getting the full evidence. In practice, the sender simply has to choose $T$ big enough and send $K$ to the responder only when it has sufficient time to launch the recovery protocol. In addition, the responder can be temporarily in an advantageous position, but both of them will be in a fair position at the end of the protocol run.

## 5 Discussion and Future Work

In this paper, we have modelled and analyzed the timed Zhou-Gollmann non-repudiation protocol. Fairness, an important property in a non-repudiation protocol, requires that neither of two parties can establish evidence of origin or evidence of receipt while still preventing the other party from obtaining such evidence. In the CSP modelling, fairness is naturally described as a liveness property in the stable failures model.

Although the introduction of the deadline $T$ makes the protocol closer to reality, it compromises the fairness of the parties. There are also two minor hidden issues: one is that the responder can be temporarily in a advantageous position, the other is that the sender may initiate the recovery protocol even when it has got the evidence. The evidence will mean the same to a judge regardless of whether it has been obtained through the main protocol or the recovery protocol, but it might be considered problematic that it is easy for the responder to prove that the initiator asked the TTP to intervene in the protocol execution. In the context of electronic commerce, it may result in bad publicity if it is known that the parties had to resort to the trusted third party to get the required evidence.

Some related work can be found in the literature concerning verification of non-repudiation protocols using different approaches. Zhou et al. in [ZG98] firstly use 'BAN-like' belief logic to check only safety properties of the non-repudiation protocols. Schneider [Sch98] gives an excellent overview of the CSP modelling and proves the correctness of properties using stable failures and rank functions; however, the proofs are constructed by hand. Shmatikov and Mitchell in [SM01] verify fairness as a monotonic property using Mur$\varphi$; that is, if fairness is broken at one point of the protocol, the protocol will remain unfair. This approach also cannot deal with liveness properties. Kremer and Raskin [KR01] use the finite state model checker MOCHA to verify non-repudiation and fair exchange protocols. This approach, which is rather different from ours here, can also cope with liveness properties as well as safety properties. However, they have modelled networks in which A and B can engage in only one run of the protocol.

We have shown that the combination of CSP and FDR is an excellent tool to verify non-repudiation protocols. We also wish to cover timeliness; that is, we wish to verify that all honest parties can reach a point where they can stop the protocol while preserving fairness. We will extend our current model to cover this issue in future work.

We still have some distance to go towards our aim of proving fairness of the protocol in its full generality, with an unbounded number of participants and atomic messages. Evans in[Eva03] gives a useful start on this issue by using rank functions and a theorem prover, PVS, to verify safety properties. This approach allows one to deal with networks with an infinite number of states and even a infinite number of parties. In the future, we will investigate this approach and apply it in the analysis of liveness properties of non-repudiation protocols.

# References

[Eva03]   Neil Evans. *Investigating Security through Proof*. PhD thesis, Royal Holloway, University of London, 2003.

[For97]   Formal Systems (Europe) Ltd. Failures-Divergence Refinement—FDR 2 user manual, 1997. Available from Formal Systems' web site at `http://www.formal.demon.co.uk/FDR2.html`.

[KMZ02]   Steve Kremer, Olivier Markowitch, and Jianying Zhou. An intensive survey of non-repudiation protocols. Technical Report 473, 2002.

[KR01]    Steve Kremer and Jean-François Raskin. A game-based verification of non-repudiation and fair exchange protocols. *Lecture Notes in Computer Science*, 2154, 2001.

[MR99]    Olivier Markowitch and Yves Roggeman. Probabilistic non-repudiation without trusted third party. In *Second Workshop on Security in Communication Network 99*, 1999.

[Ros98]   A. W. Roscoe. *The Theory and Practice of Concurrency*. Prentice-Hall International, 1998.

[Sch98]   Steve A. Schneider. Formal analysis of a non-repudiation protocol. In *Proceedings of the 11th IEEE Computer Security Foundations Workshop*, 1998.

[Sch99]   Steve A. Schneider. *Concurrent and real-time systems: the CSP approach.* John Wiley & Sons, 1999.

[SM01]    Vitaly Shmatikov and John C. Mitchell. Analysis of abuse-free contract signing. In *FC '00: Proceedings of the 4th International Conference on Financial Cryptography*, pages 174–191, London, UK, 2001. Springer-Verlag.

[Ted83]   Tom Tedrick. How to exchange half a bit. In *CRYPTO*, pages 147–151, 1983.

[ZG96]    Jianying Zhou and Dieter Gollmann. A fair non-repudiation protocol. In *Proceedings of the IEEE Symposium on Research in Security and Privacy*, pages 55–61, Oakland, CA, 1996. IEEE Computer Society Press.

[ZG97]    J. Zhou and D. Gollmann. An efficient non-repudiation protocol. In *Proceedings of The 10th Computer Security Foundations Workshop*. IEEE Computer Society Press, 1997.

[ZG98]    J. Zhou and D. Gollmann. Towards verification of non-repudiation protocols. In *Proceedings of 1998 International Refinement Workshop and Formal Methods Pacific*, pages 370–380, Canberra, Australia, September 1998.

# Author Index

# Lecture Notes in Computer Science

For information about Vols. 1–3798

please contact your bookseller or Springer

Vol. 3843: P. Healy, N.S. Nikolov (Eds.), Graph Drawing. XVII, 536 pages. 2006.

Vol. 3842: H.T. Shen, J. Li, M. Li, J. Ni, W. Wang (Eds.), Advanced Web and Network Technologies, and Applications. XXVII, 1057 pages. 2006.

Vol. 3841: X. Zhou, J. Li, H.T. Shen, M. Kitsuregawa, Y. Zhang (Eds.), Frontiers of WWW Research and Development - APWeb 2006. XXIV, 1223 pages. 2006.

Vol. 3840: M. Li, B. Boehm, L.J. Osterweil (Eds.), Unifying the Software Process Spectrum. XVI, 522 pages. 2006.

Vol. 3839: J.-C. Filliâtre, C. Paulin-Mohring, B. Werner (Eds.), Types for Proofs and Programs. VIII, 275 pages. 2006.

Vol. 3838: A. Middeldorp, V. van Oostrom, F. van Raamsdonk, R. de Vrijer (Eds.), Processes, Terms and Cycles: Steps on the Road to Infinity. XVIII, 639 pages. 2005.

Vol. 3837: K. Cho, P. Jacquet (Eds.), Technologies for Advanced Heterogeneous Networks. IX, 307 pages. 2005.

Vol. 3836: J.-M. Pierson (Ed.), Data Management in Grids. X, 143 pages. 2006.

Vol. 3835: G. Sutcliffe, A. Voronkov (Eds.), Logic for Programming, Artificial Intelligence, and Reasoning. XIV, 744 pages. 2005. (Sublibrary LNAI).

Vol. 3834: D.G. Feitelson, E. Frachtenberg, L. Rudolph, U. Schwiegelshohn (Eds.), Job Scheduling Strategies for Parallel Processing. VIII, 283 pages. 2005.

Vol. 3833: K.-J. Li, C. Vangenot (Eds.), Web and Wireless Geographical Information Systems. XI, 309 pages. 2005.

Vol. 3832: D. Zhang, A.K. Jain (Eds.), Advances in Biometrics. XX, 796 pages. 2005.

Vol. 3831: J. Wiedermann, G. Tel, J. Pokorný, M. Bieliková, J. Štuller (Eds.), SOFSEM 2006: Theory and Practice of Computer Science. XV, 576 pages. 2006.

Vol. 3830: D. Weyns, H. V.D. Parunak, F. Michel (Eds.), Environments for Multi-Agent Systems II. VIII, 291 pages. 2006. (Sublibrary LNAI).

Vol. 3829: P. Pettersson, W. Yi (Eds.), Formal Modeling and Analysis of Timed Systems. IX, 305 pages. 2005.

Vol. 3828: X. Deng, Y. Ye (Eds.), Internet and Network Economics. XVII, 1106 pages. 2005.

Vol. 3827: X. Deng, D.-Z. Du (Eds.), Algorithms and Computation. XX, 1190 pages. 2005.

Vol. 3826: B. Benatallah, F. Casati, P. Traverso (Eds.), Service-Oriented Computing - ICSOC 2005. XVIII, 597 pages. 2005.

Vol. 3824: L.T. Yang, M. Amamiya, Z. Liu, M. Guo, F.J. Rammig (Eds.), Embedded and Ubiquitous Computing - EUC 2005. XXIII, 1204 pages. 2005.

Vol. 3823: T. Enokido, L. Yan, B. Xiao, D. Kim, Y. Dai, L.T. Yang (Eds.), Embedded and Ubiquitous Computing - EUC 2005 Workshops. XXXII, 1317 pages. 2005.

Vol. 3822: D. Feng, D. Lin, M. Yung (Eds.), Information Security and Cryptology. XII, 420 pages. 2005.

Vol. 3821: R. Ramanujam, S. Sen (Eds.), FSTTCS 2005: Foundations of Software Technology and Theoretical Computer Science. XIV, 566 pages. 2005.

Vol. 3820: L.T. Yang, X.-s. Zhou, W. Zhao, Z. Wu, Y. Zhu, M. Lin (Eds.), Embedded Software and Systems. XXVIII, 779 pages. 2005.

Vol. 3819: P. Van Hentenryck (Ed.), Practical Aspects of Declarative Languages. X, 231 pages. 2005.

Vol. 3818: S. Grumbach, L. Sui, V. Vianu (Eds.), Advances in Computer Science - ASIAN 2005. XIII, 294 pages. 2005.

Vol. 3817: M. Faundez-Zanuy, L. Janer, A. Esposito, A. Satue-Villar, J. Roure, V. Espinosa-Duro (Eds.), Nonlinear Analyses and Algorithms for Speech Processing. XII, 380 pages. 2006. (Sublibrary LNAI).

Vol. 3816: G. Chakraborty (Ed.), Distributed Computing and Internet Technology. XXI, 606 pages. 2005.

Vol. 3815: E.A. Fox, E.J. Neuhold, P. Premsmit, V. Wuwongse (Eds.), Digital Libraries: Implementing Strategies and Sharing Experiences. XVII, 529 pages. 2005.

Vol. 3814: M. Maybury, O. Stock, W. Wahlster (Eds.), Intelligent Technologies for Interactive Entertainment. XV, 342 pages. 2005. (Sublibrary LNAI).

Vol. 3813: R. Molva, G. Tsudik, D. Westhoff (Eds.), Security and Privacy in Ad-hoc and Sensor Networks. VIII, 219 pages. 2005.

Vol. 3812: C. Bussler, A. Haller (Eds.), Business Process Management Workshops. XIII, 520 pages. 2006.

Vol. 3811: C. Bussler, M.-C. Shan (Eds.), Technologies for E-Services. VIII, 127 pages. 2006.

Vol. 3810: Y.G. Desmedt, H. Wang, Y. Mu, Y. Li (Eds.), Cryptology and Network Security. XI, 349 pages. 2005.

Vol. 3809: S. Zhang, R. Jarvis (Eds.), AI 2005: Advances in Artificial Intelligence. XXVII, 1344 pages. 2005. (Sublibrary LNAI).

Vol. 3808: C. Bento, A. Cardoso, G. Dias (Eds.), Progress in Artificial Intelligence. XVIII, 704 pages. 2005. (Sublibrary LNAI).

Vol. 3807: M. Dean, Y. Guo, W. Jun, R. Kaschek, S. Krishnaswamy, Z. Pan, Q.Z. Sheng (Eds.), Web Information Systems Engineering - WISE 2005 Workshops. XV, 275 pages. 2005.

Vol. 3806: A.H. H. Ngu, M. Kitsuregawa, E.J. Neuhold, J.-Y. Chung, Q.Z. Sheng (Eds.), Web Information Systems Engineering - WISE 2005. XXI, 771 pages. 2005.

Vol. 3805: G. Subsol (Ed.), Virtual Storytelling. XII, 289 pages. 2005.

Vol. 3804: G. Bebis, R. Boyle, D. Koracin, B. Parvin (Eds.), Advances in Visual Computing. XX, 755 pages. 2005.

Vol. 3803: S. Jajodia, C. Mazumdar (Eds.), Information Systems Security. XI, 342 pages. 2005.

Vol. 3802: Y. Hao, J. Liu, Y.-P. Wang, Y.-m. Cheung, H. Yin, L. Jiao, J. Ma, Y.-C. Jiao (Eds.), Computational Intelligence and Security, Part II. XLII, 1166 pages. 2005. (Sublibrary LNAI).

Vol. 3801: Y. Hao, J. Liu, Y.-P. Wang, Y.-m. Cheung, H. Yin, L. Jiao, J. Ma, Y.-C. Jiao (Eds.), Computational Intelligence and Security, Part I. XLI, 1122 pages. 2005. (Sublibrary LNAI).

Vol. 3799: M. A. Rodríguez, I.F. Cruz, S. Levashkin, M.J. Egenhofer (Eds.), GeoSpatial Semantics. X, 259 pages. 2005.